SOUTH KOREA
in a blur

A Photographic Exploration

SCOTT SHAW

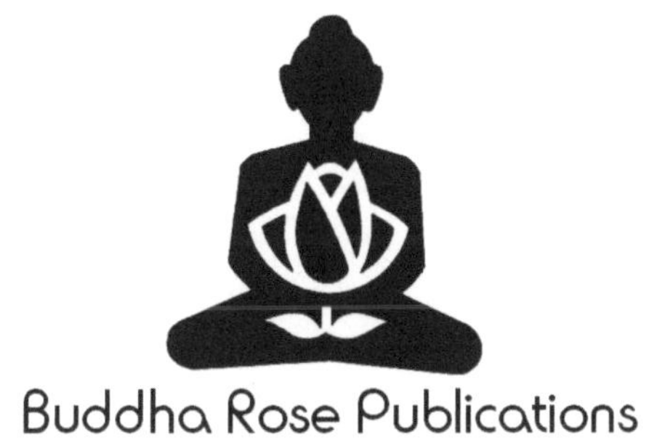

Buddha Rose Publications

South Korea in a Blur

www.scottshaw.com

First Edition

ISBN 10: 1-877792-59-4
ISBN 13: 978-1-877792-59-5

Photographed with a vintage Leica camera.

Printed in the United States of America

10 9 8 7 6 5 4 3 2 1

South Korea
in a blur

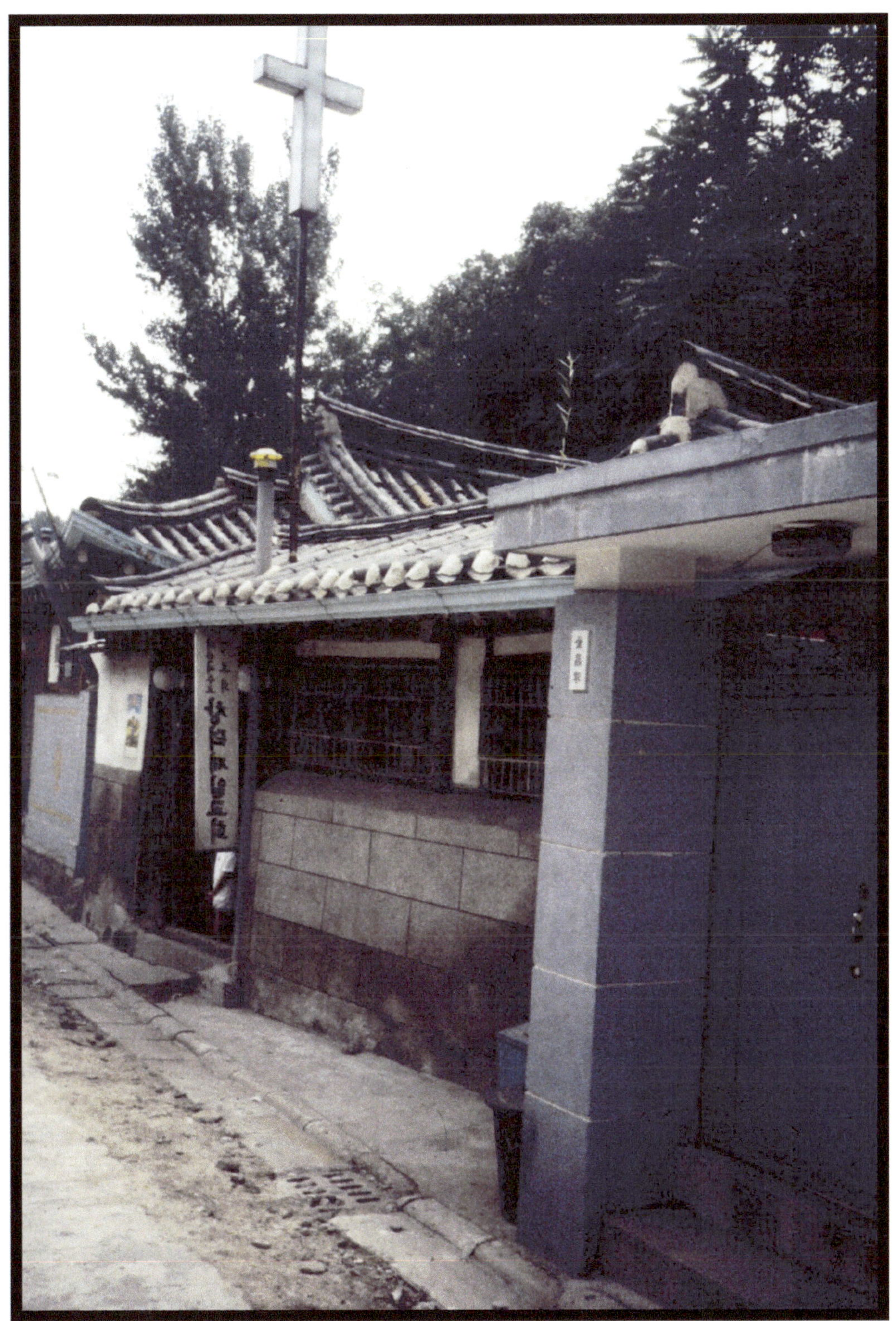

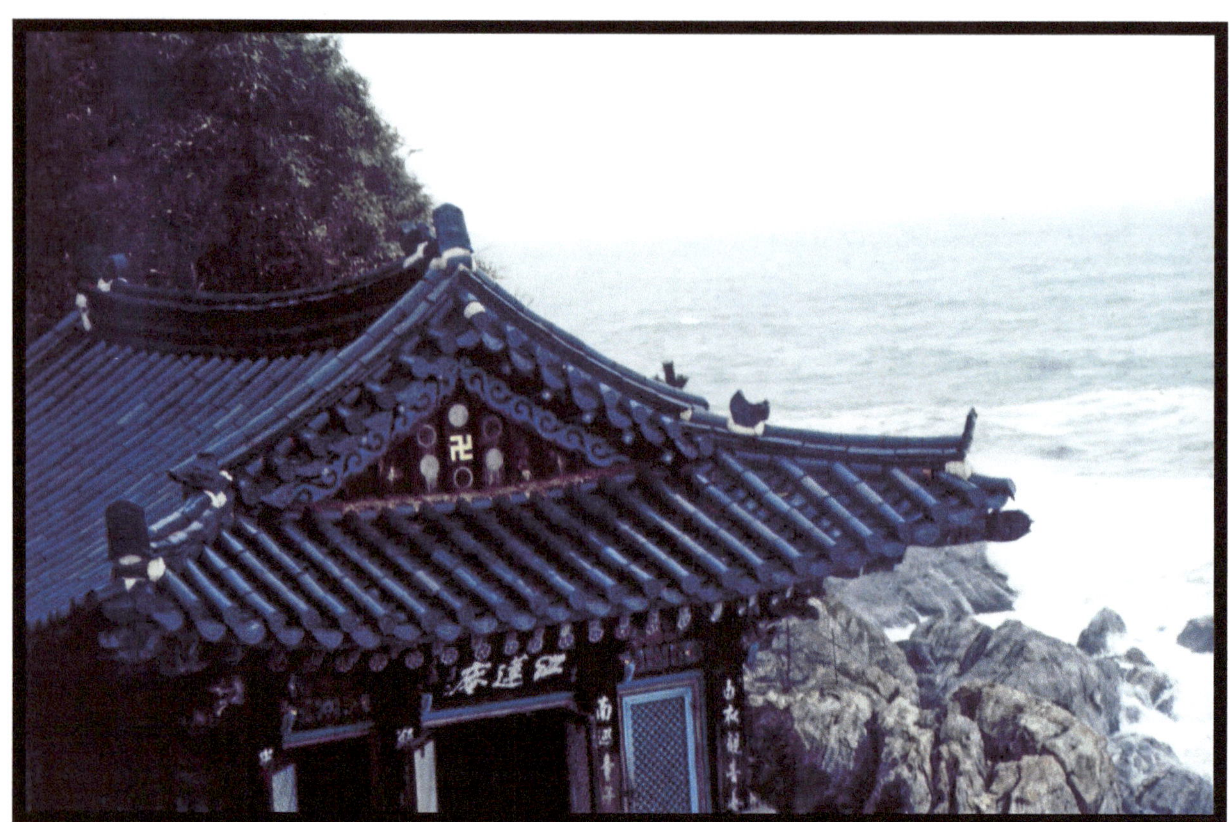

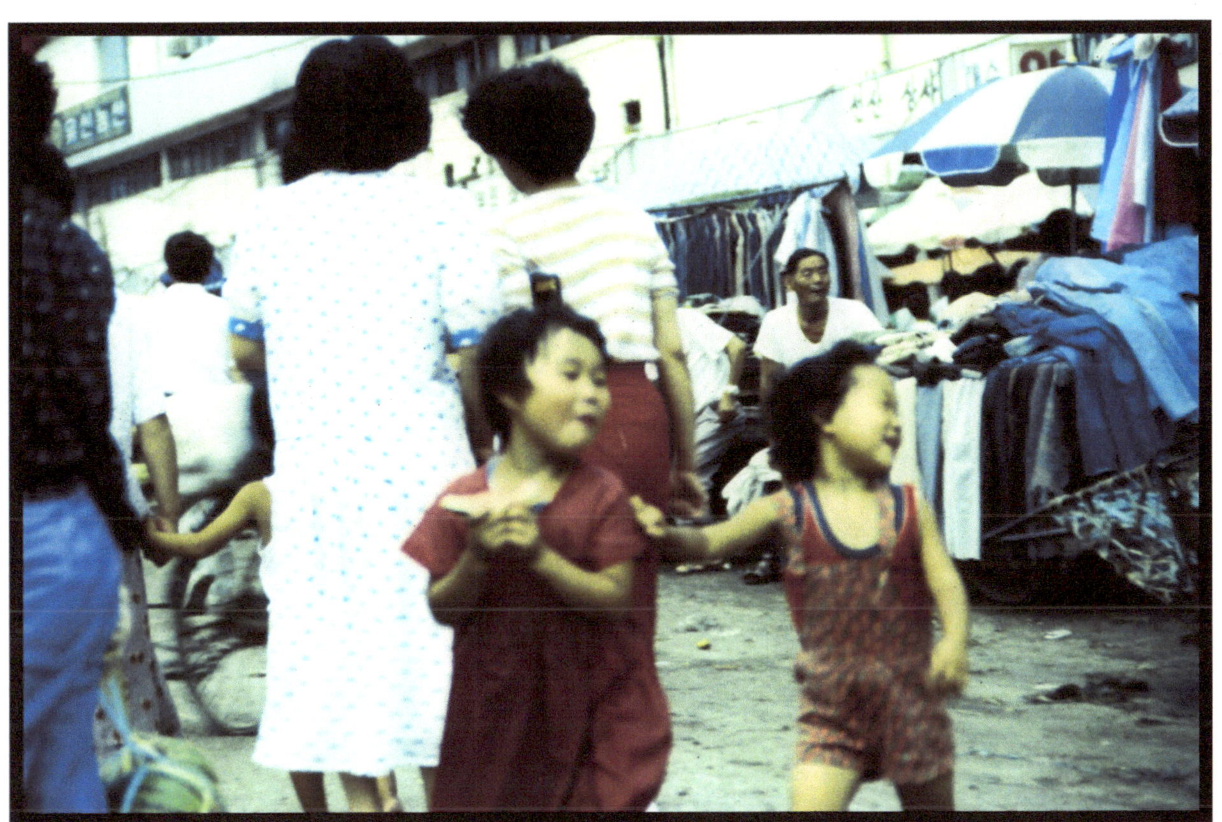

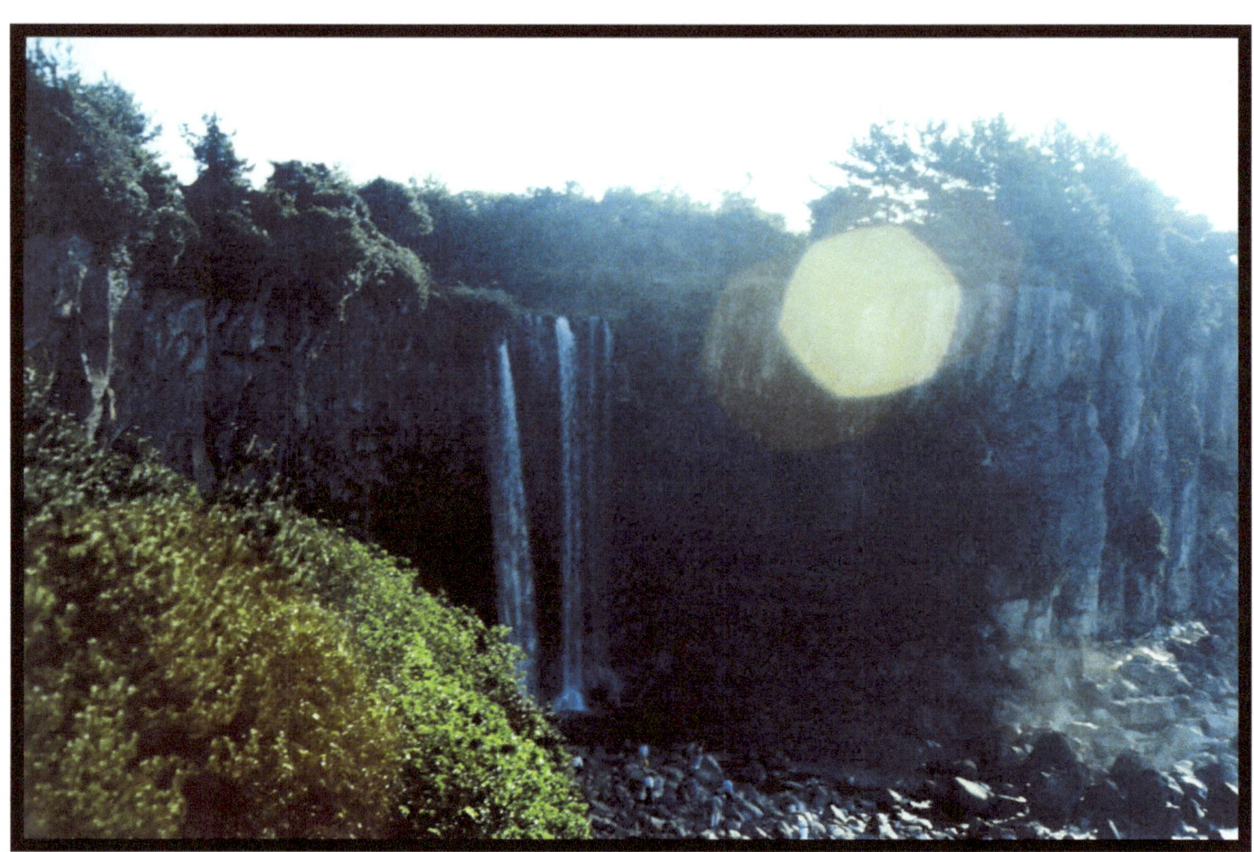

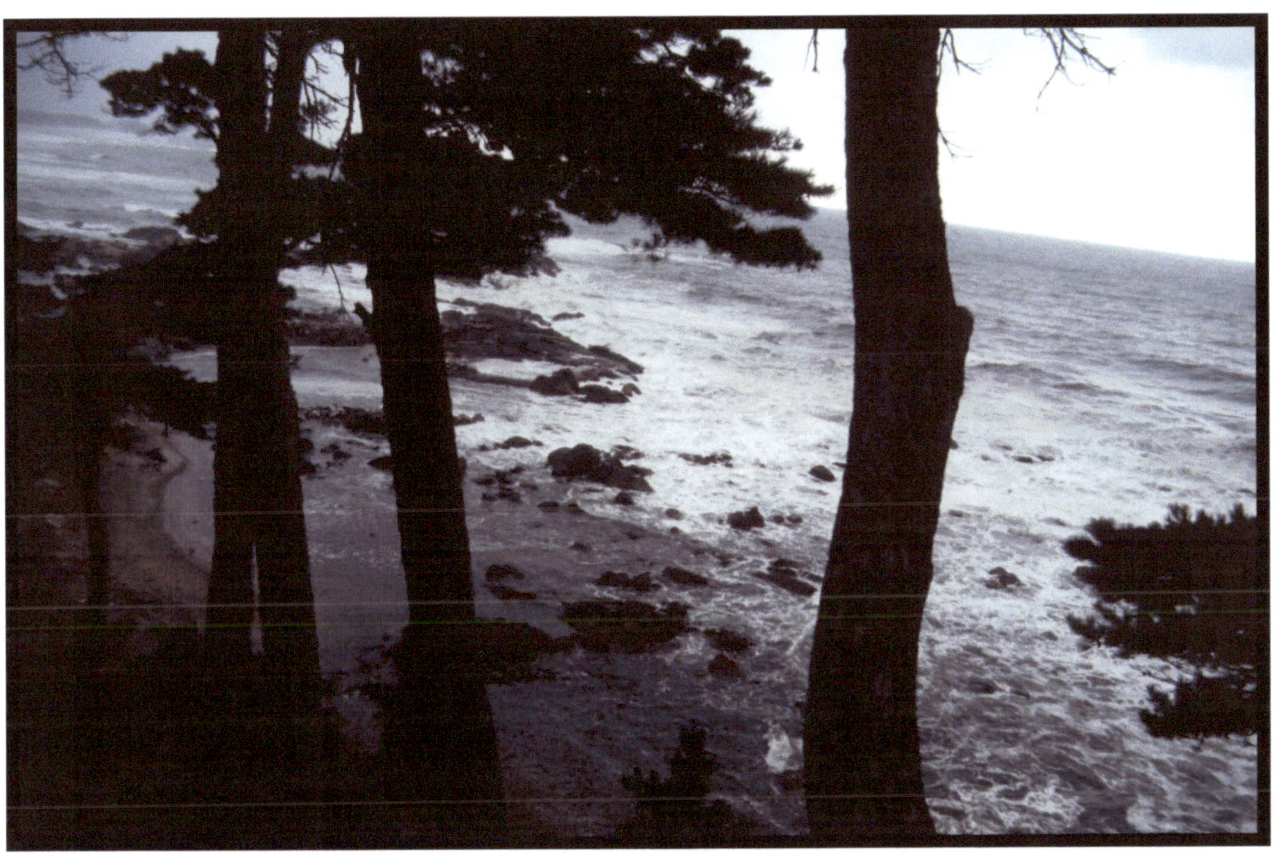

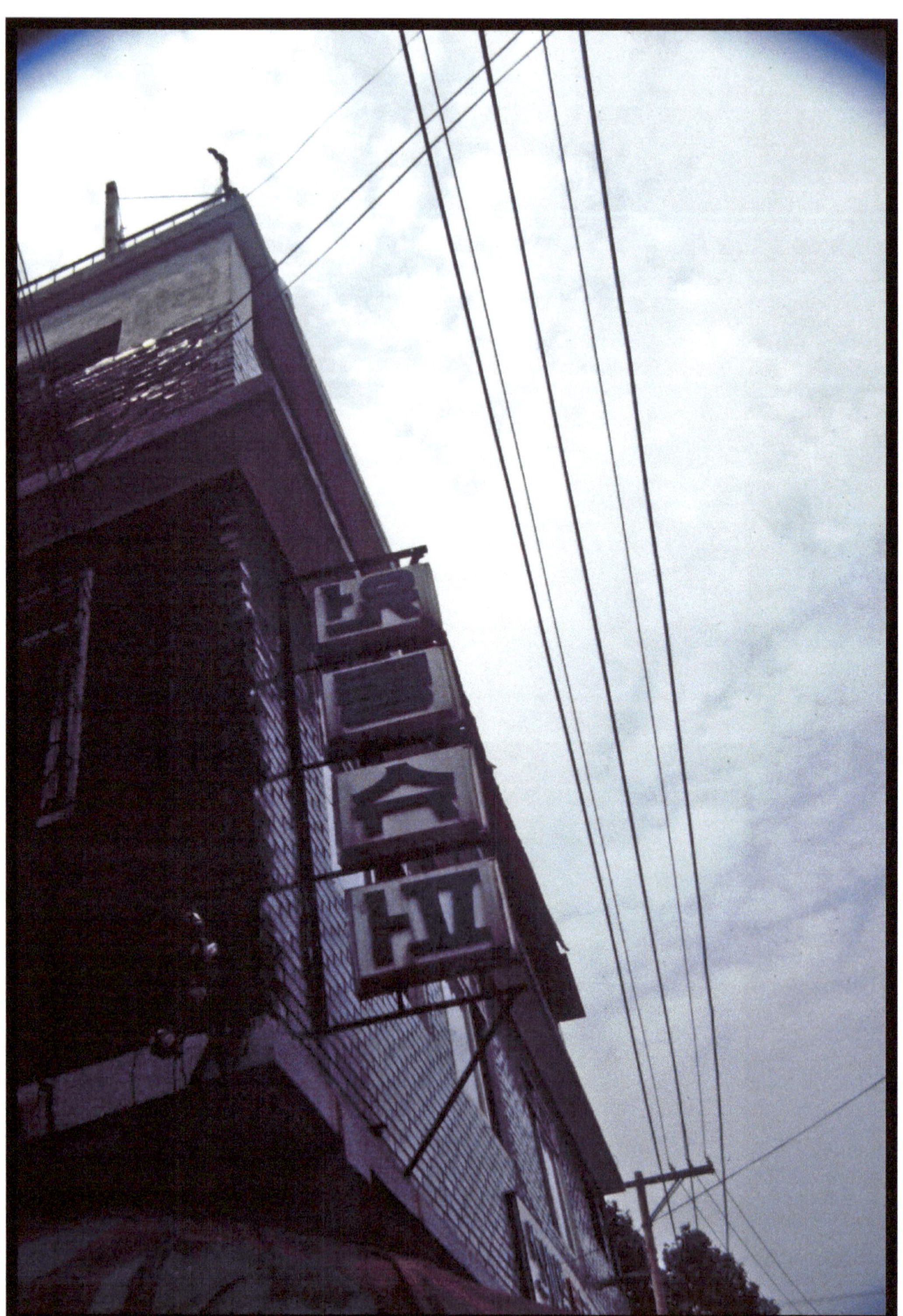

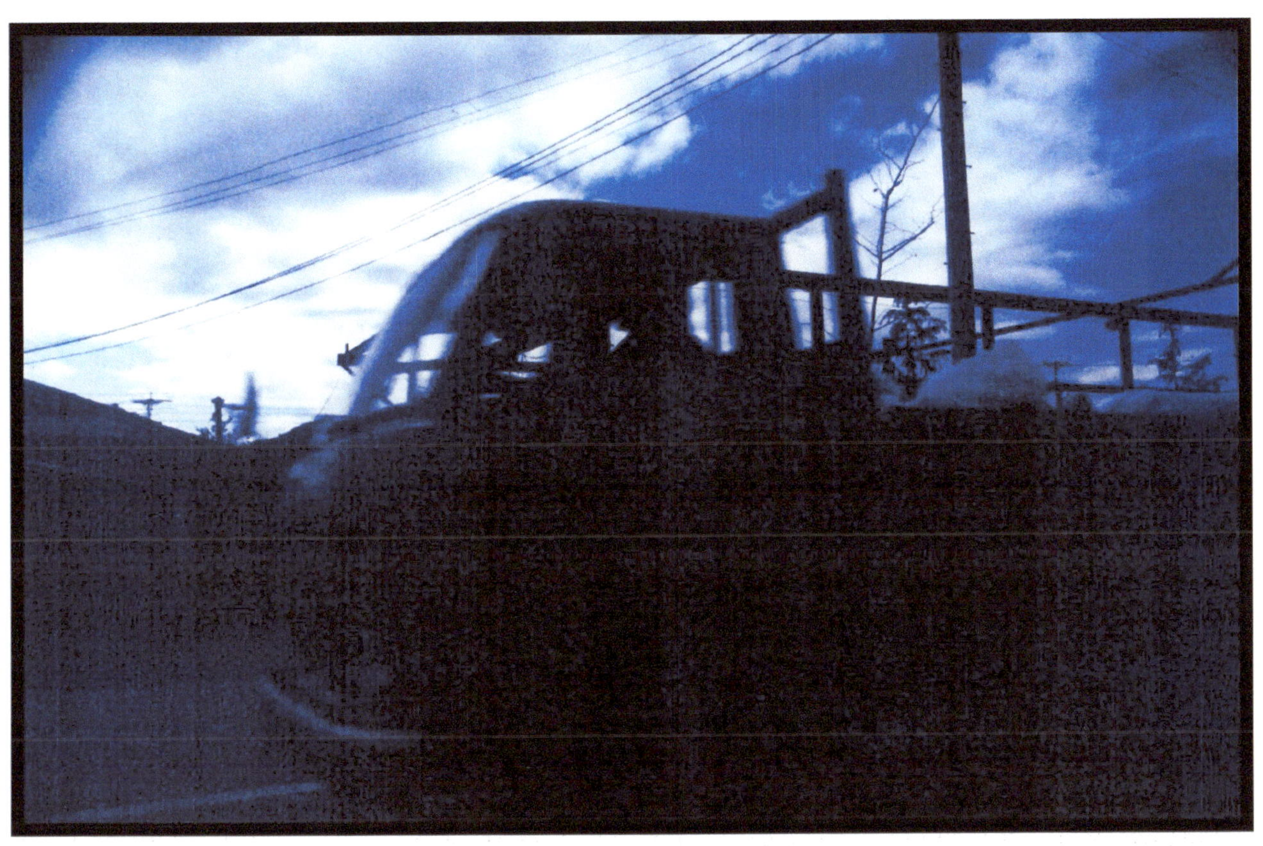

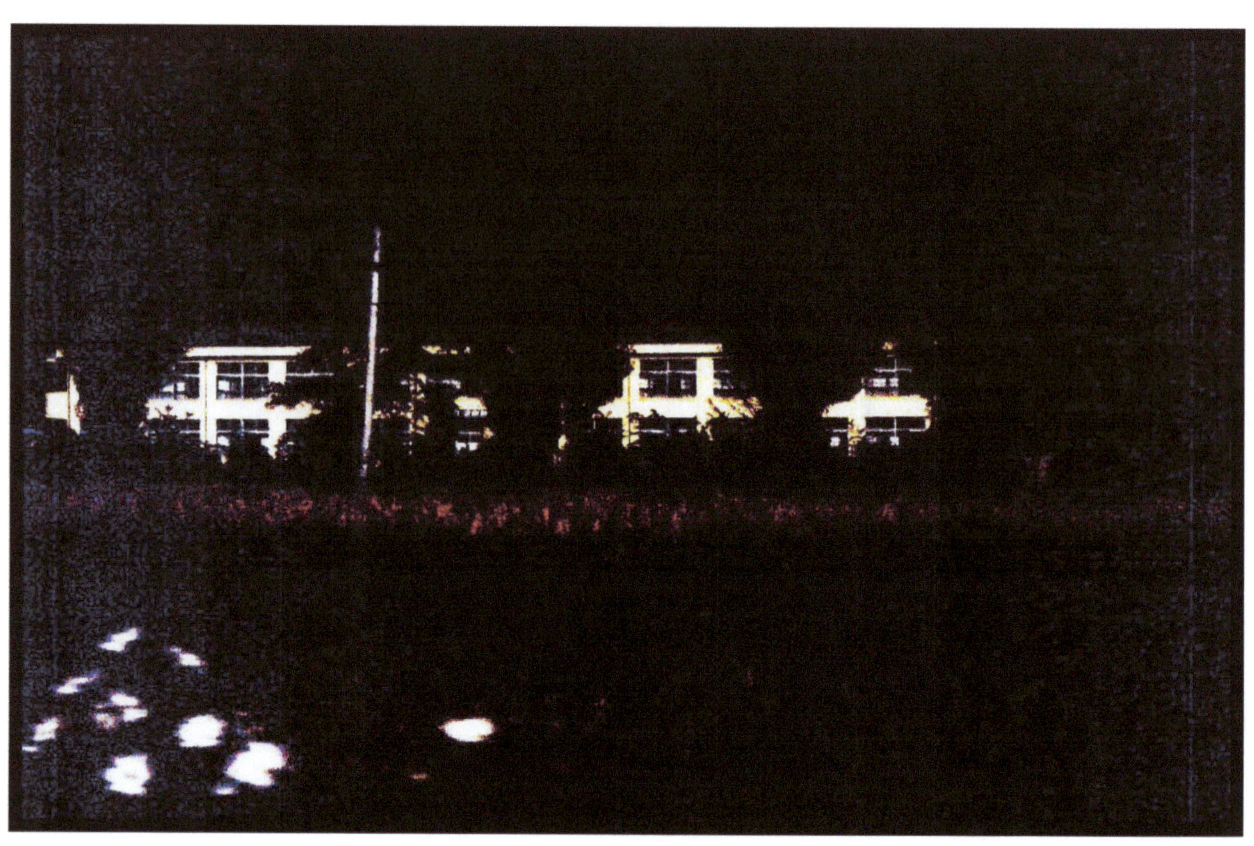

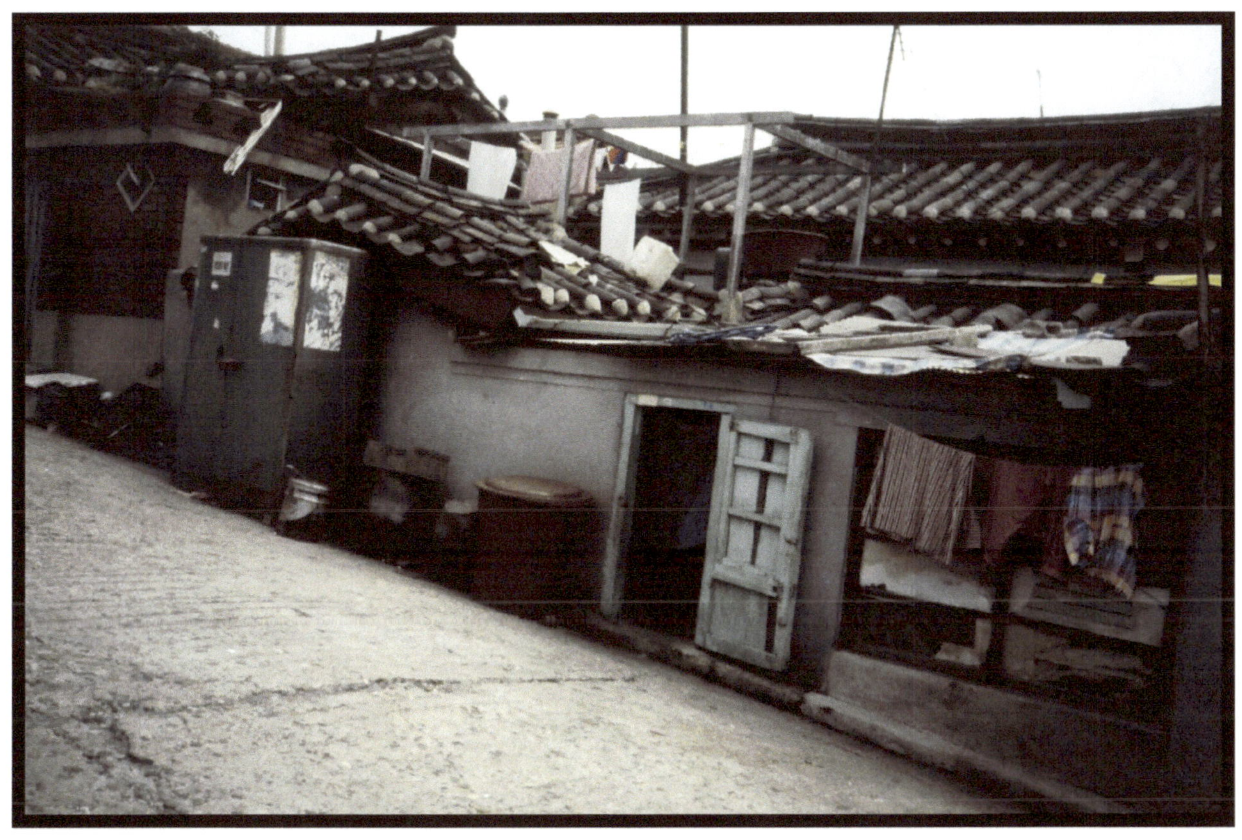

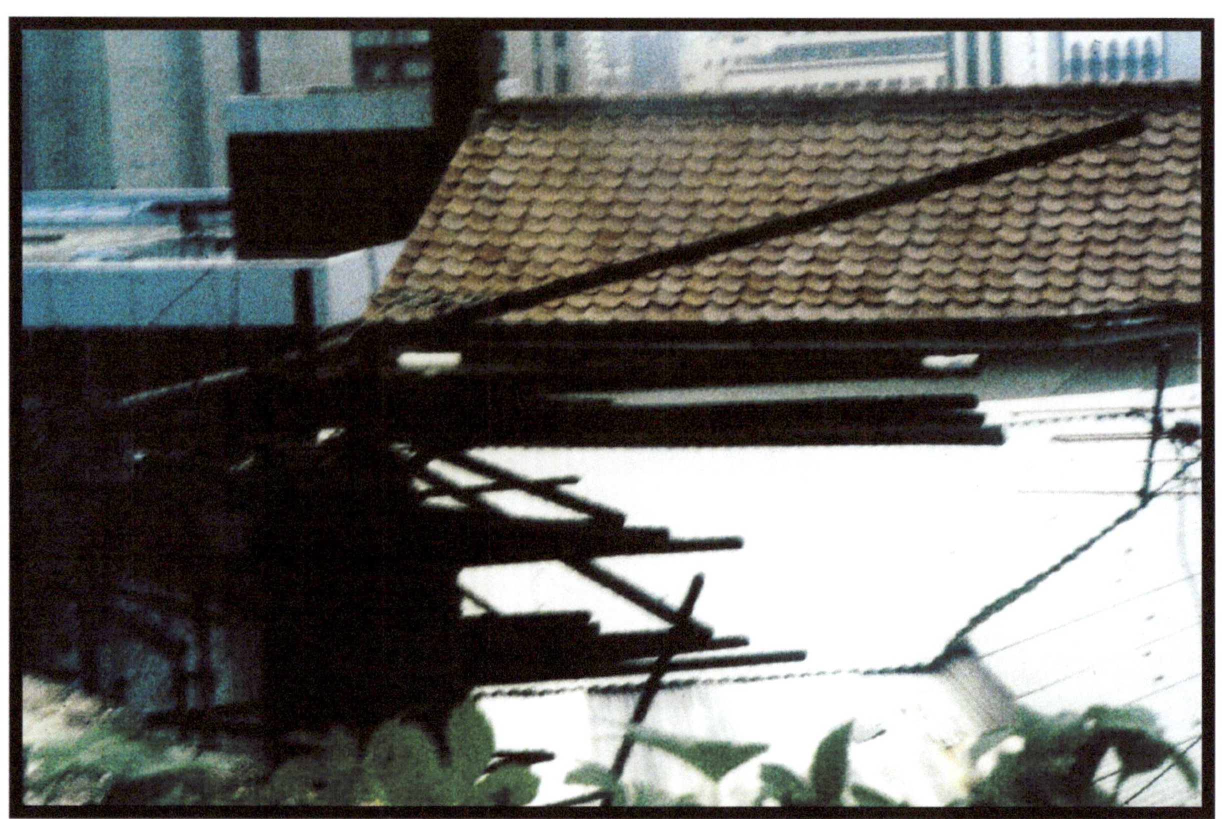

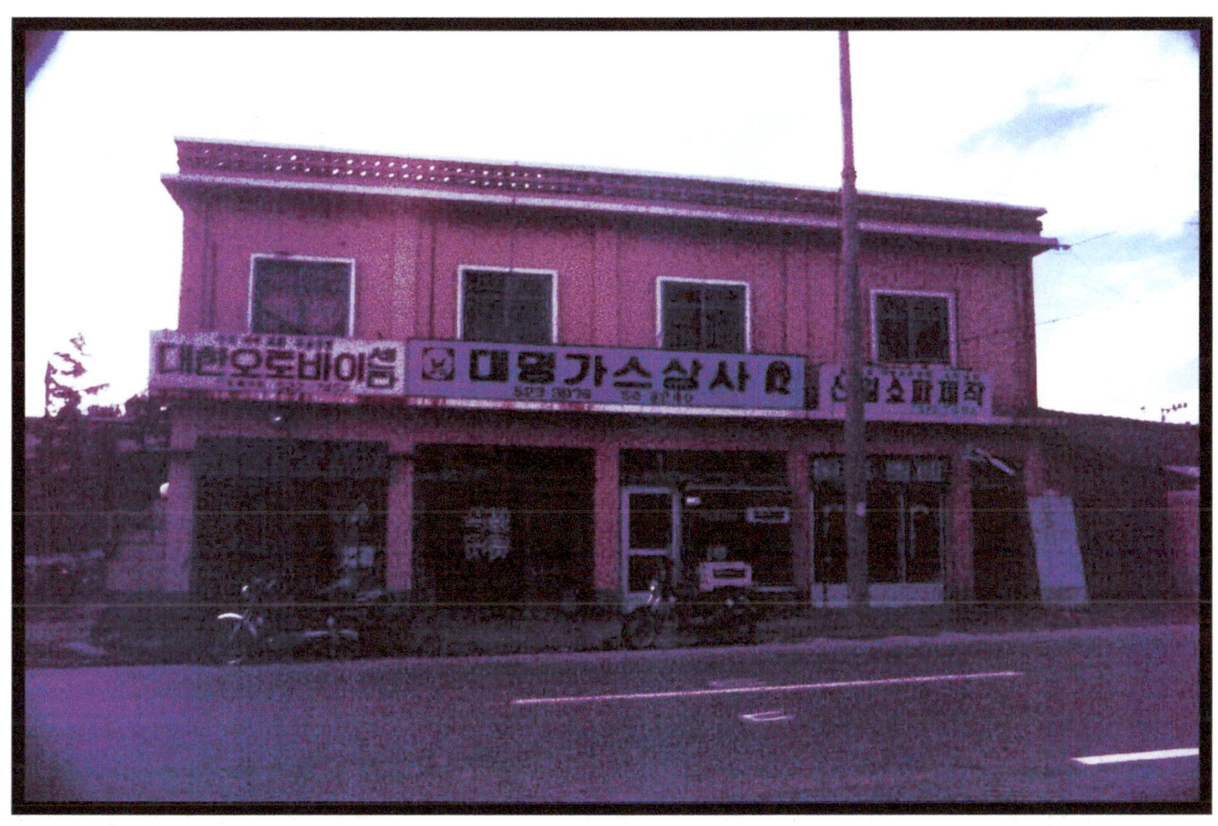
대한오토바이샵
대명가스상사

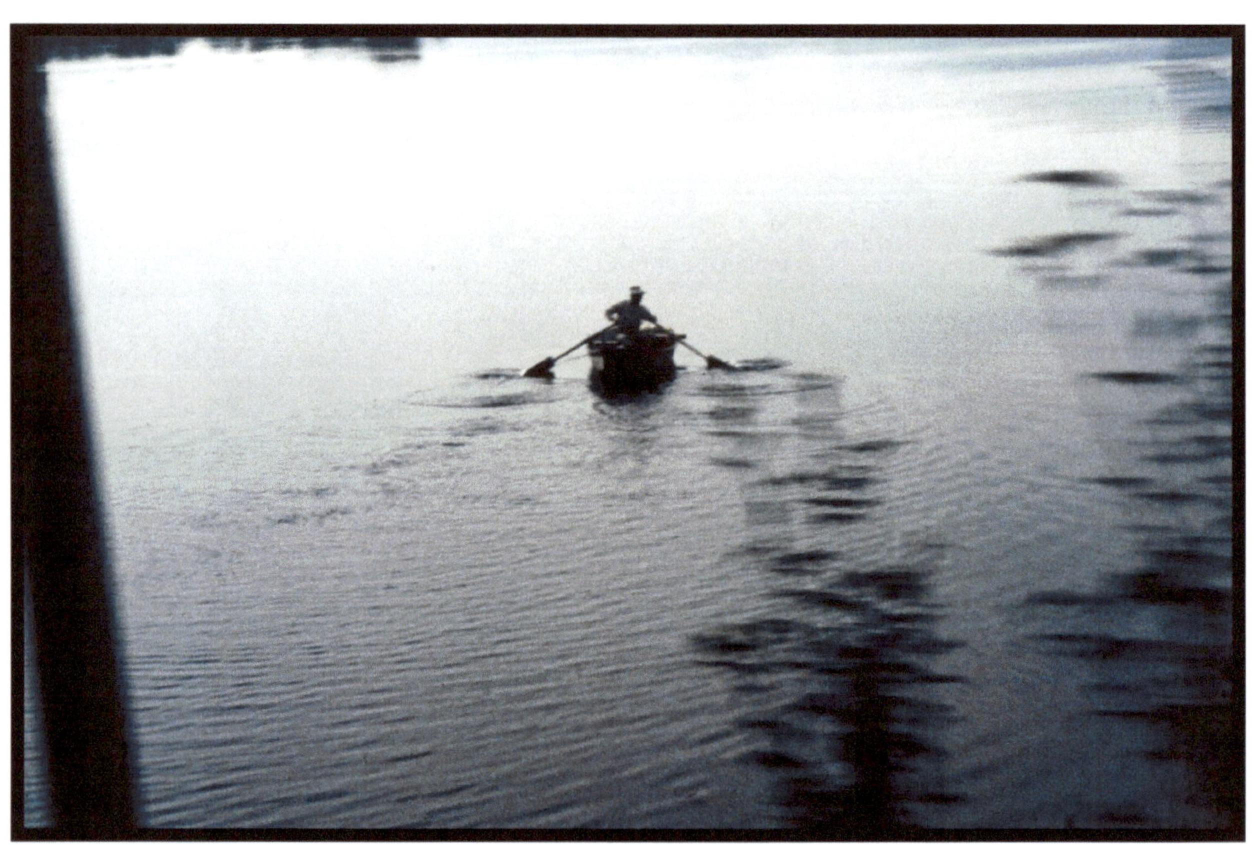

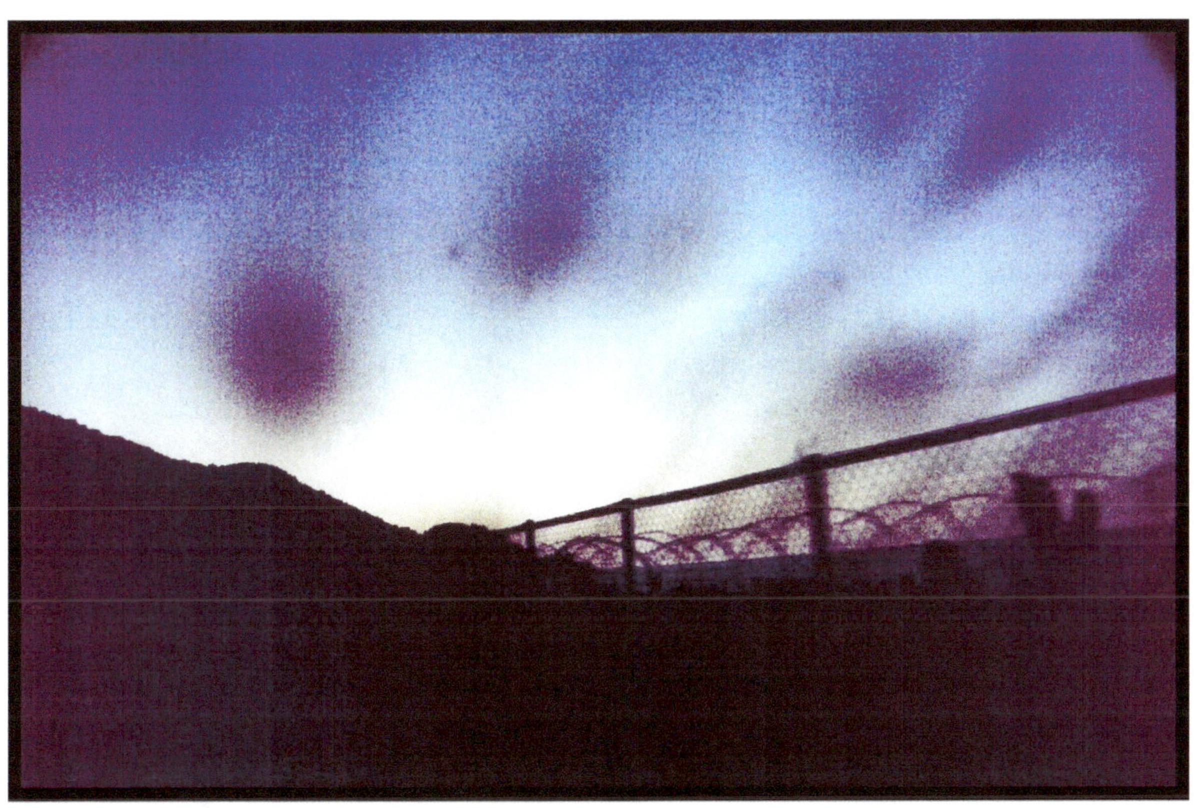

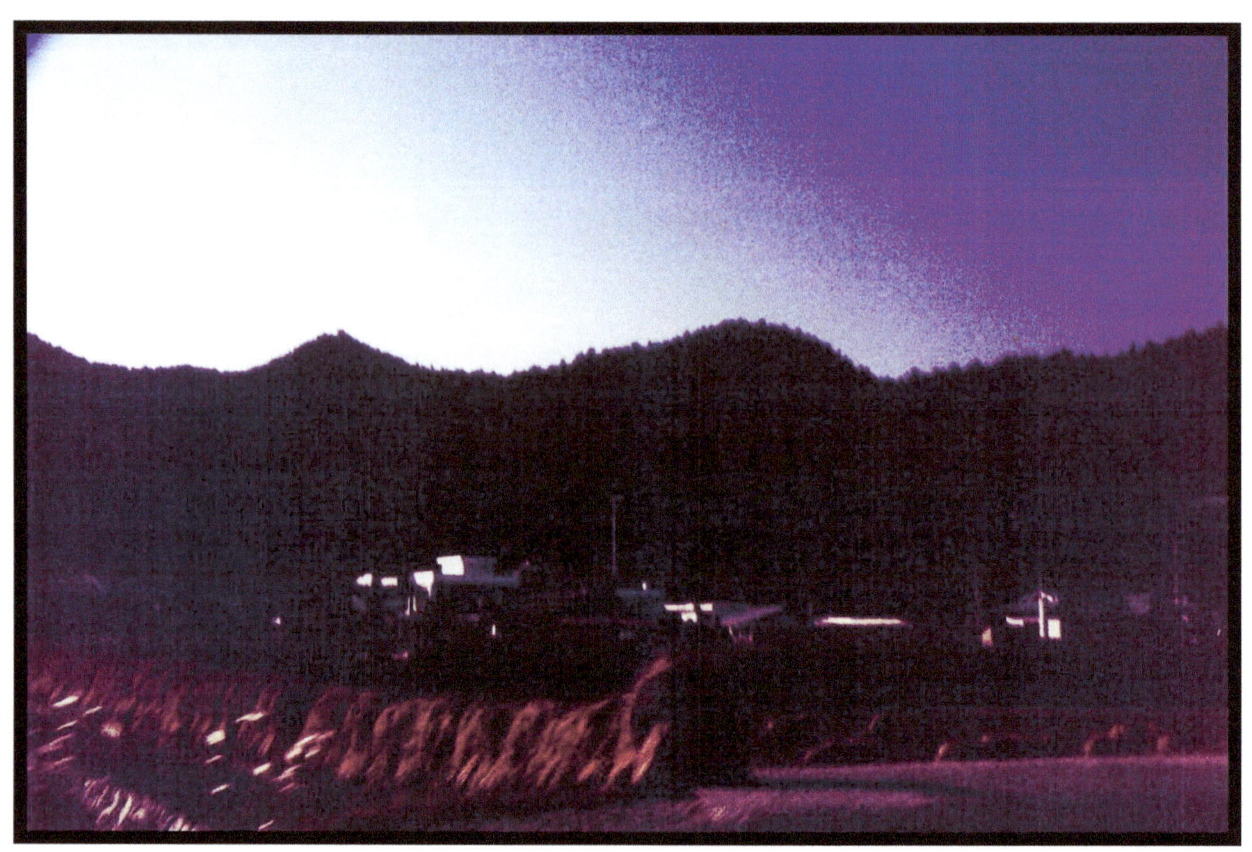

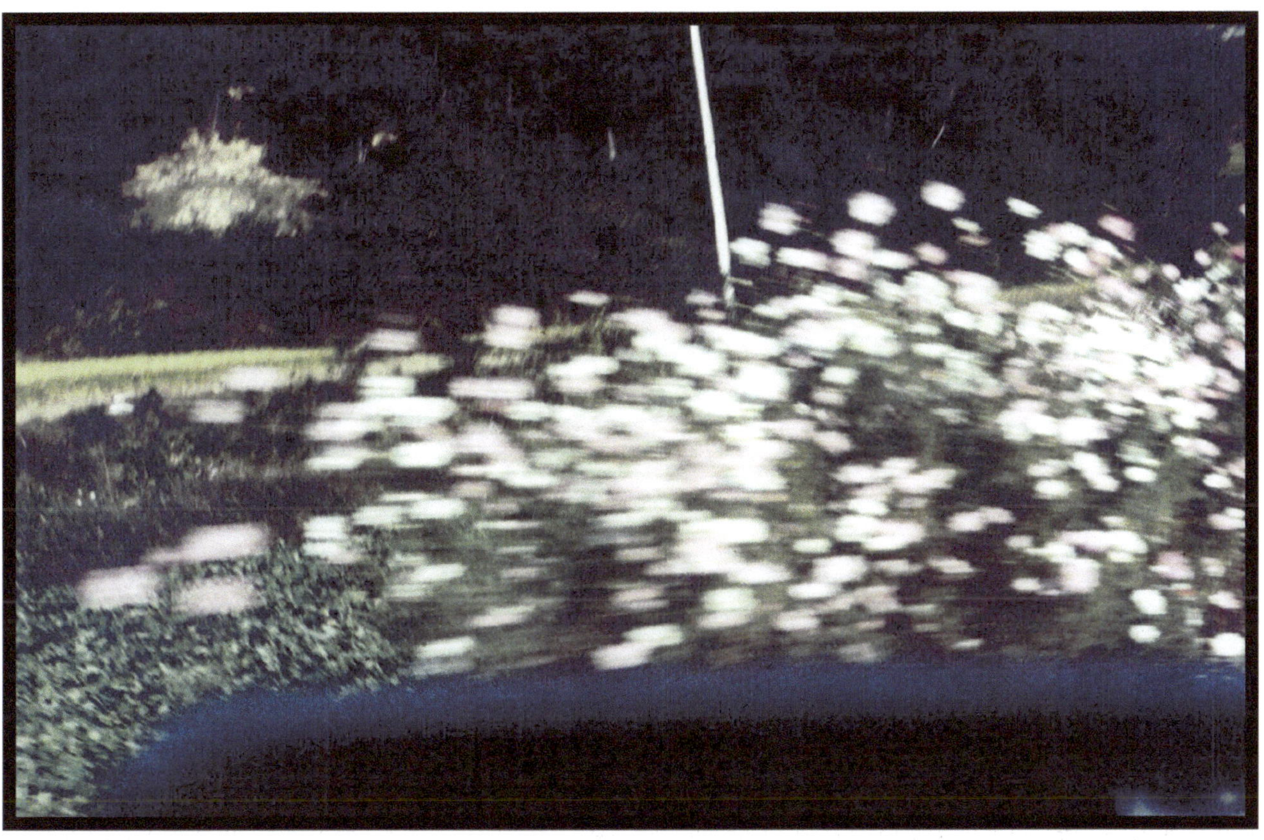

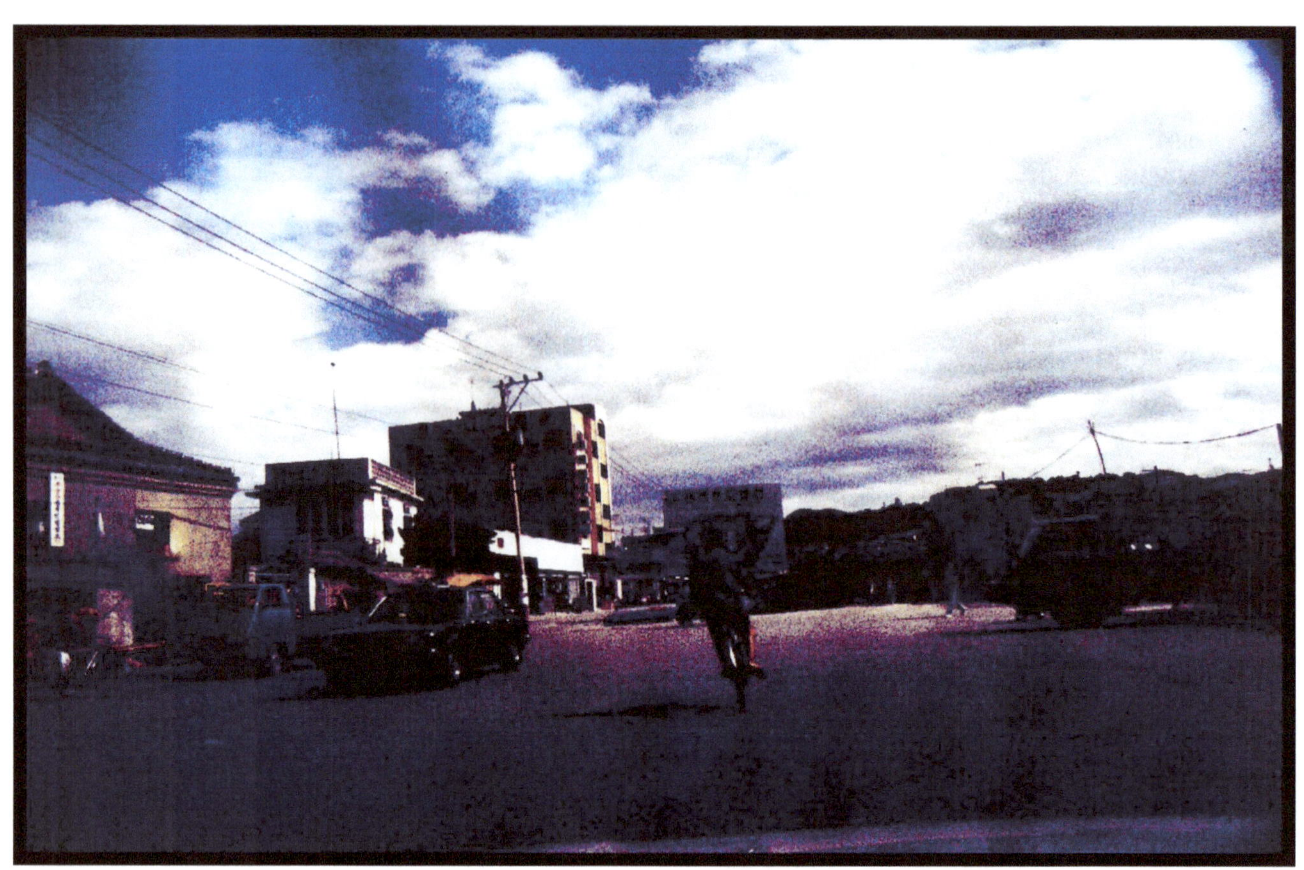

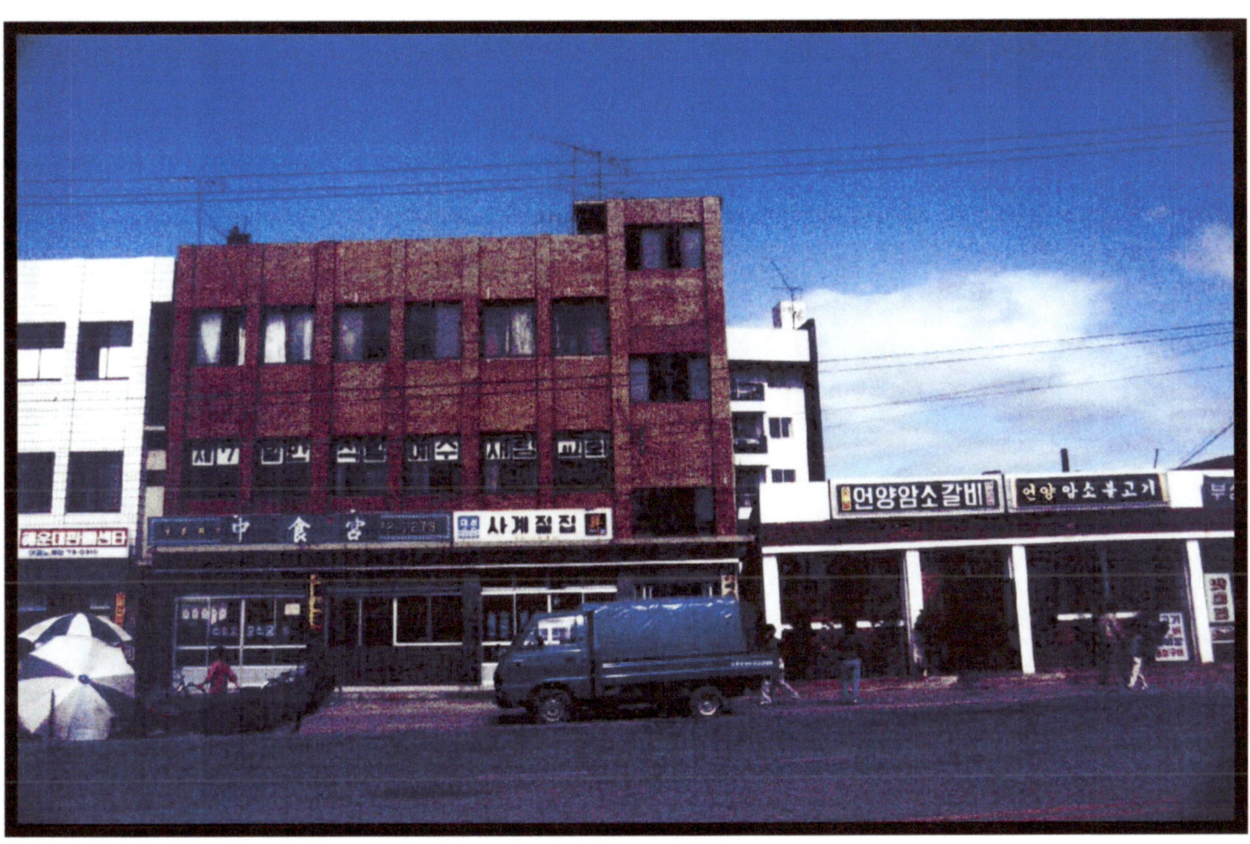
中食宮
사계절집
언양암소갈비
언양암소불고기

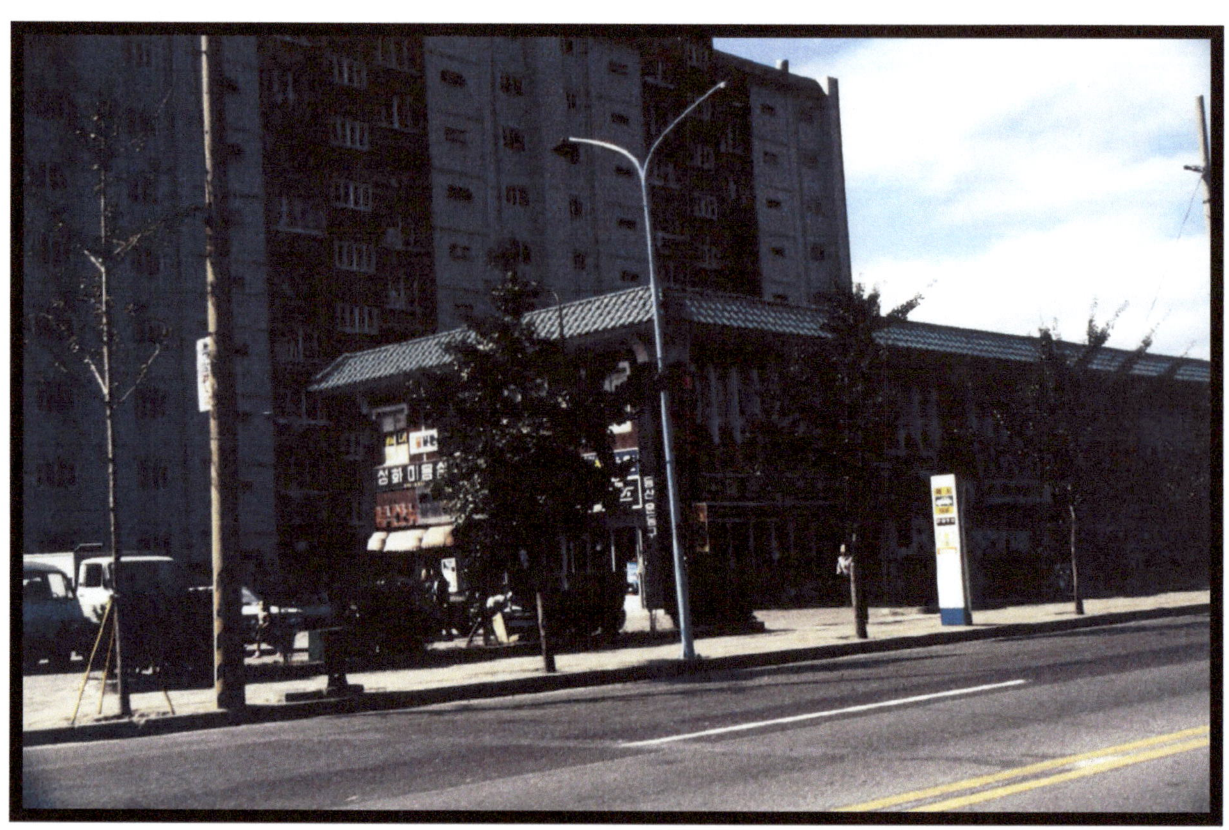

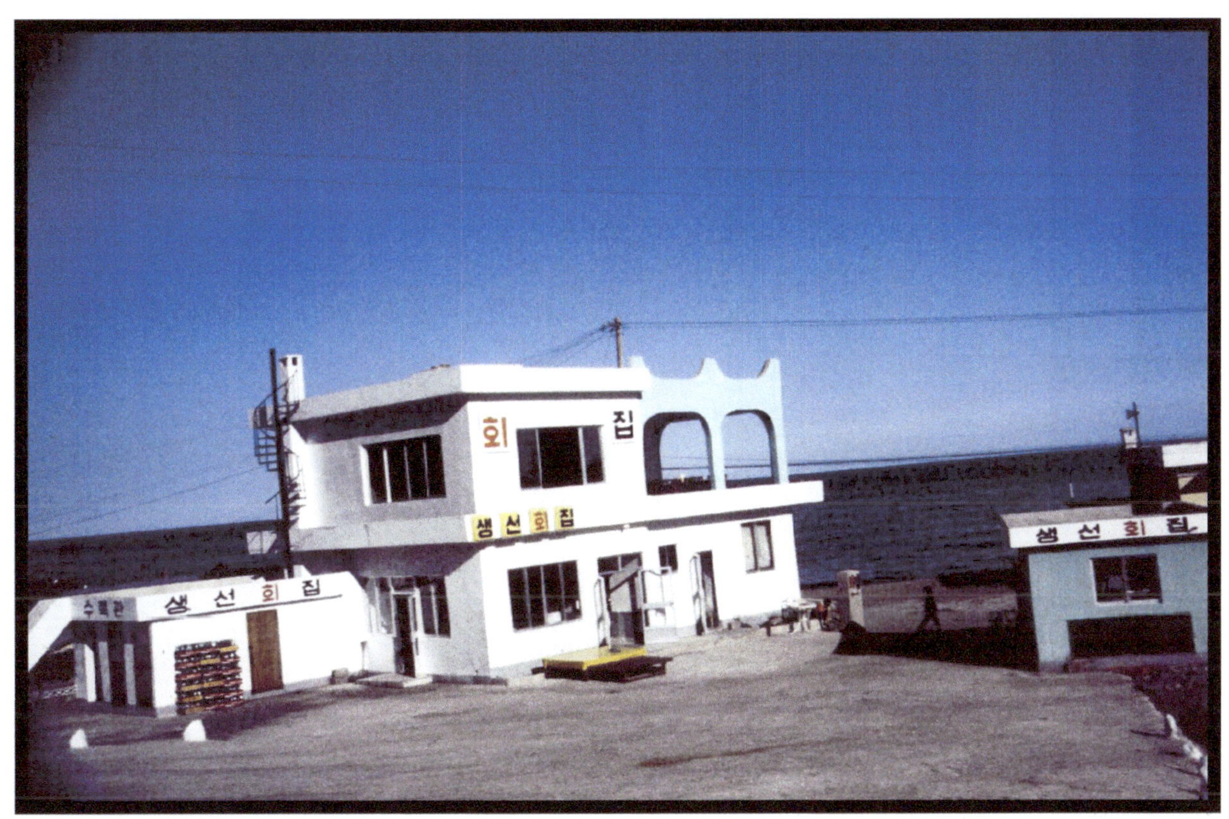
회 집
생선회집
생 선 회 집
생 선 회 집

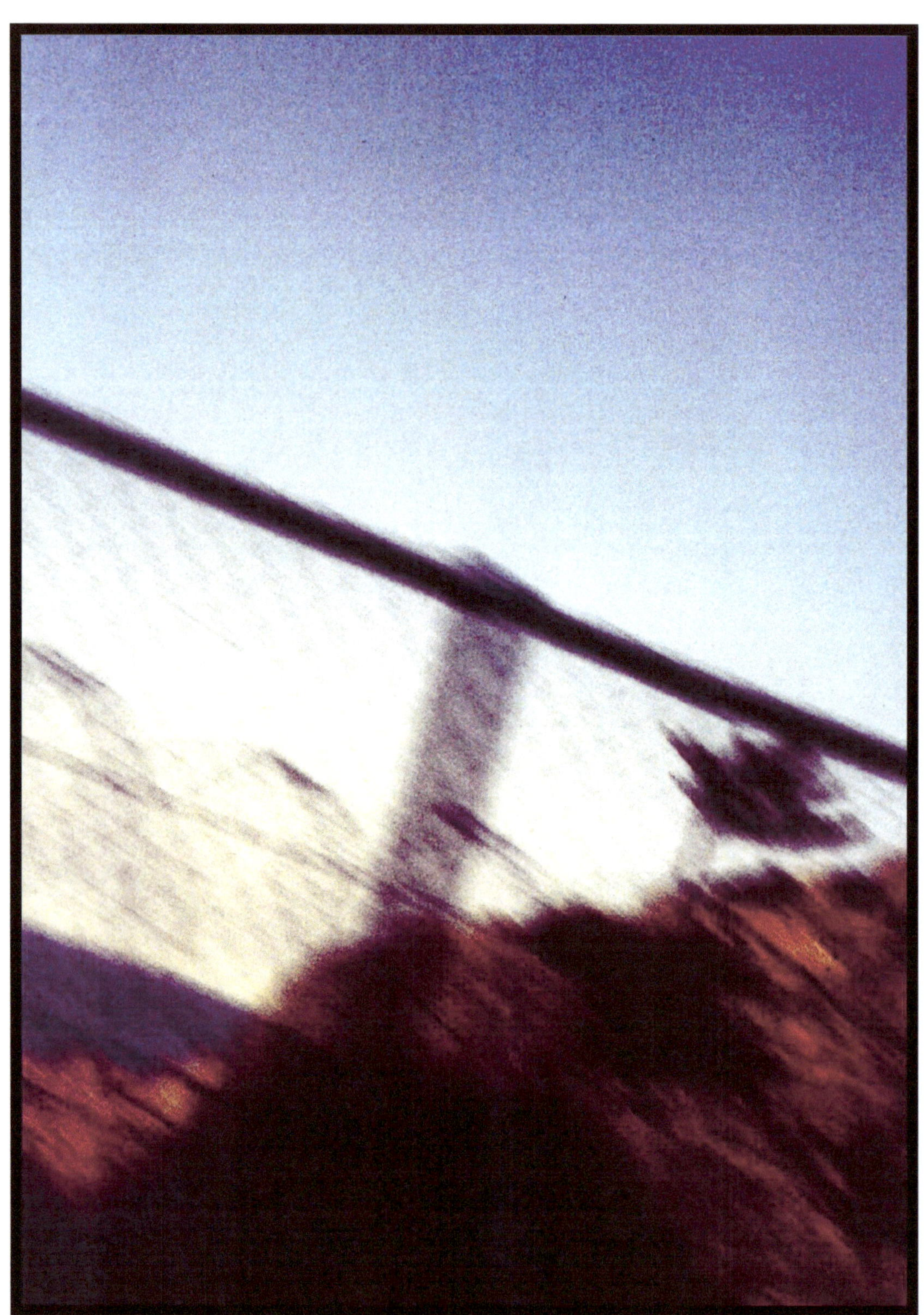

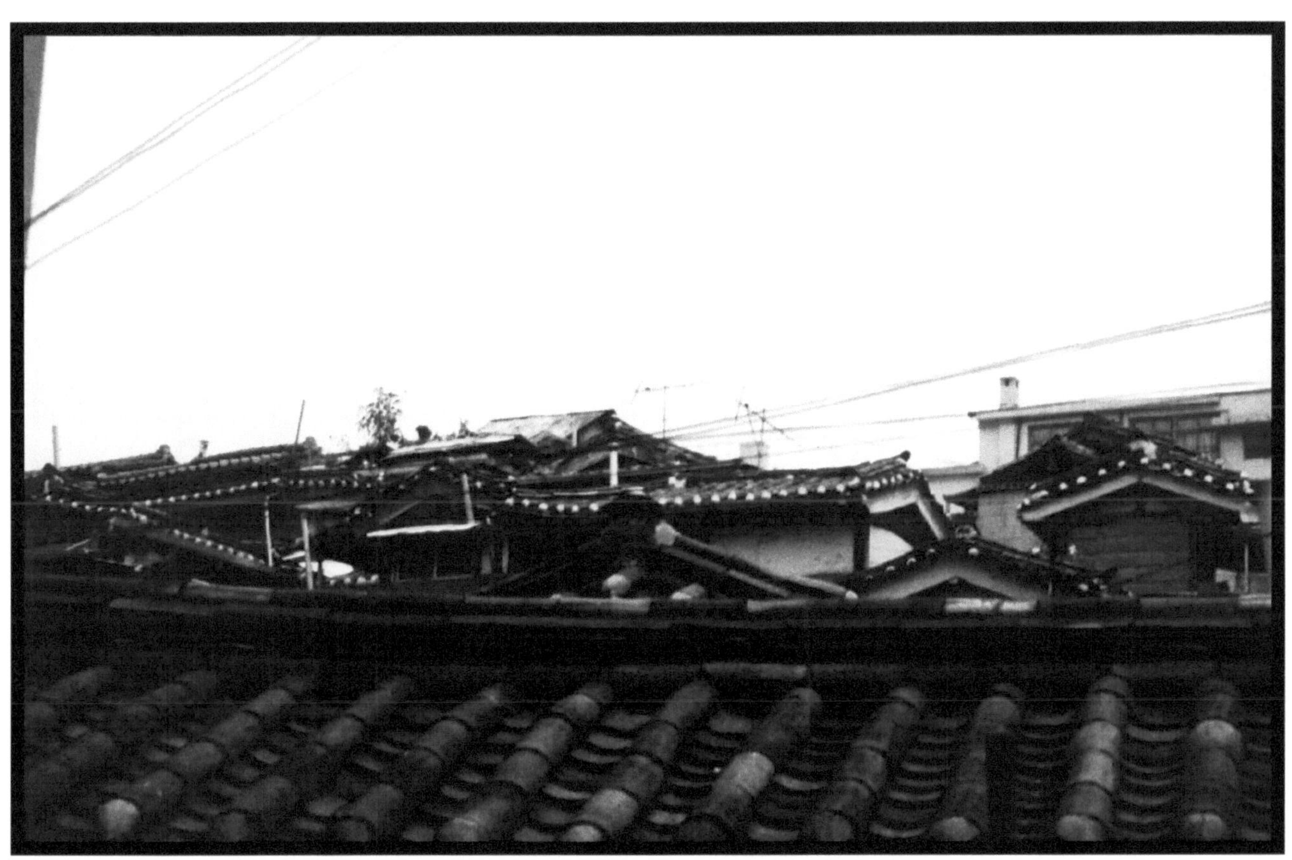

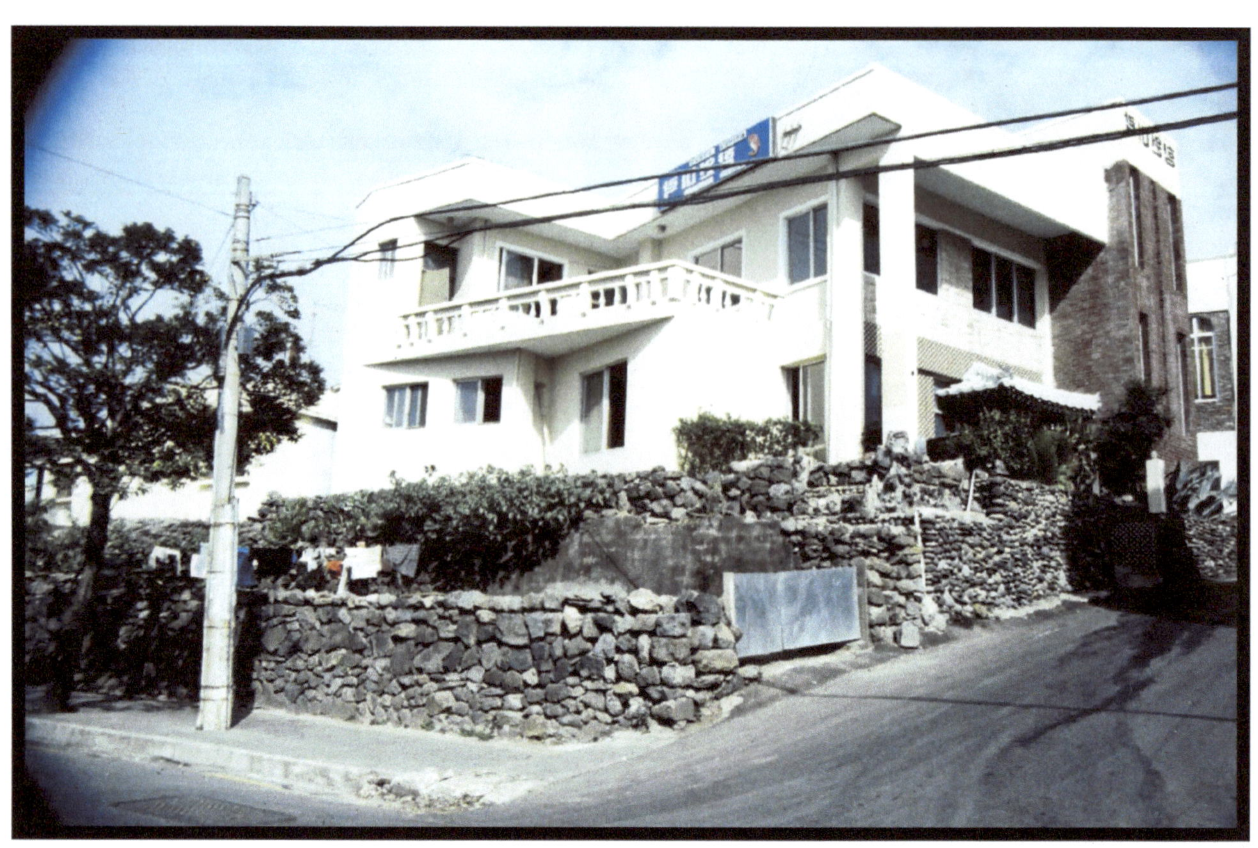

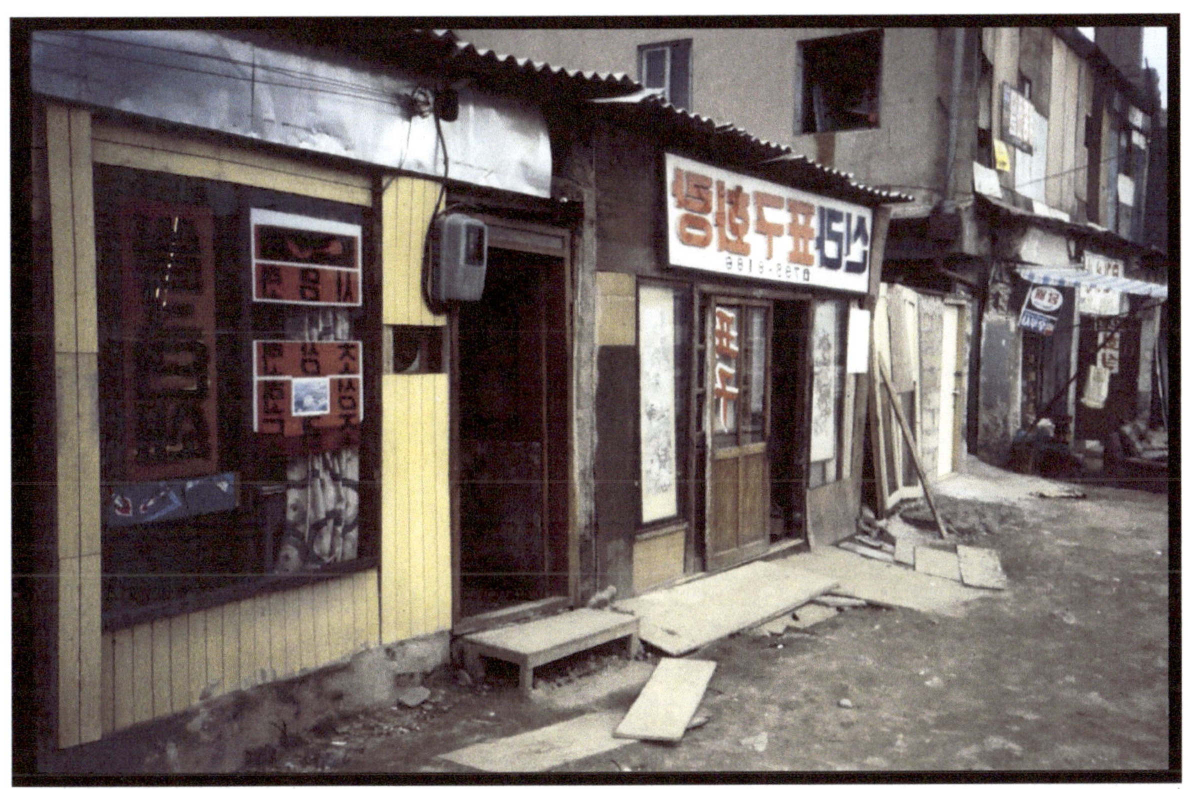

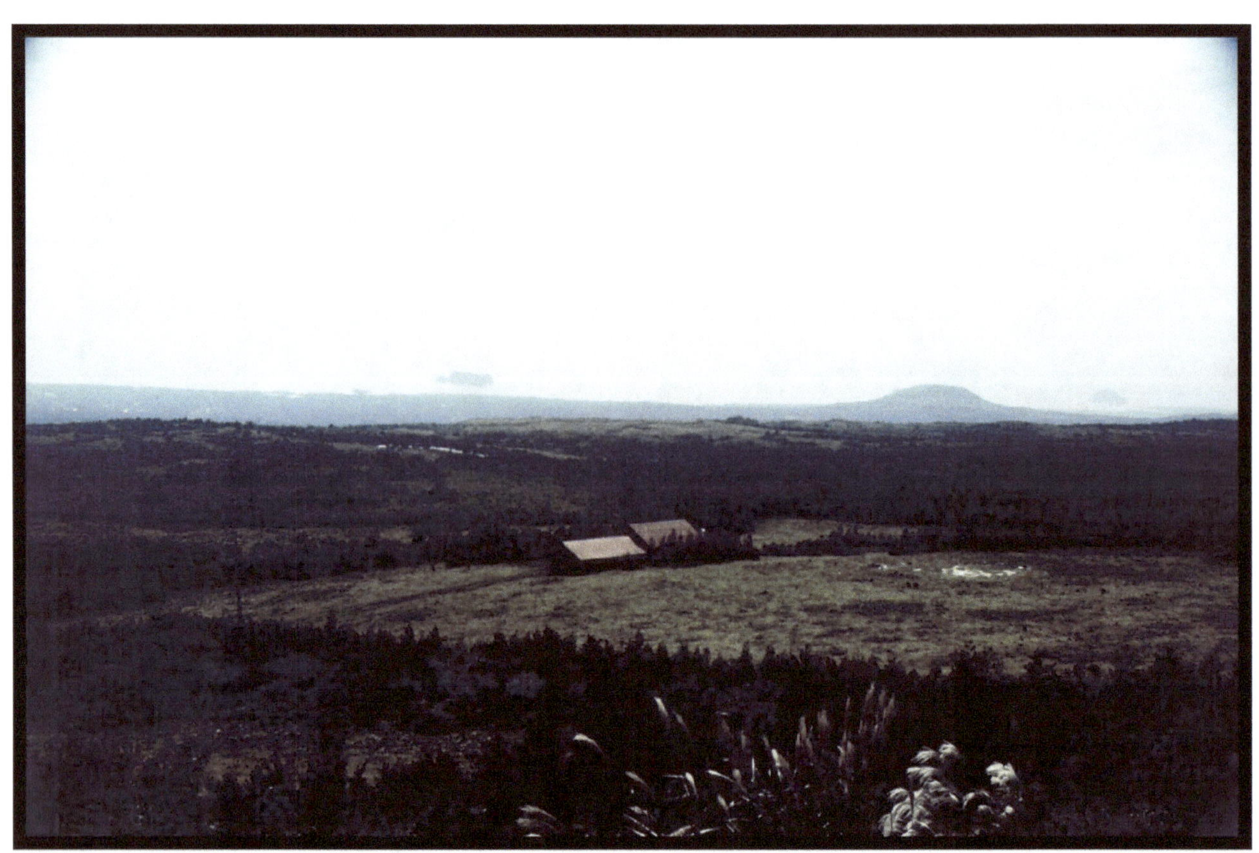

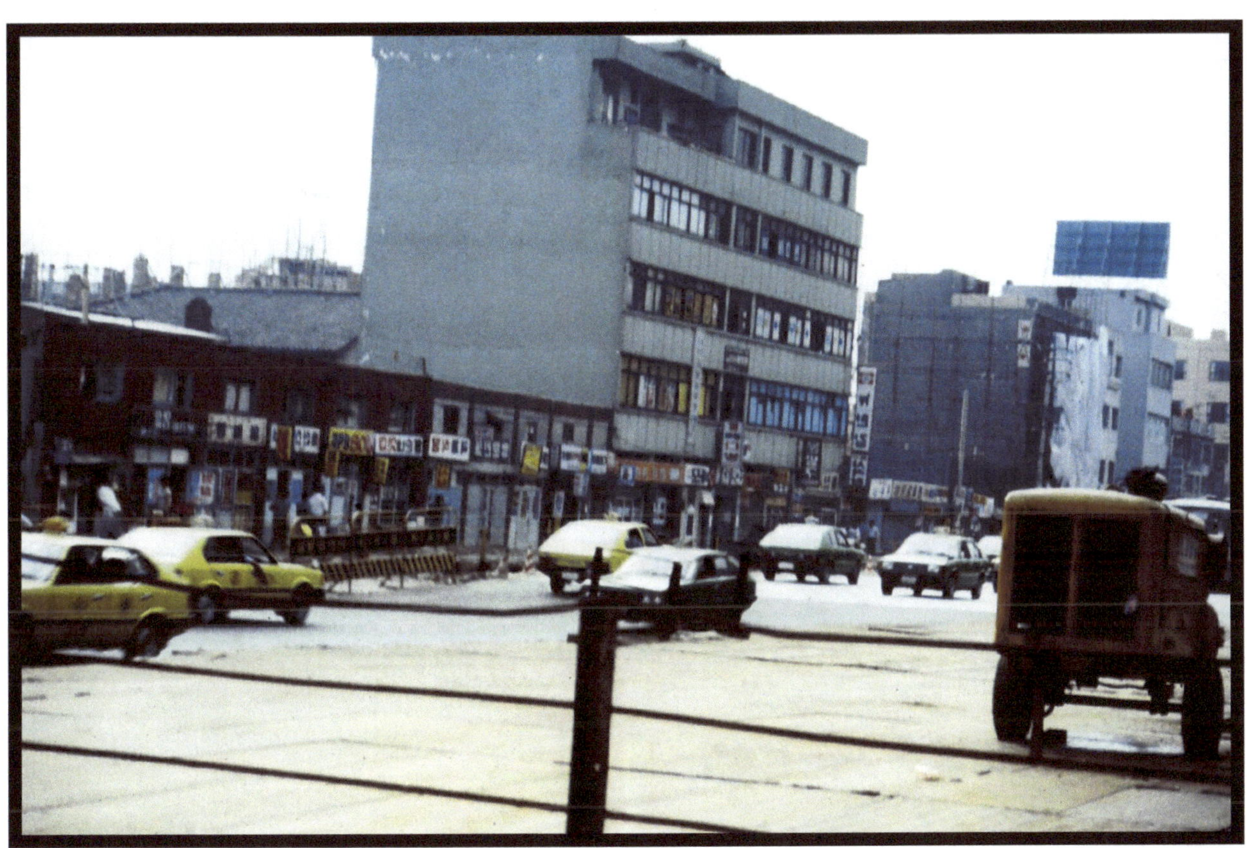

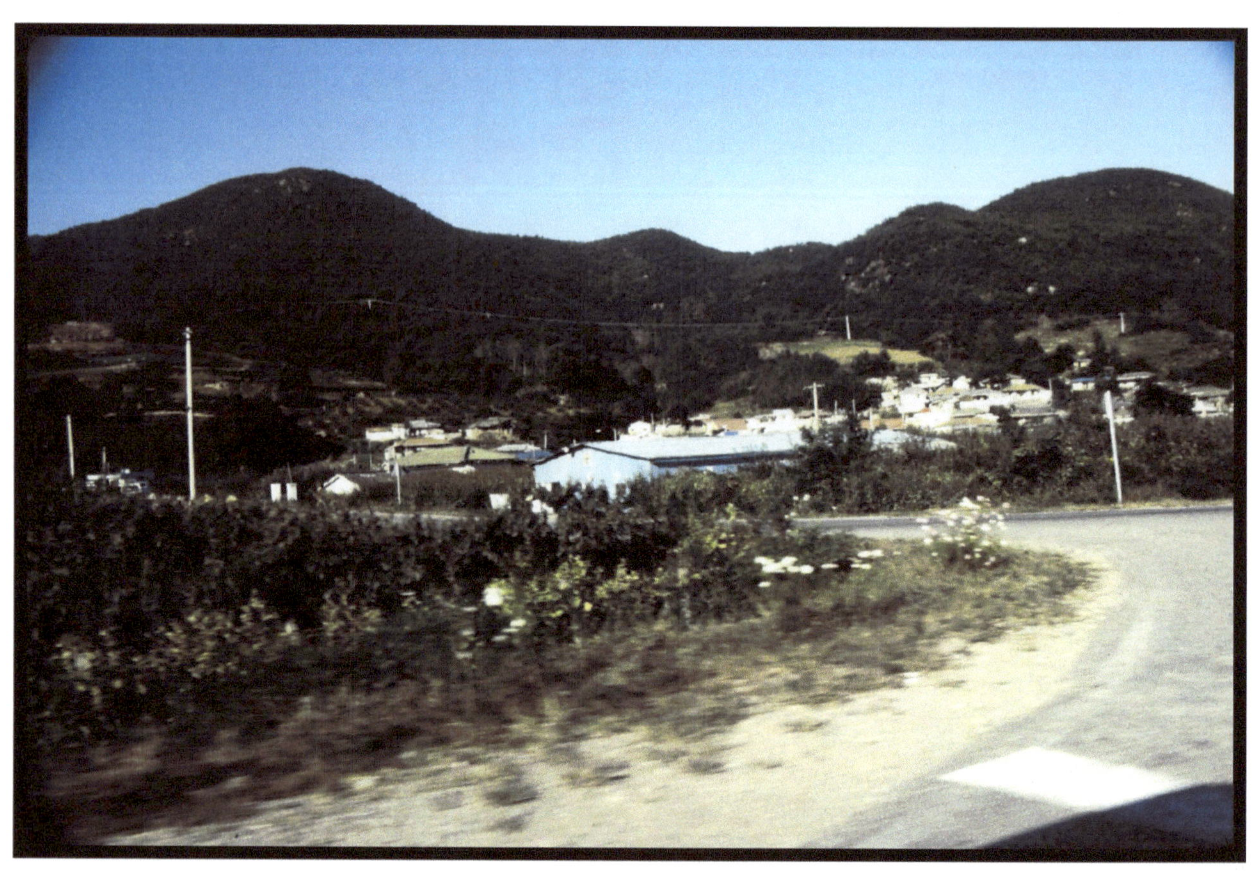

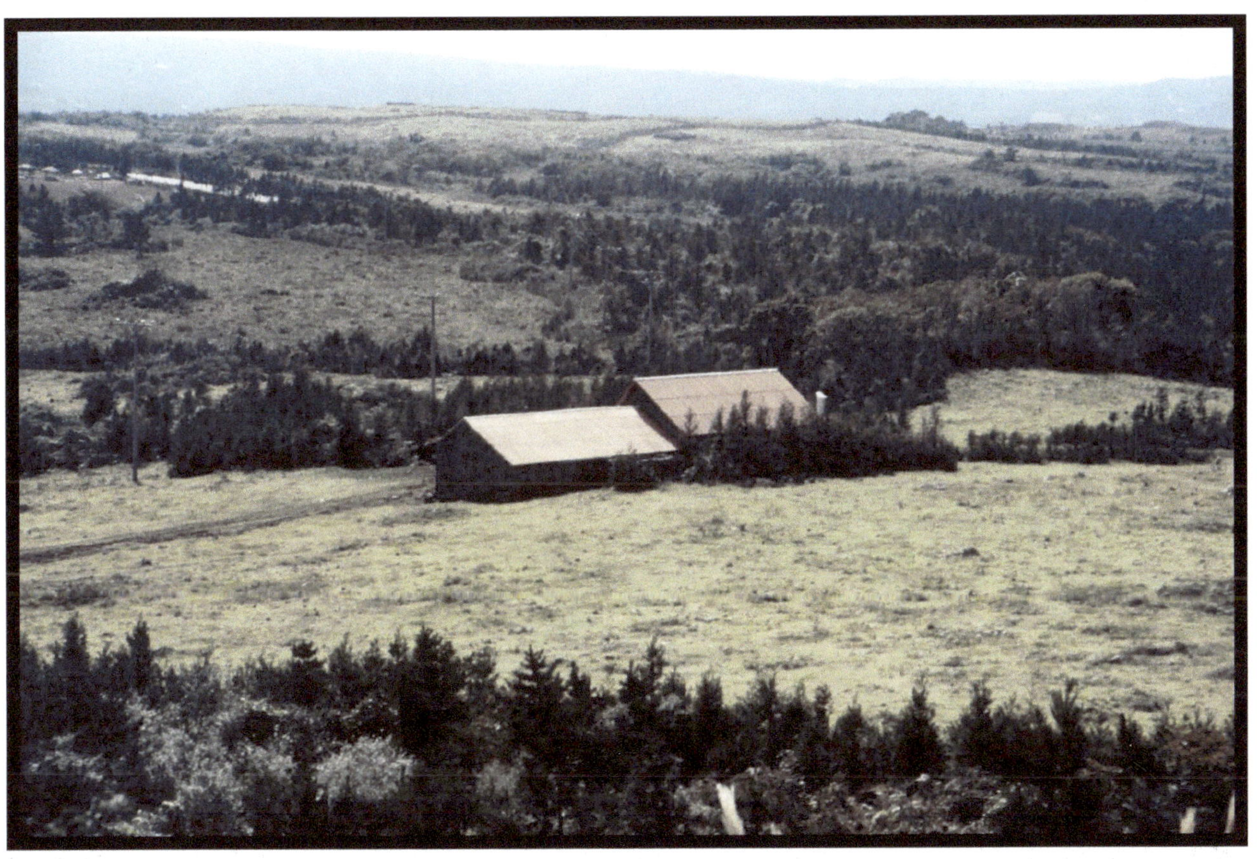

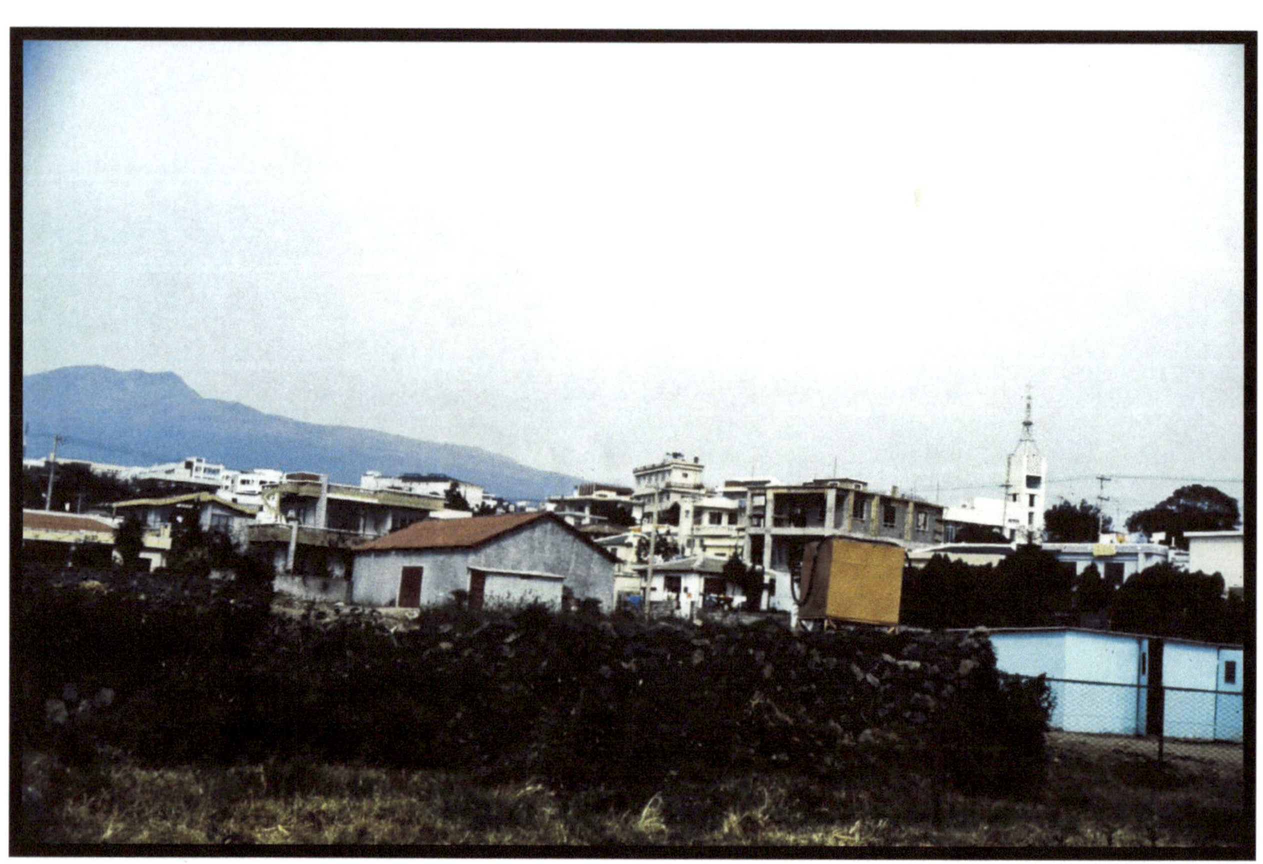

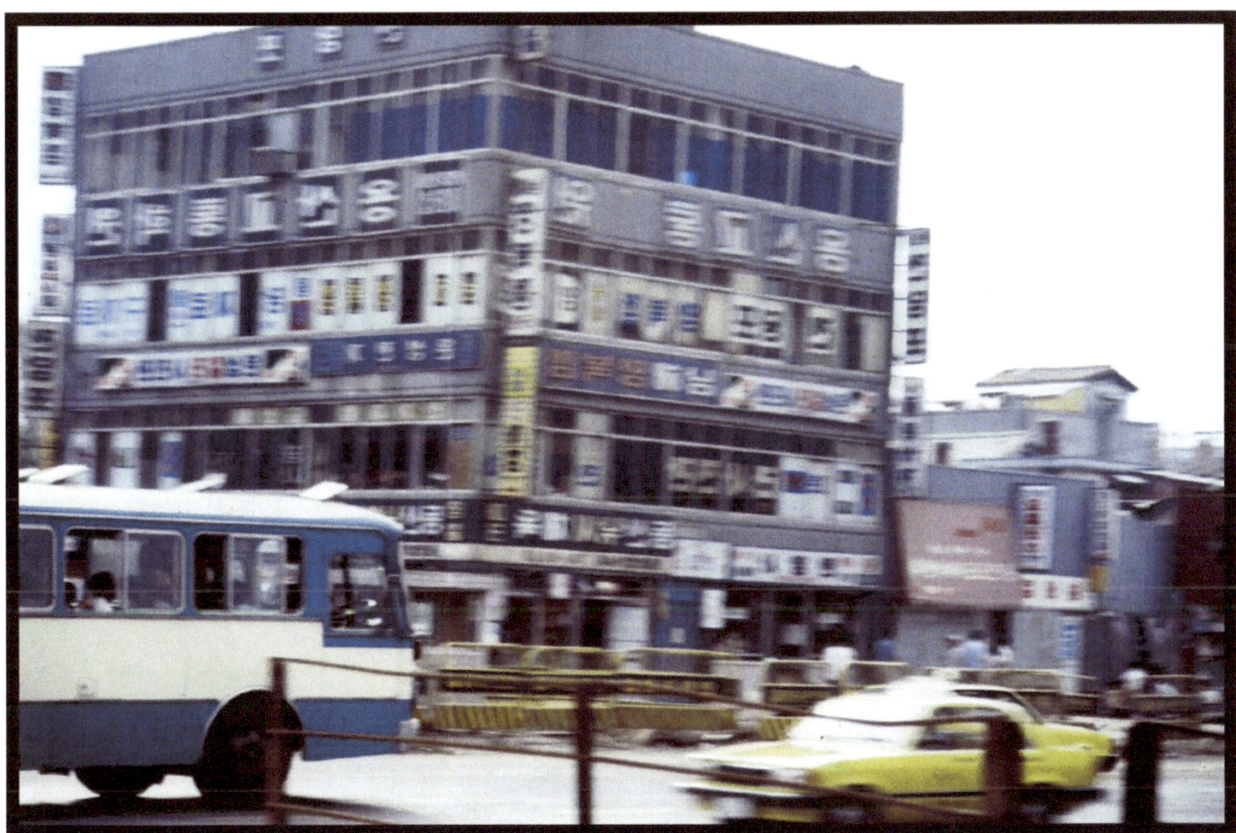

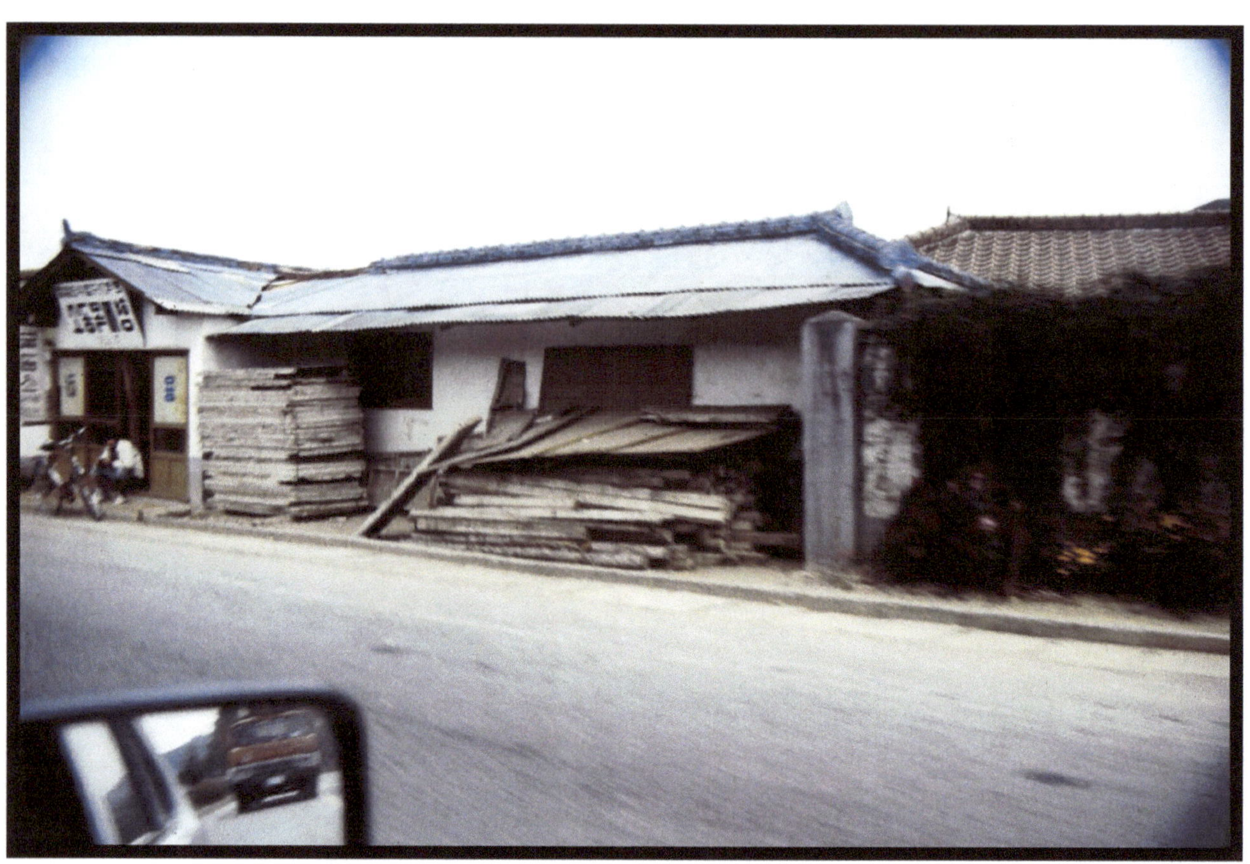

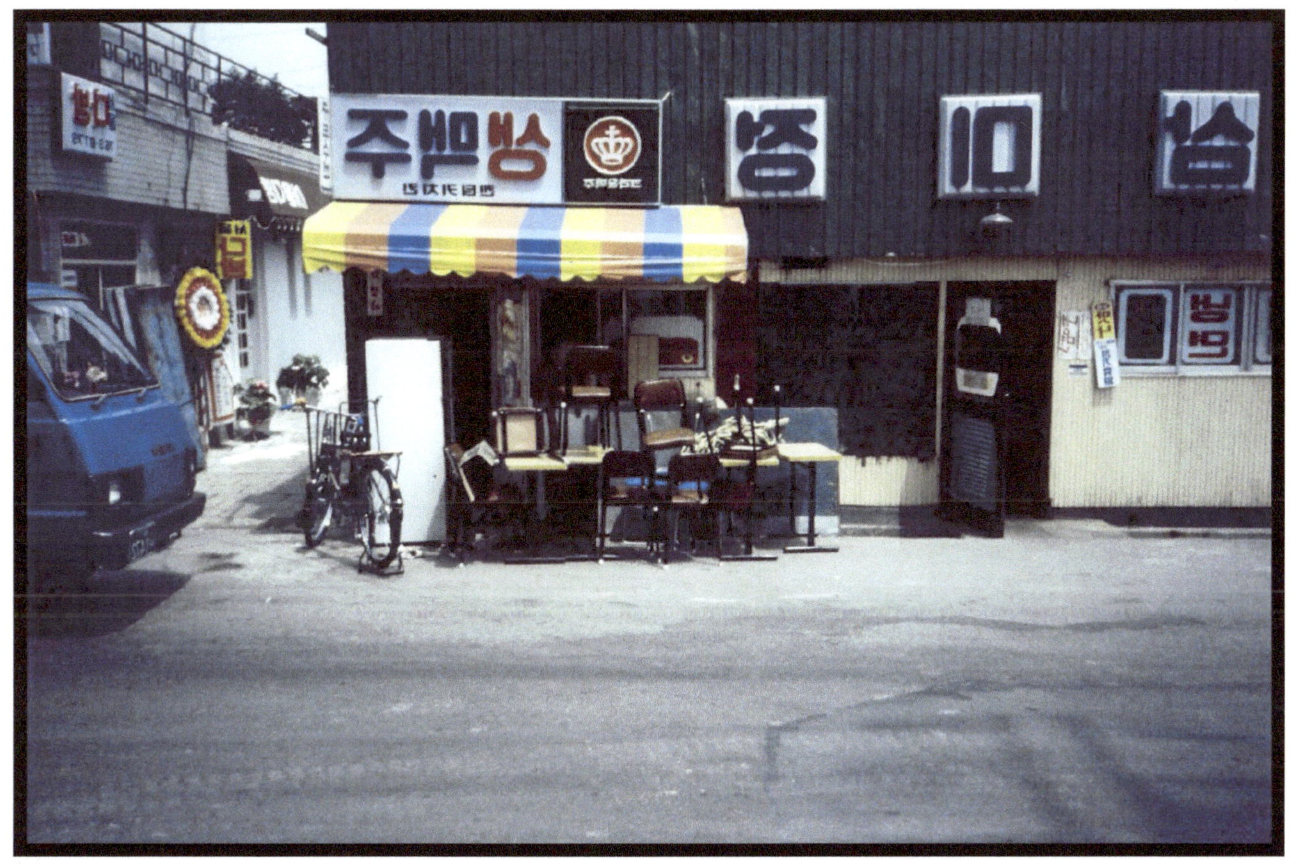

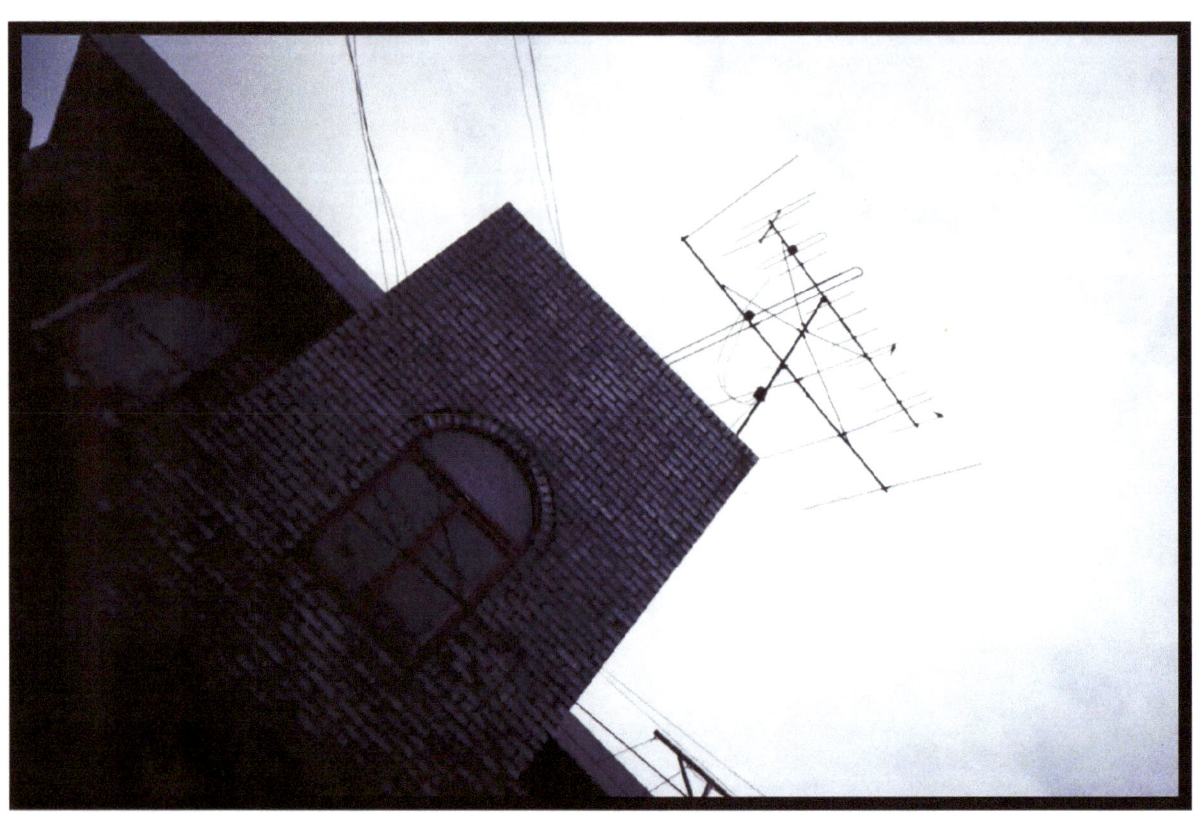

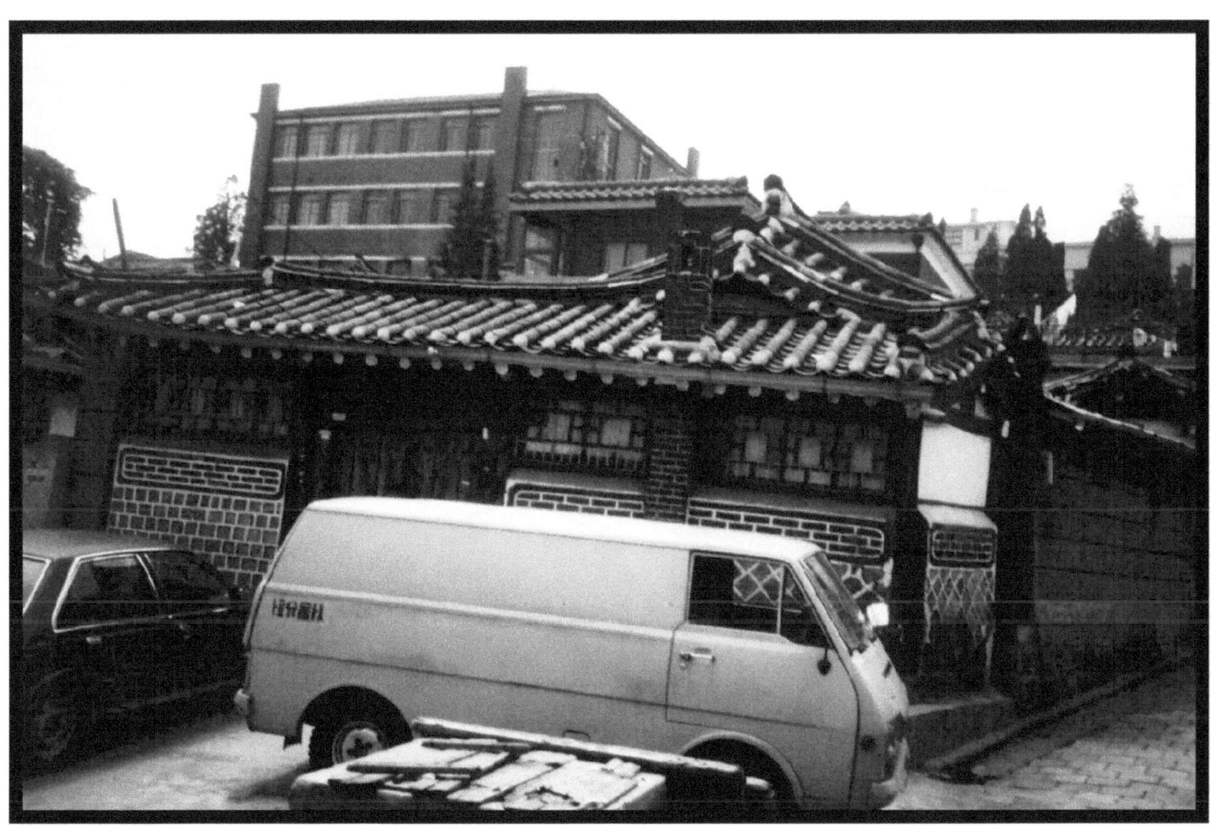

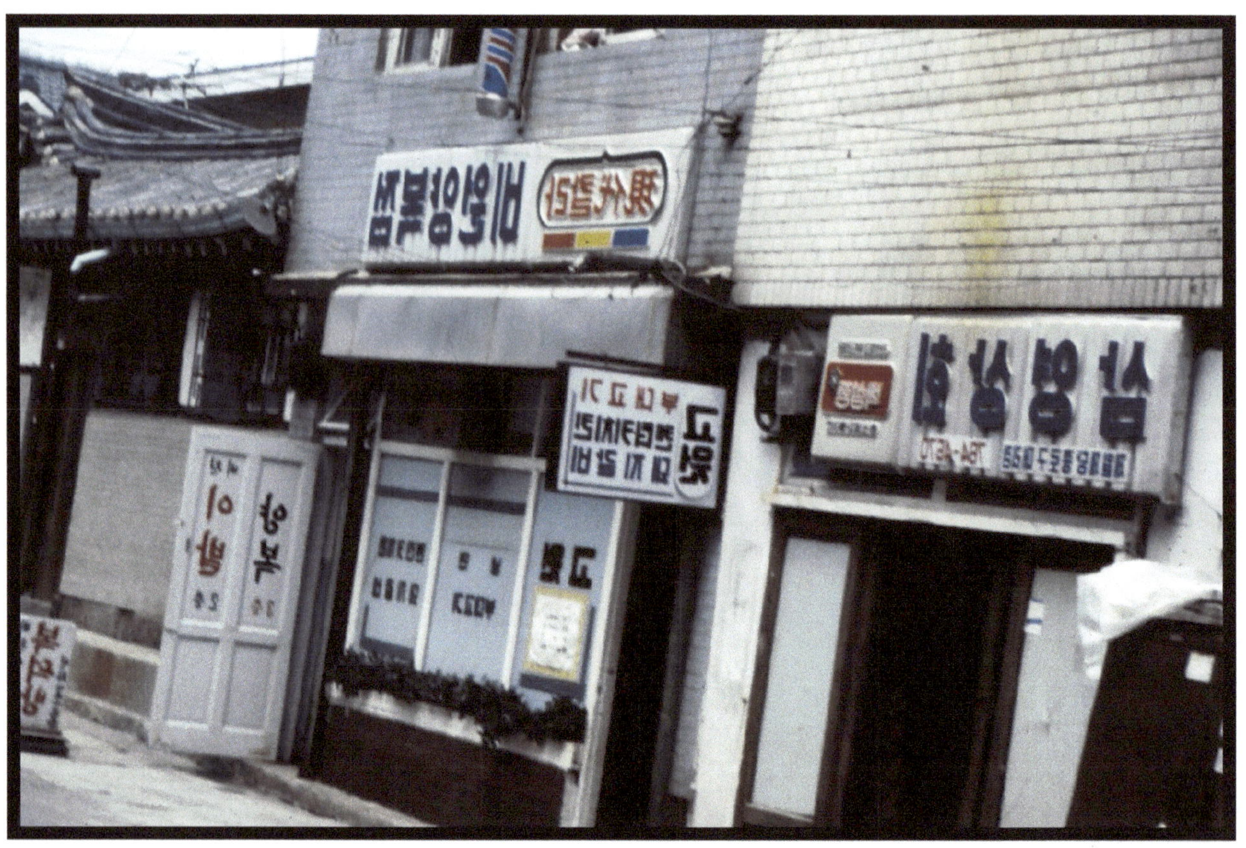

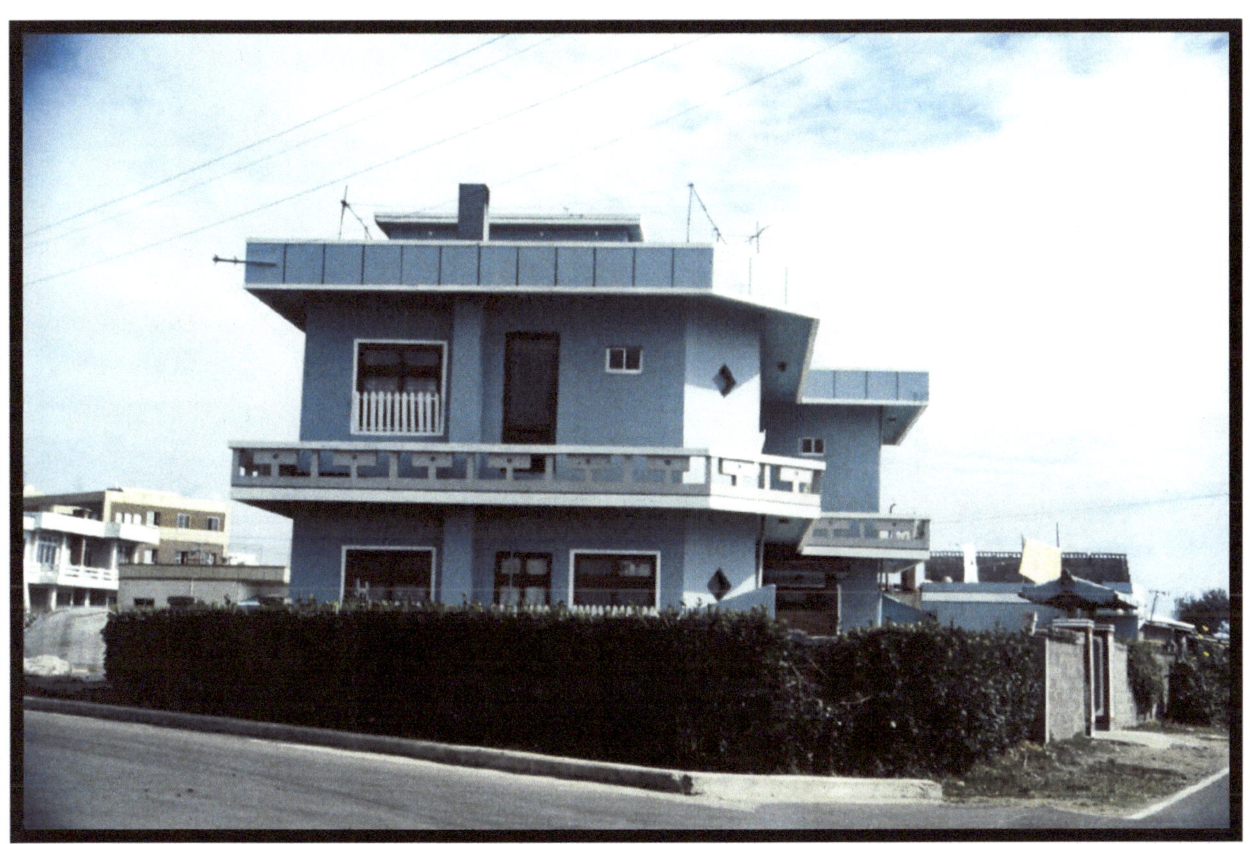

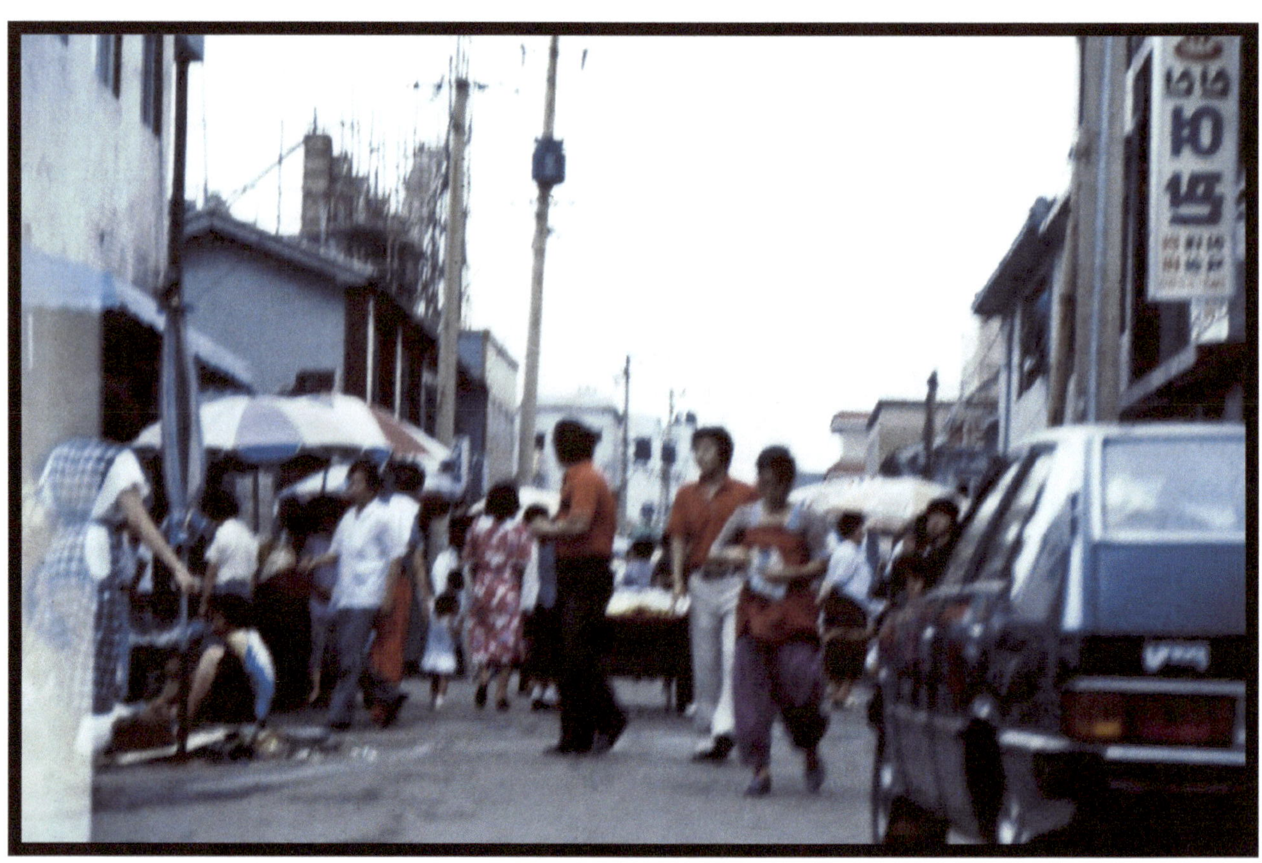

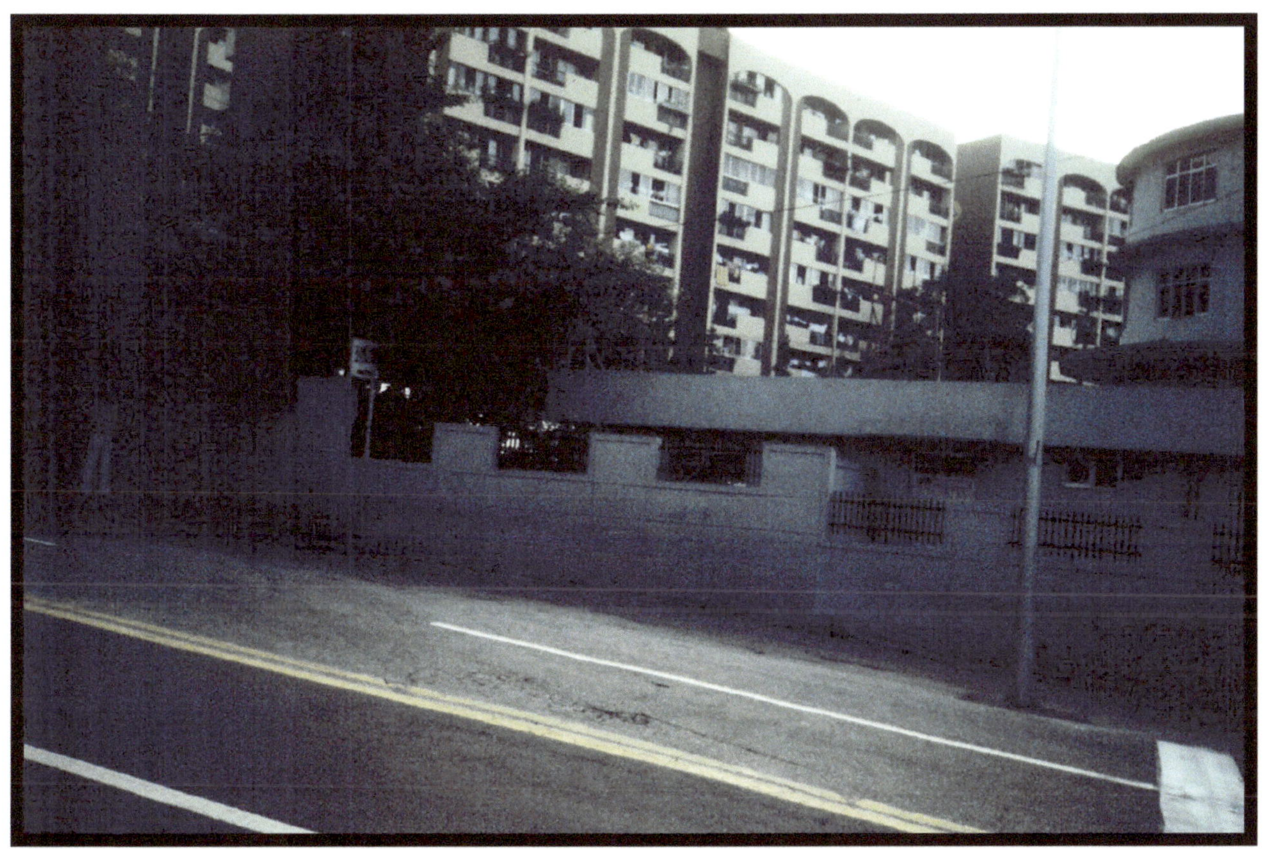

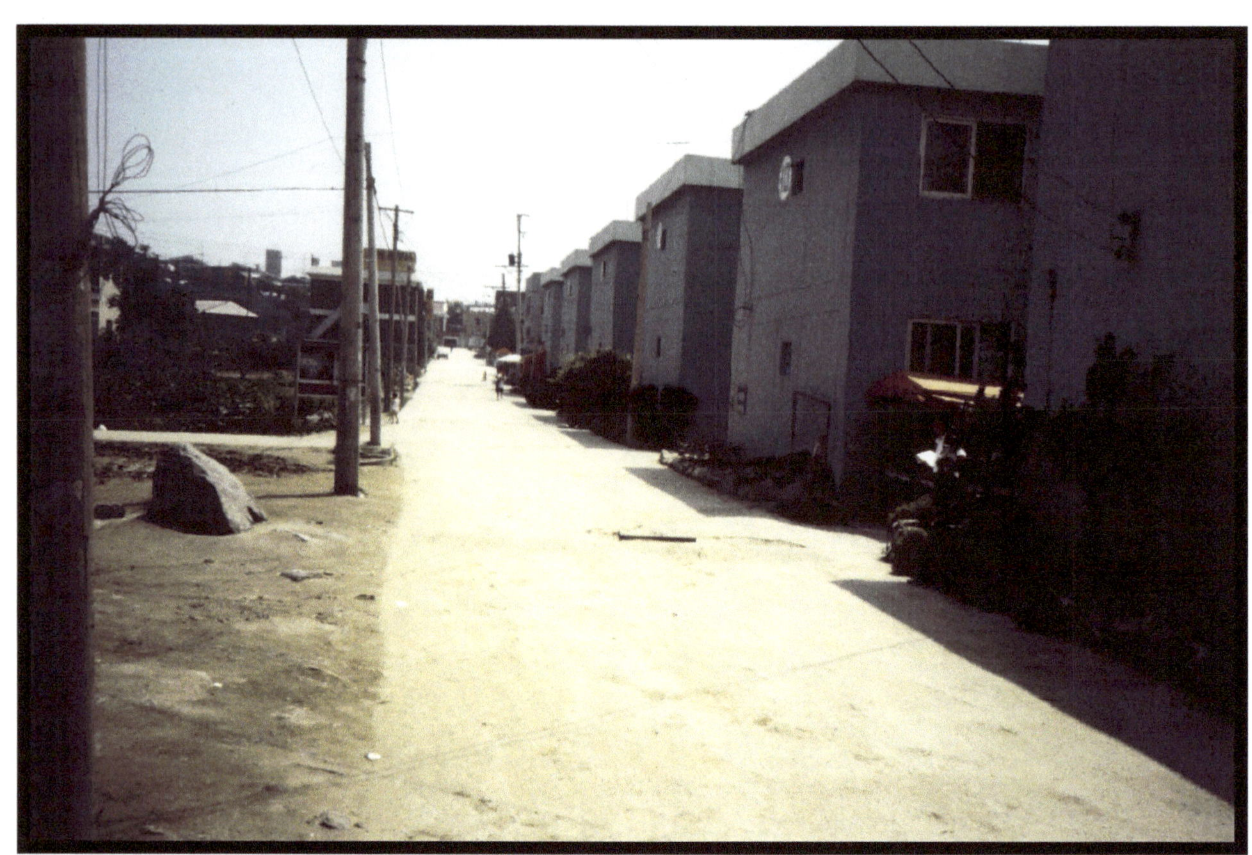

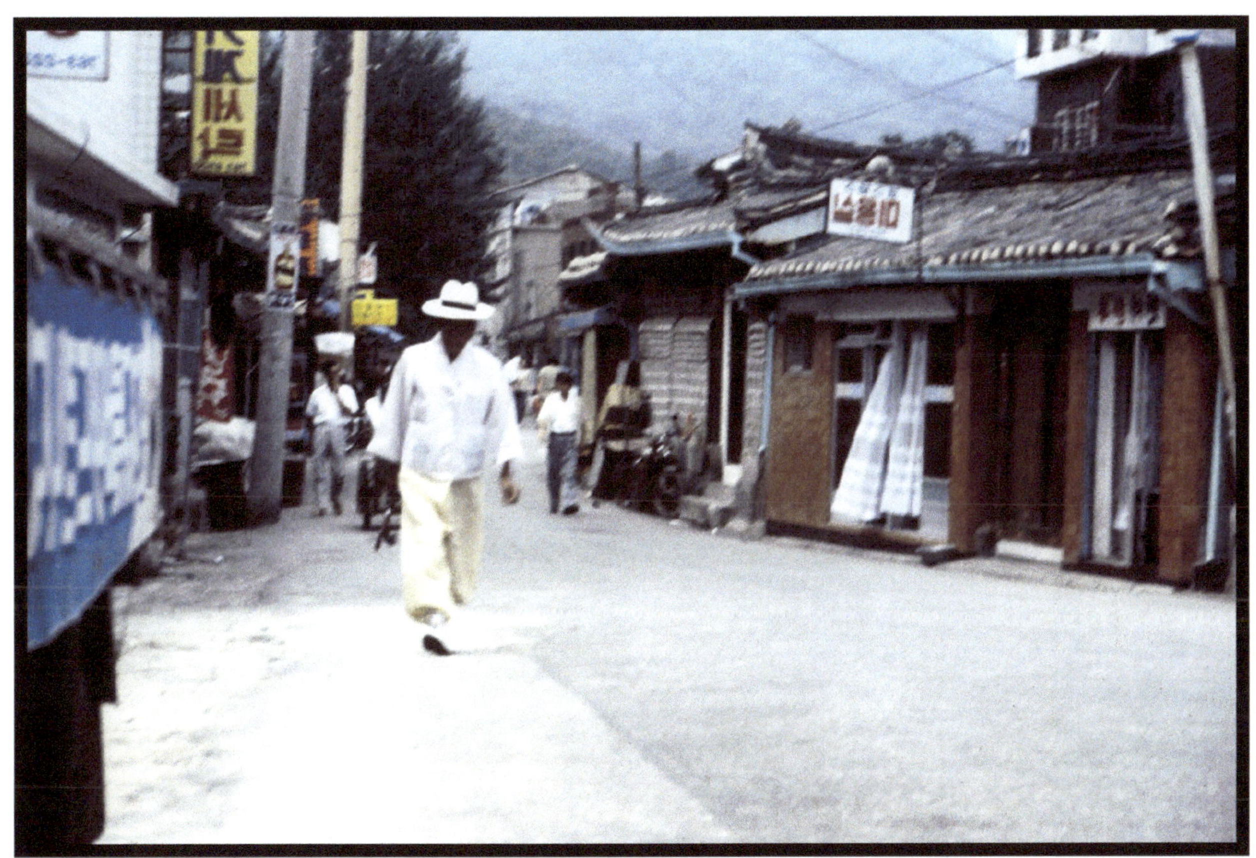

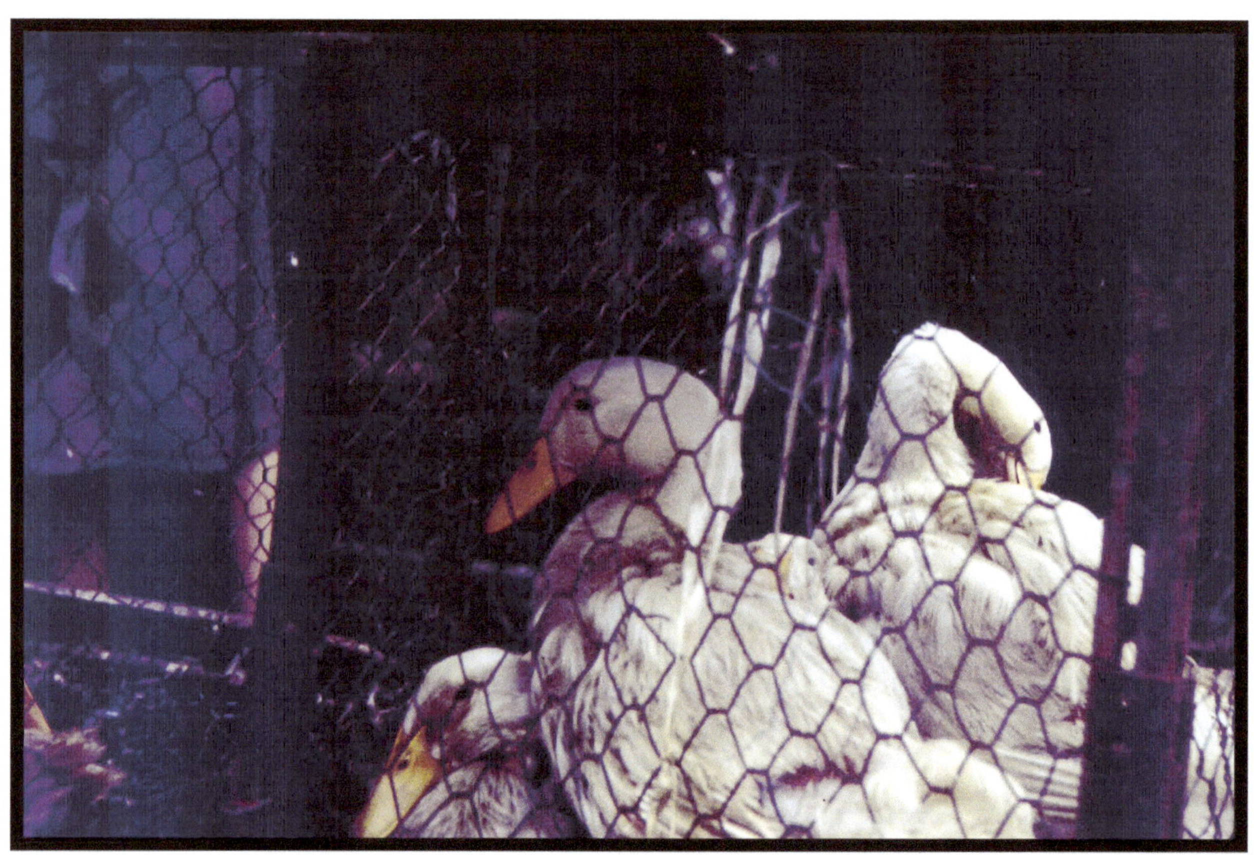

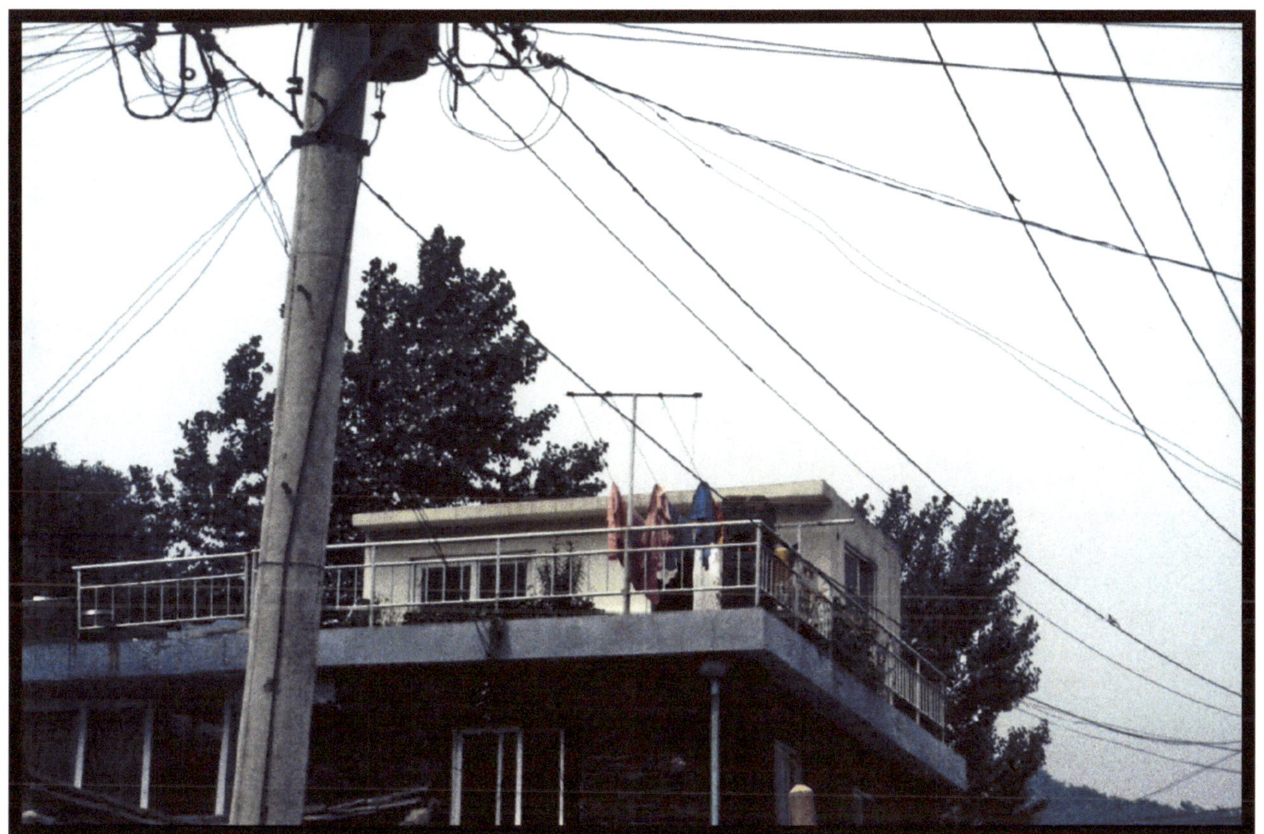

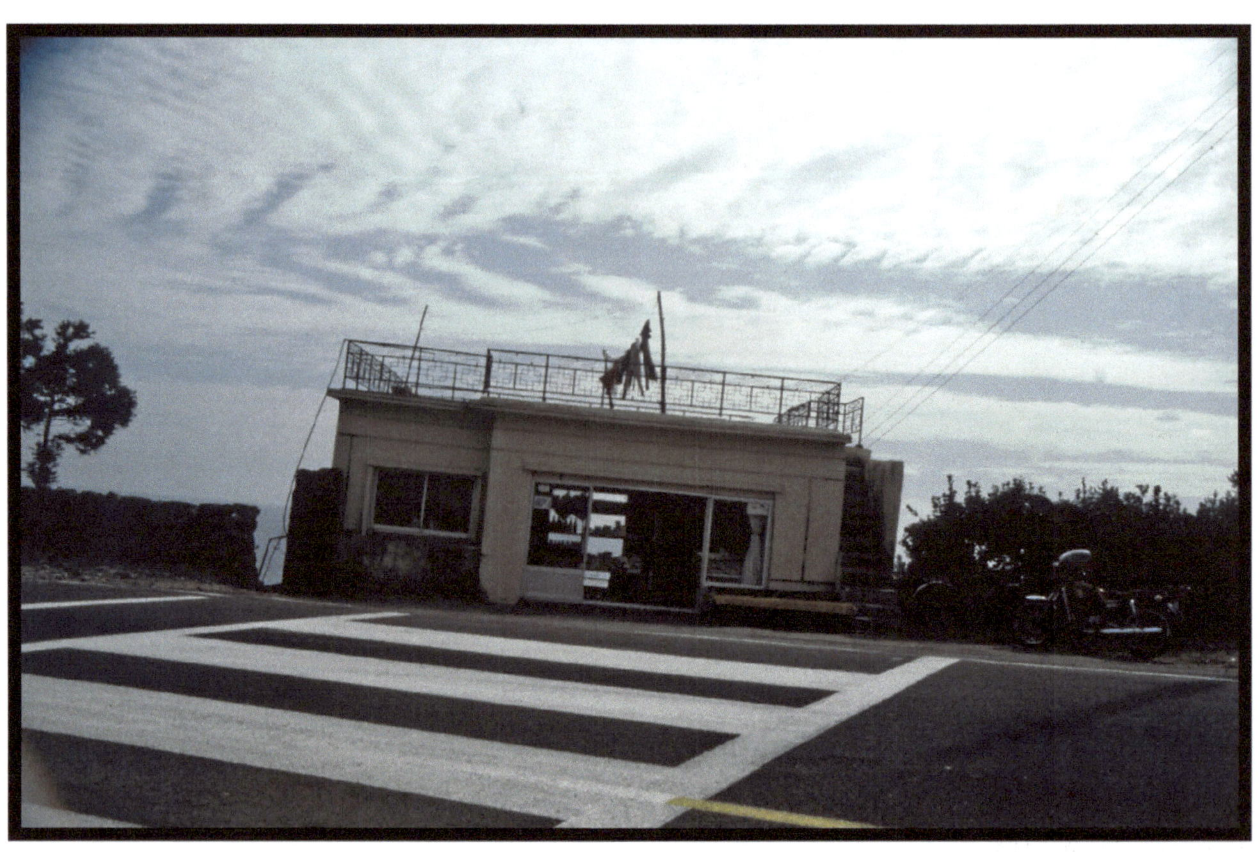

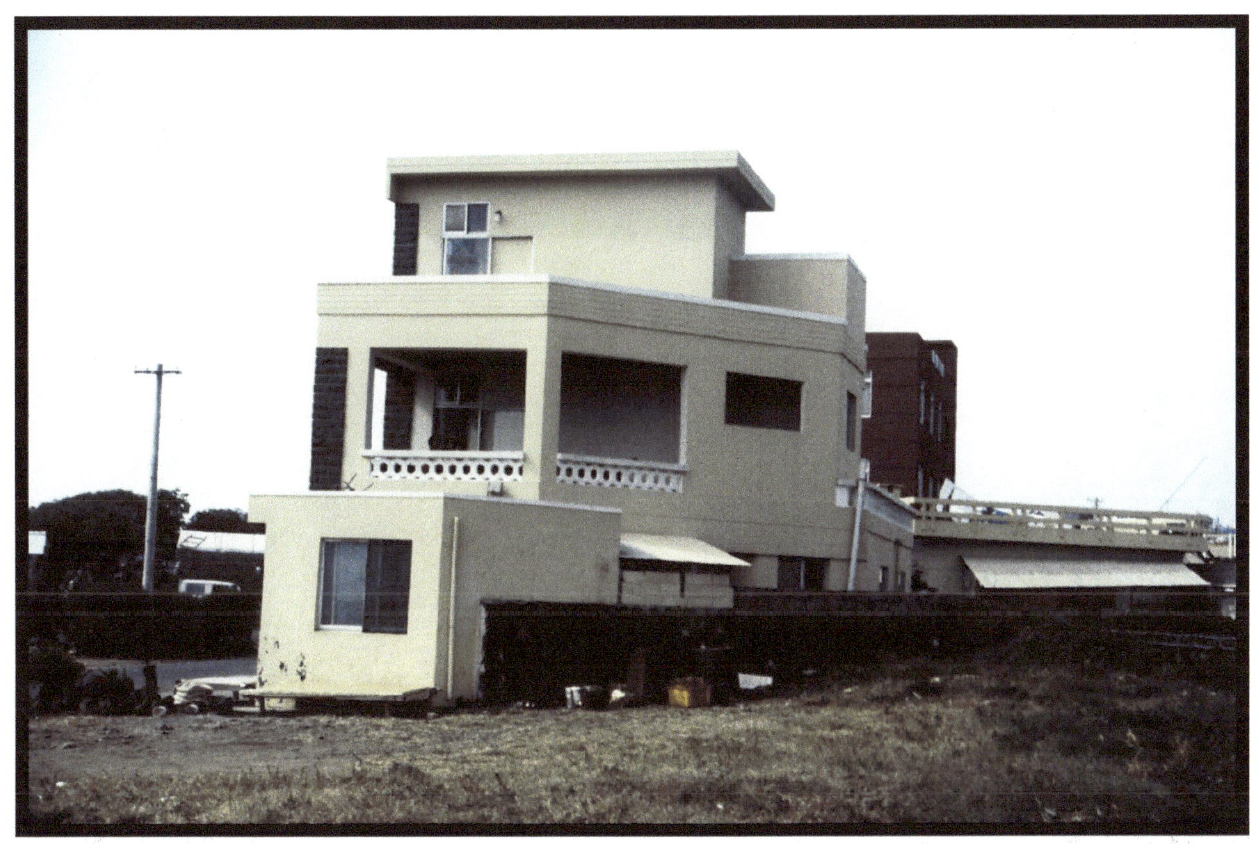

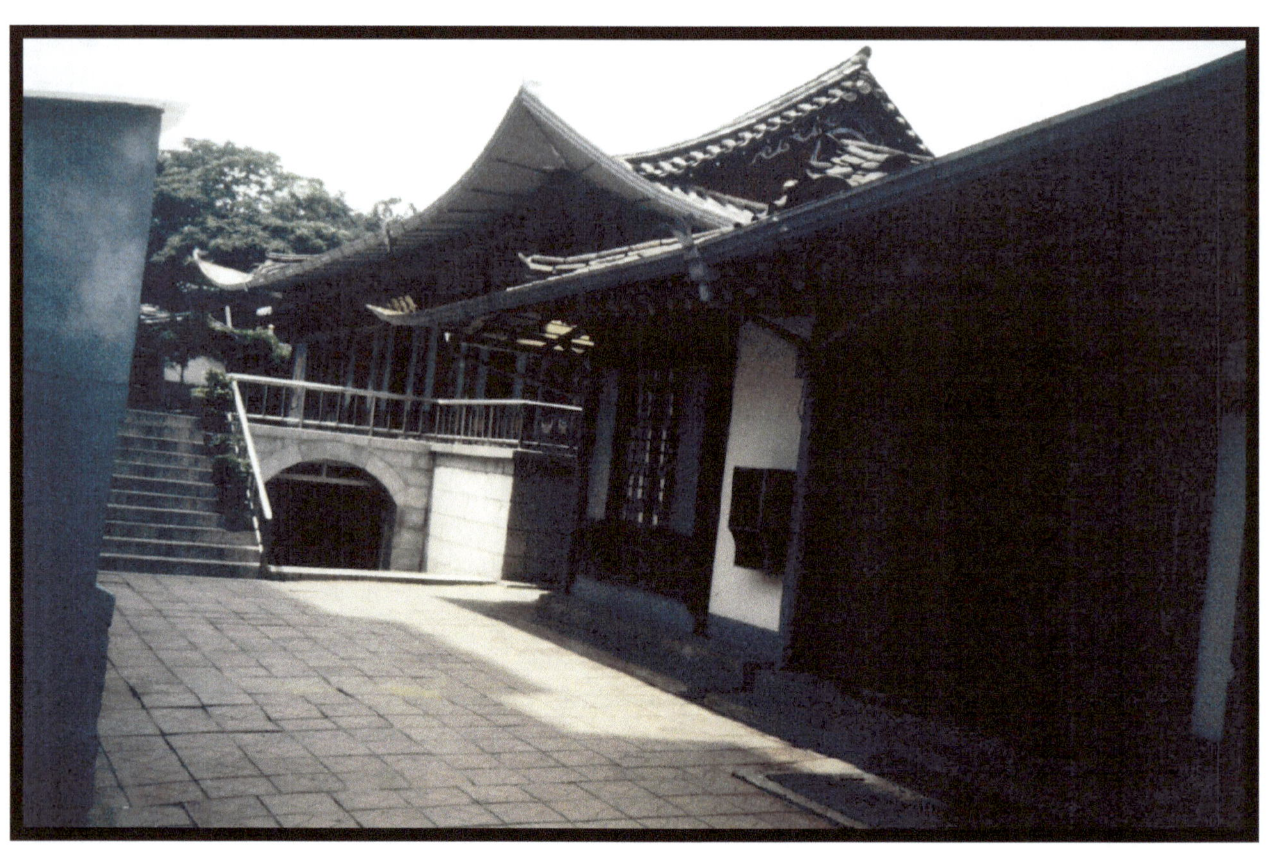

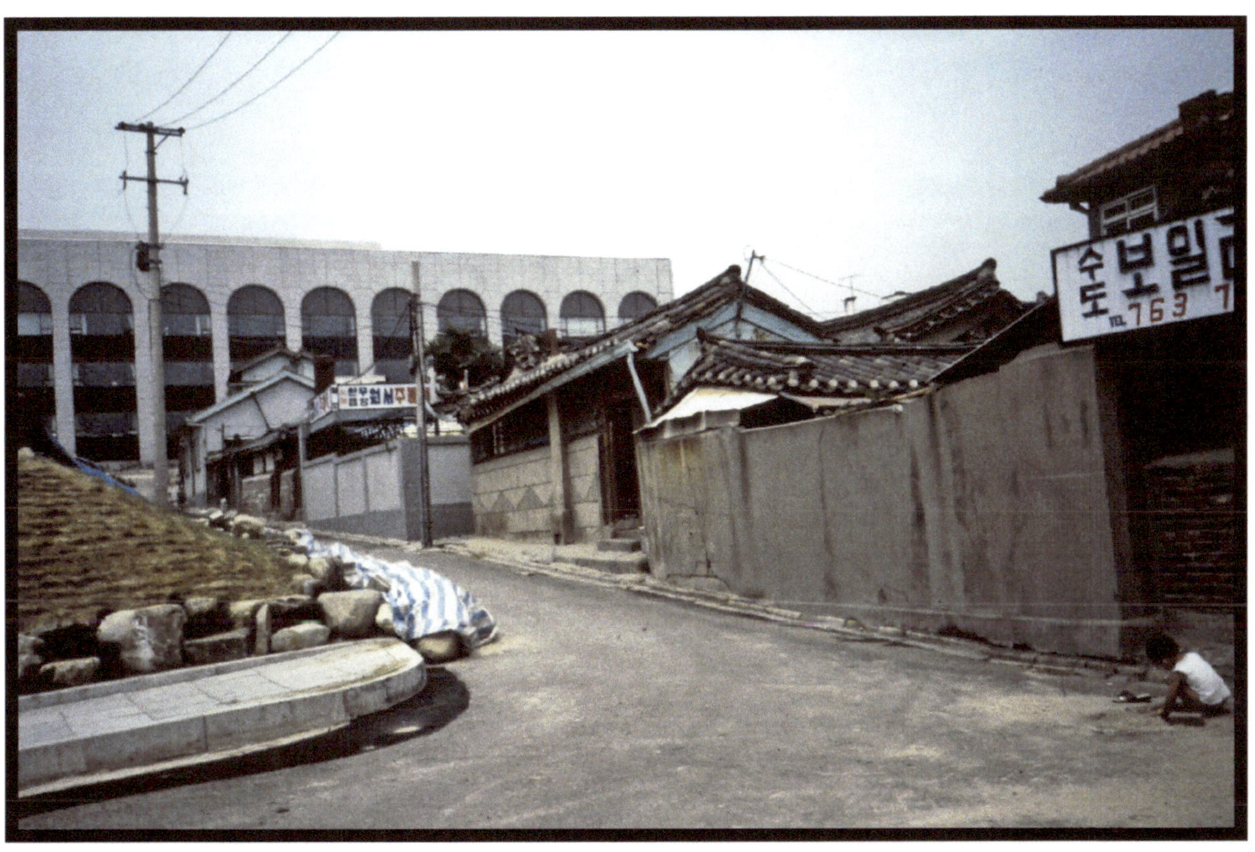
수도보일
TEL 763 7

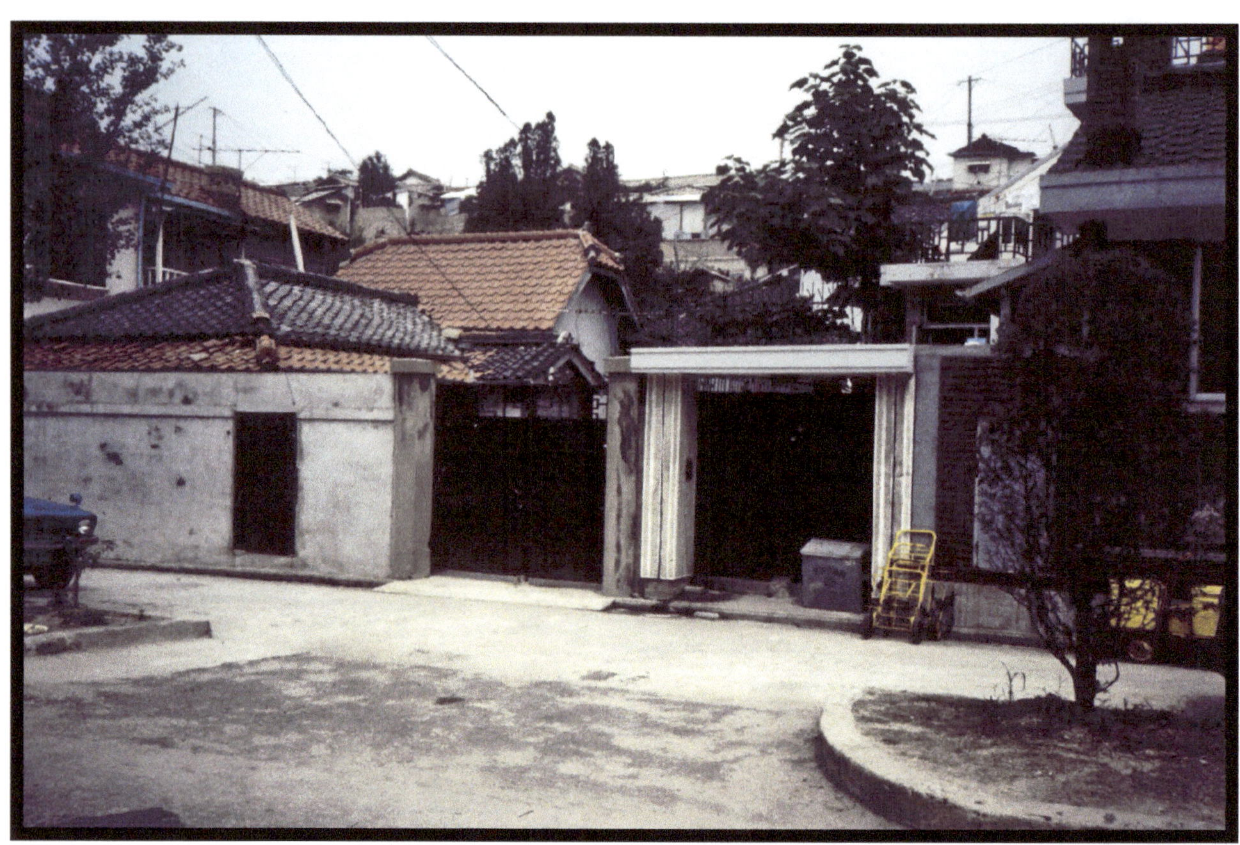

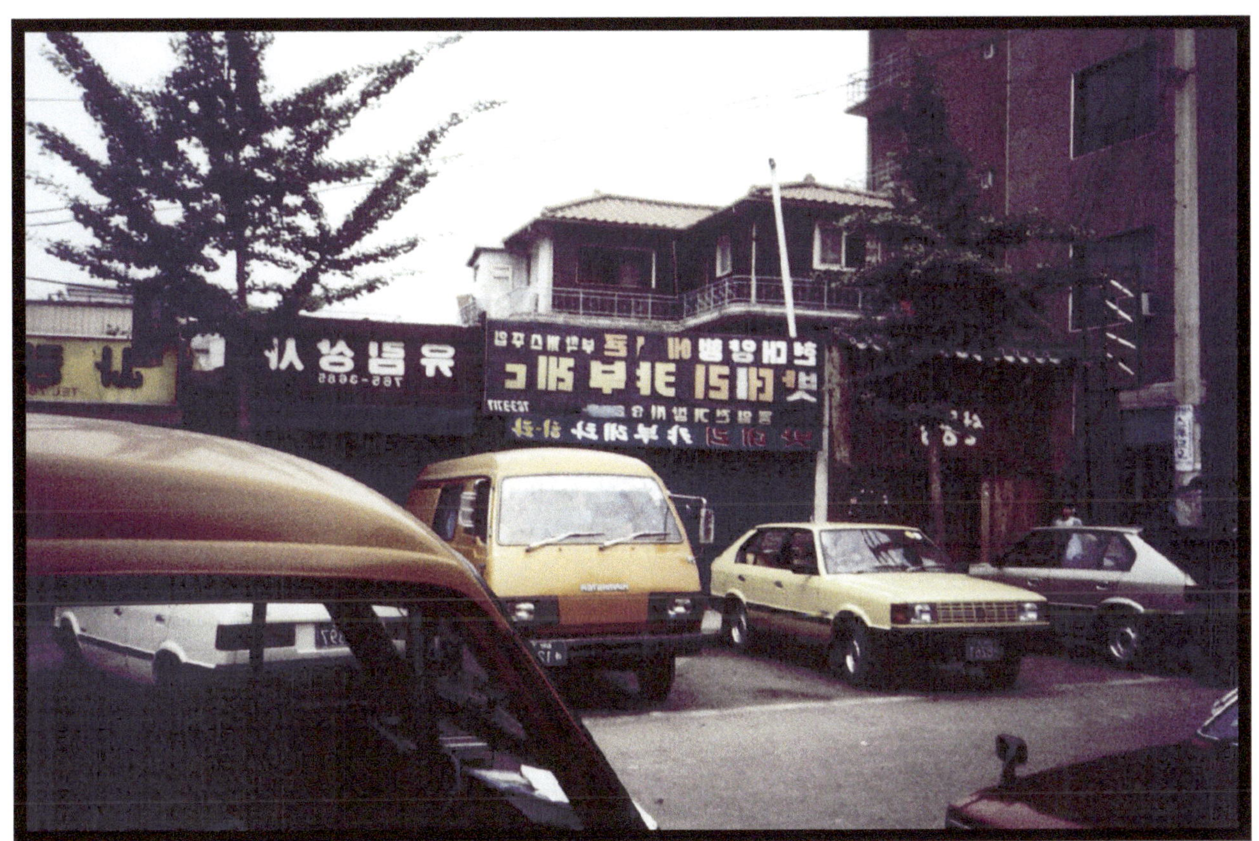

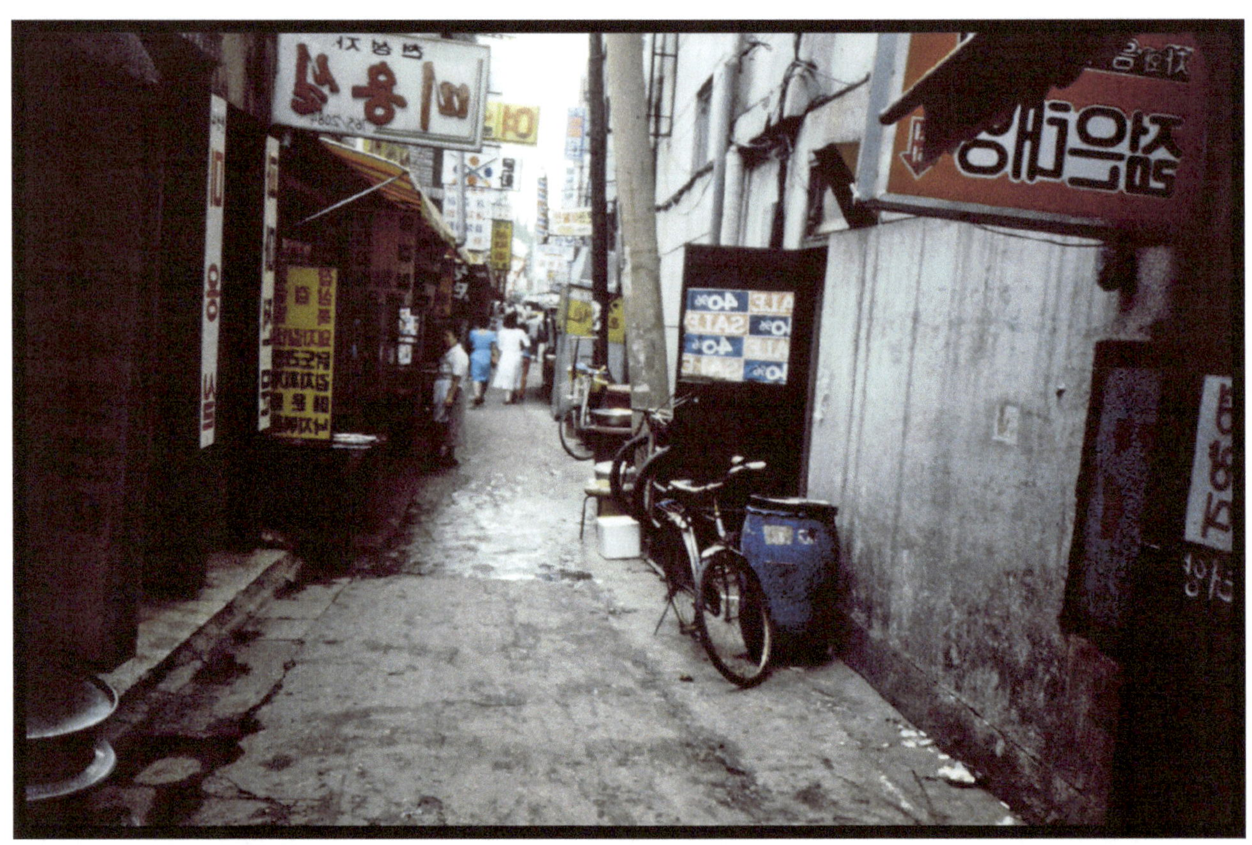

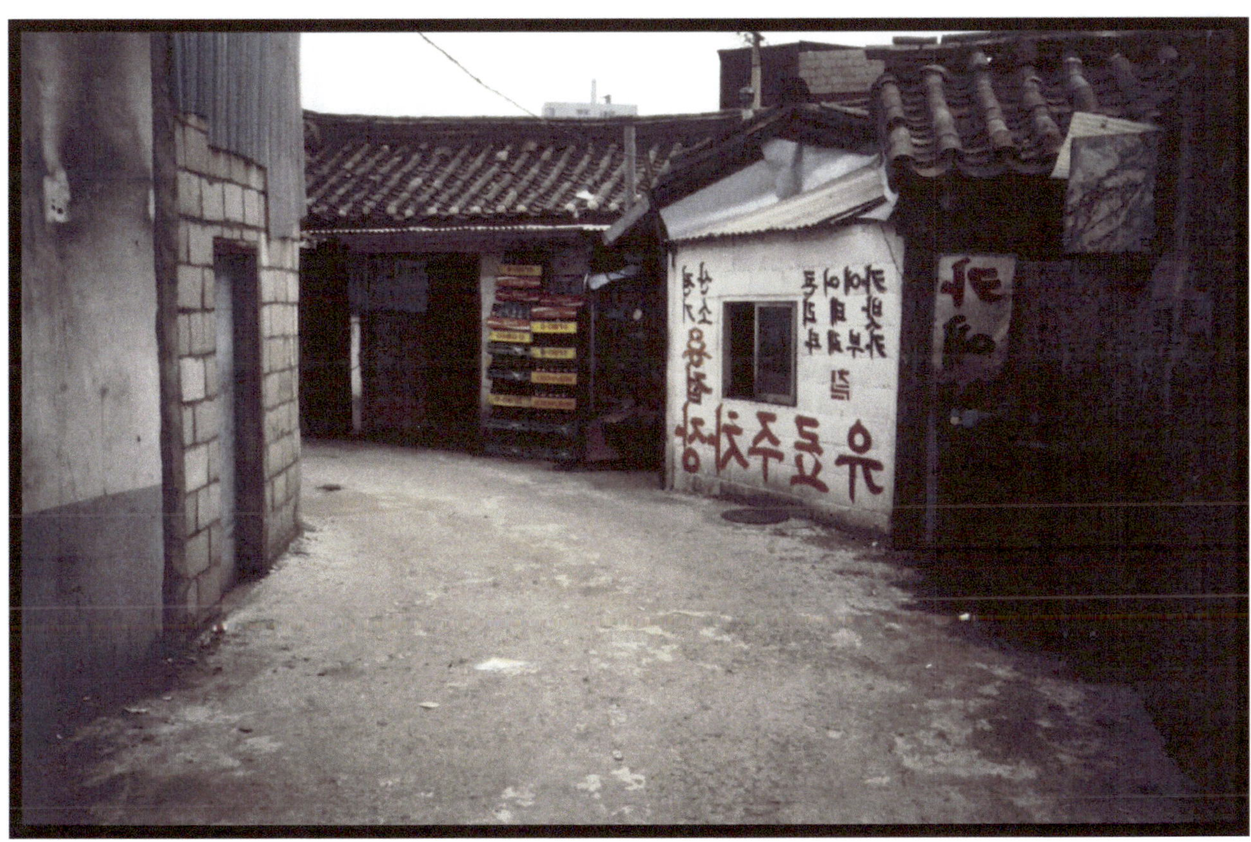
유료주차장

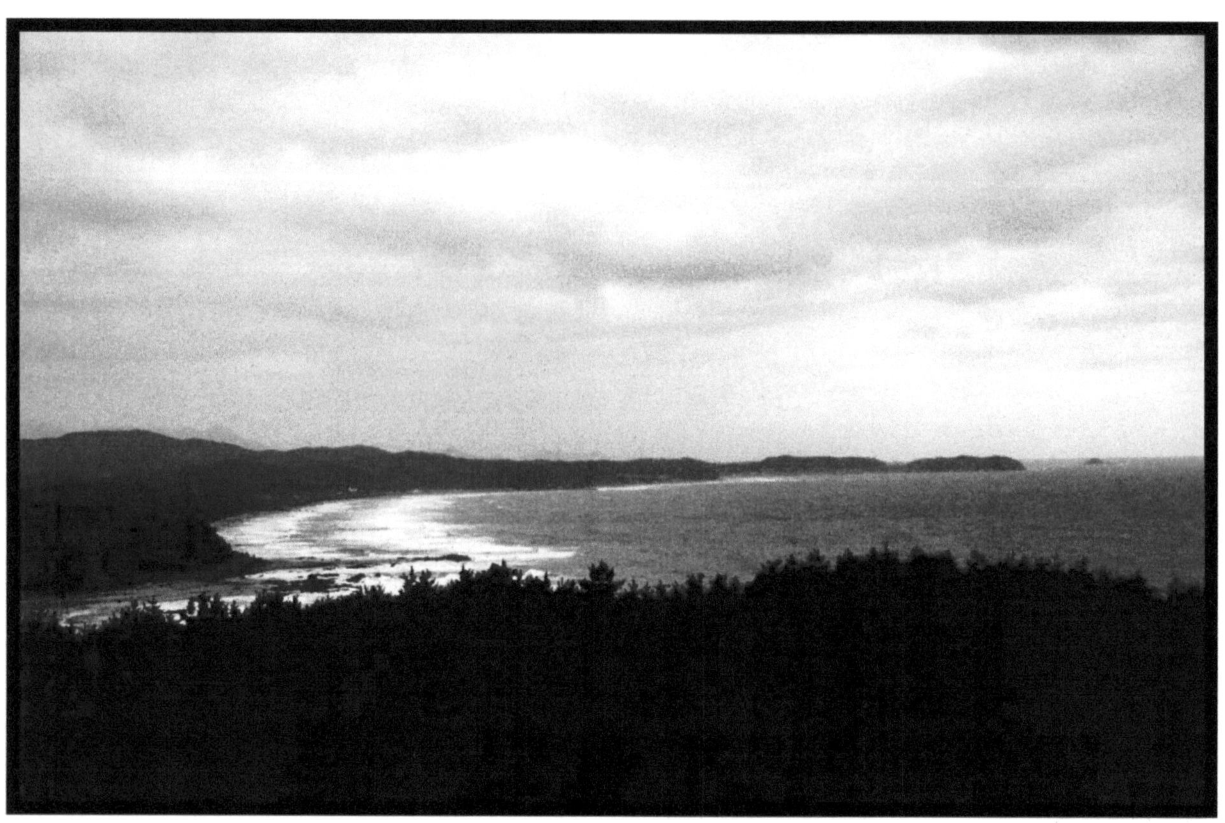

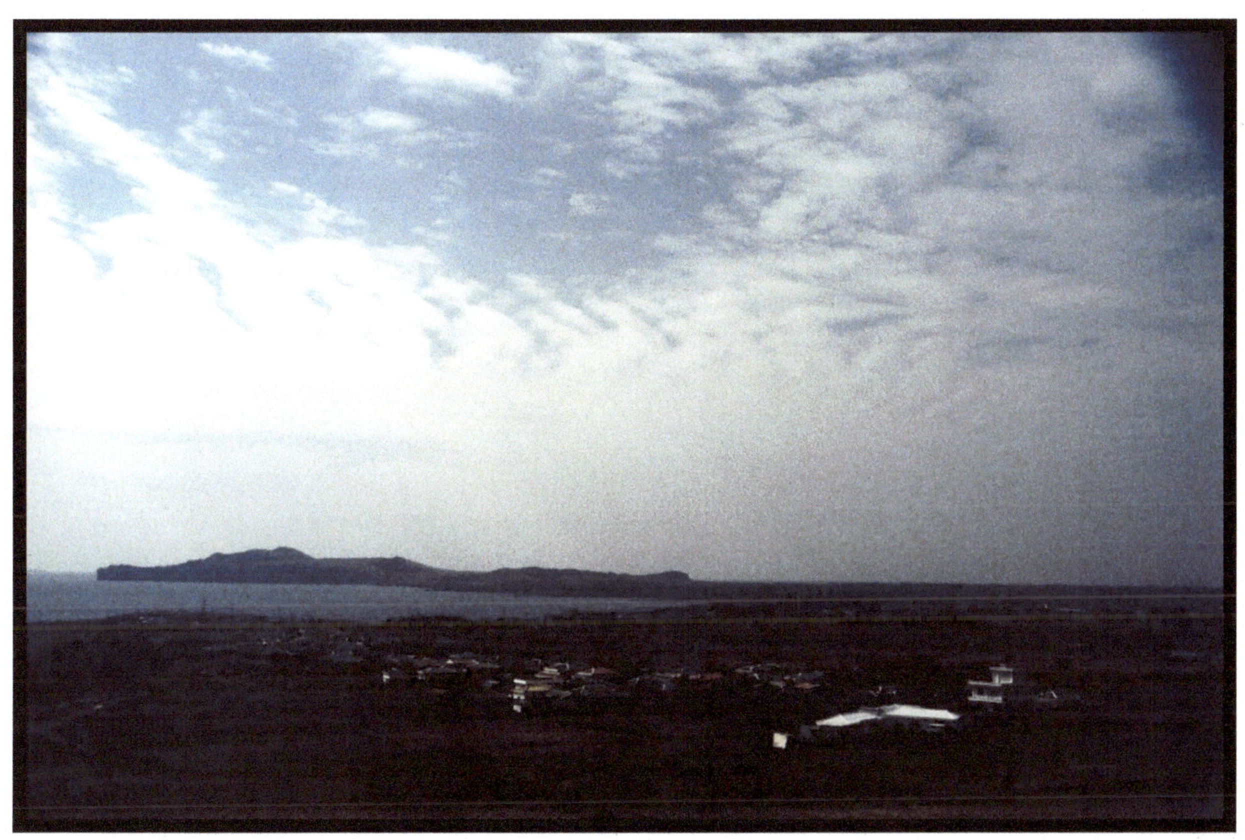

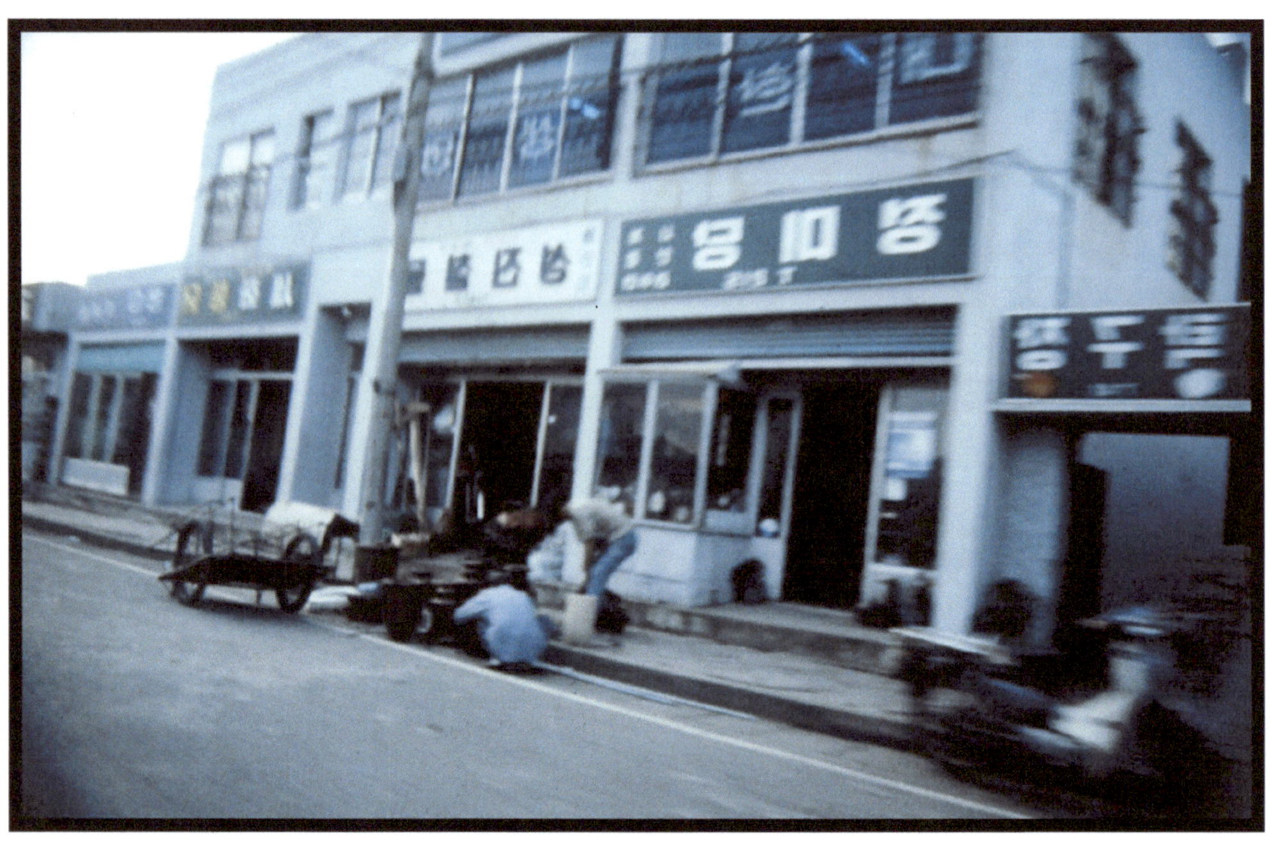

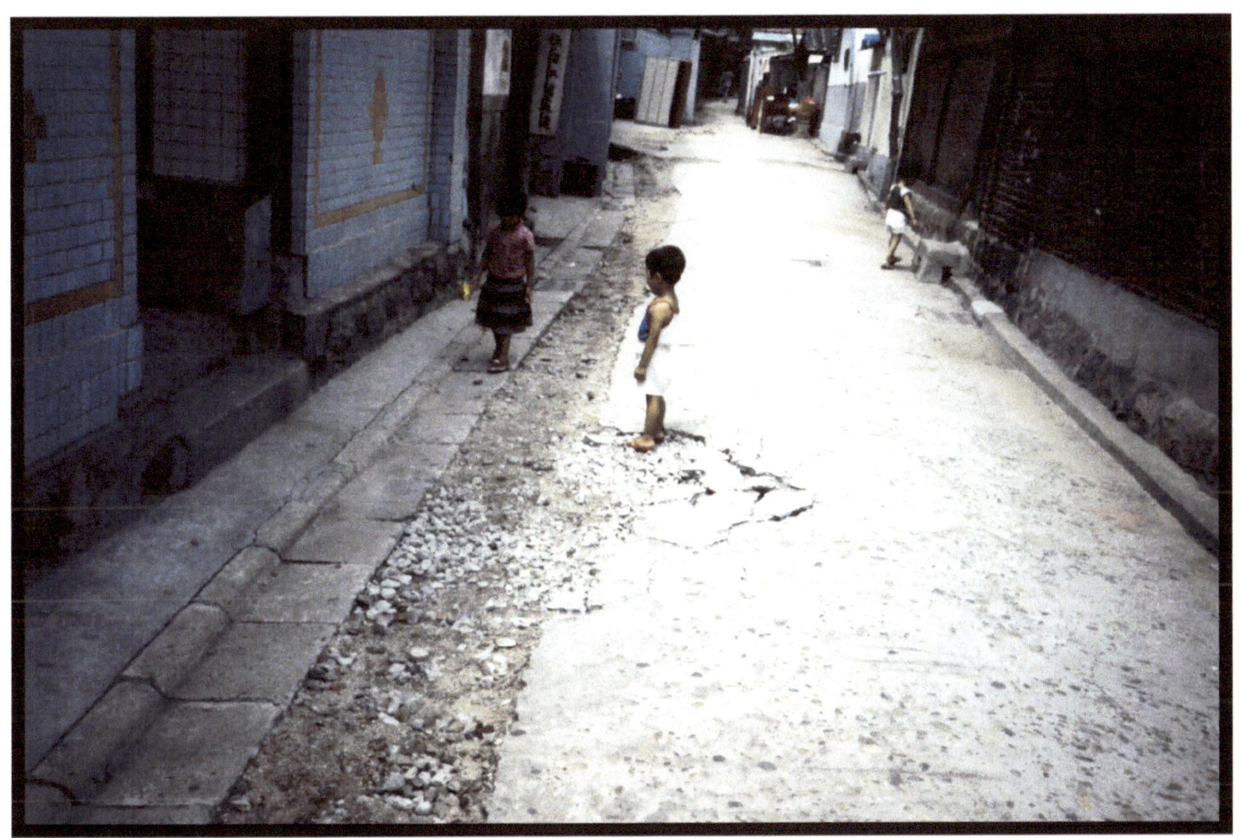

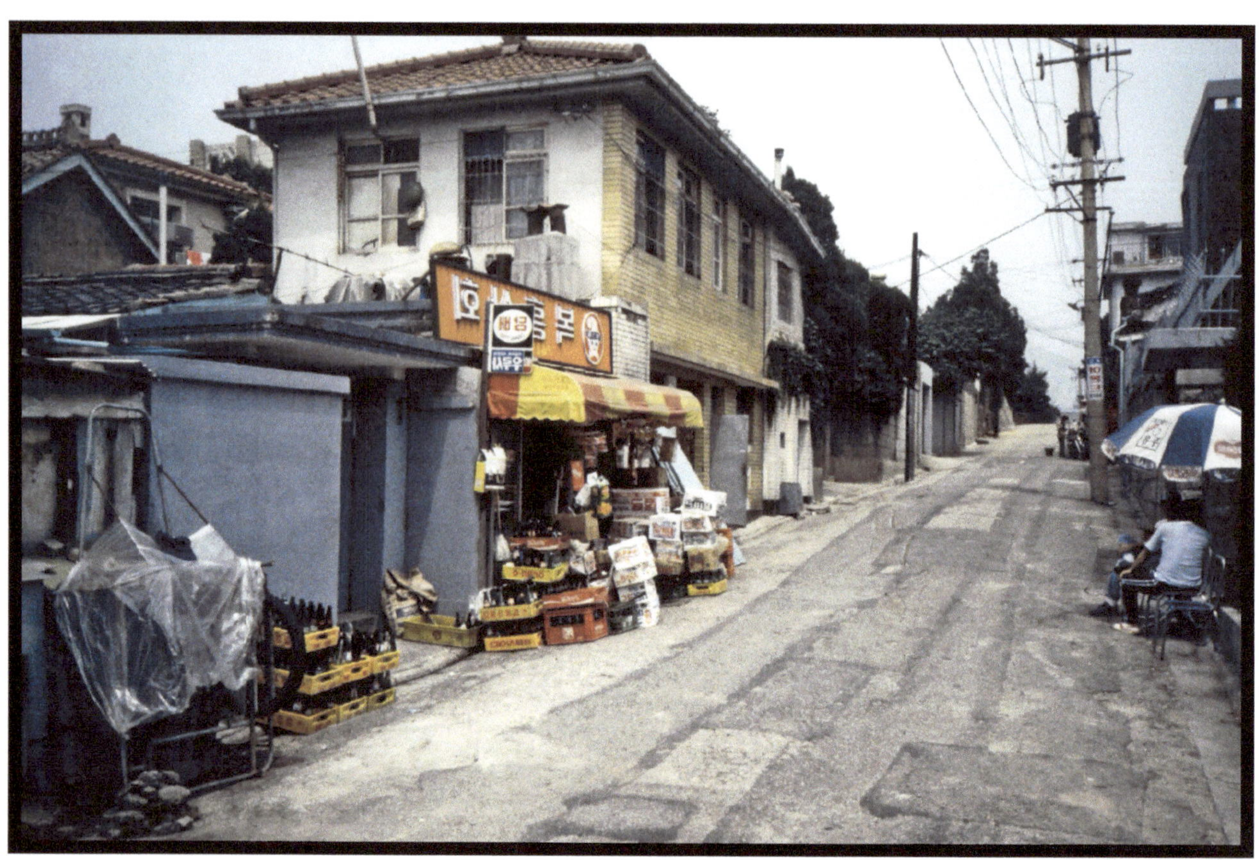

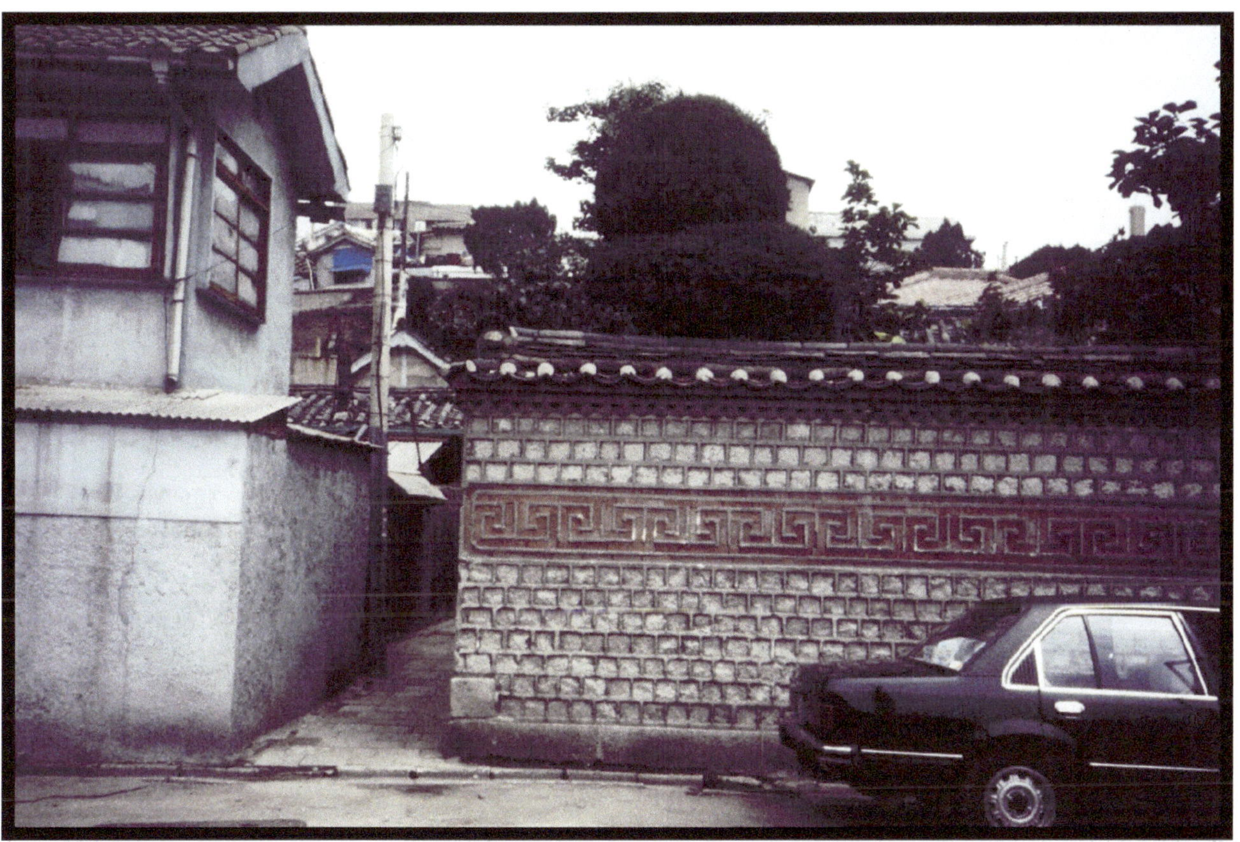

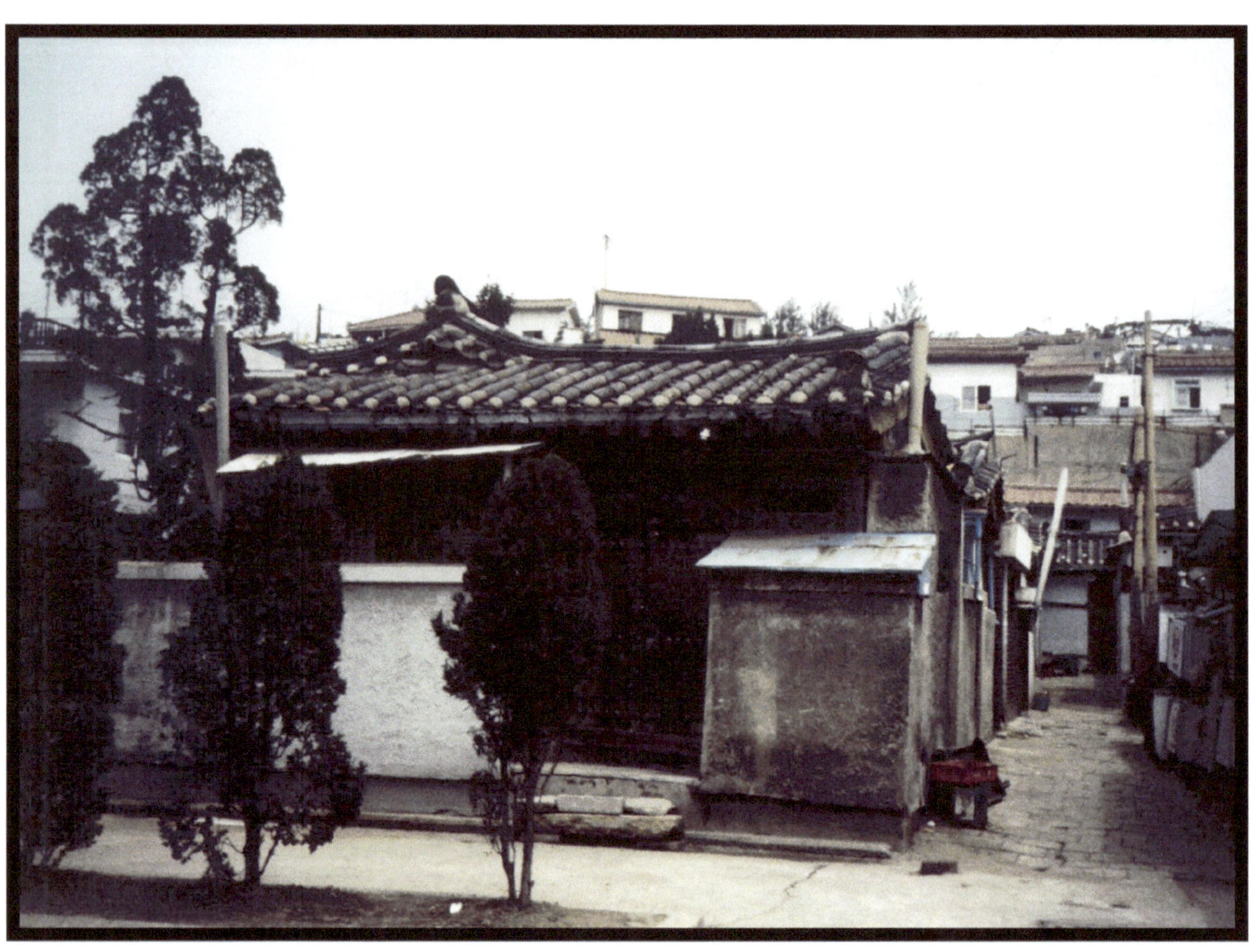

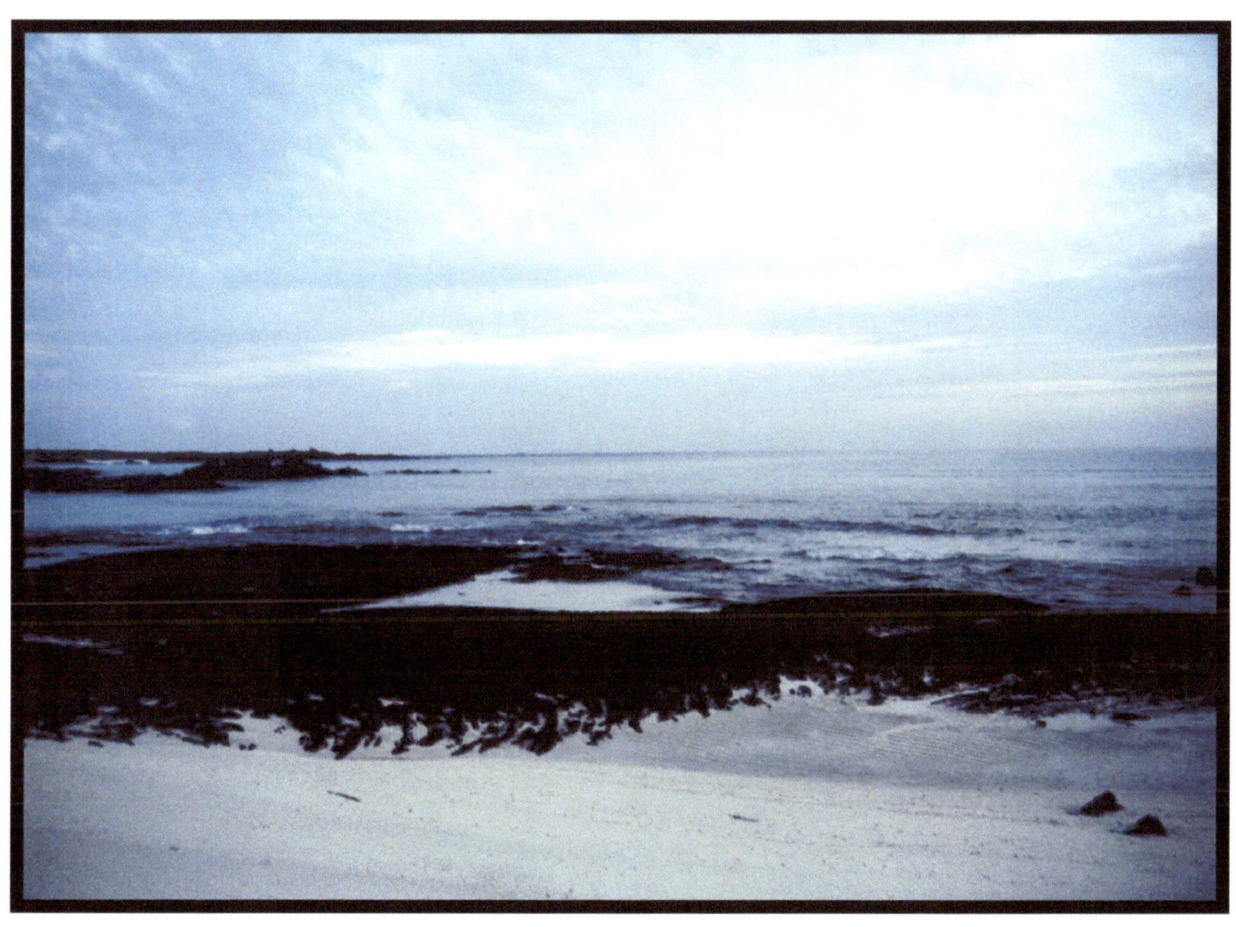

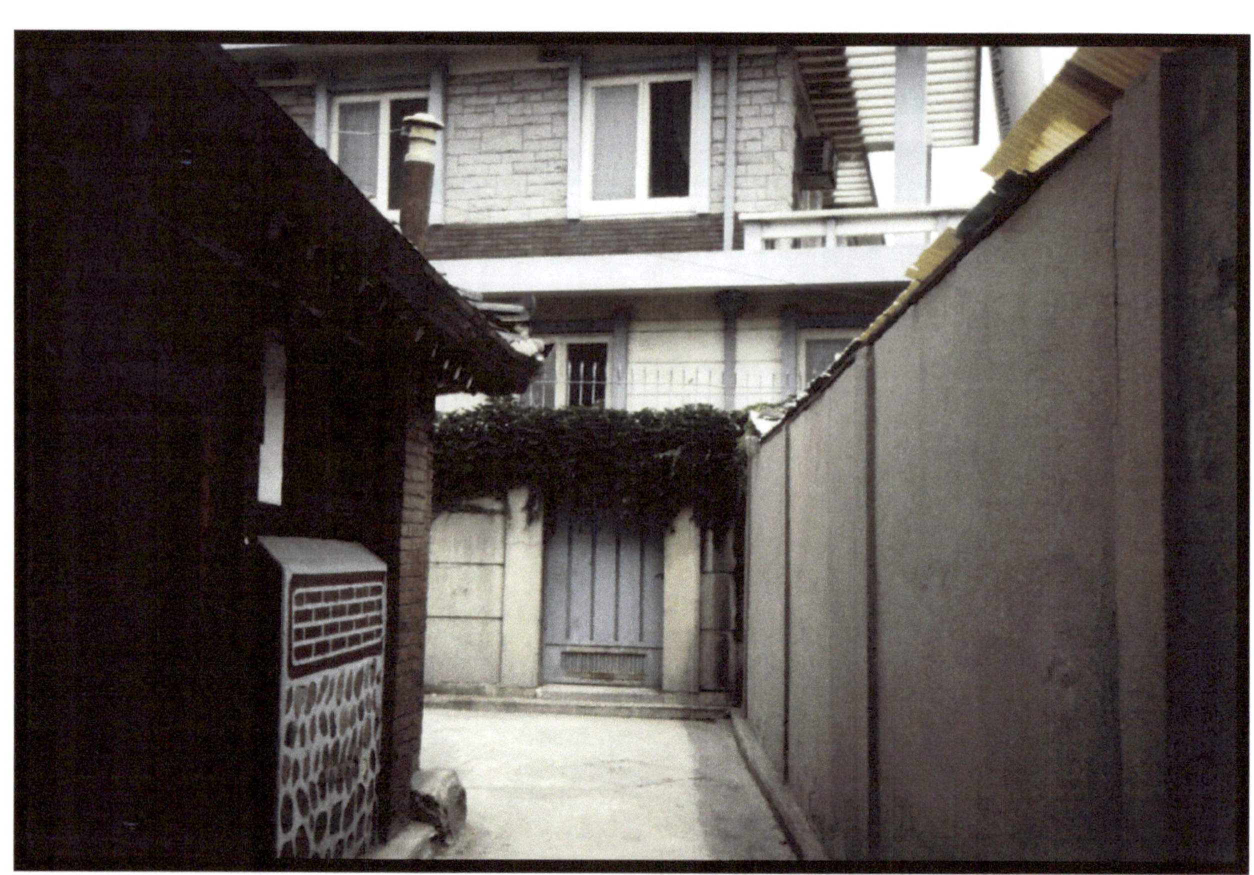

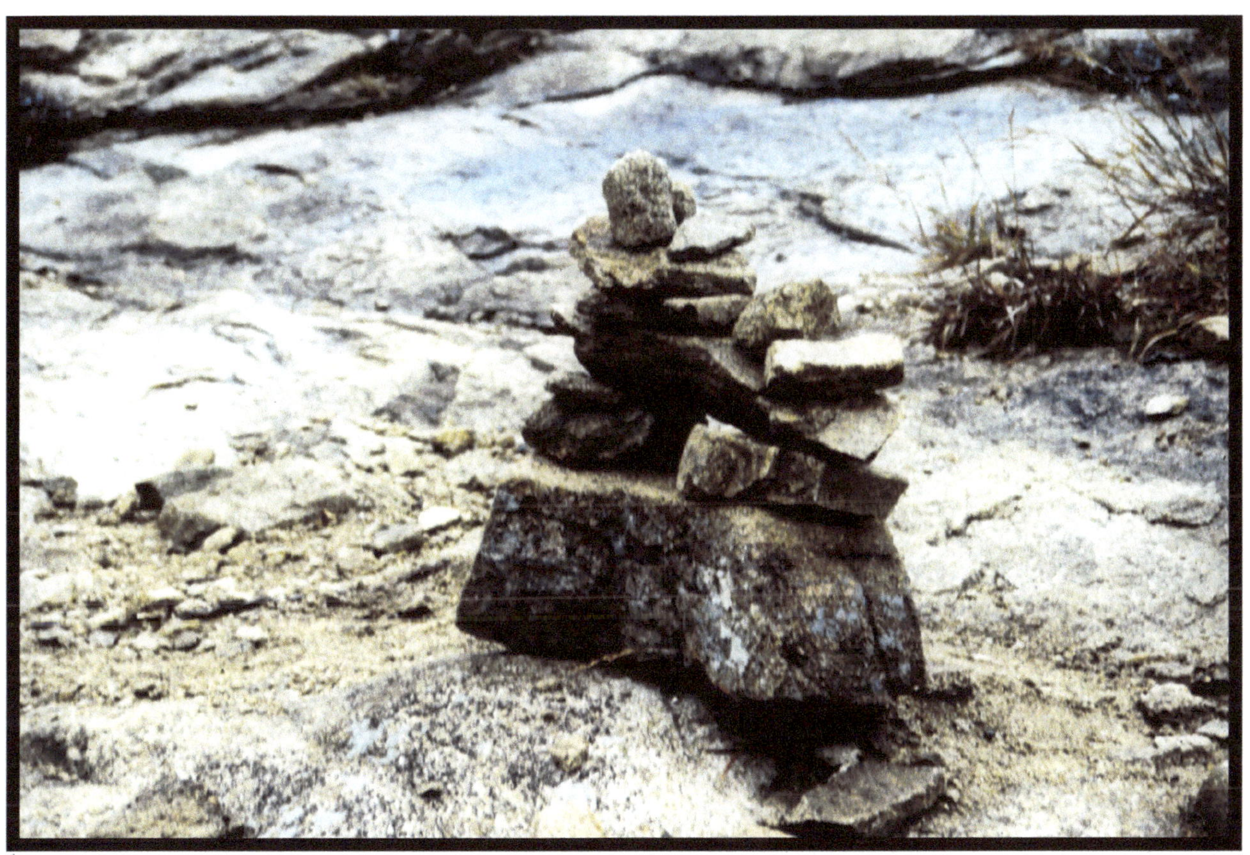

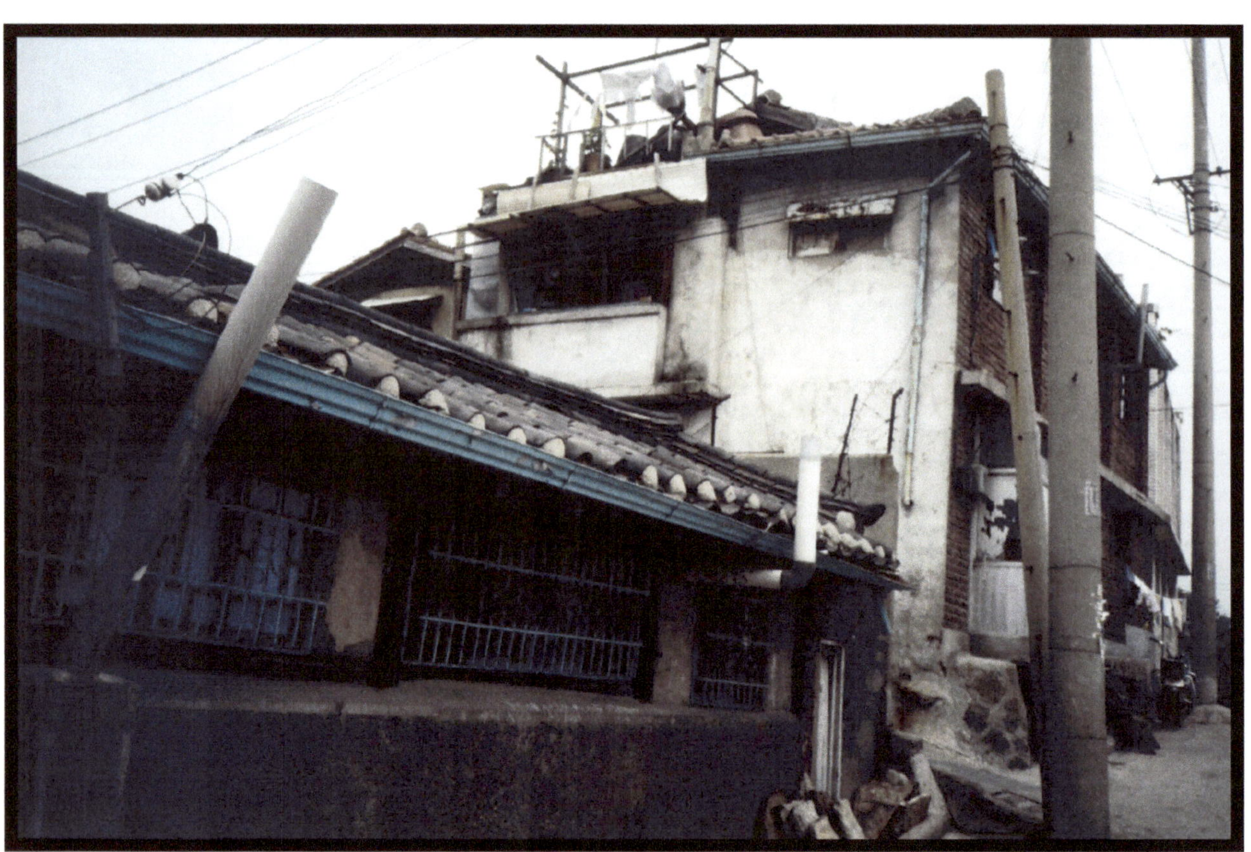

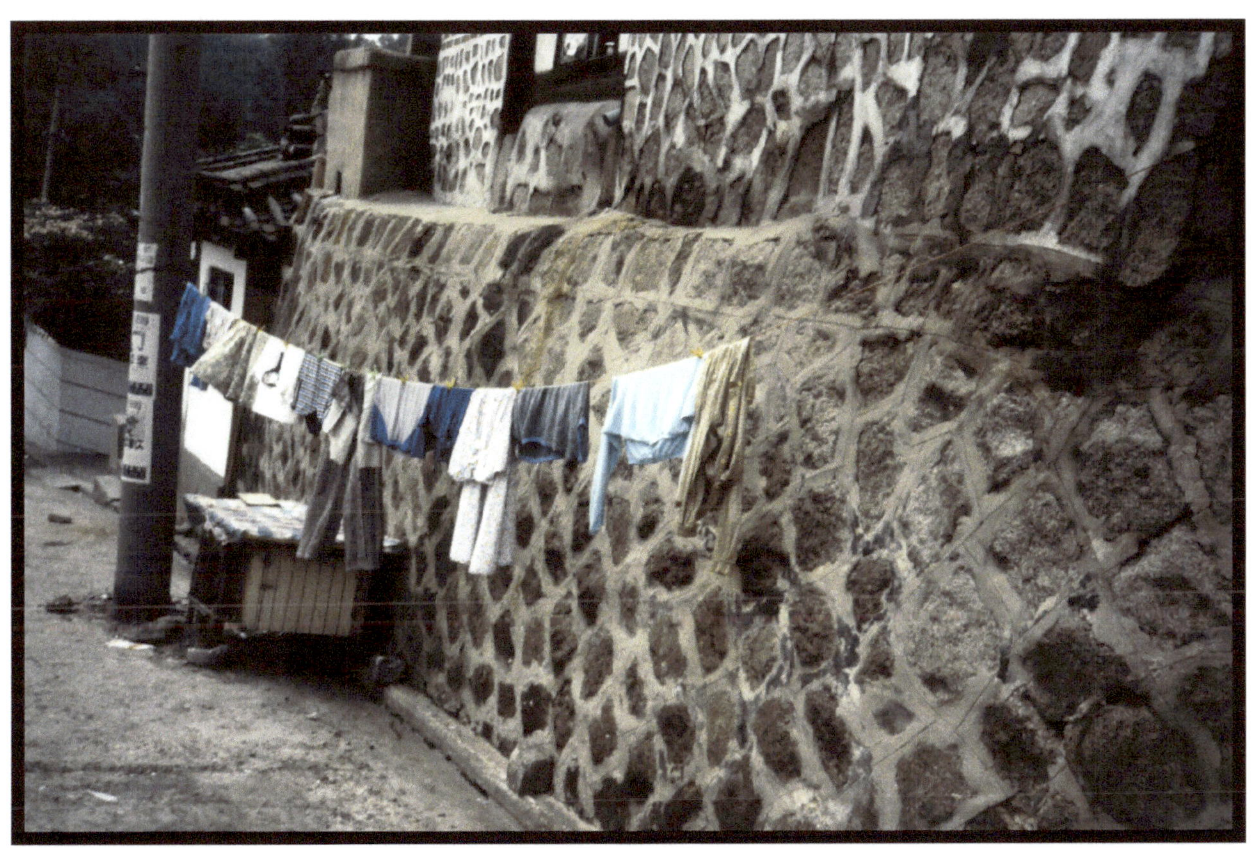

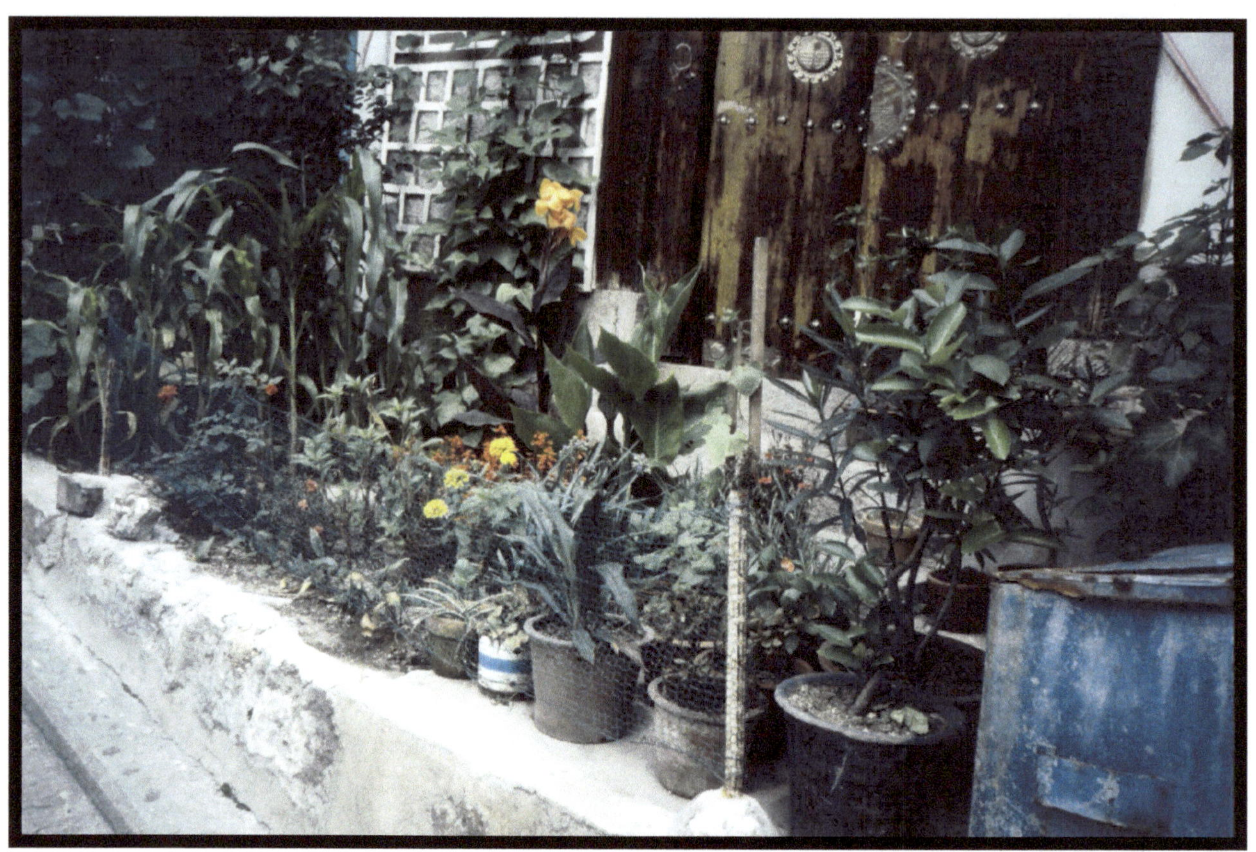

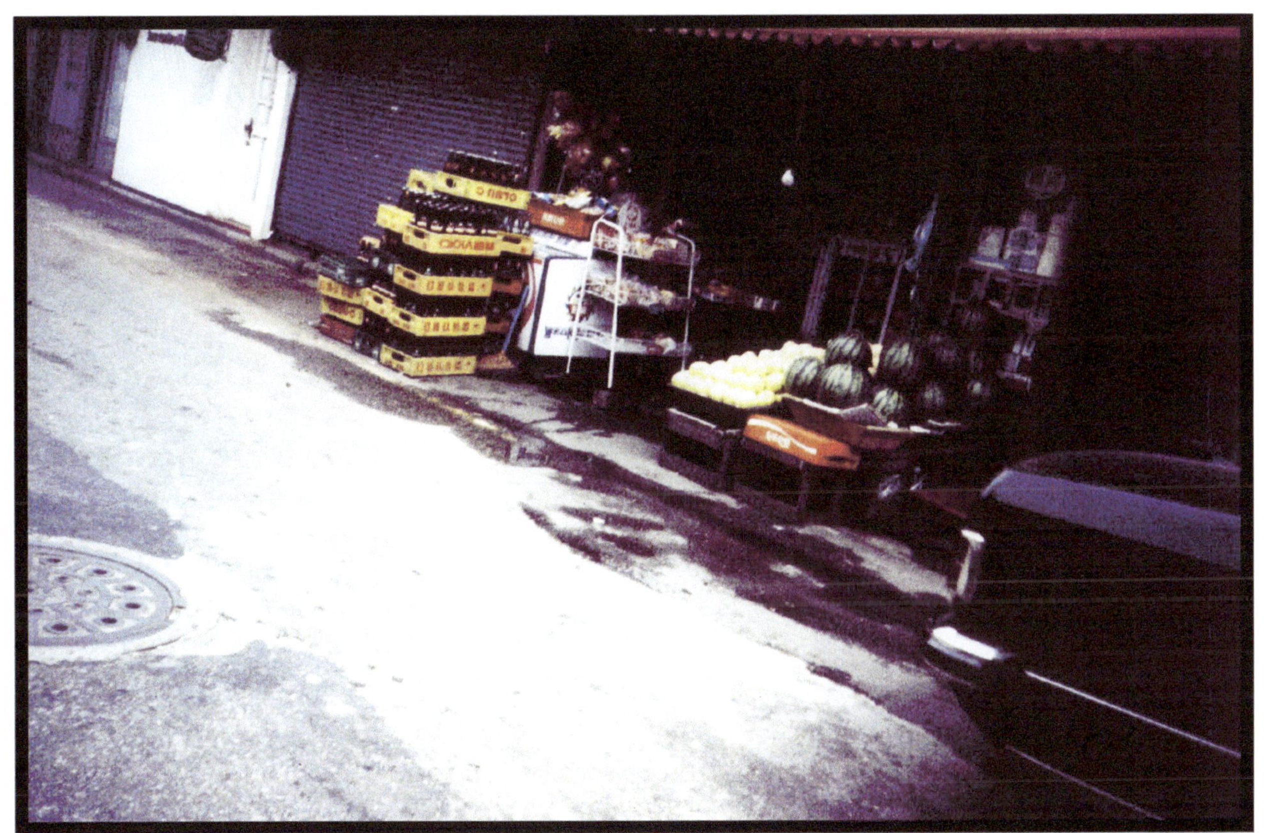

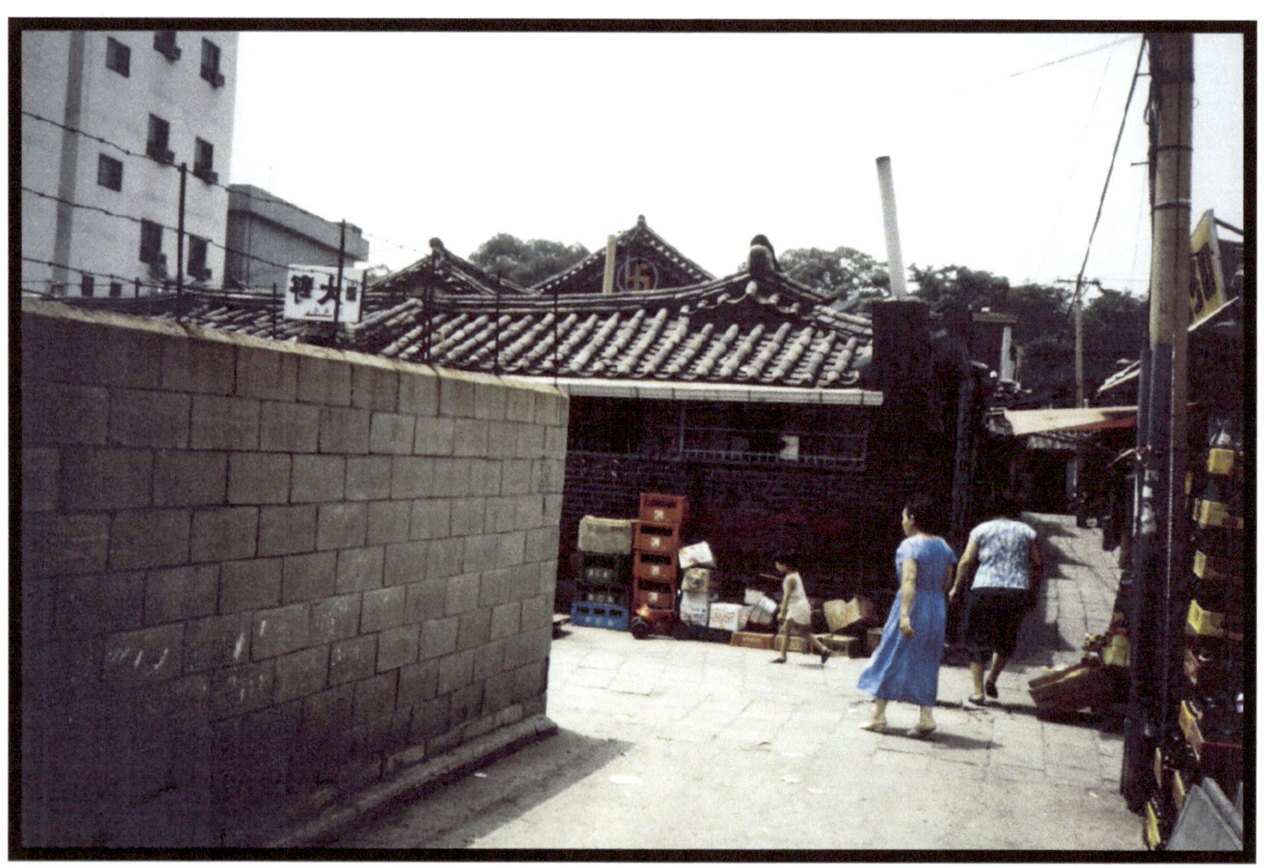

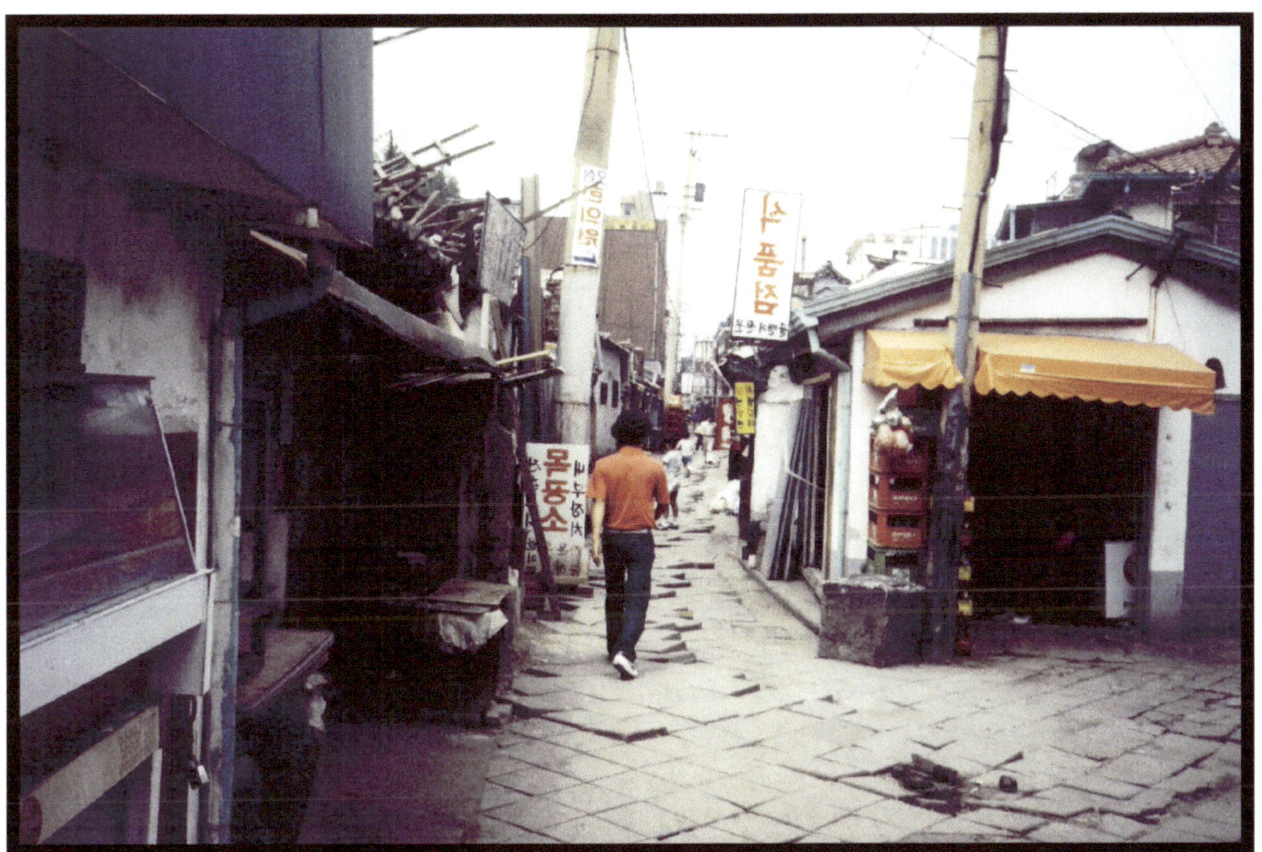

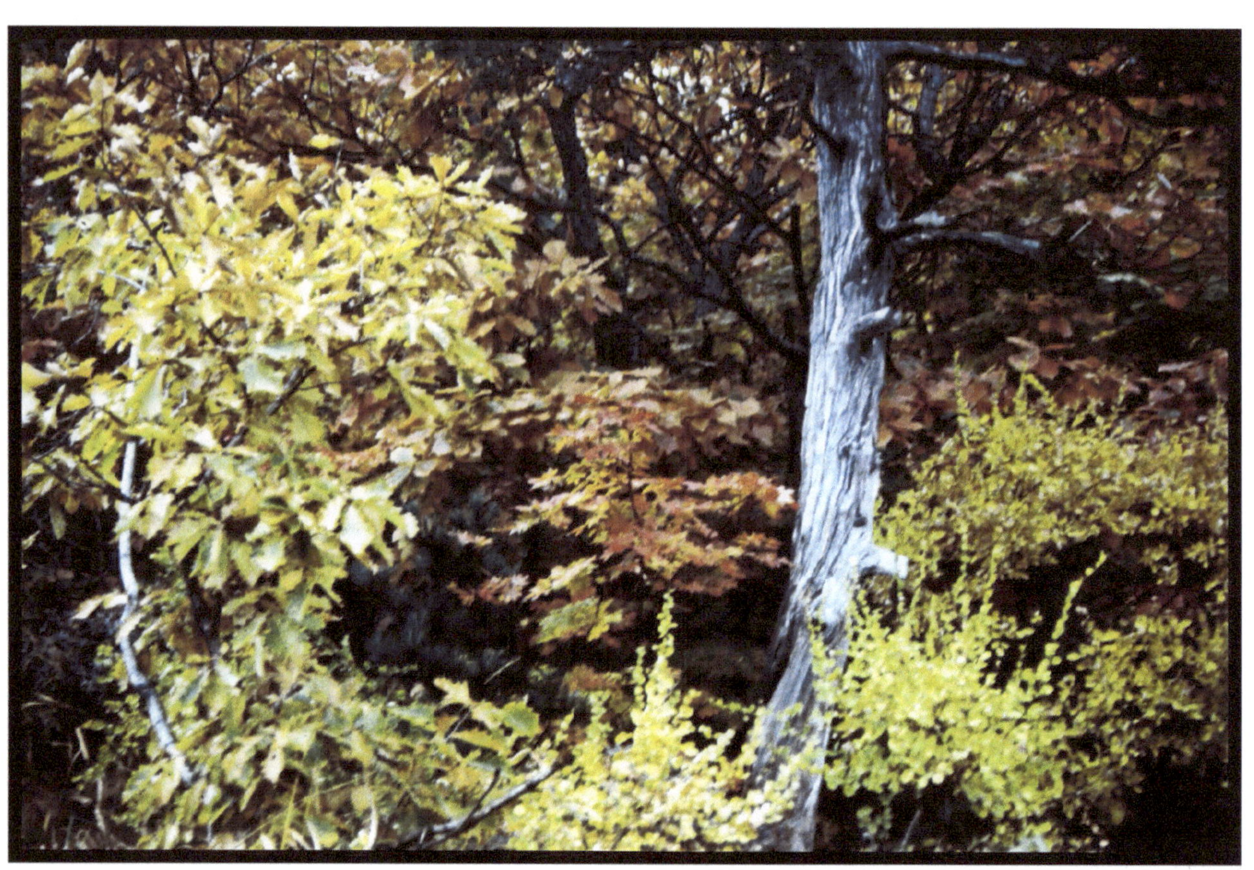

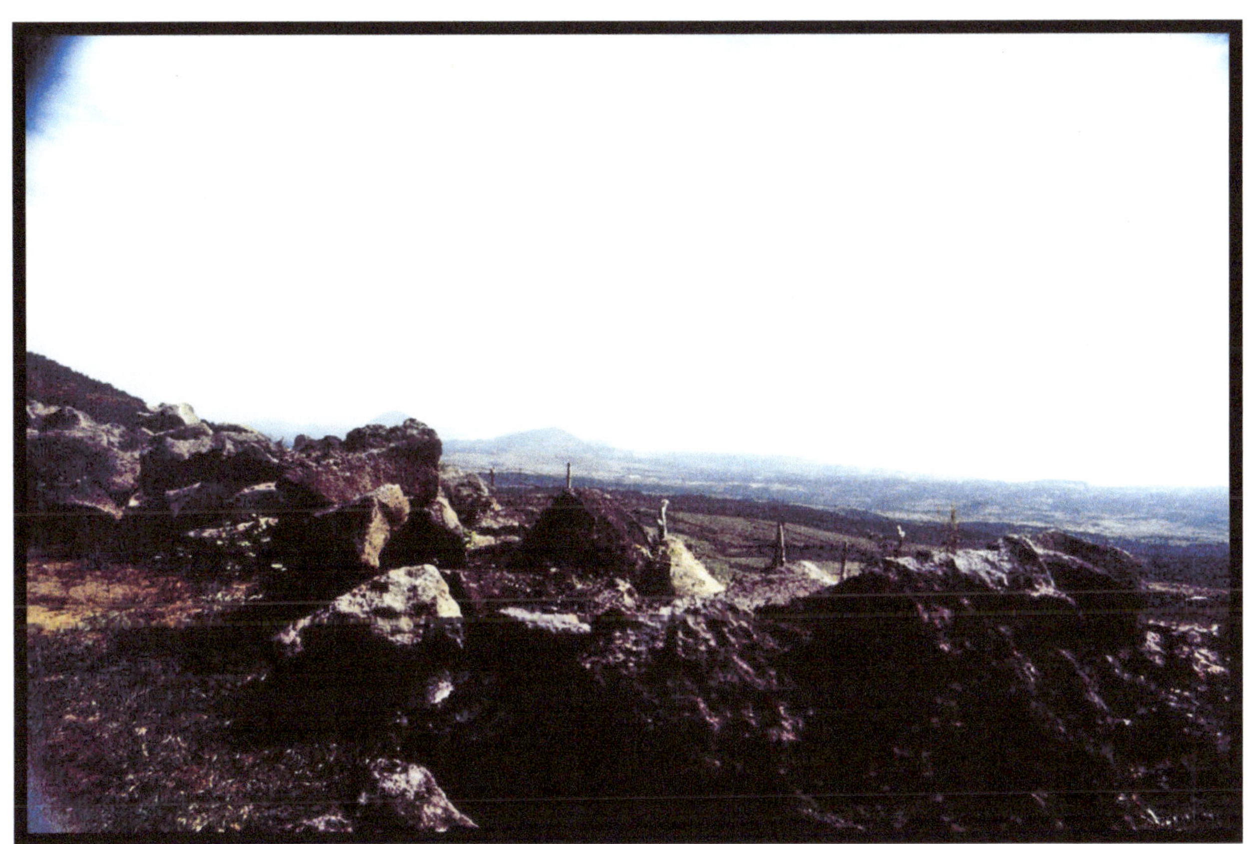

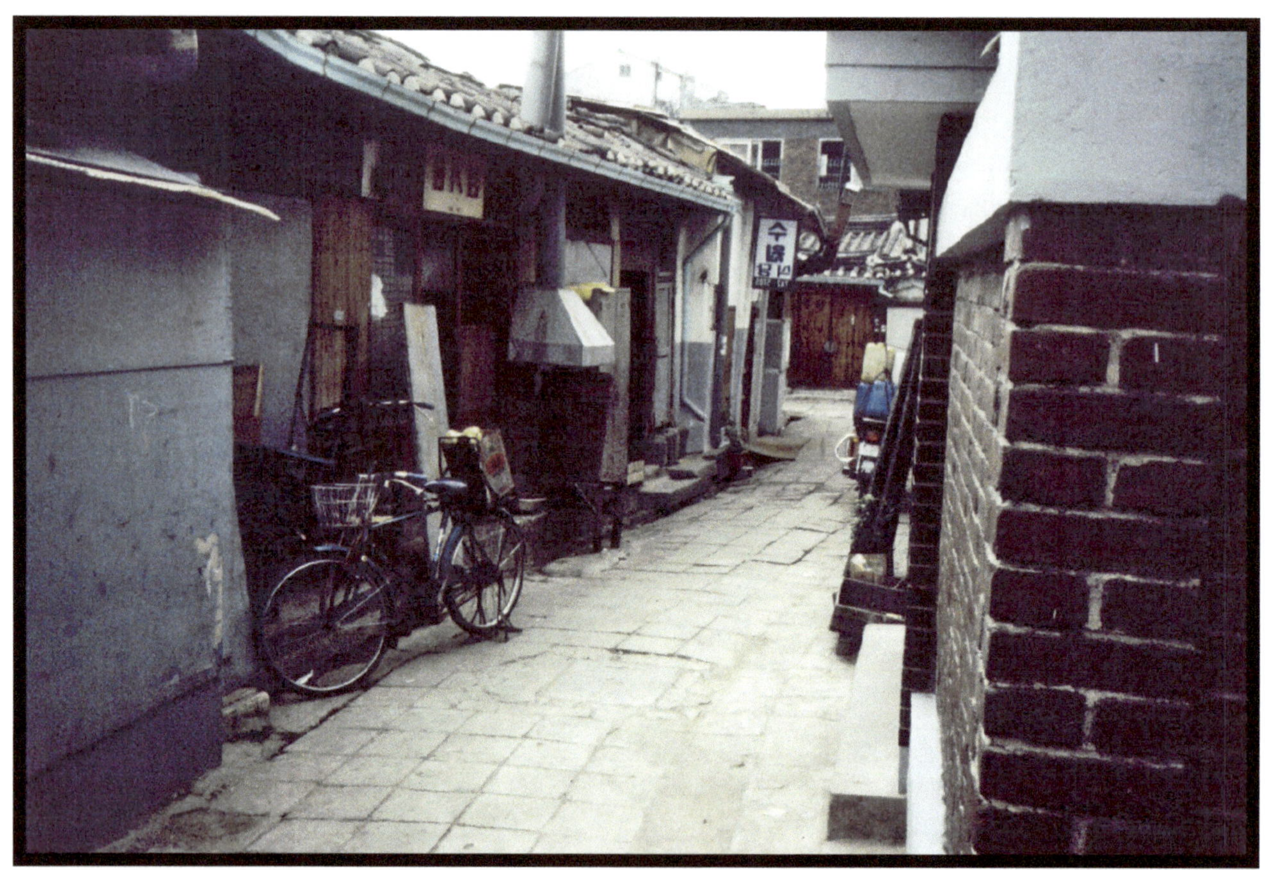

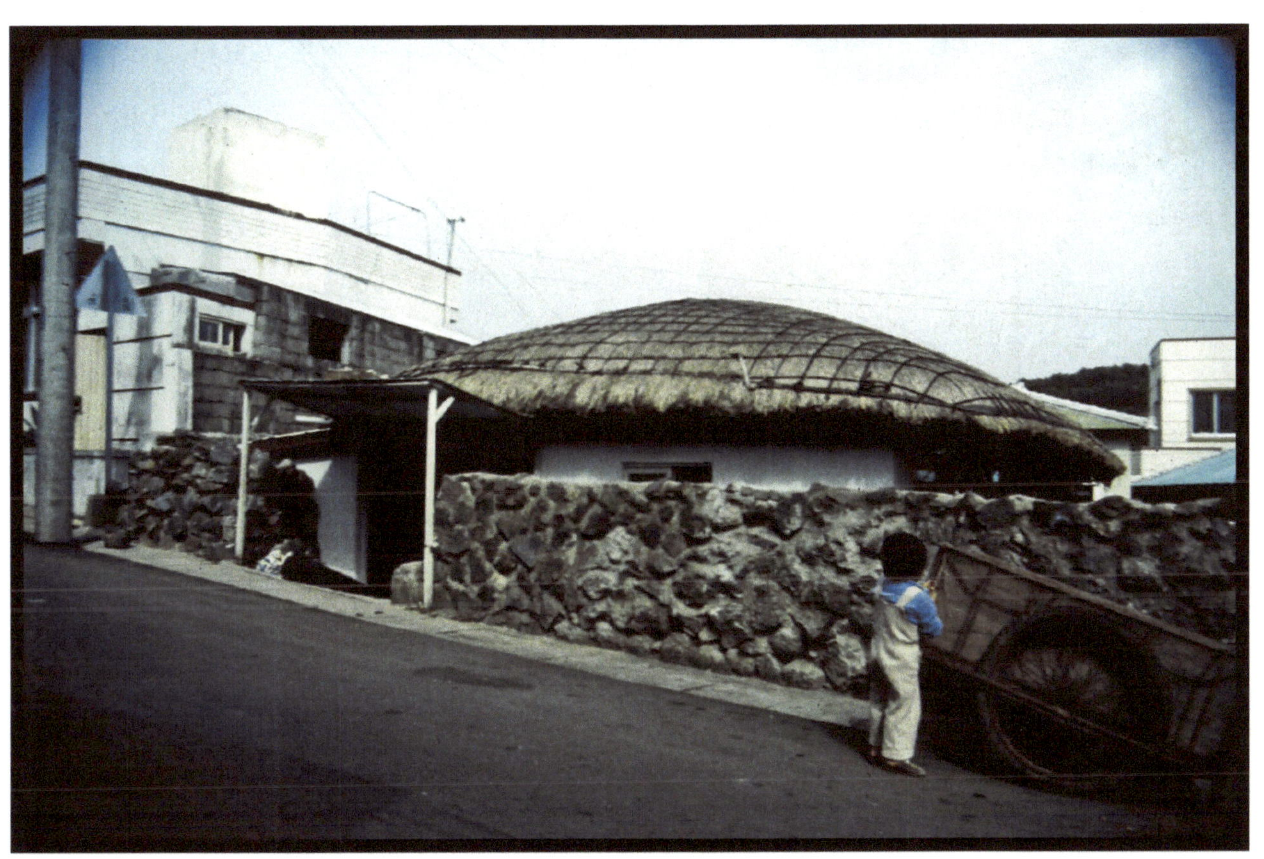

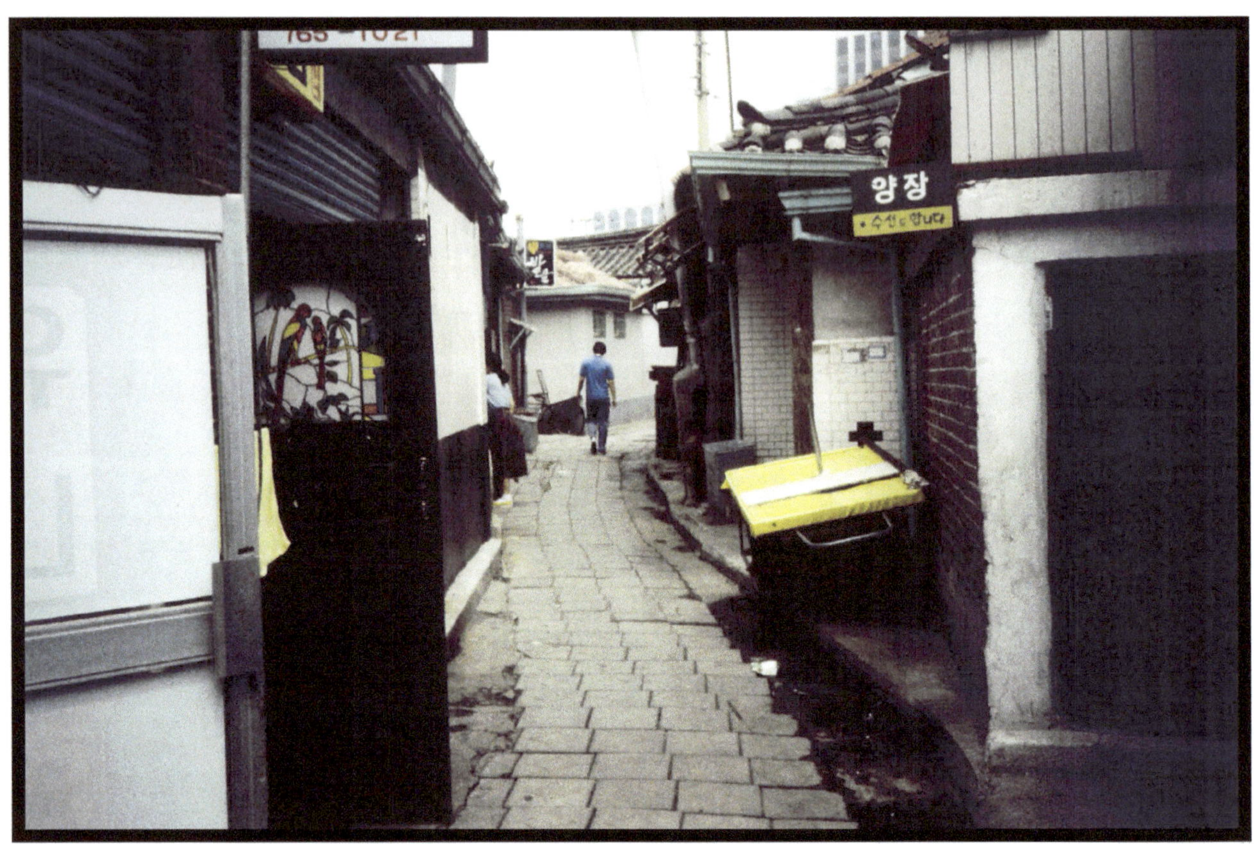
양장

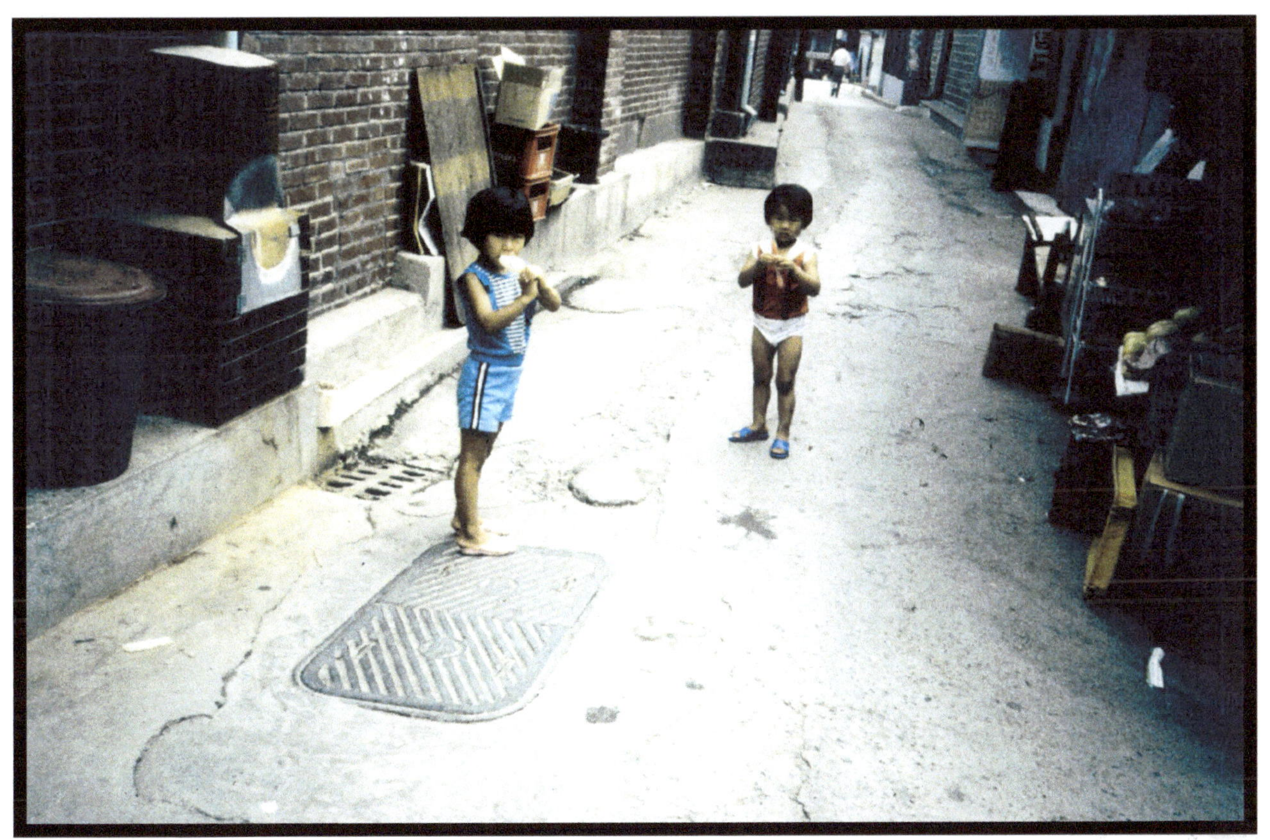

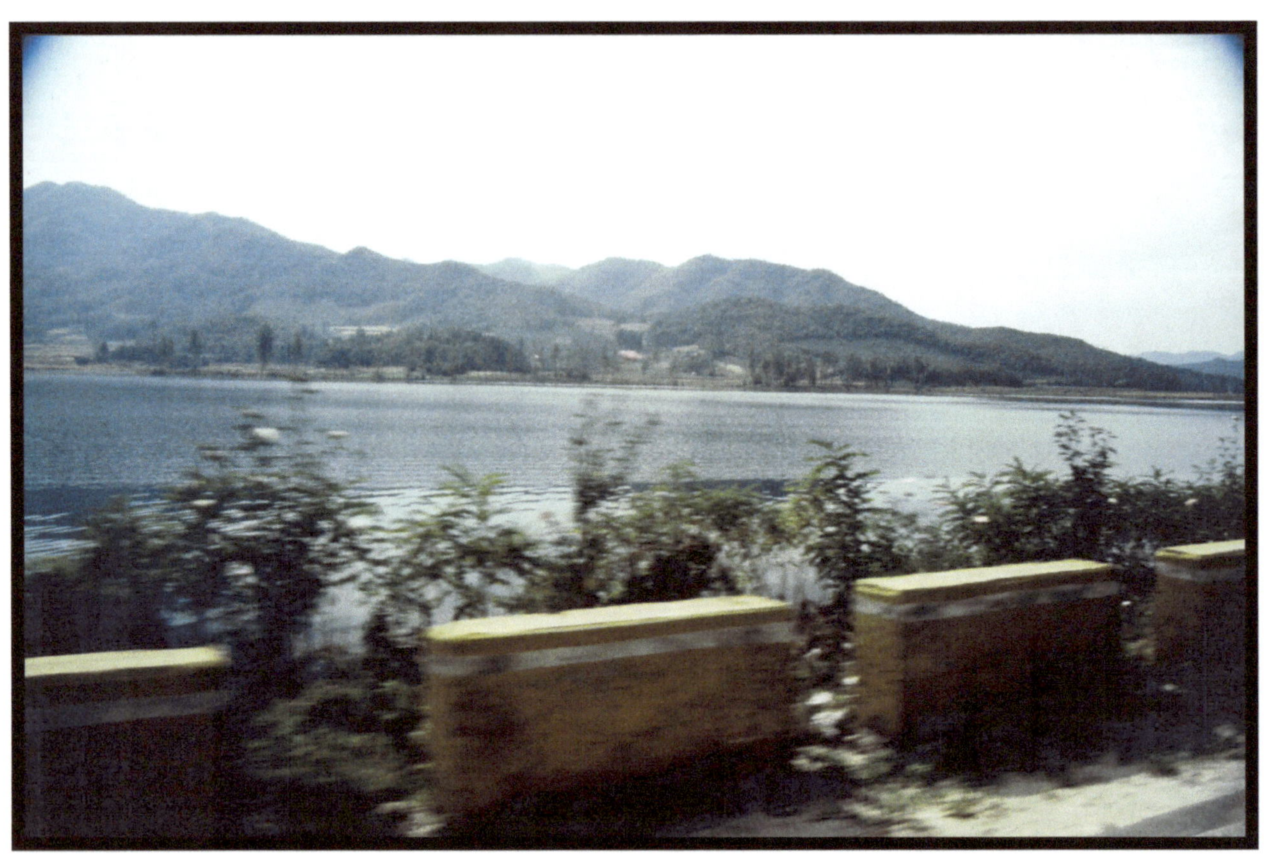

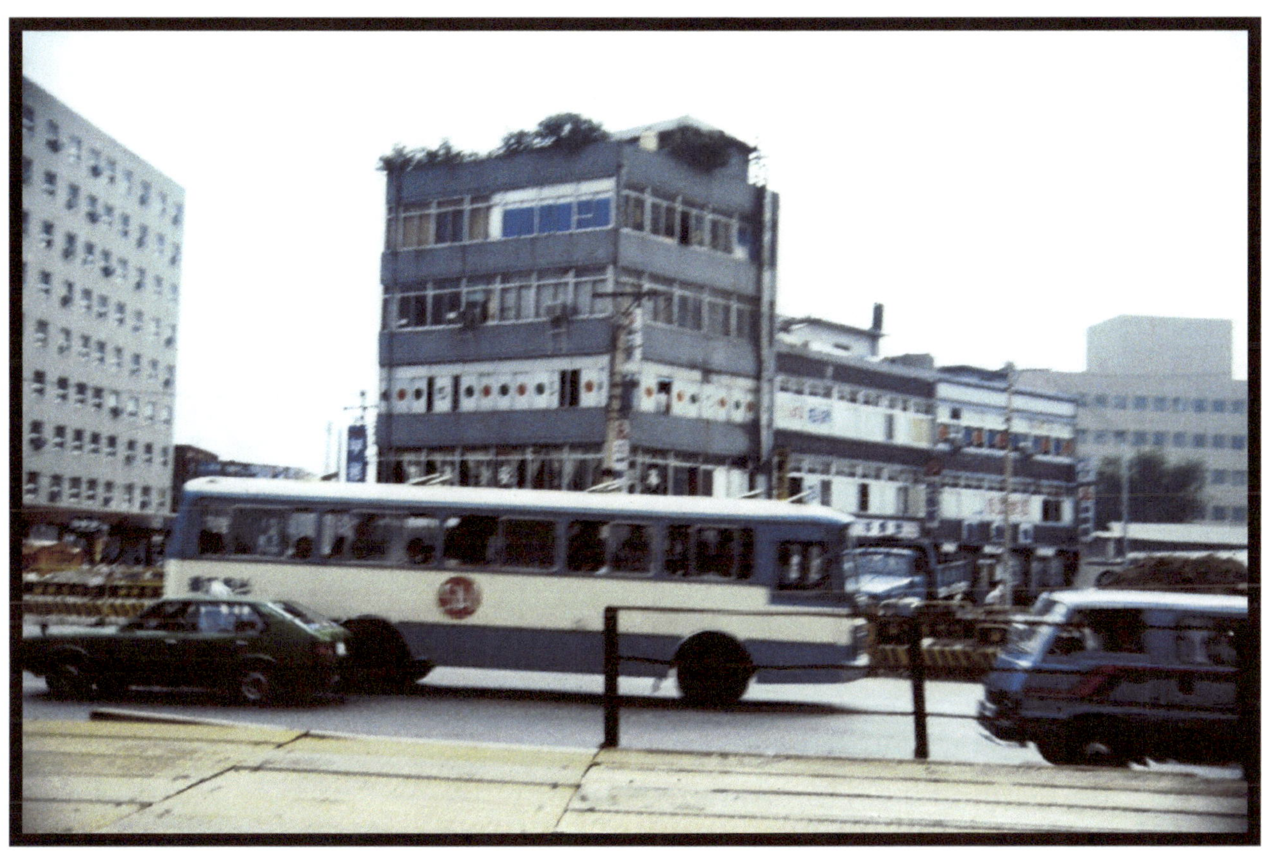

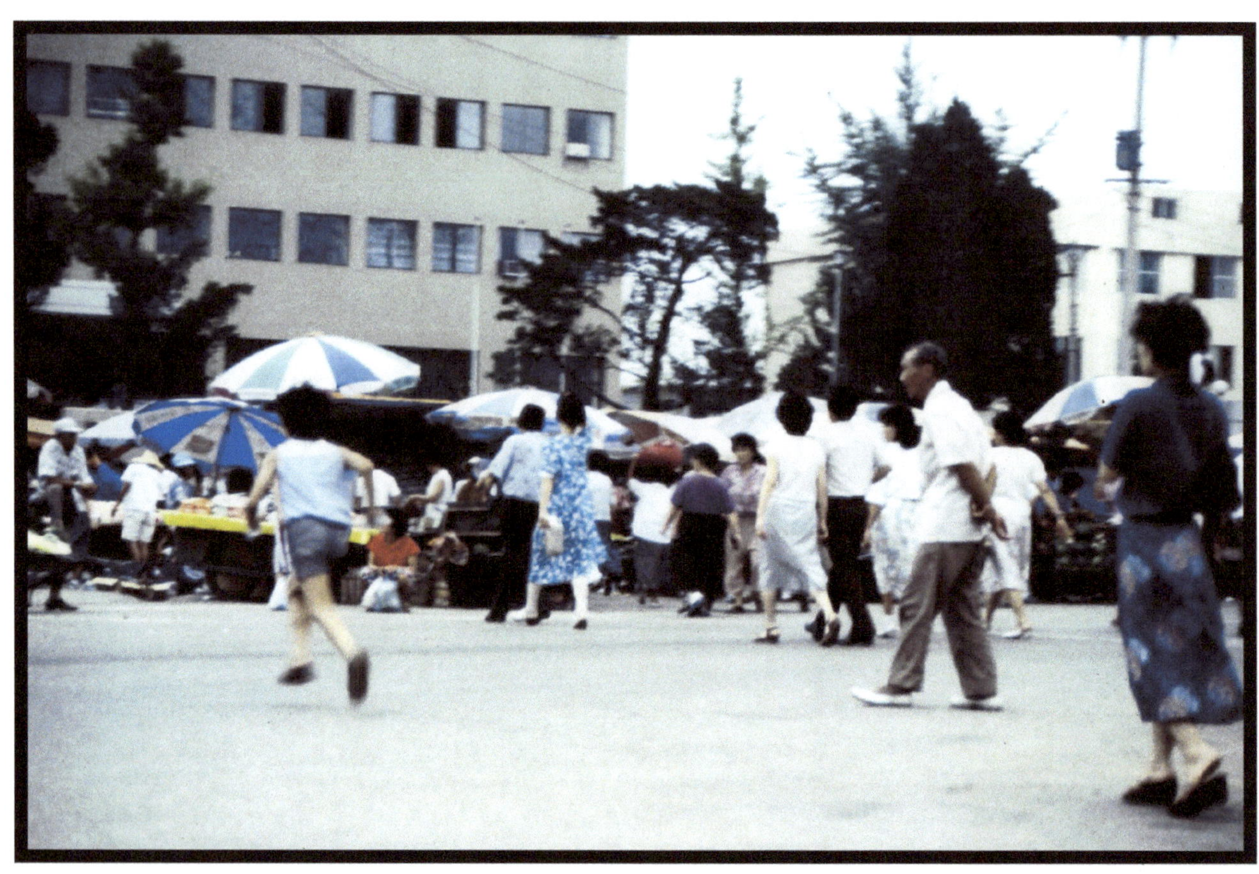

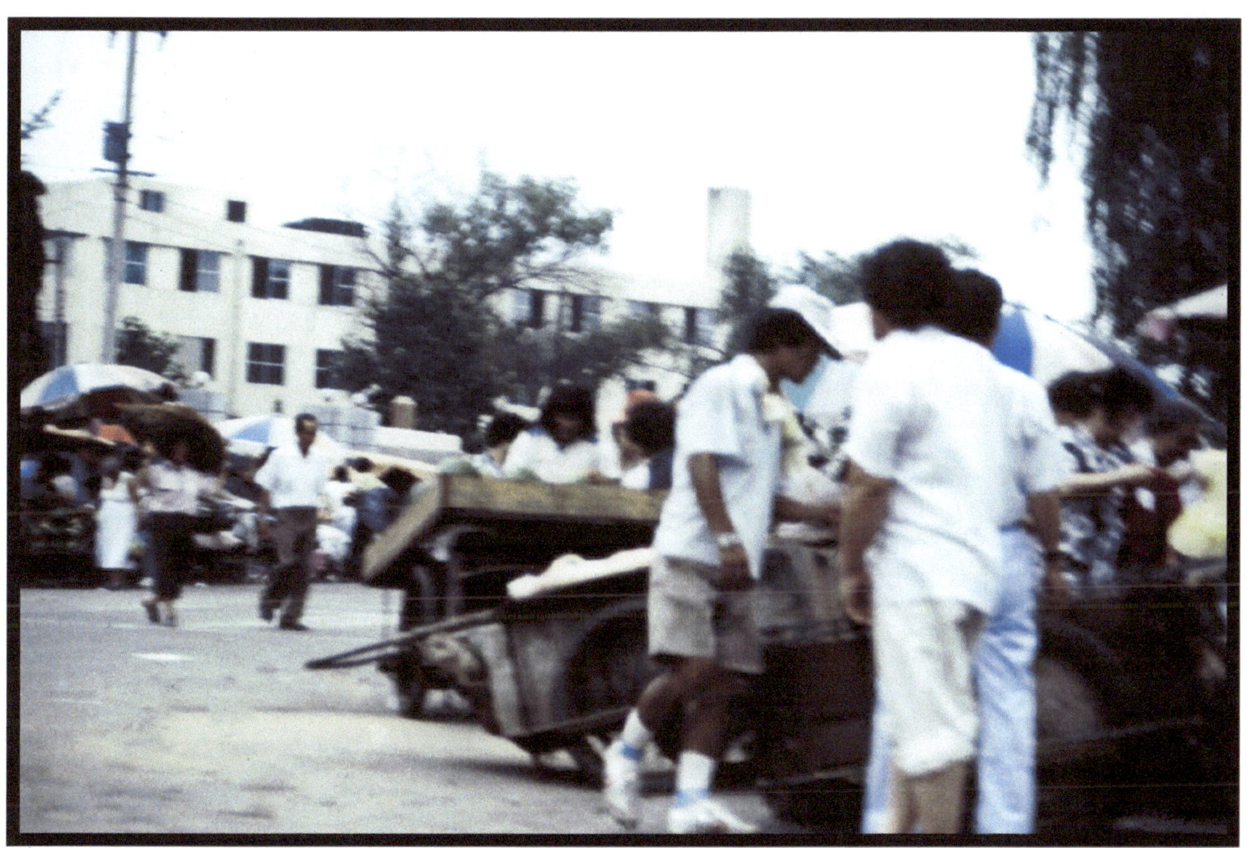

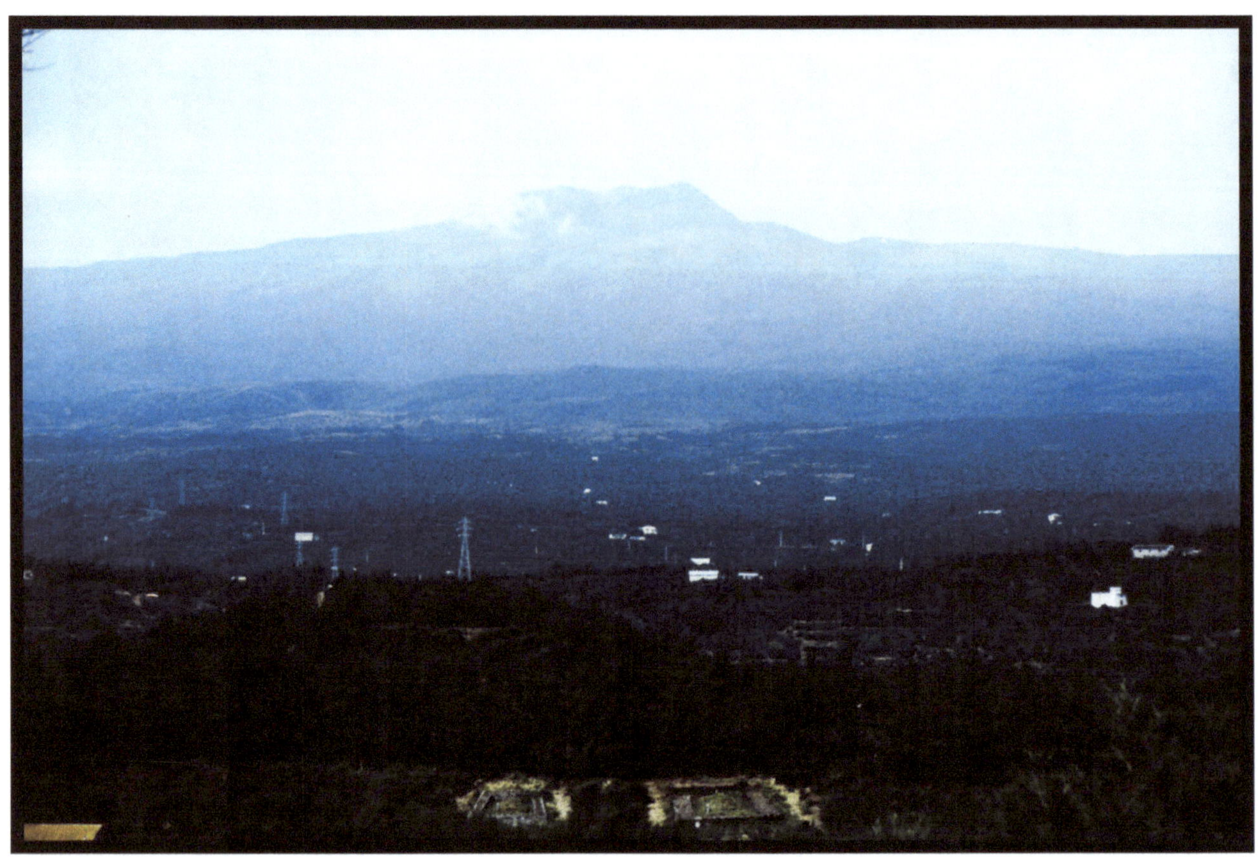

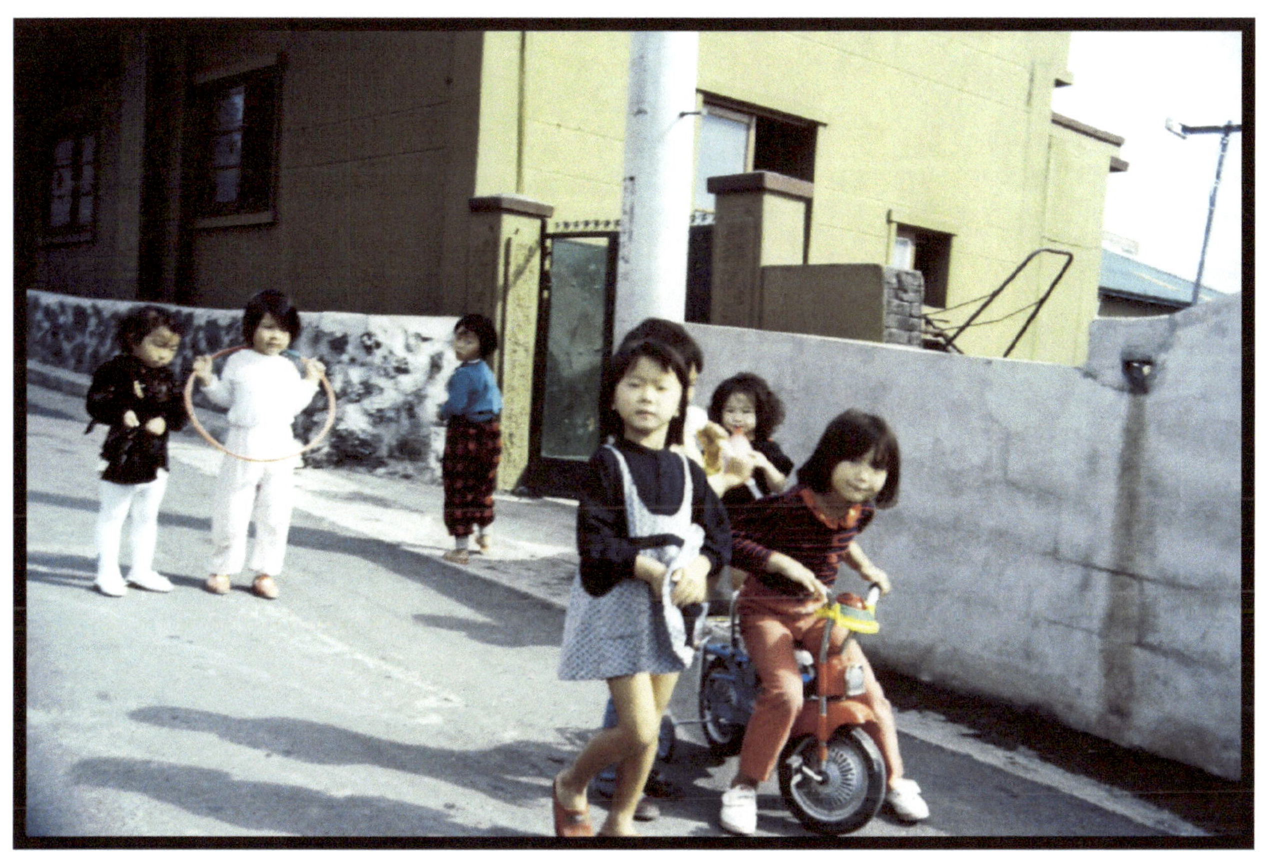

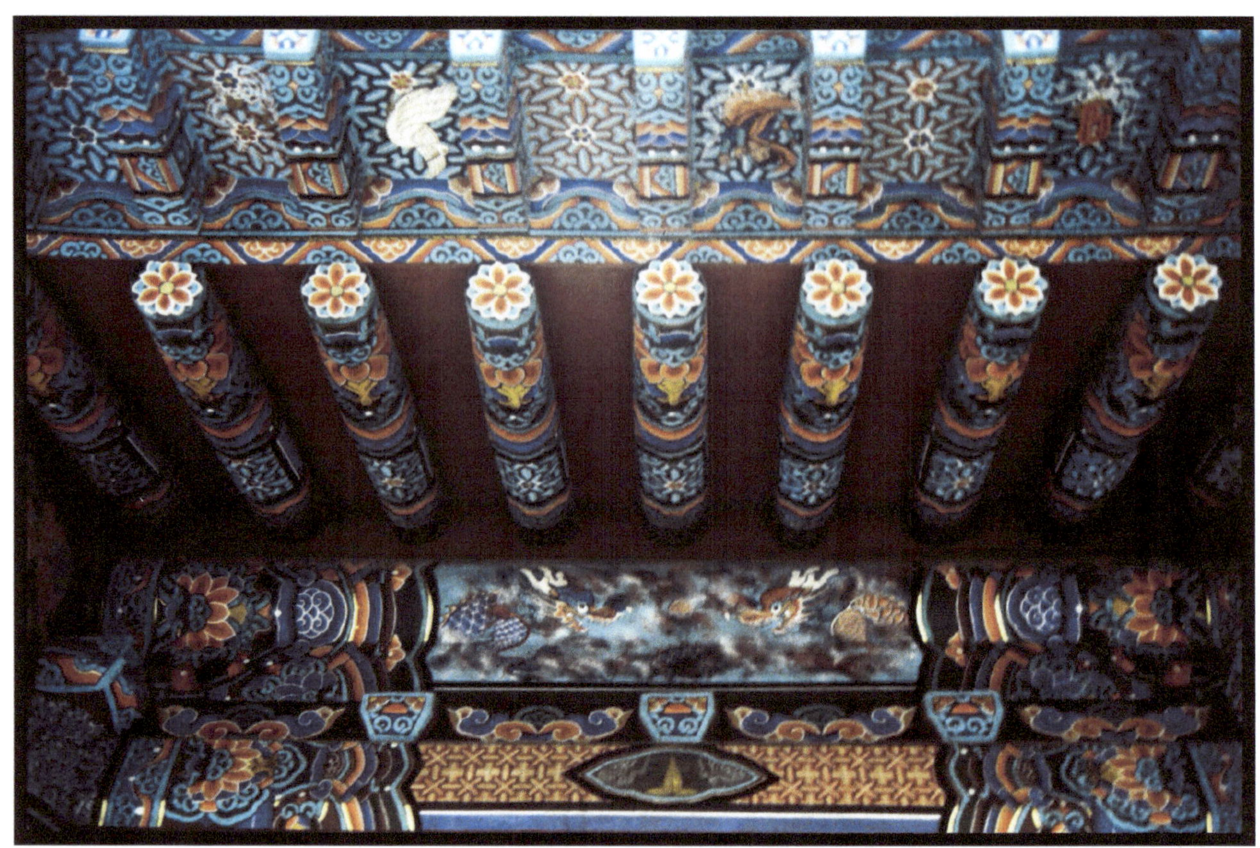

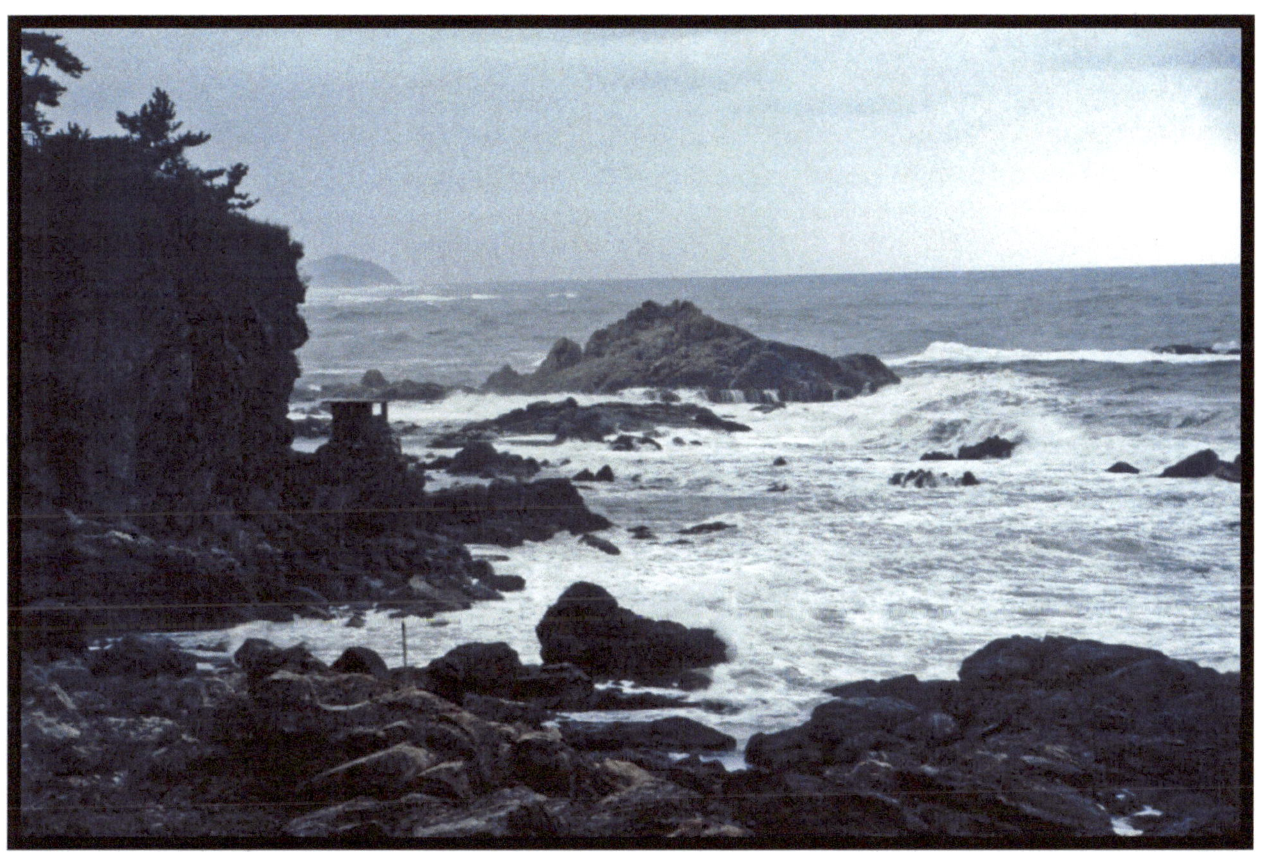

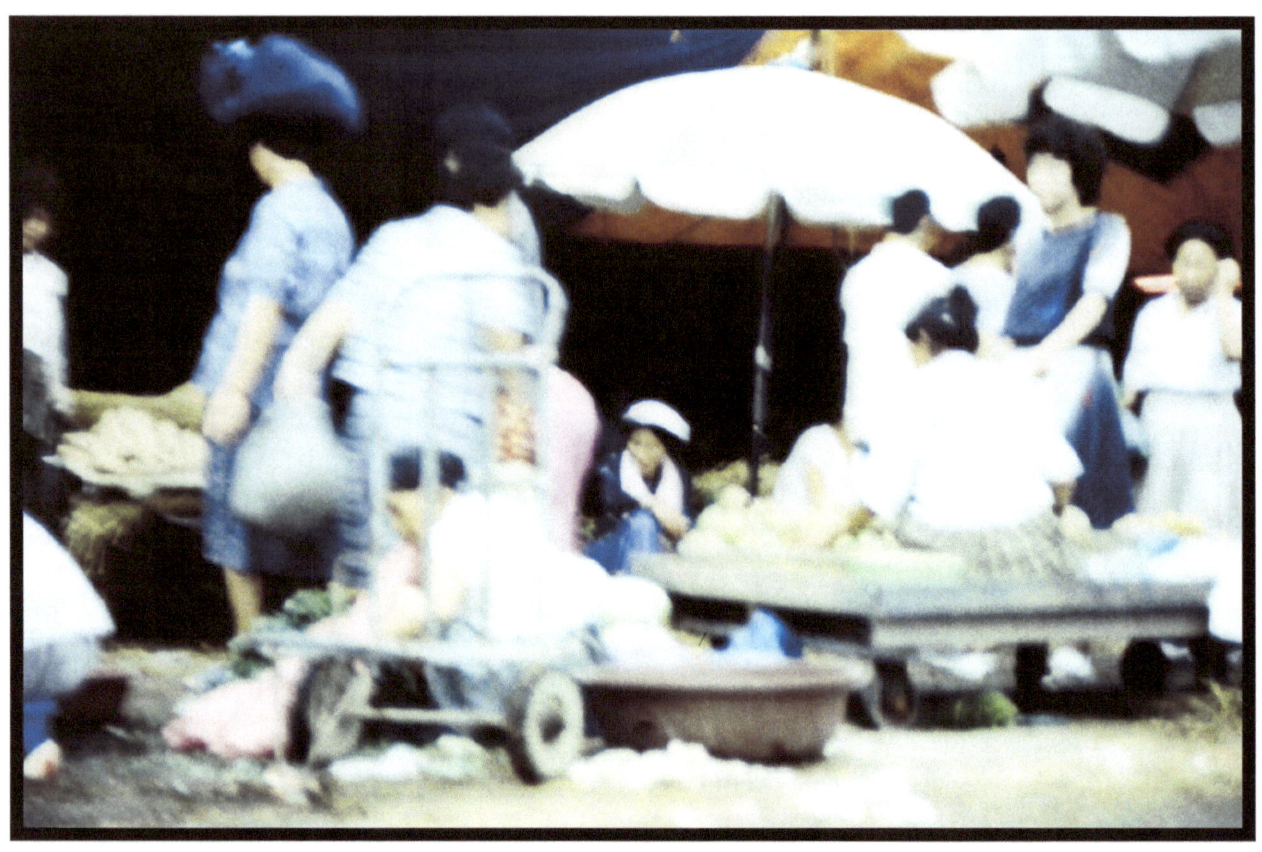

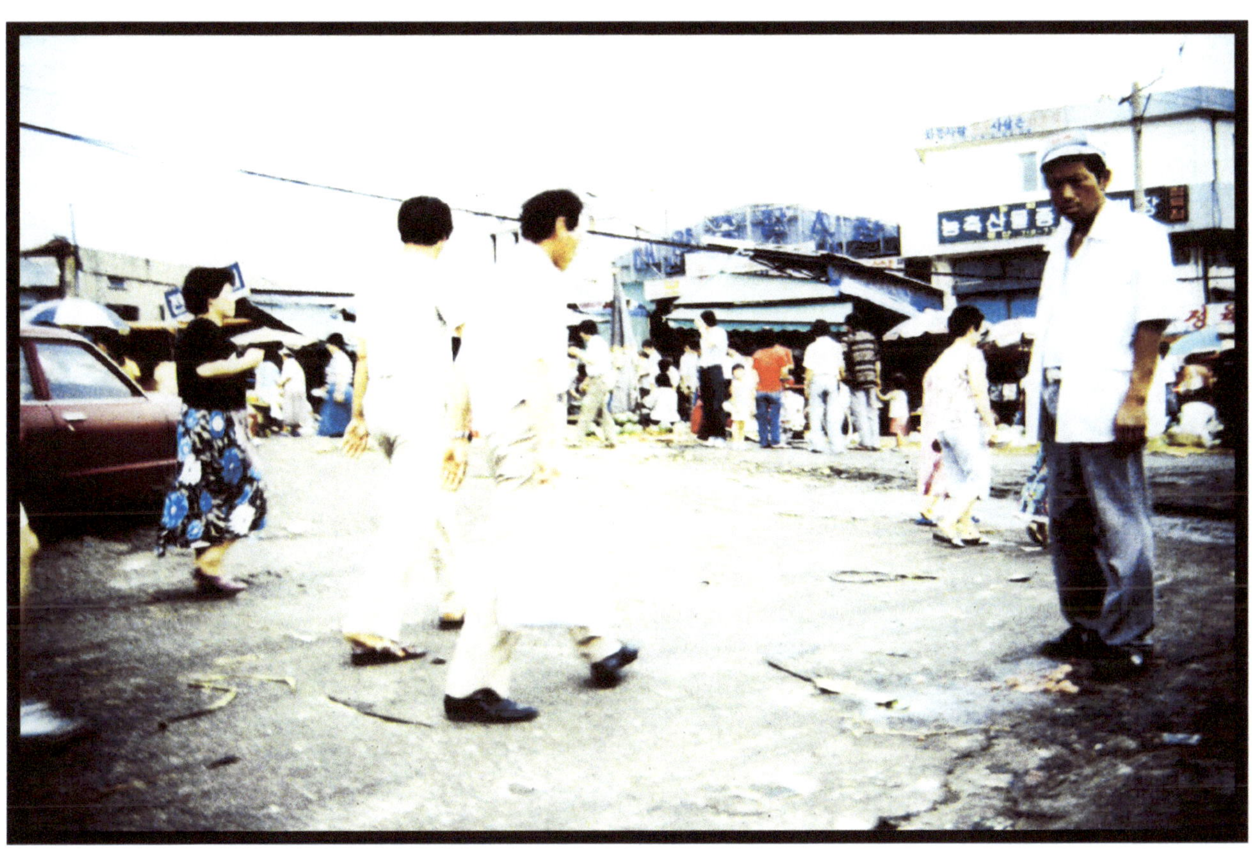

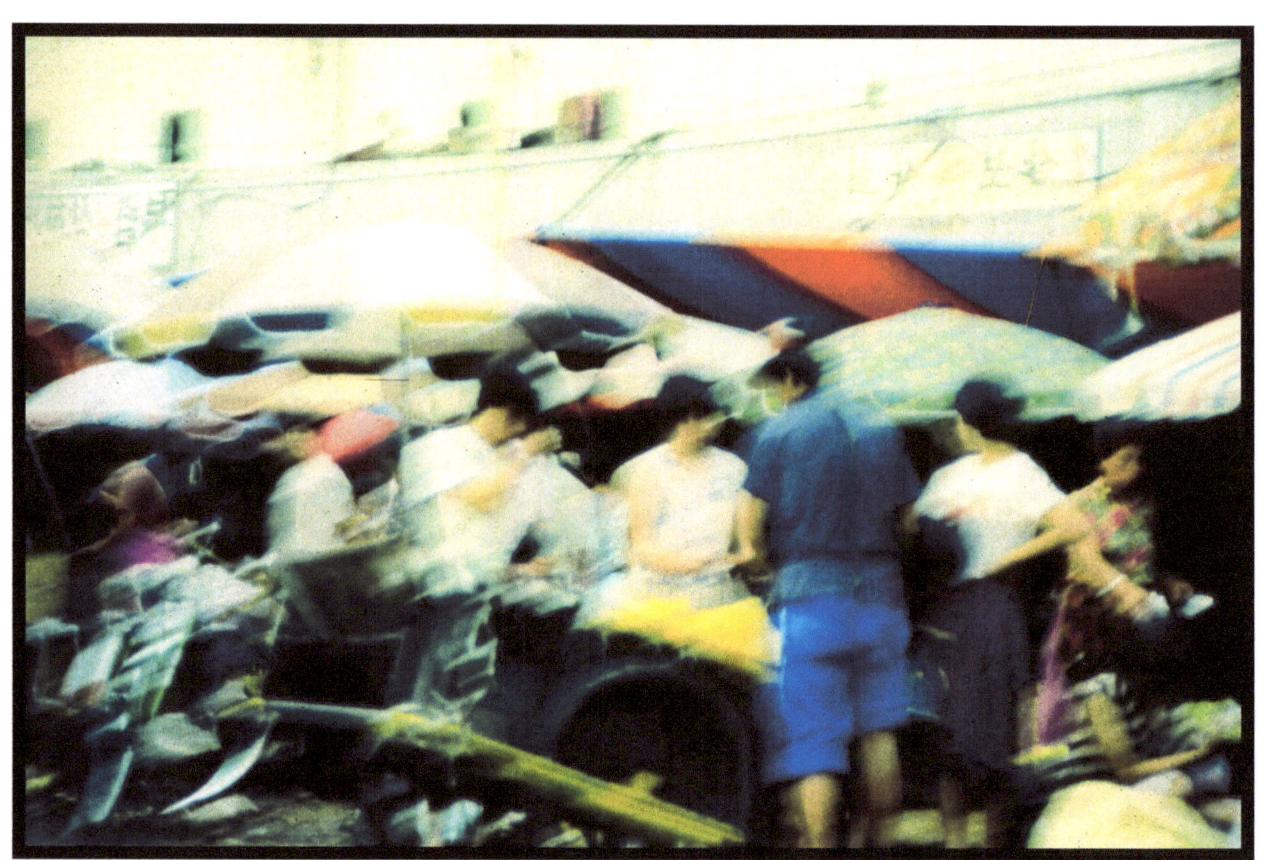

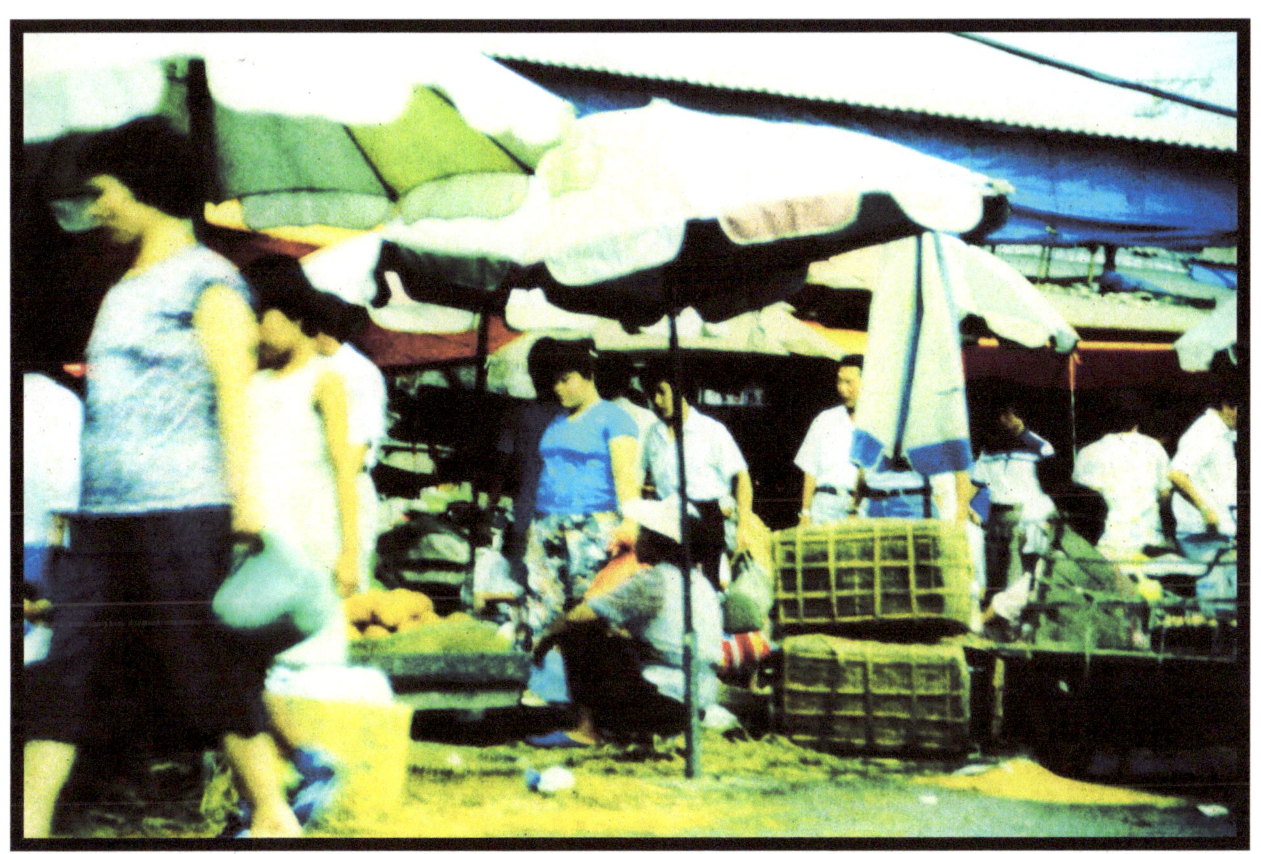

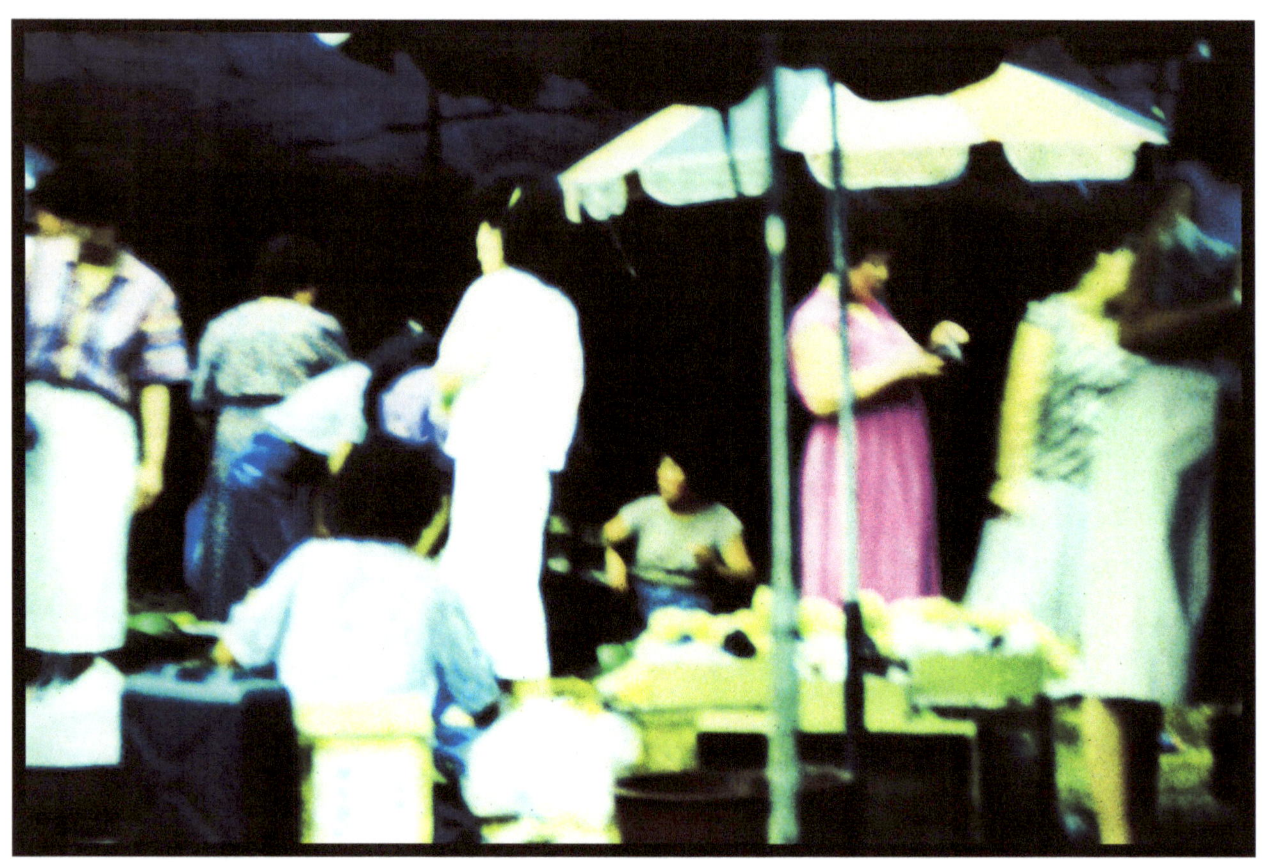

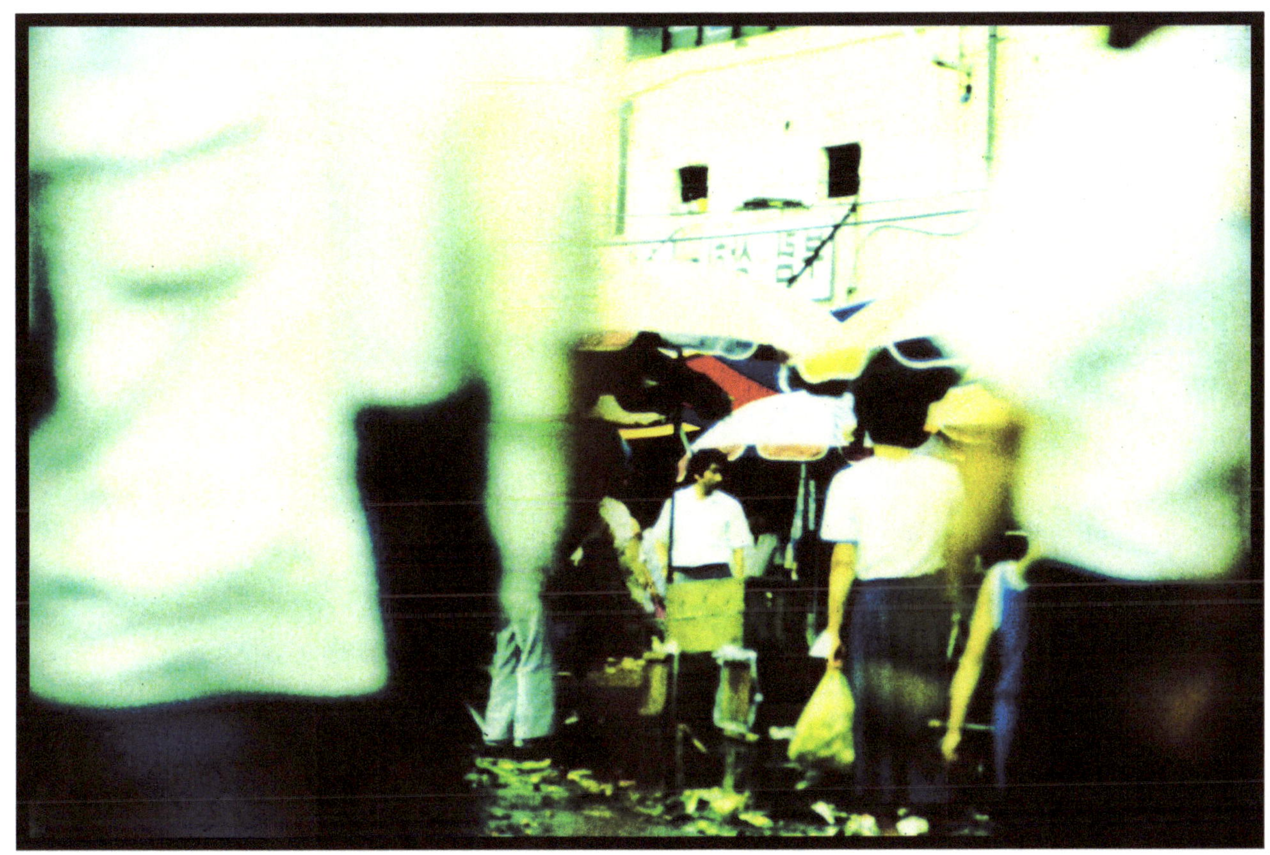

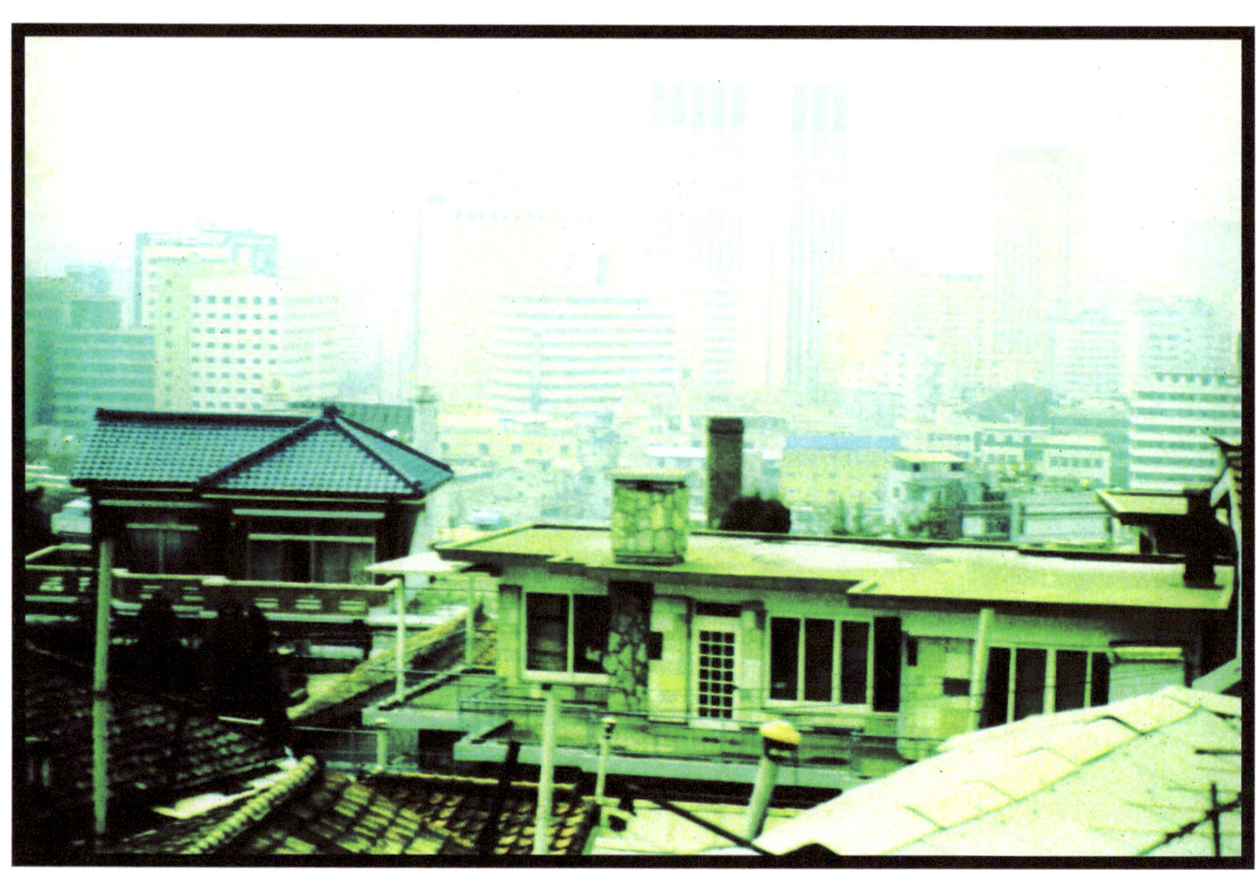

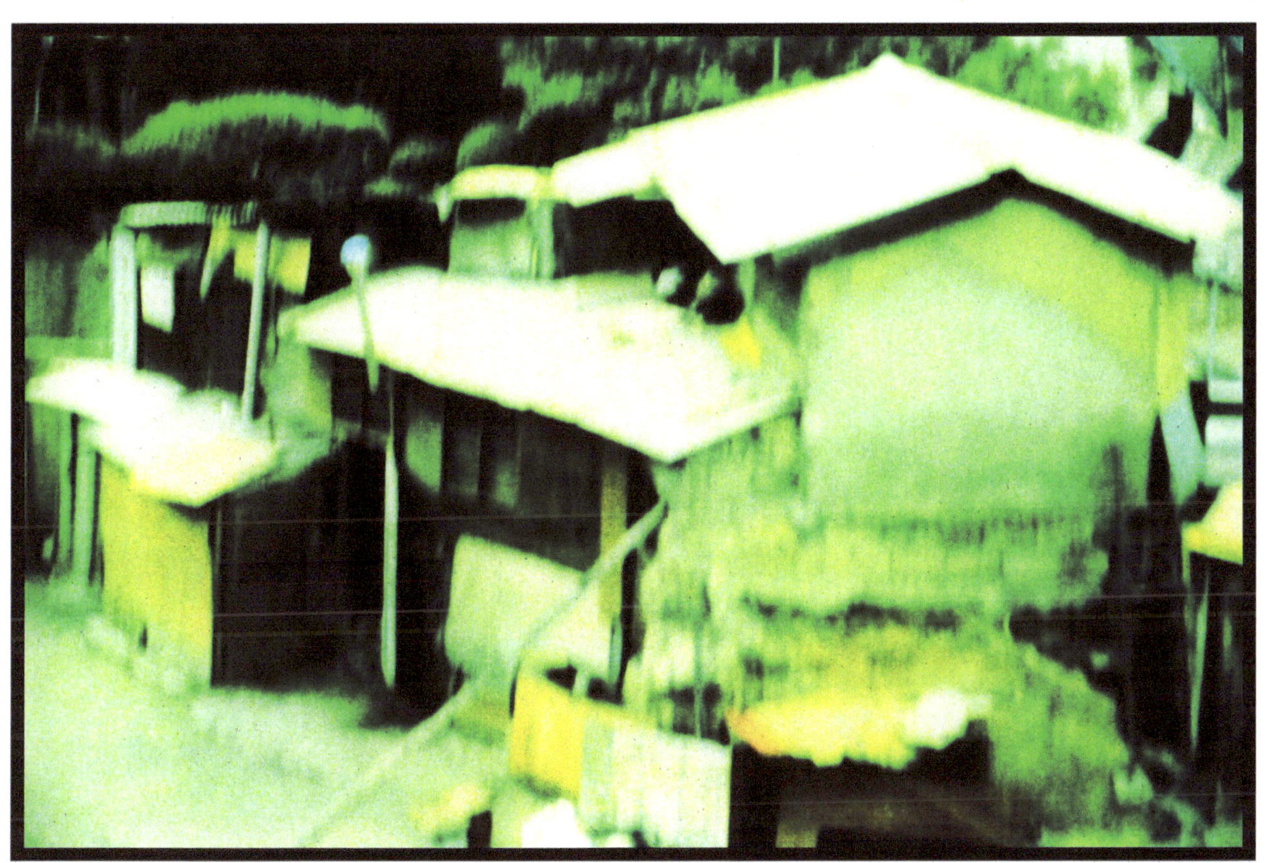

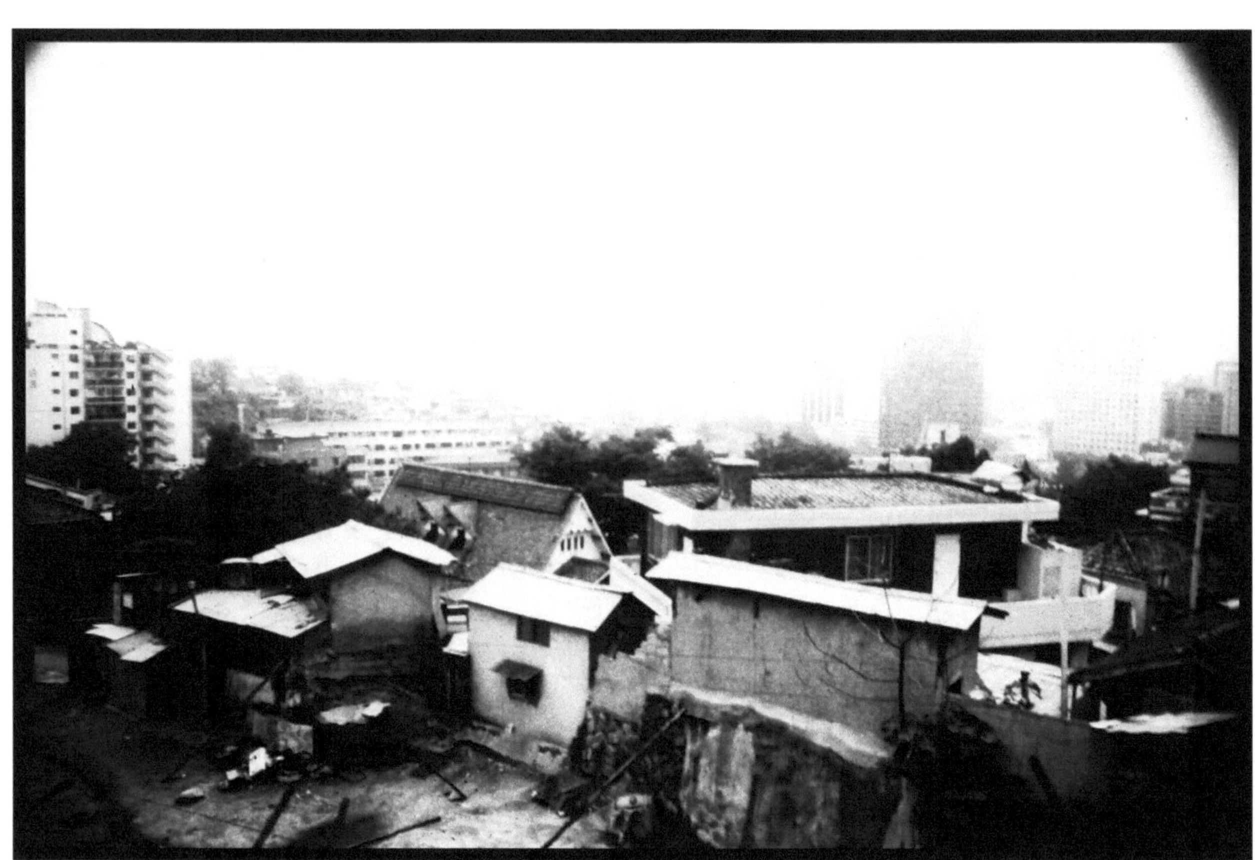

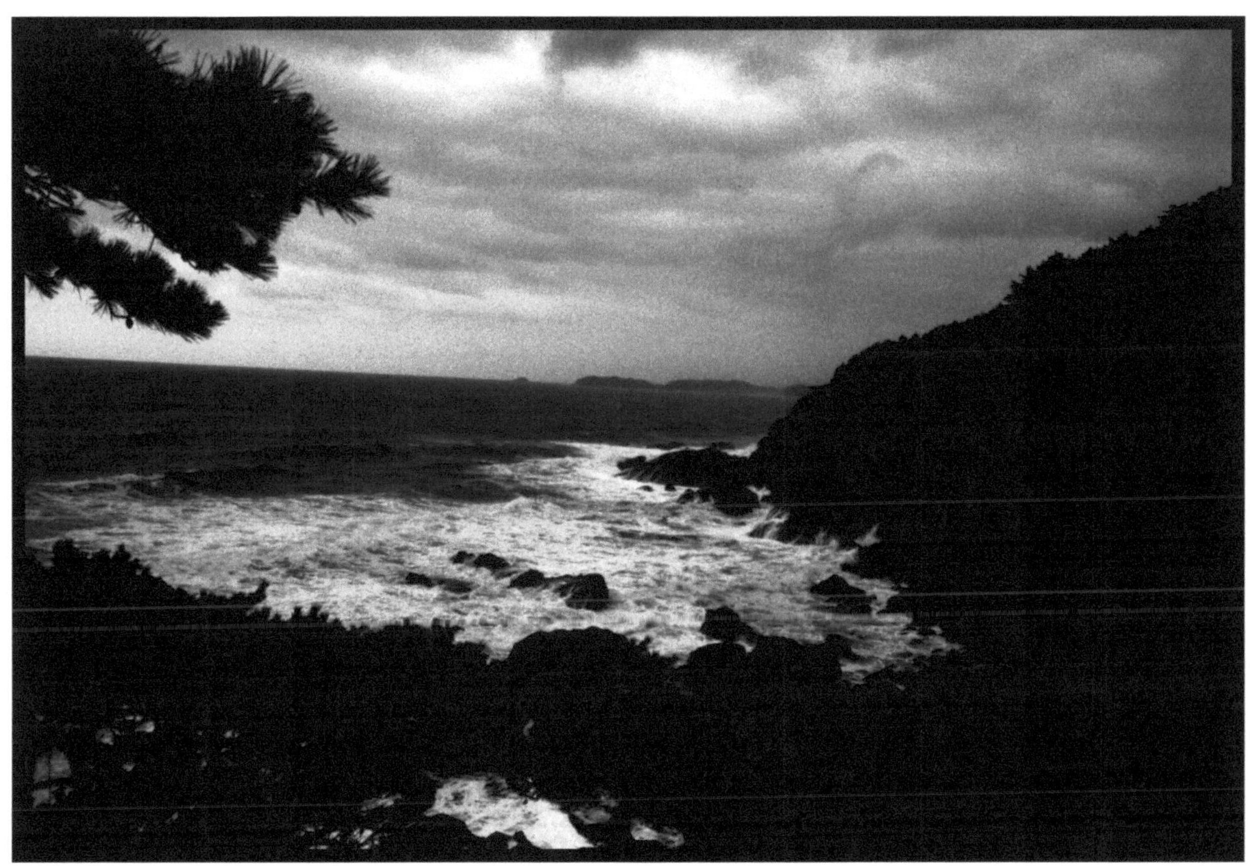

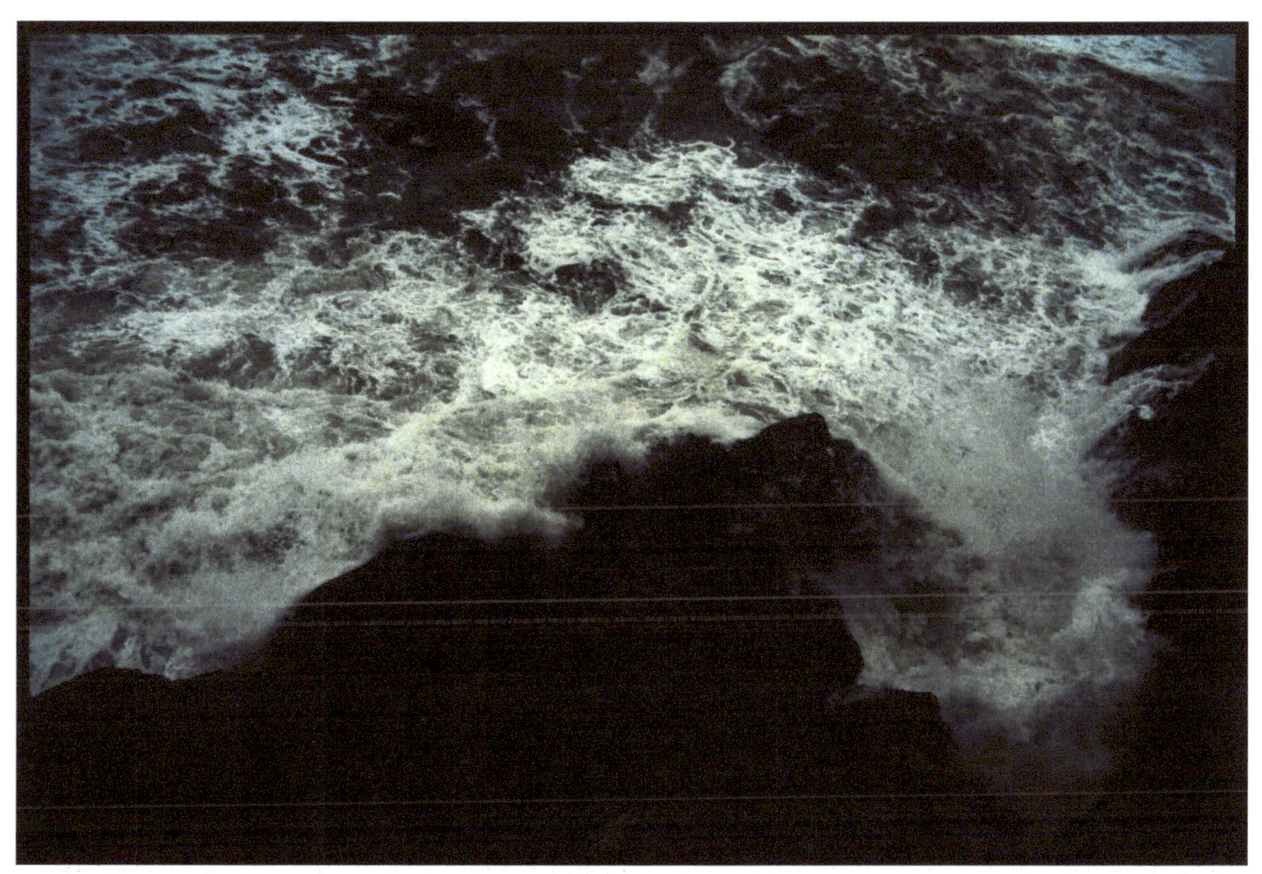

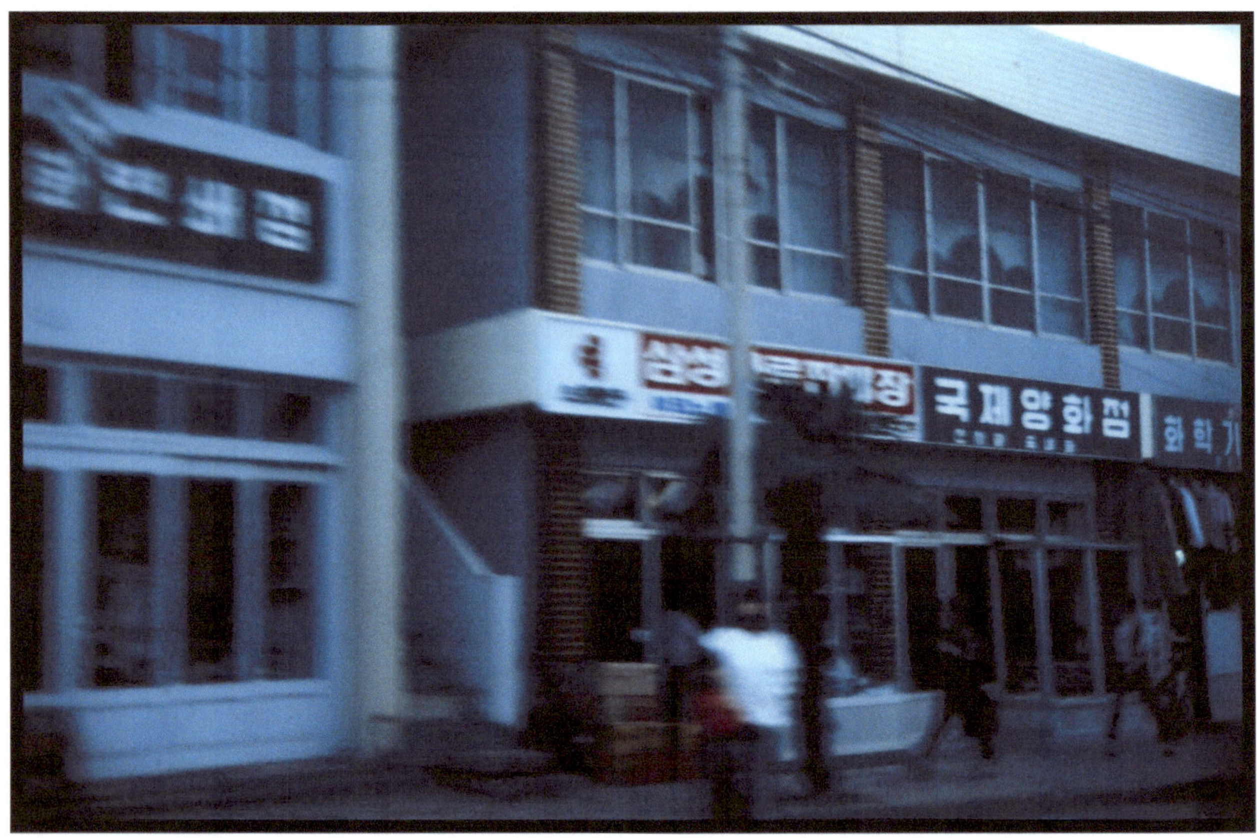

삼성
국제양화점

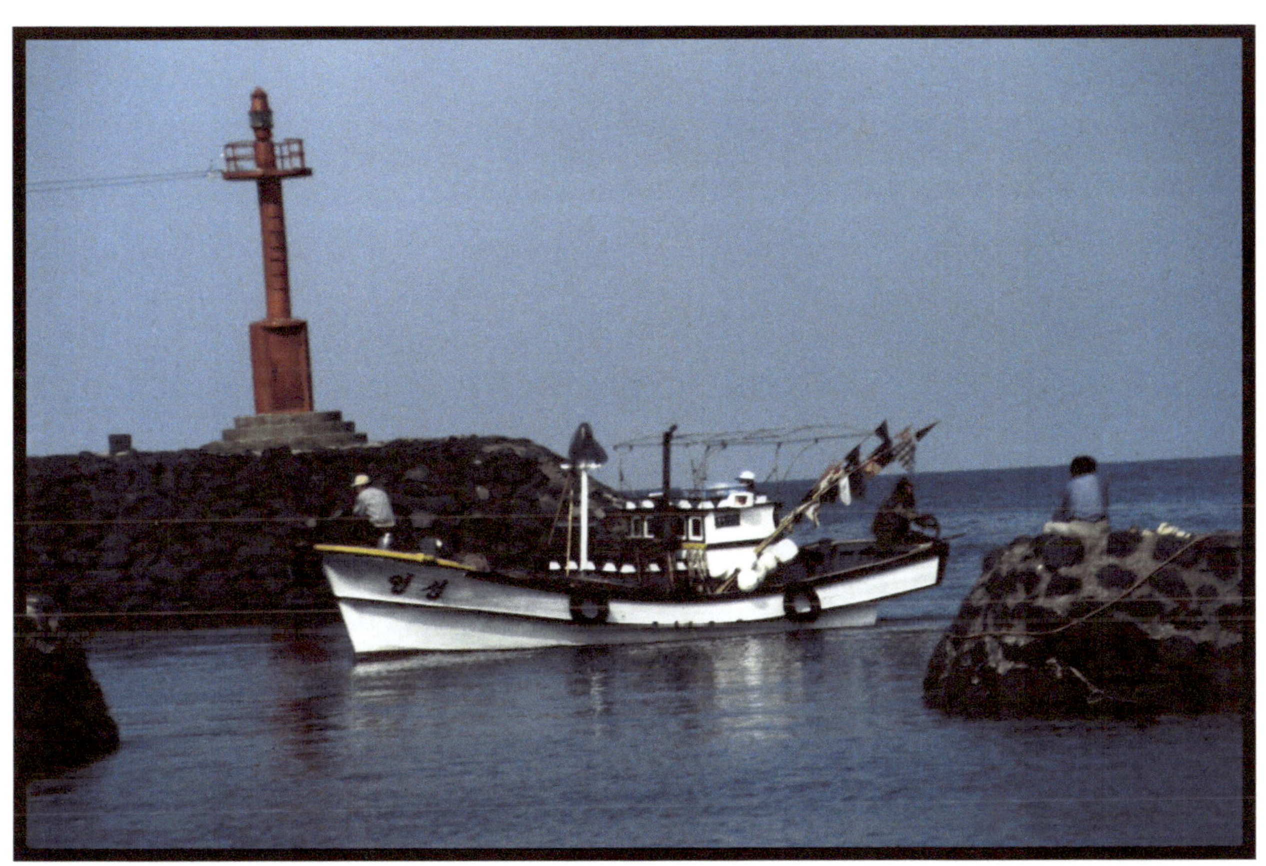

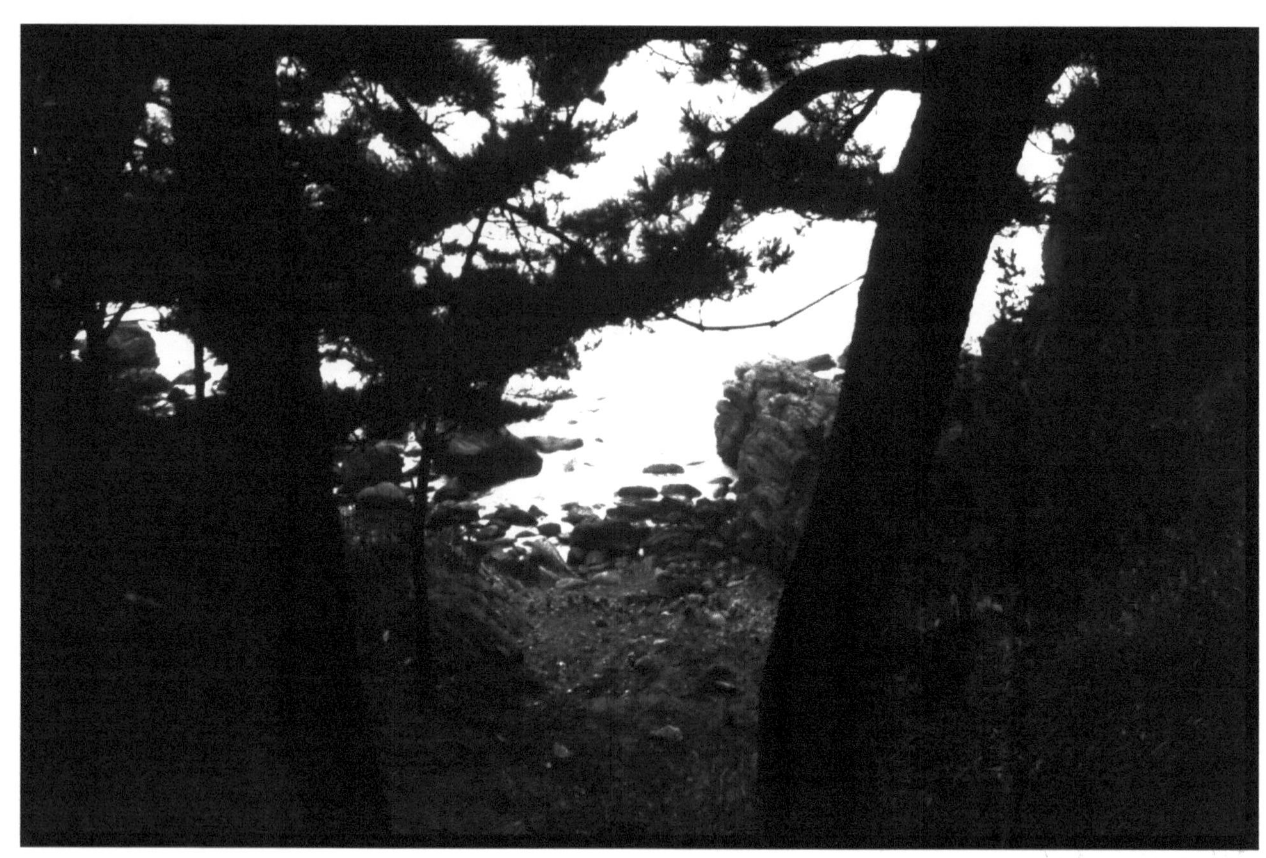

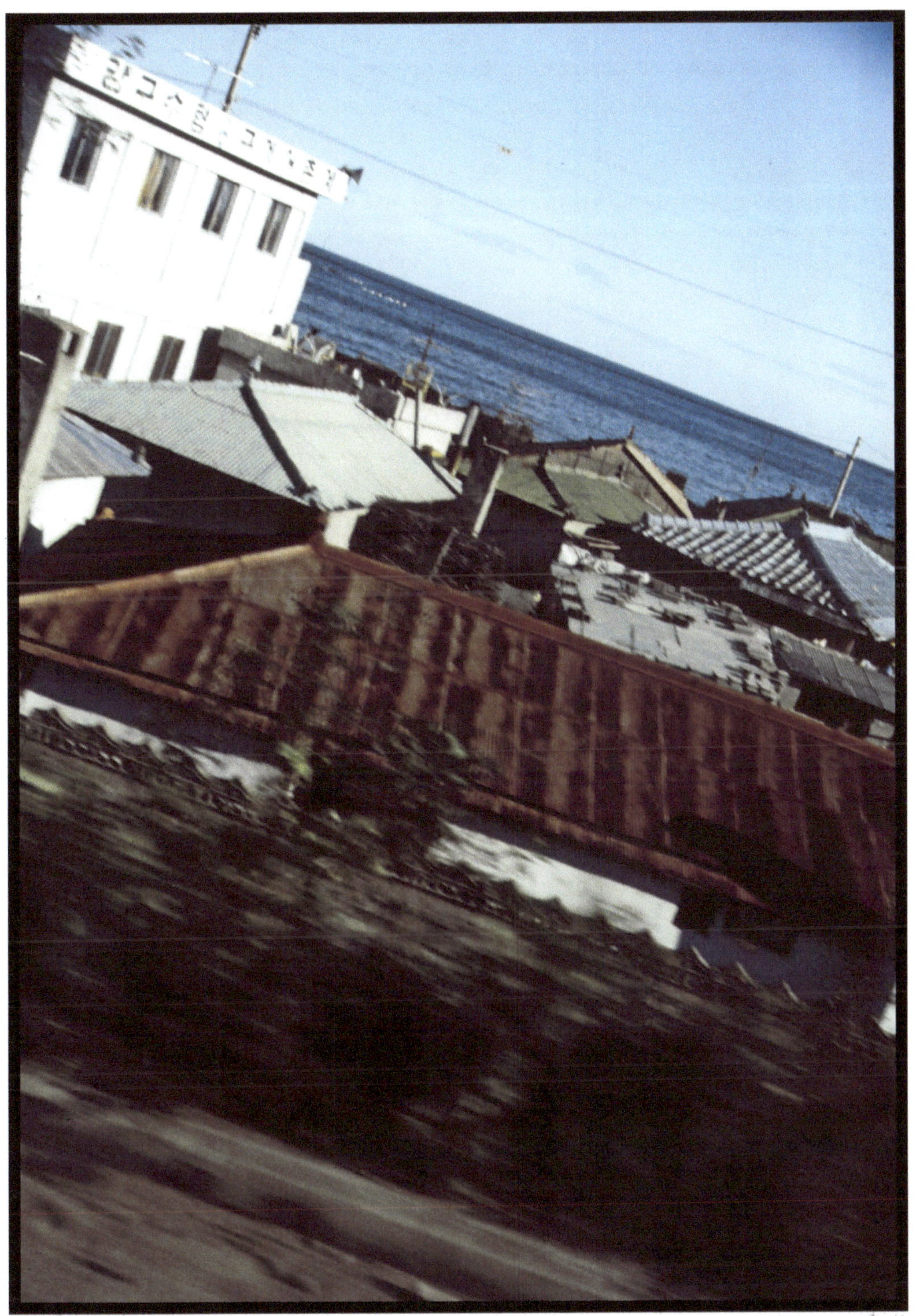

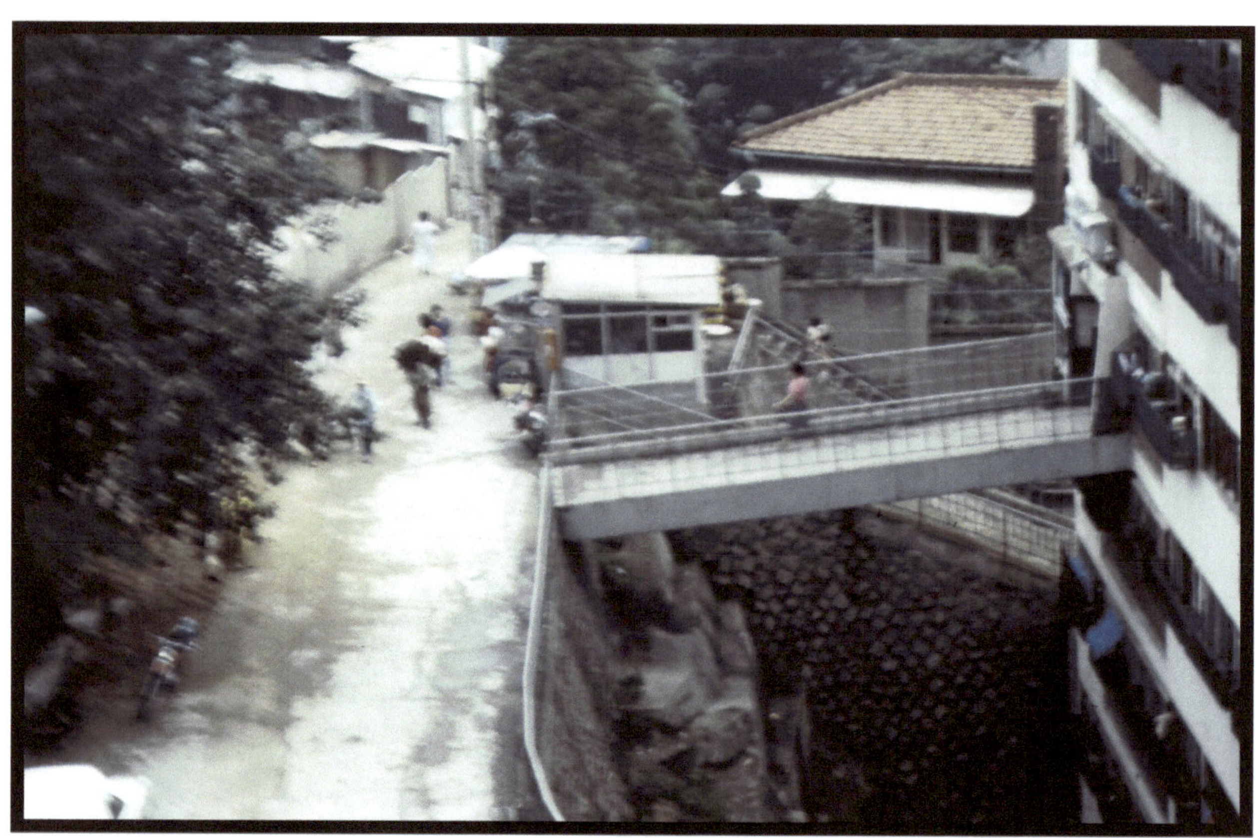

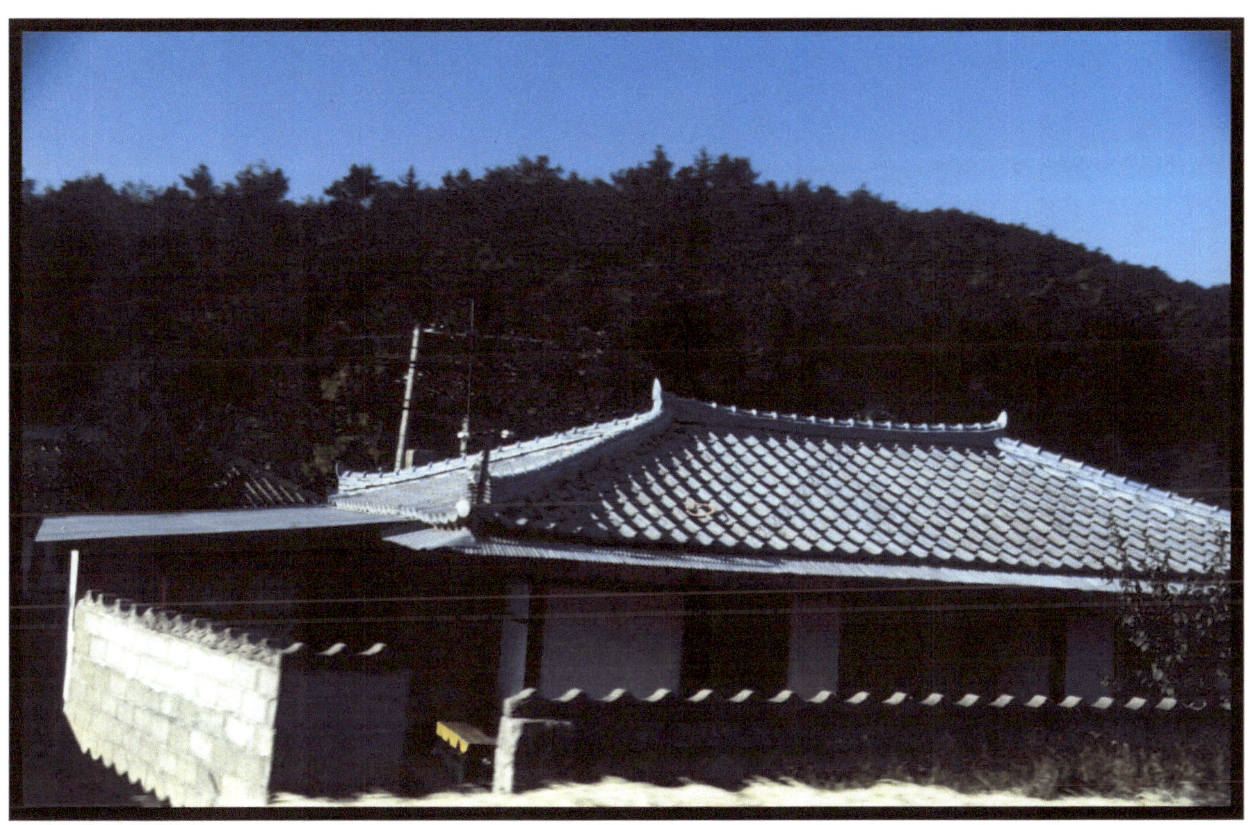

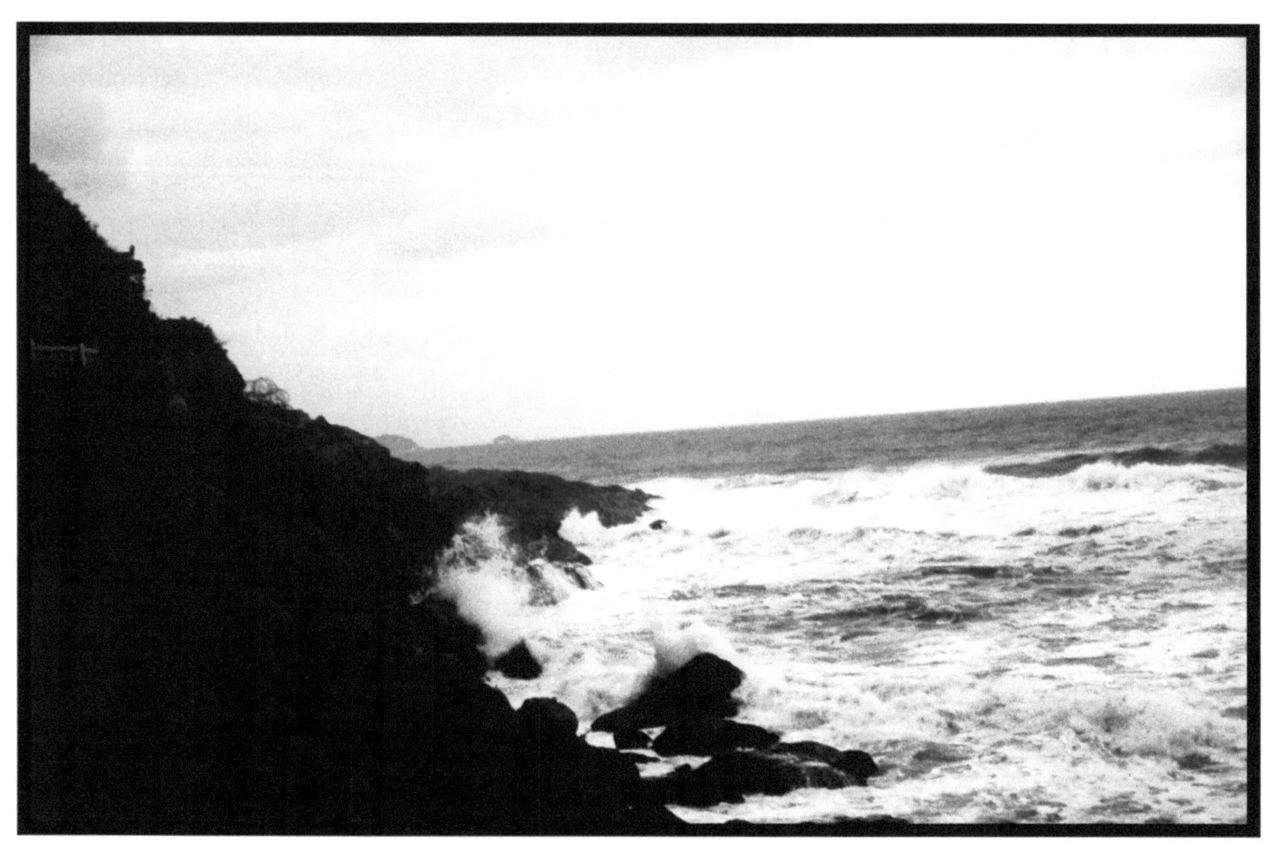

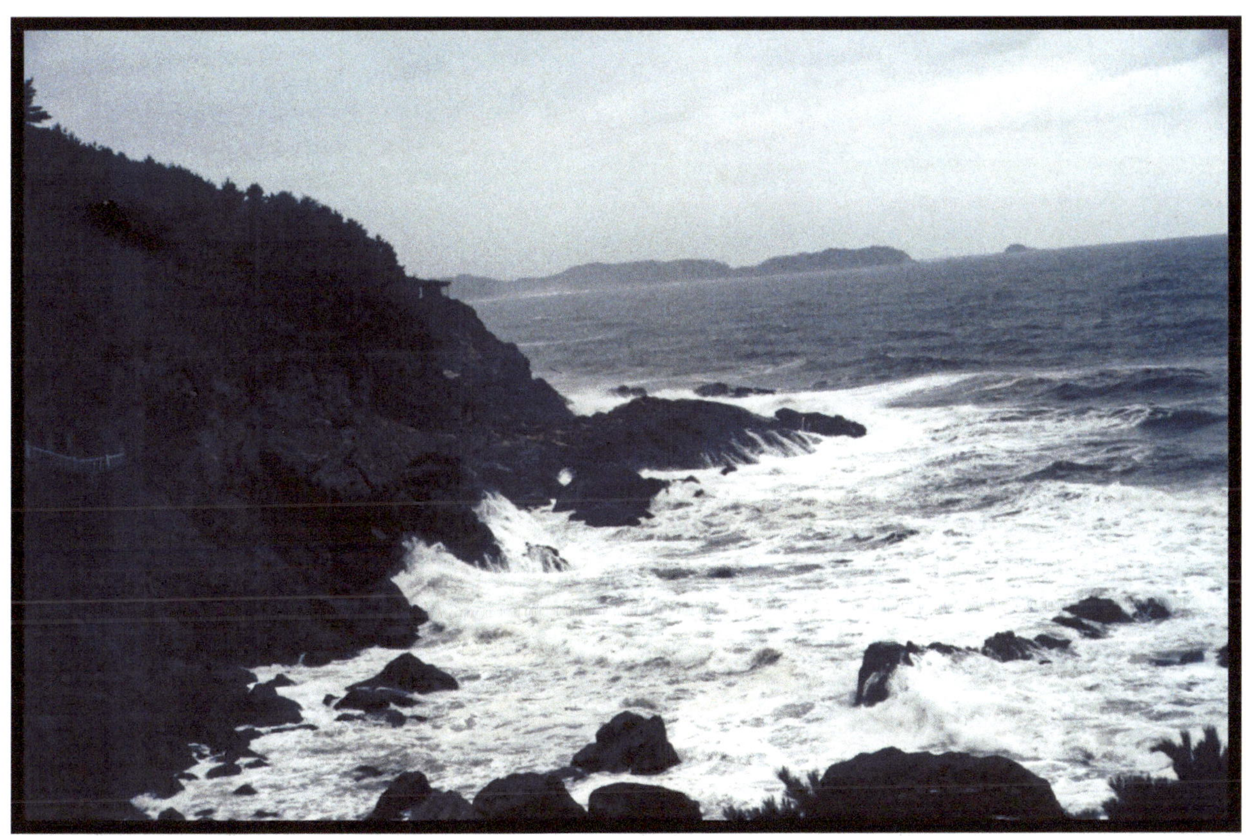

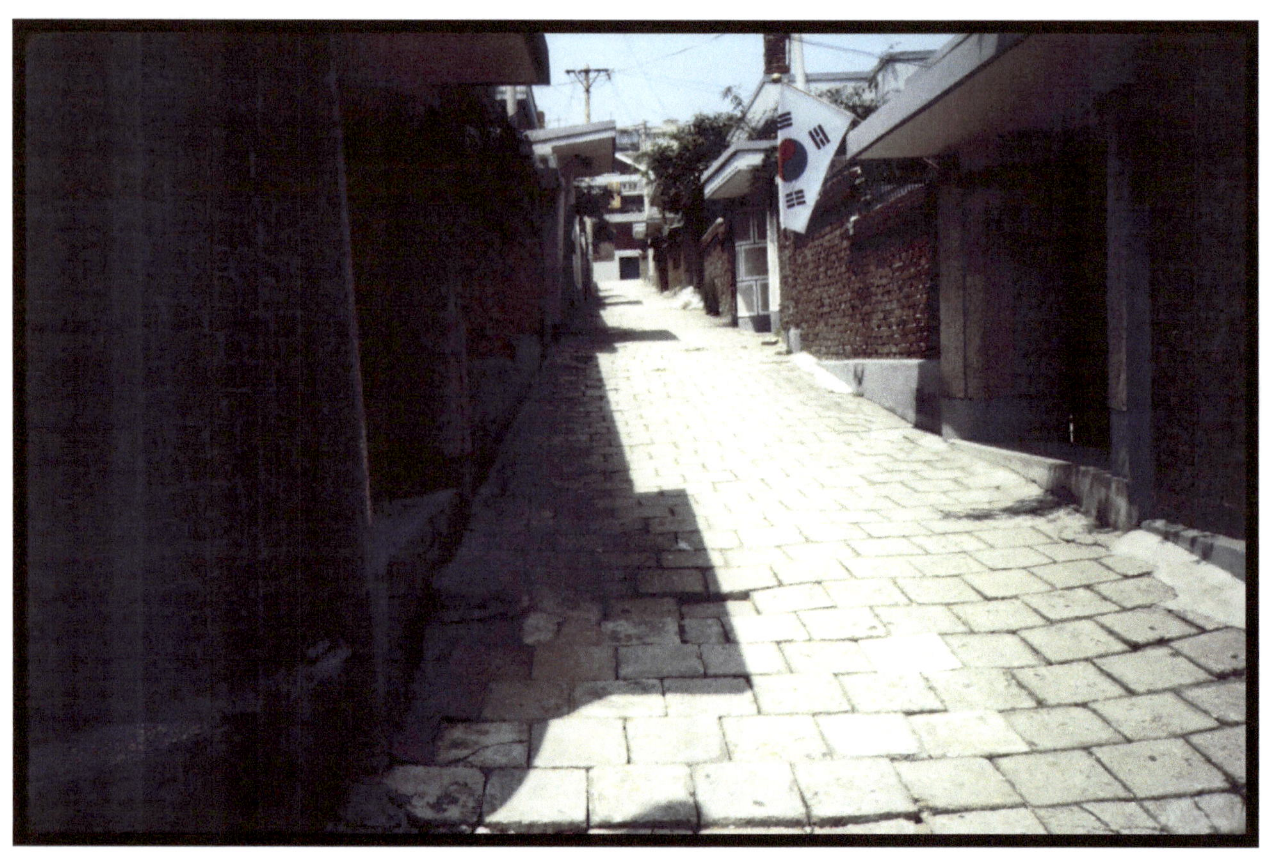

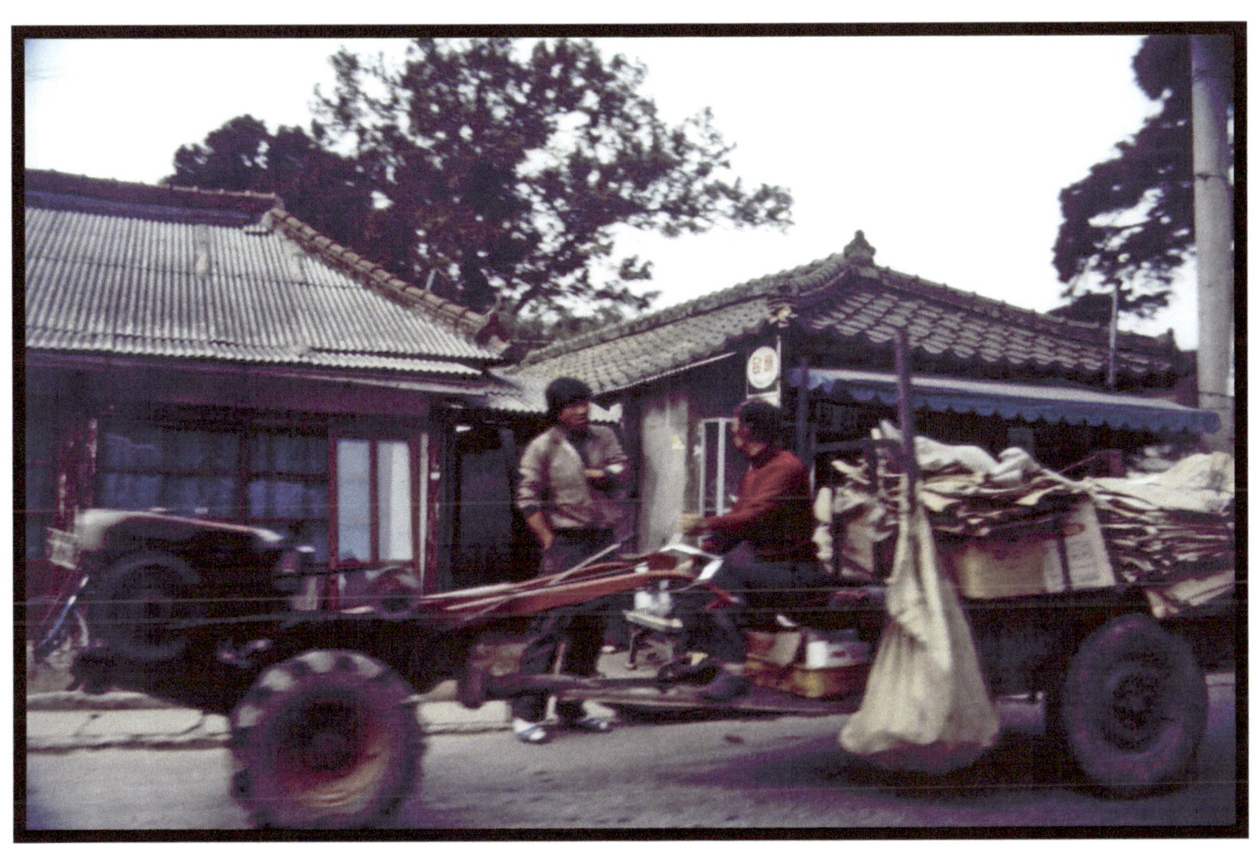

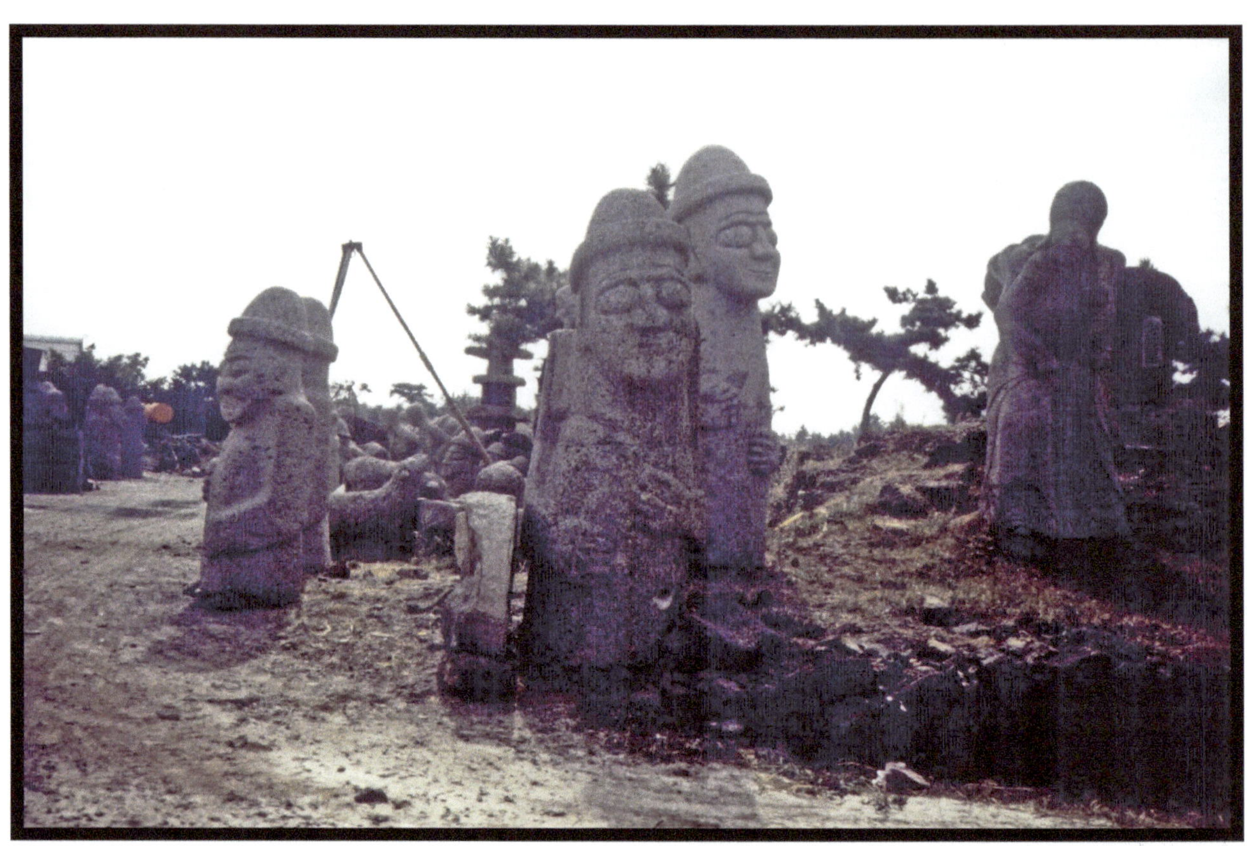

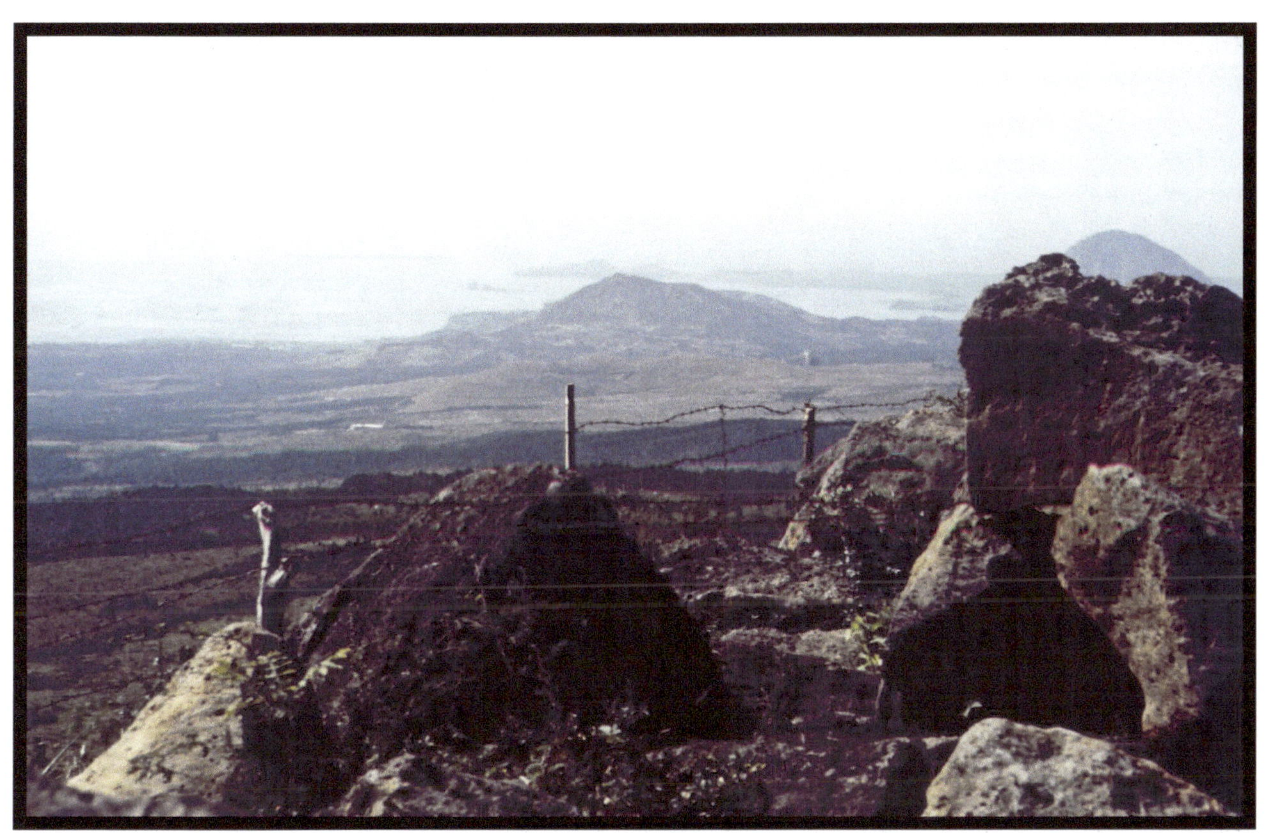

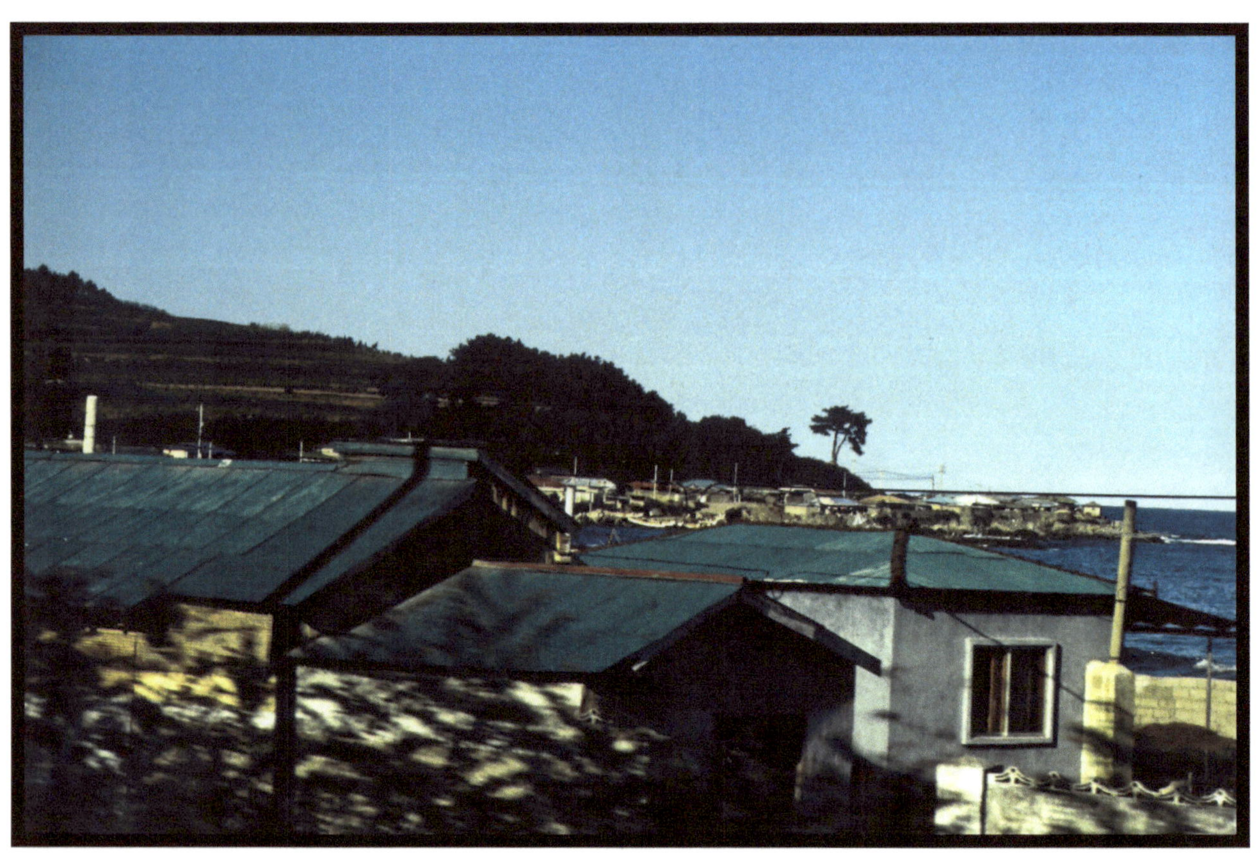

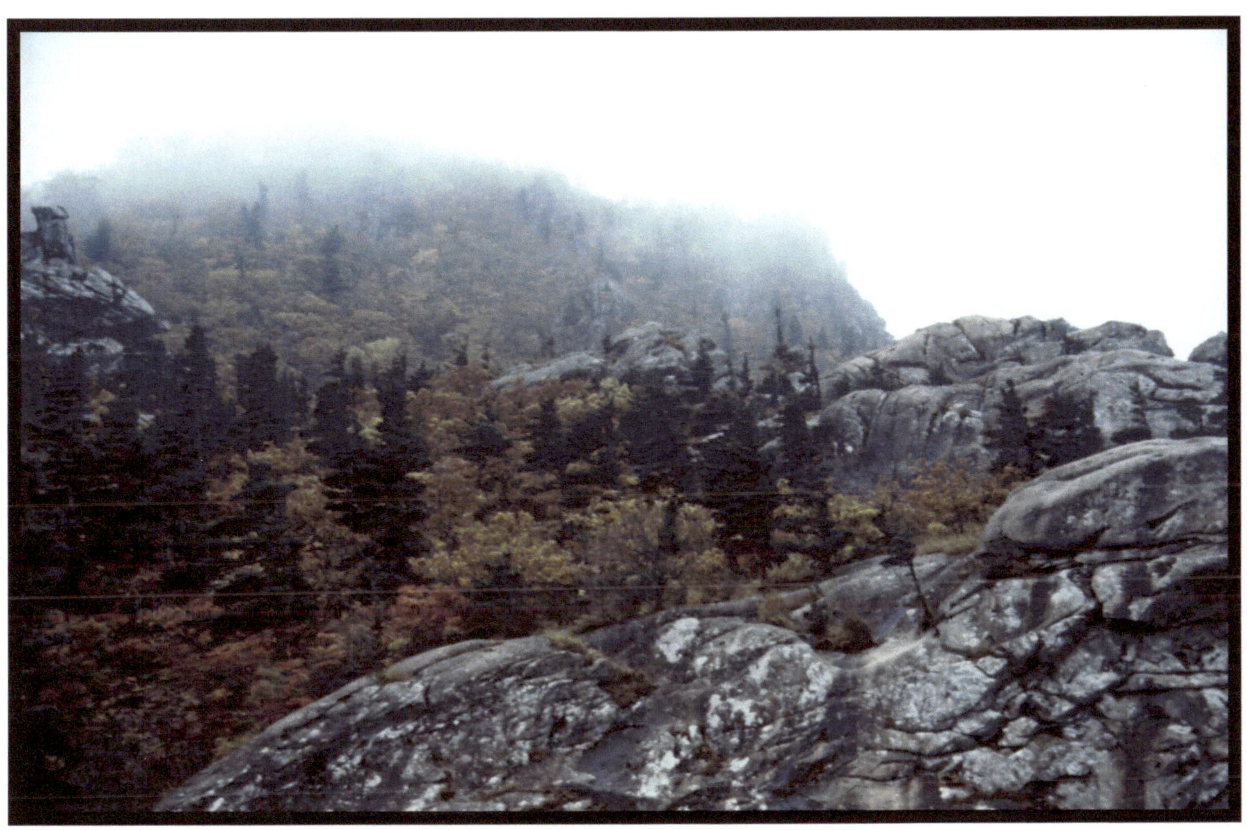

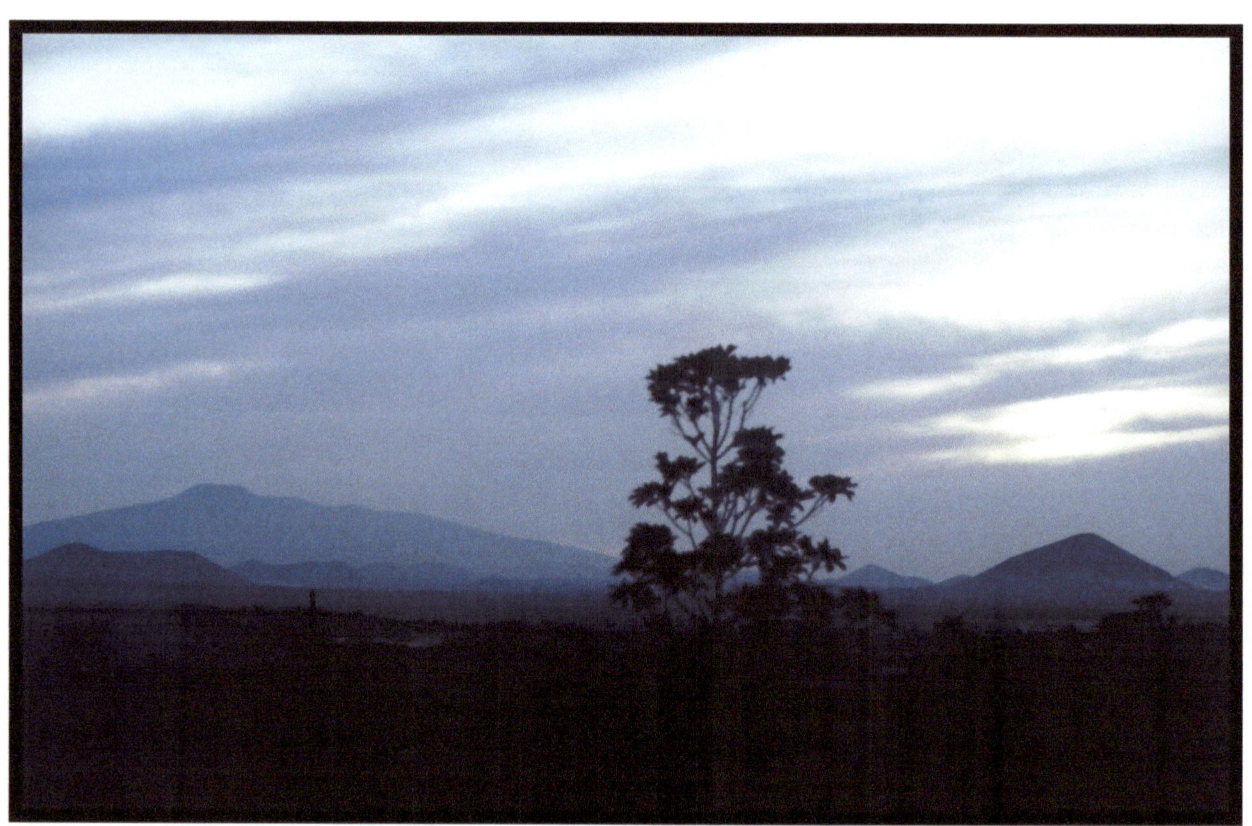

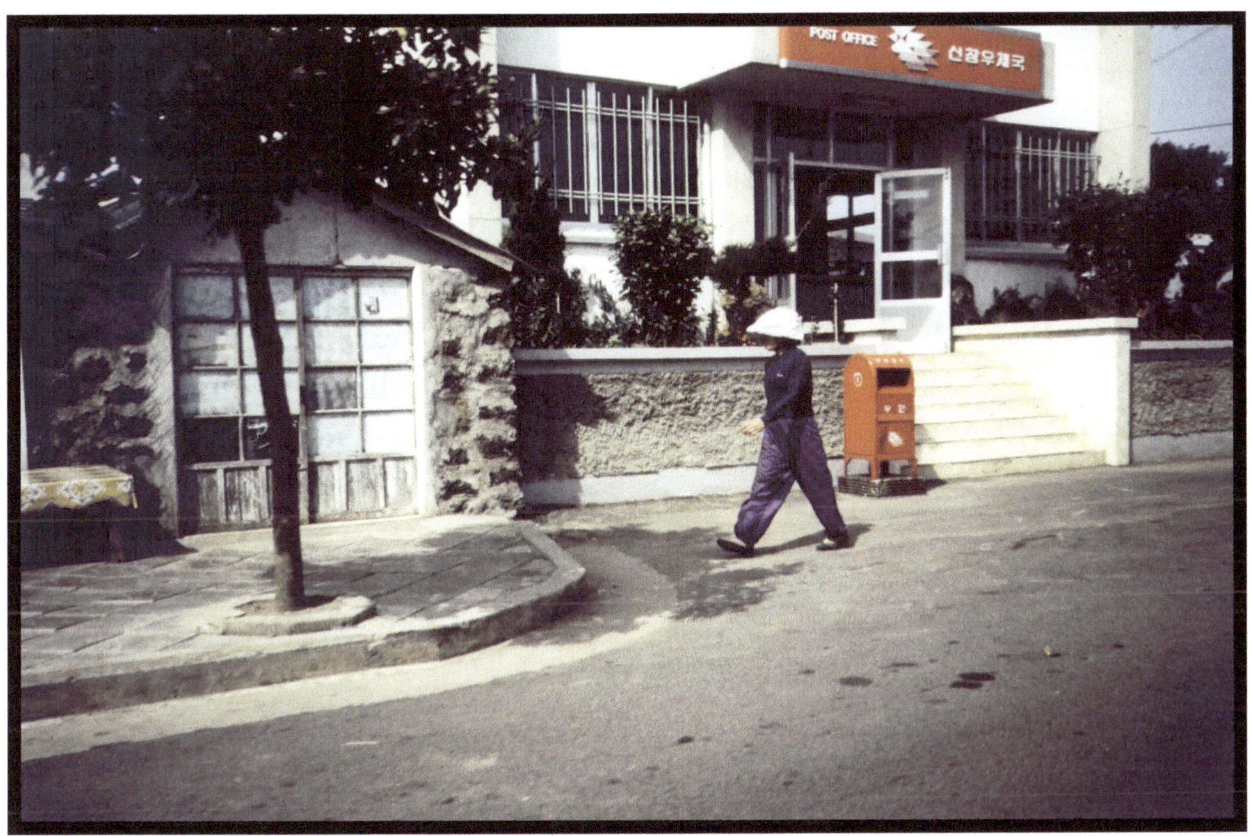
POST OFFICE
신창우체국

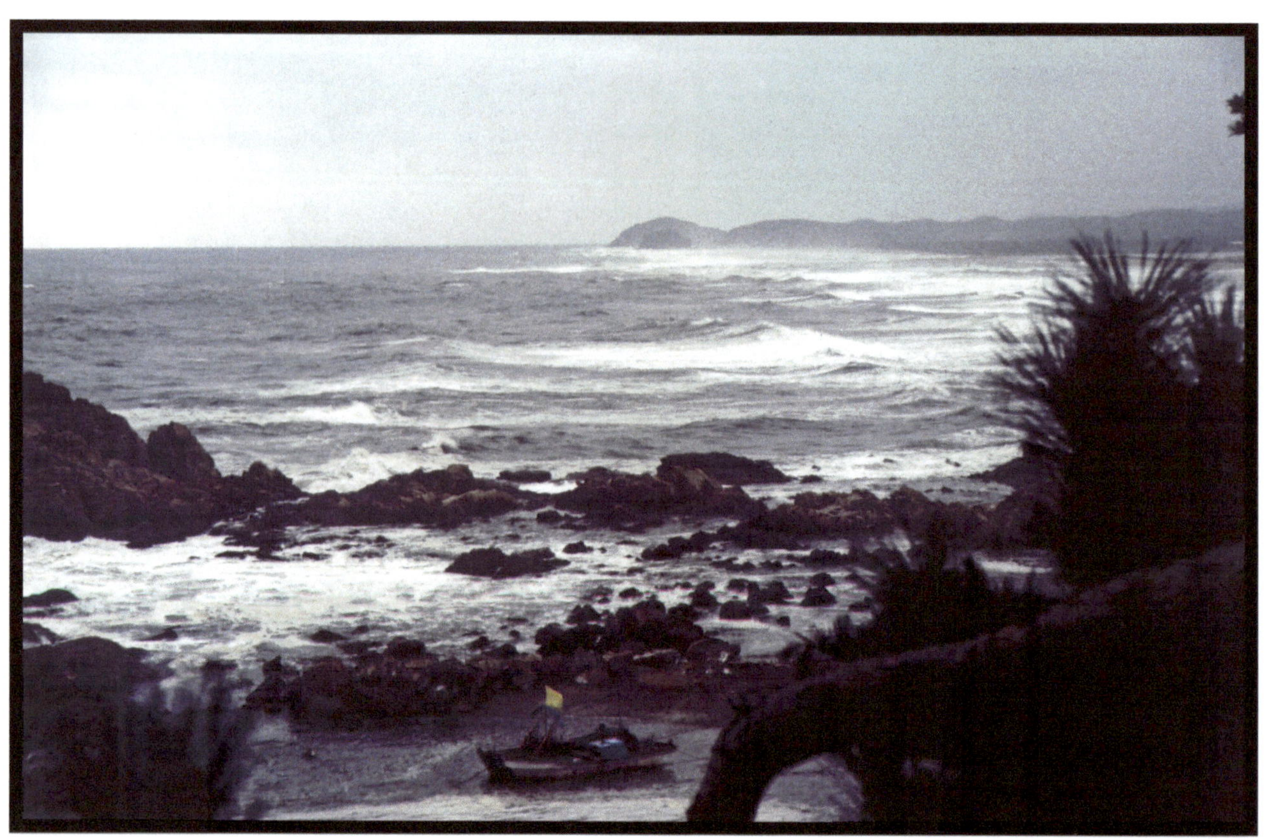

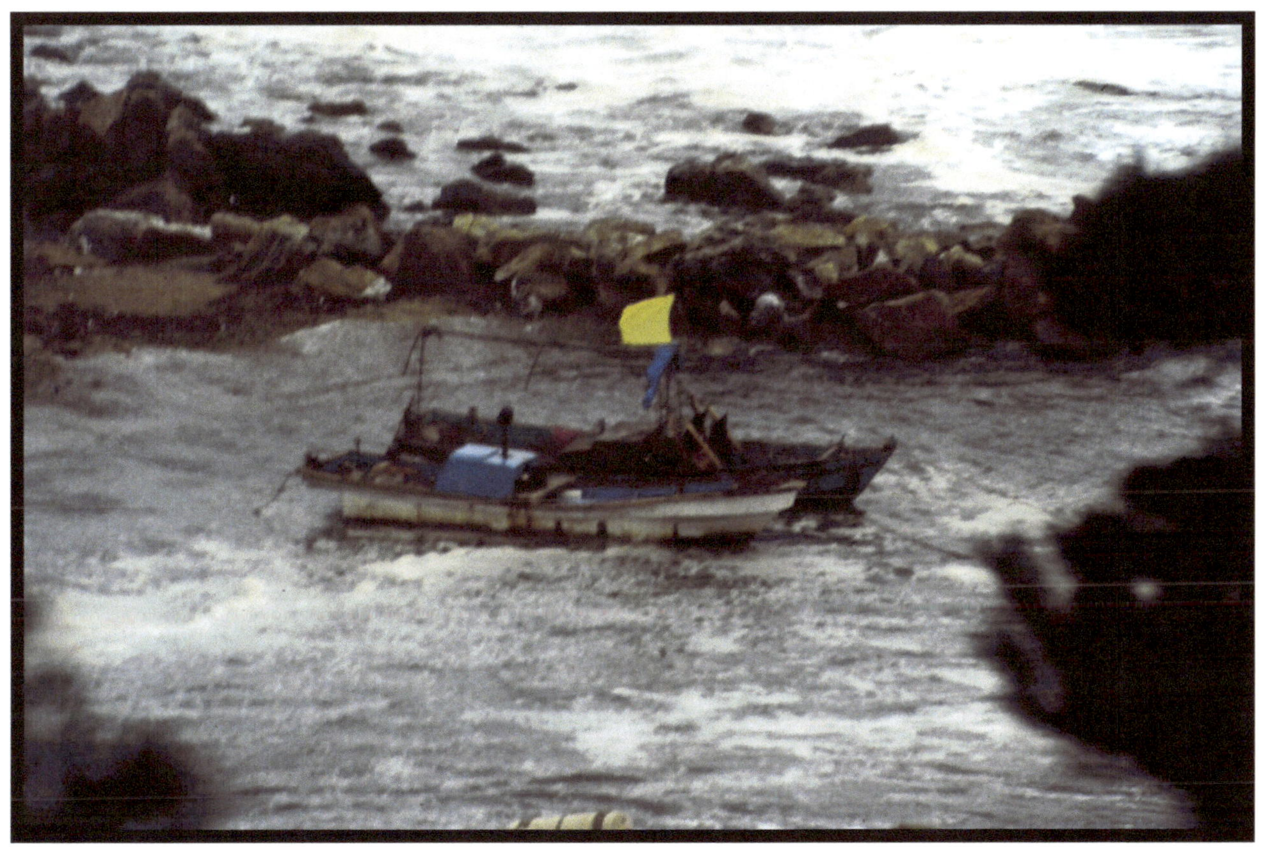

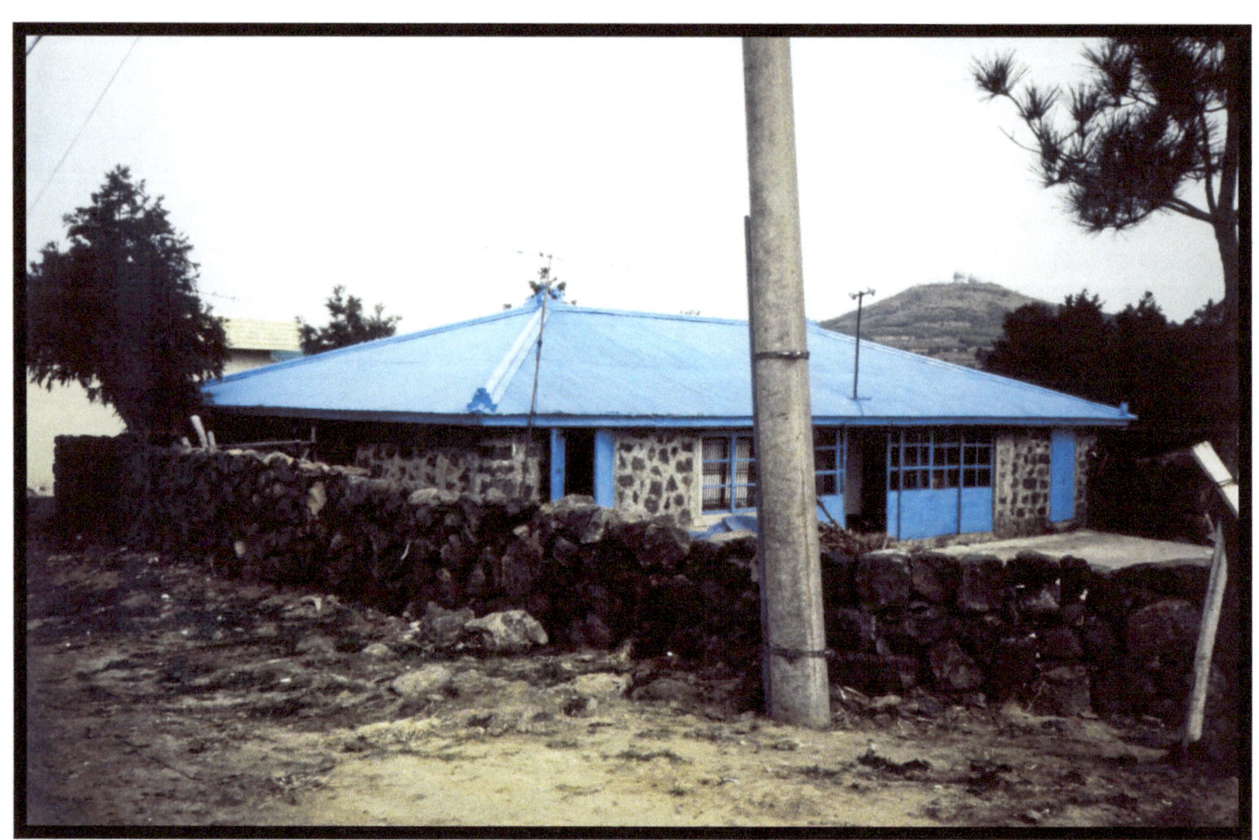

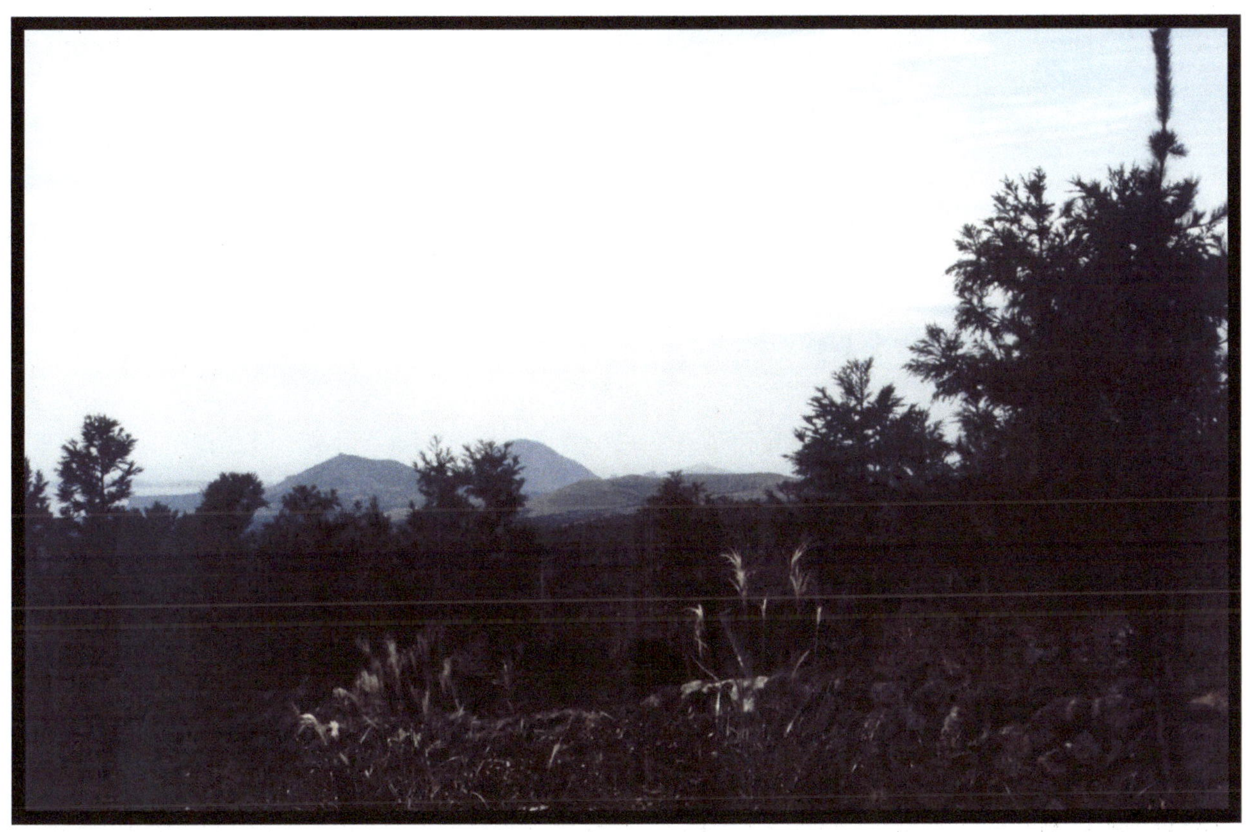

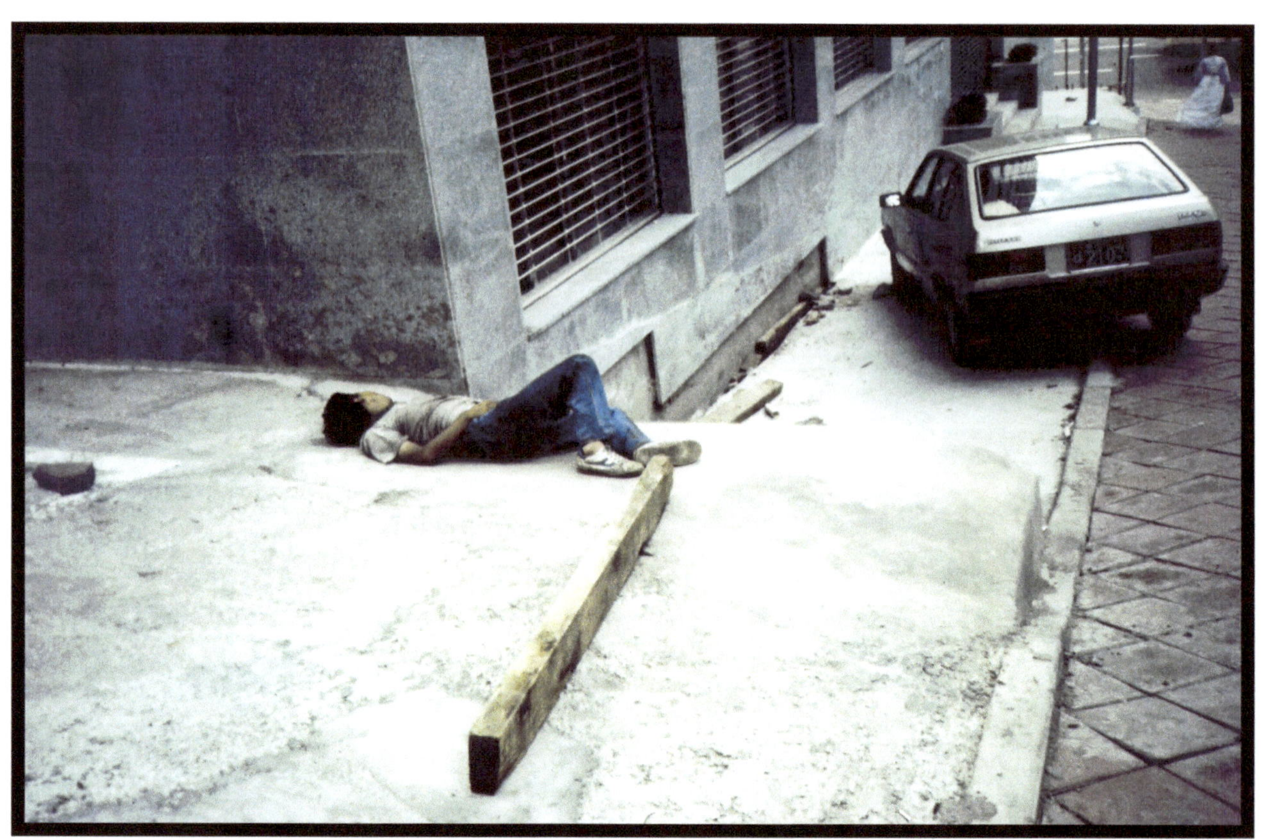

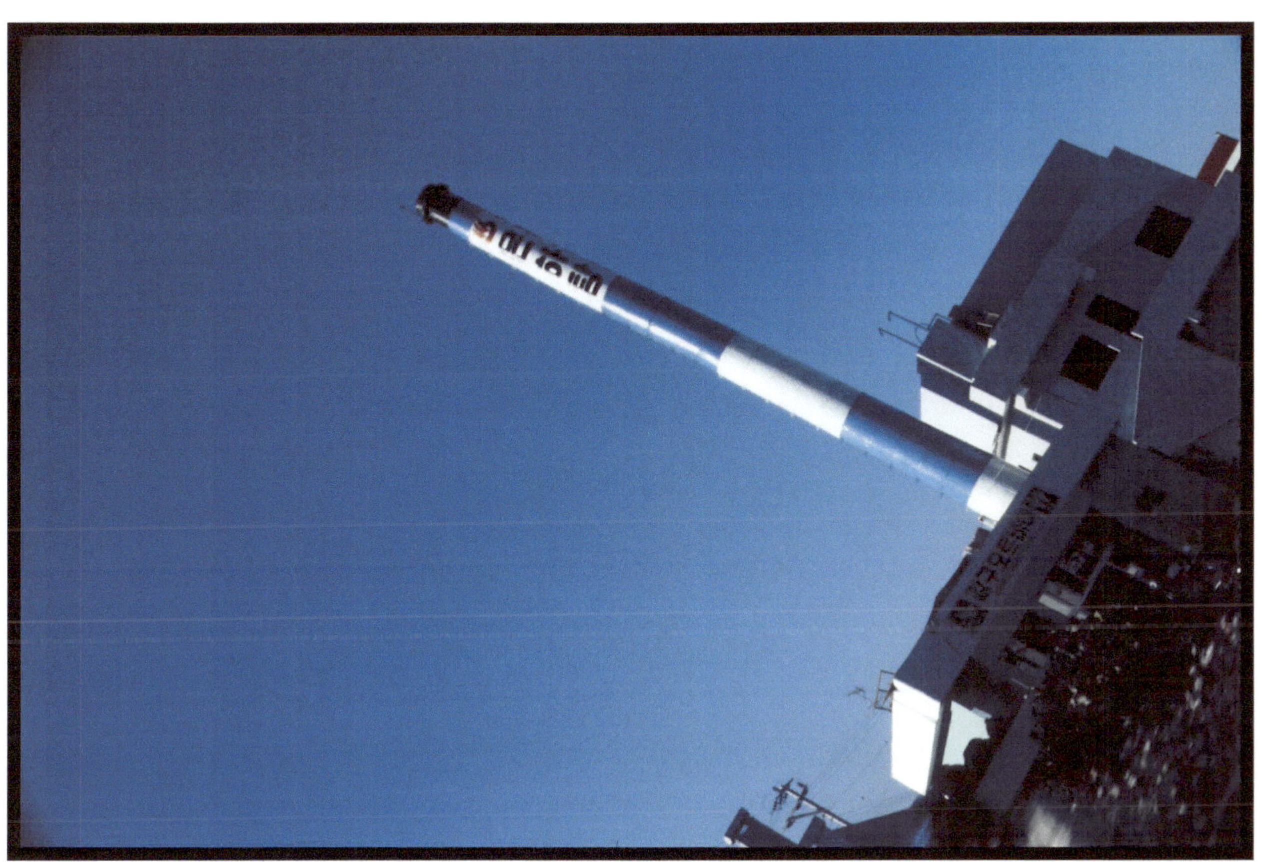

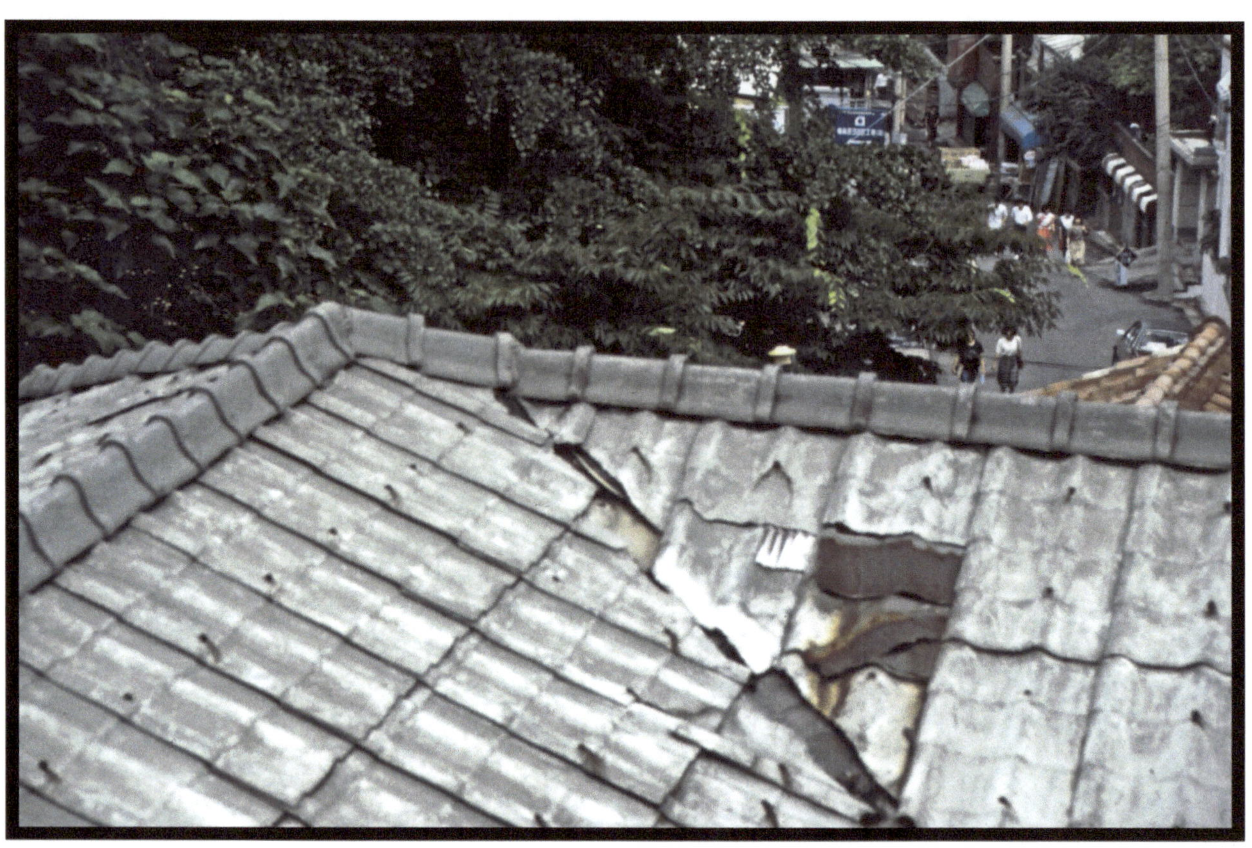

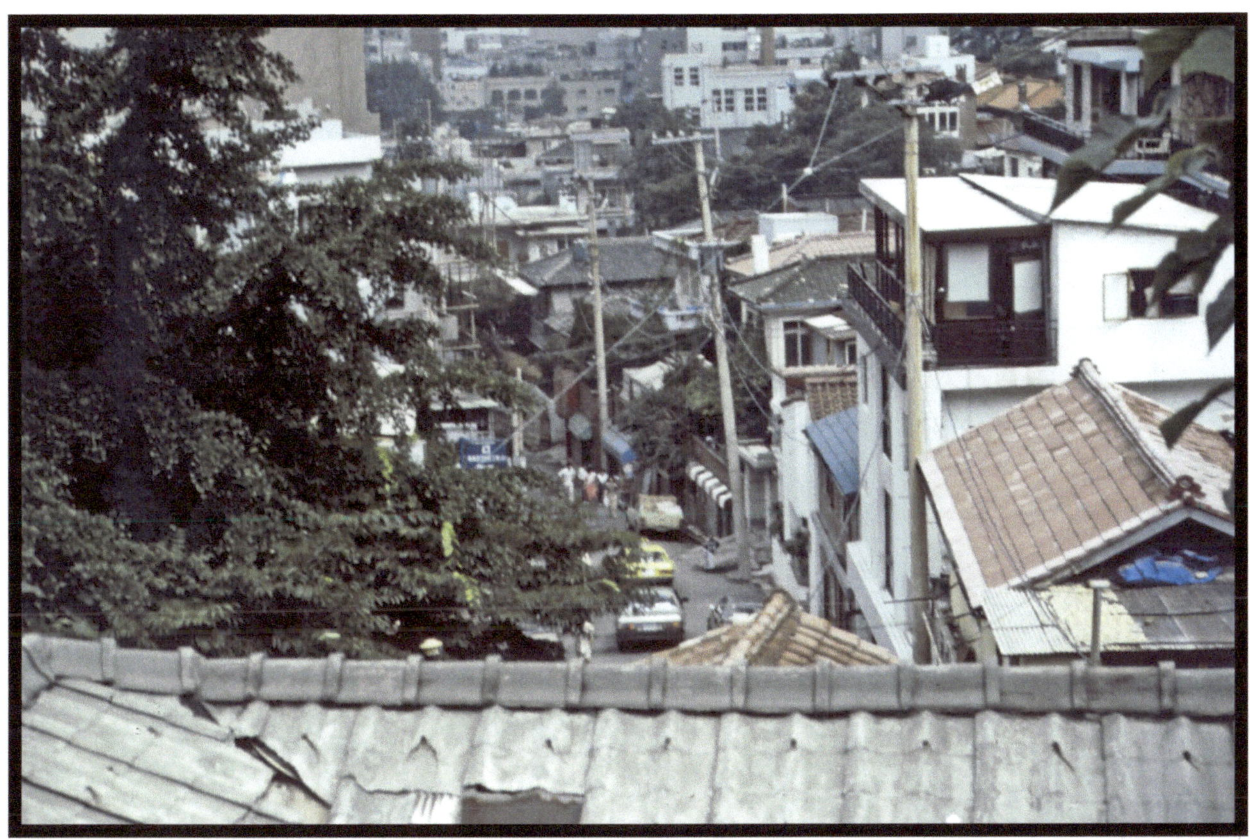

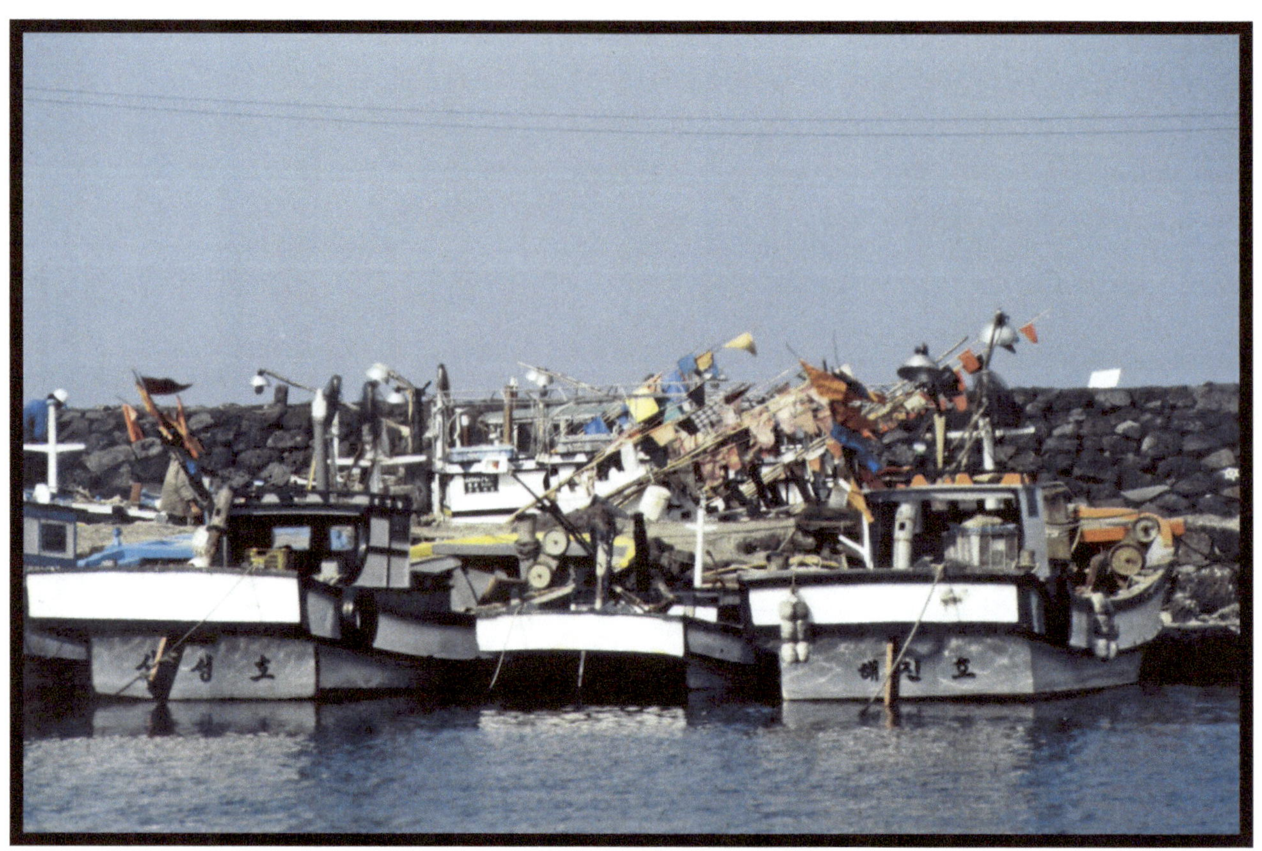
해 진 호

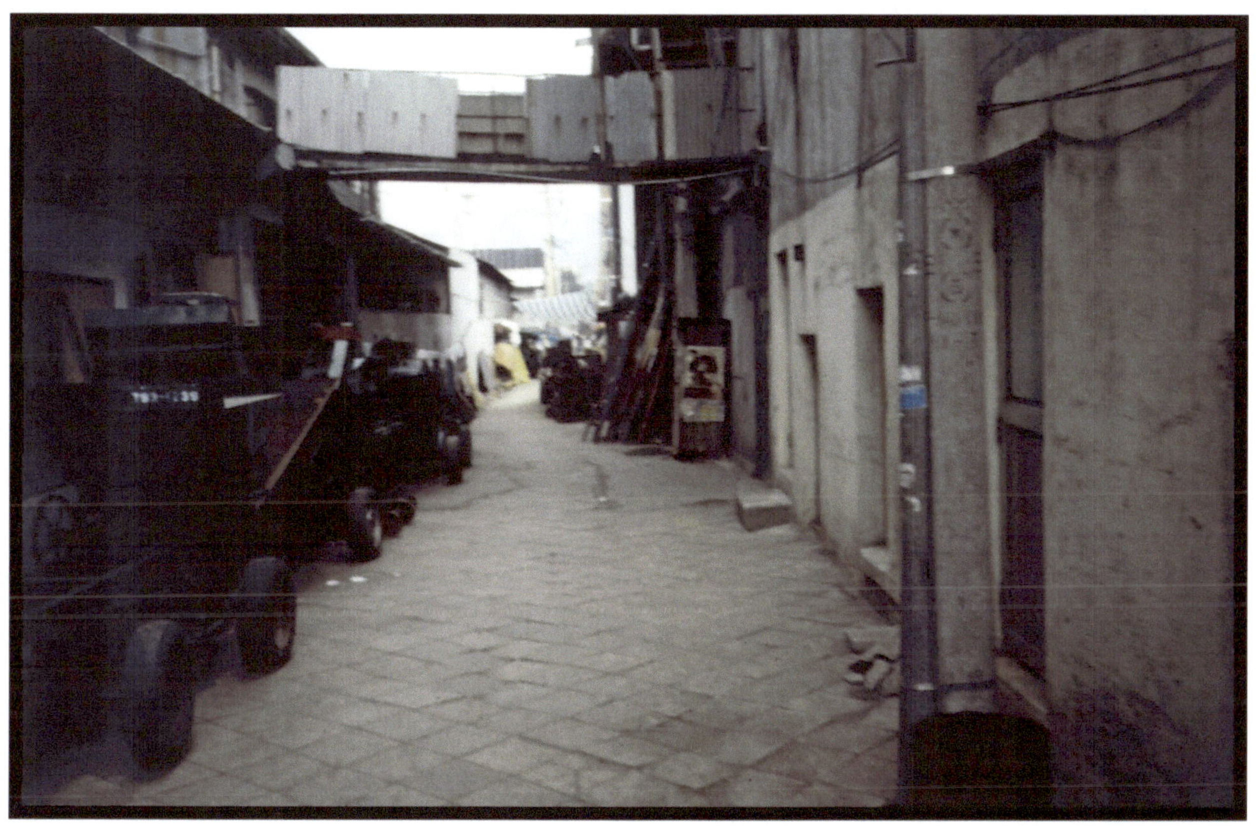

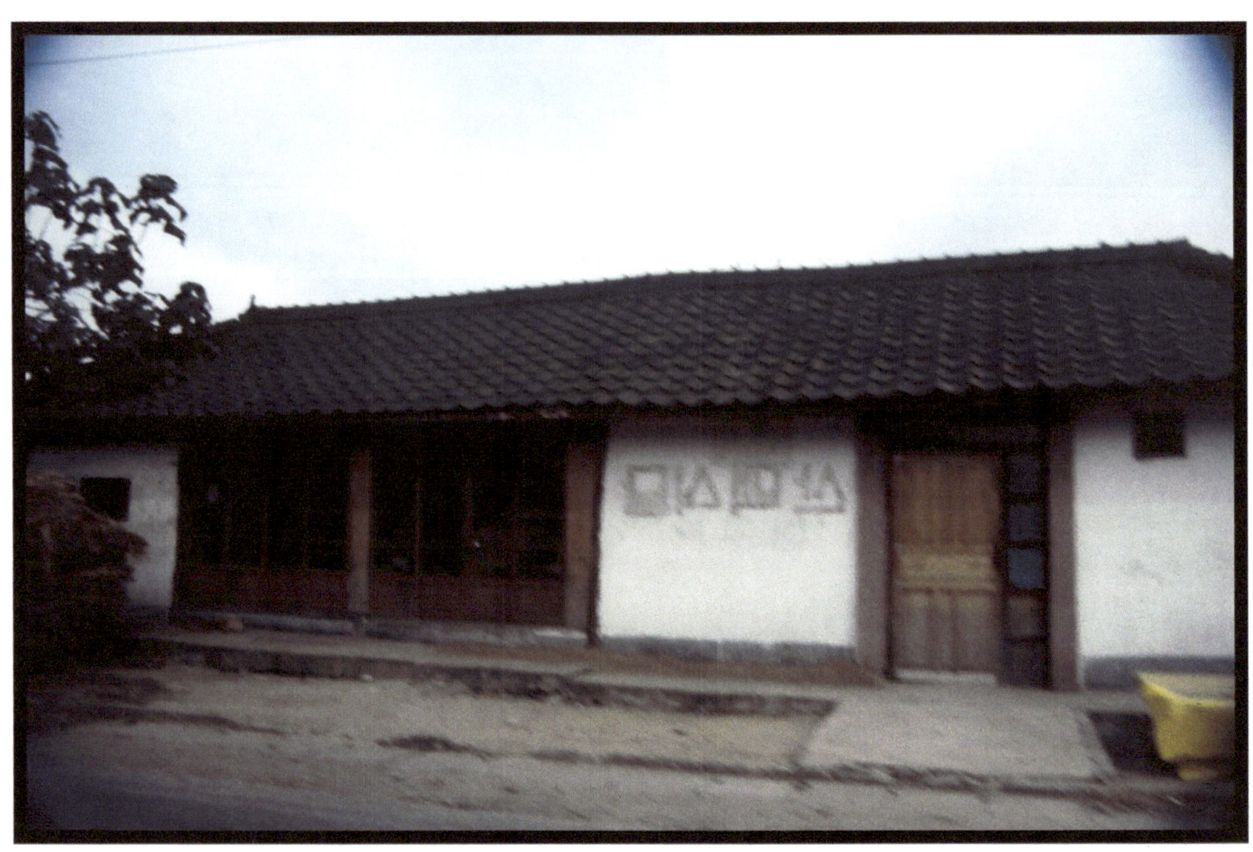

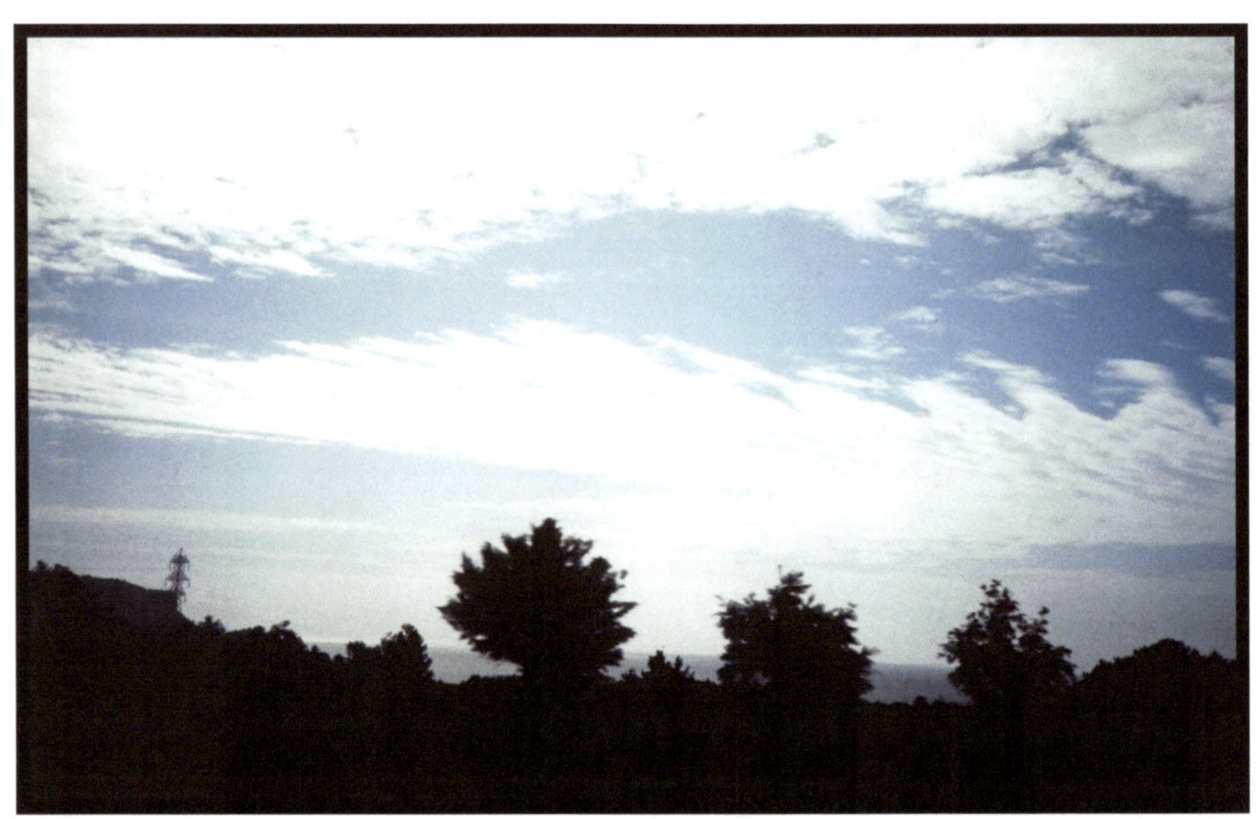

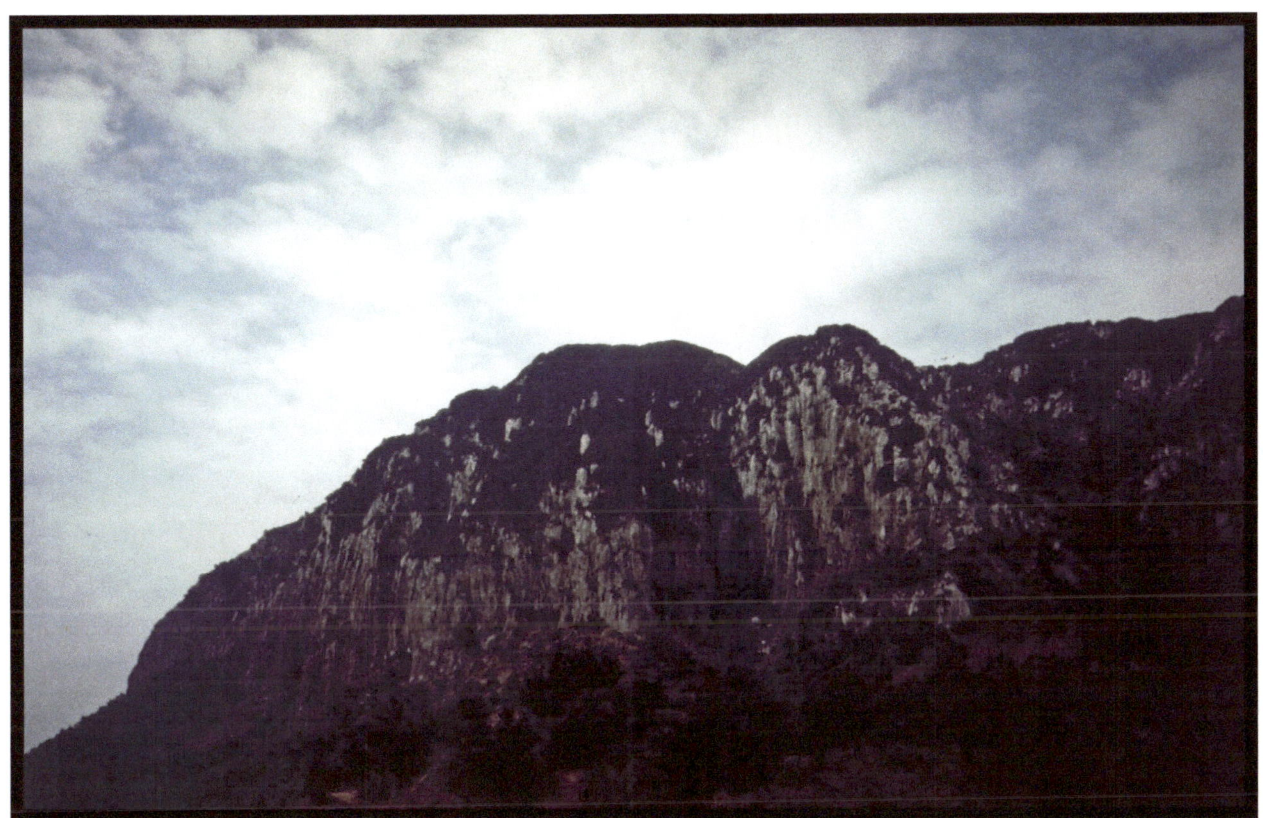

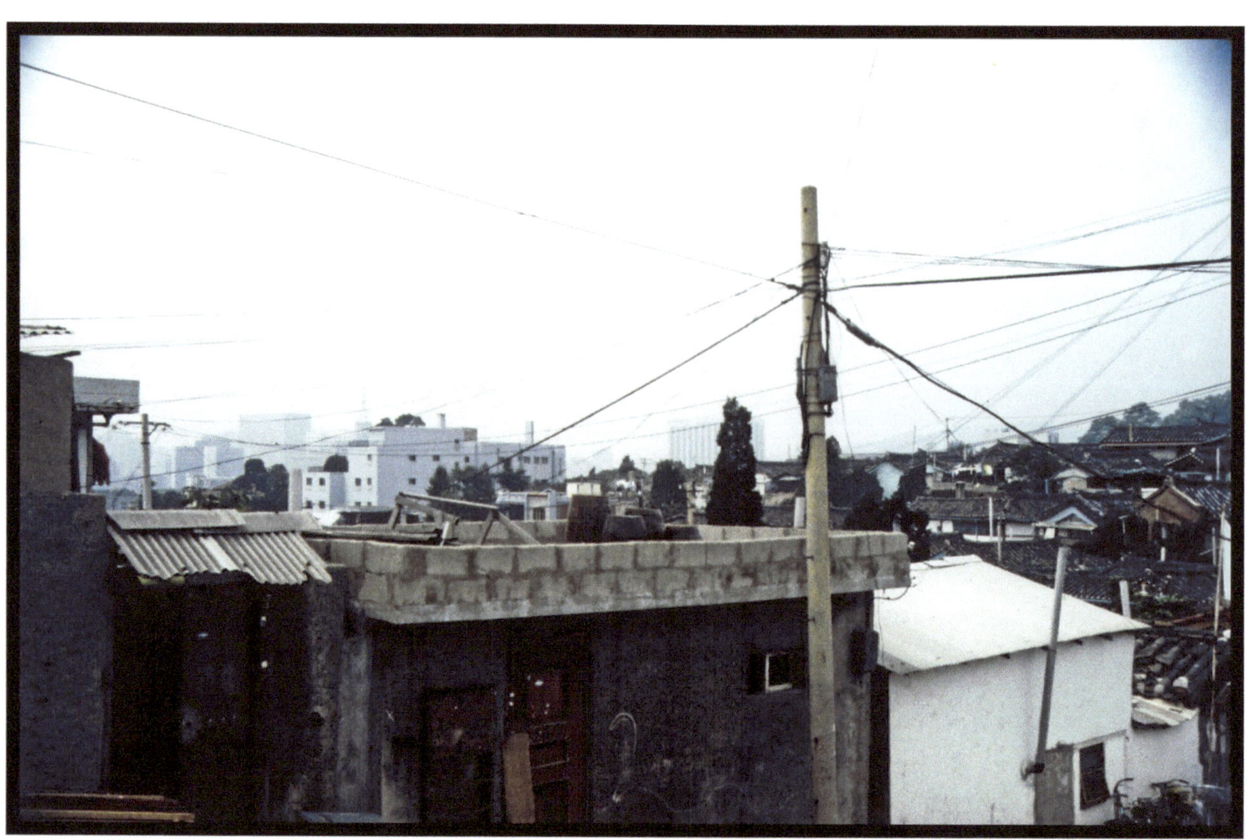

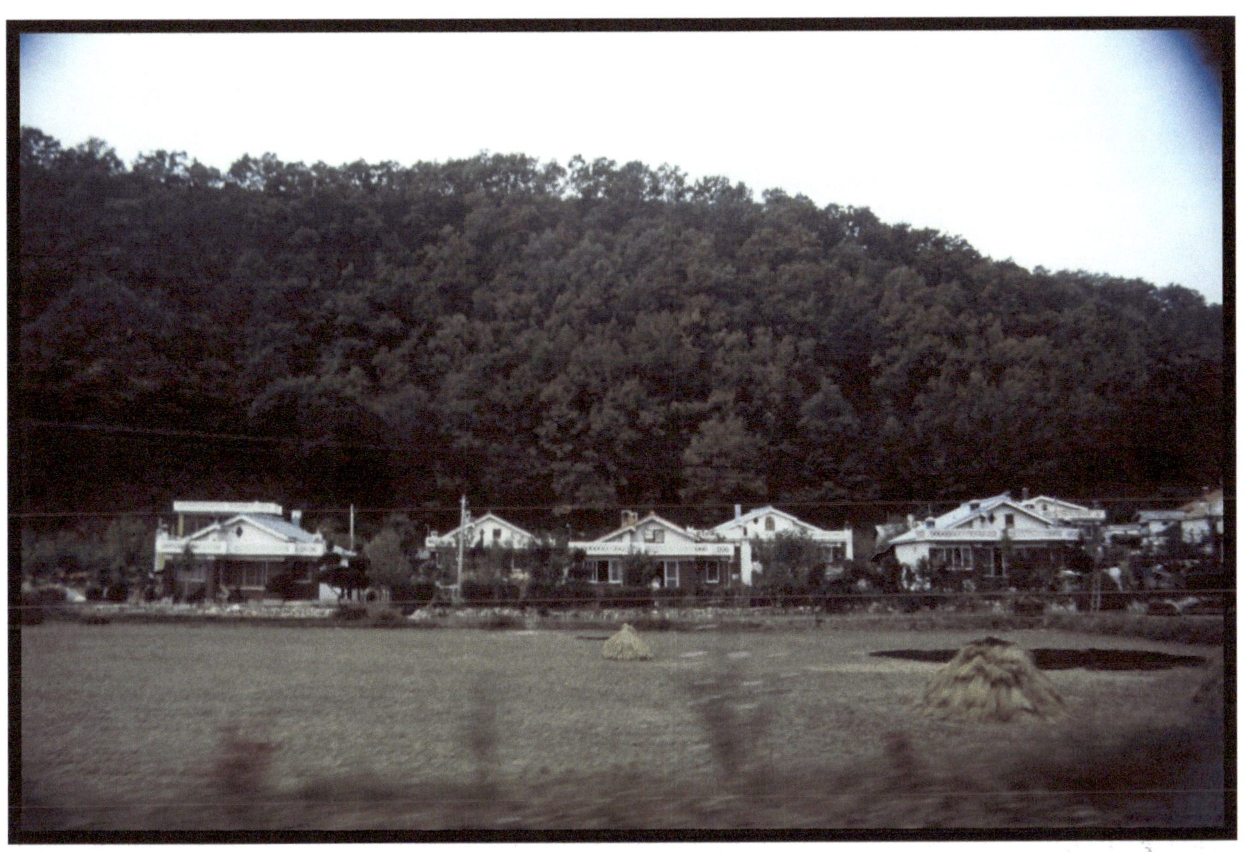

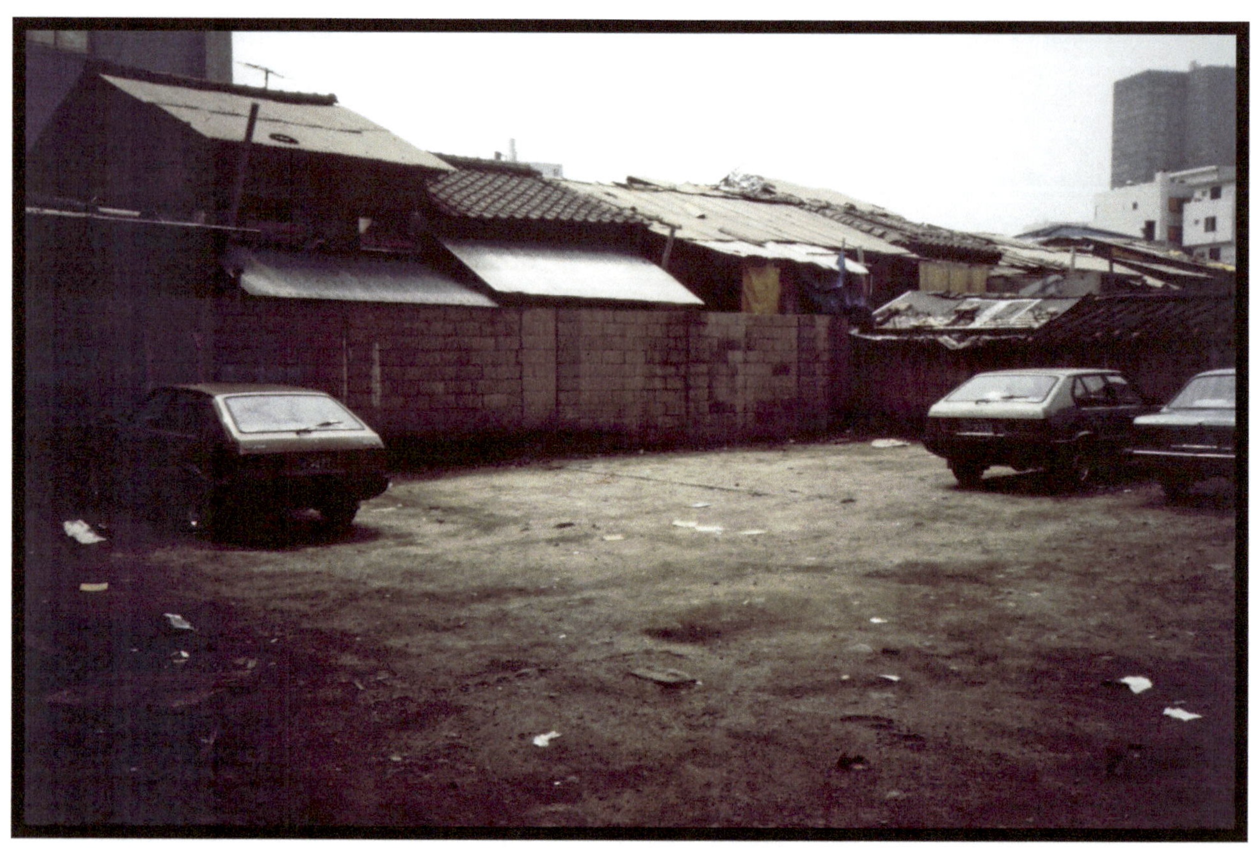

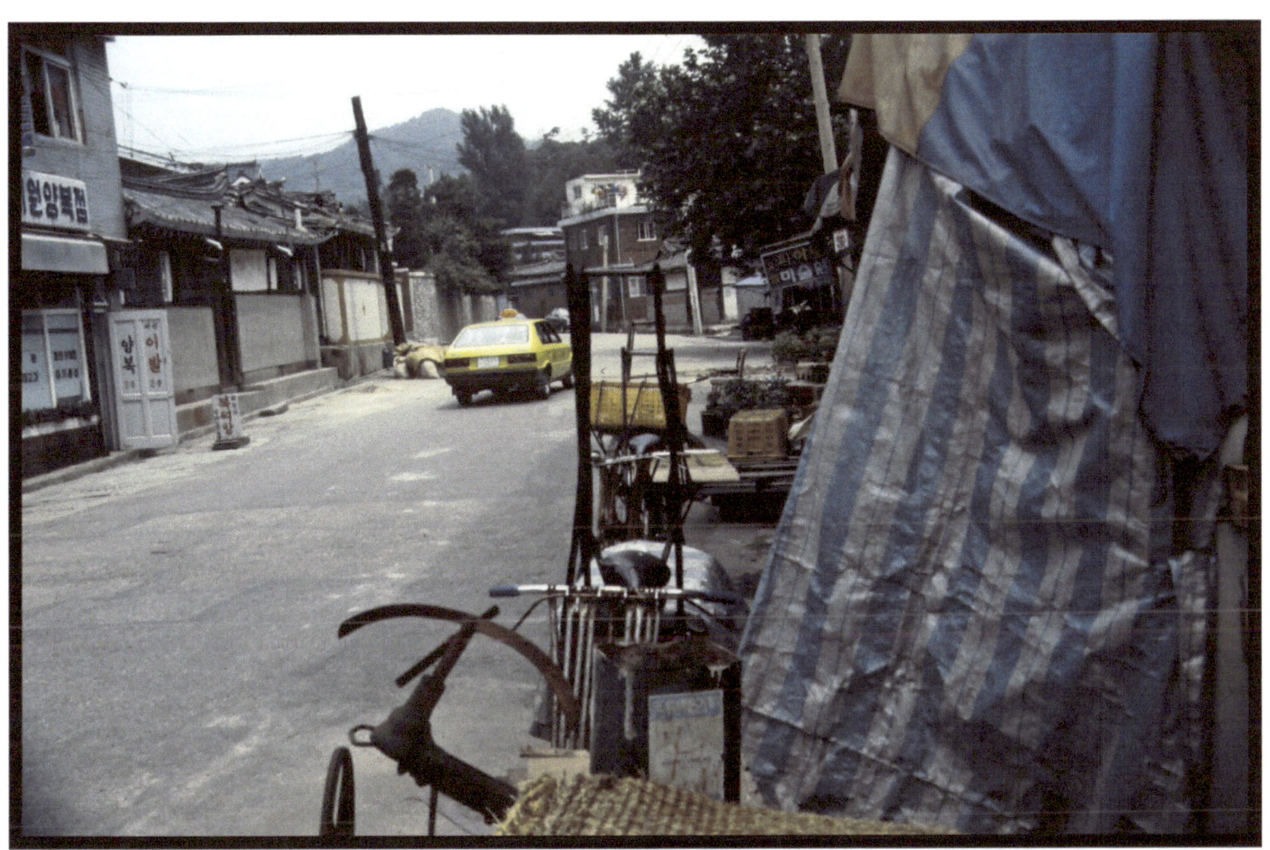
원양복점
양복
이발

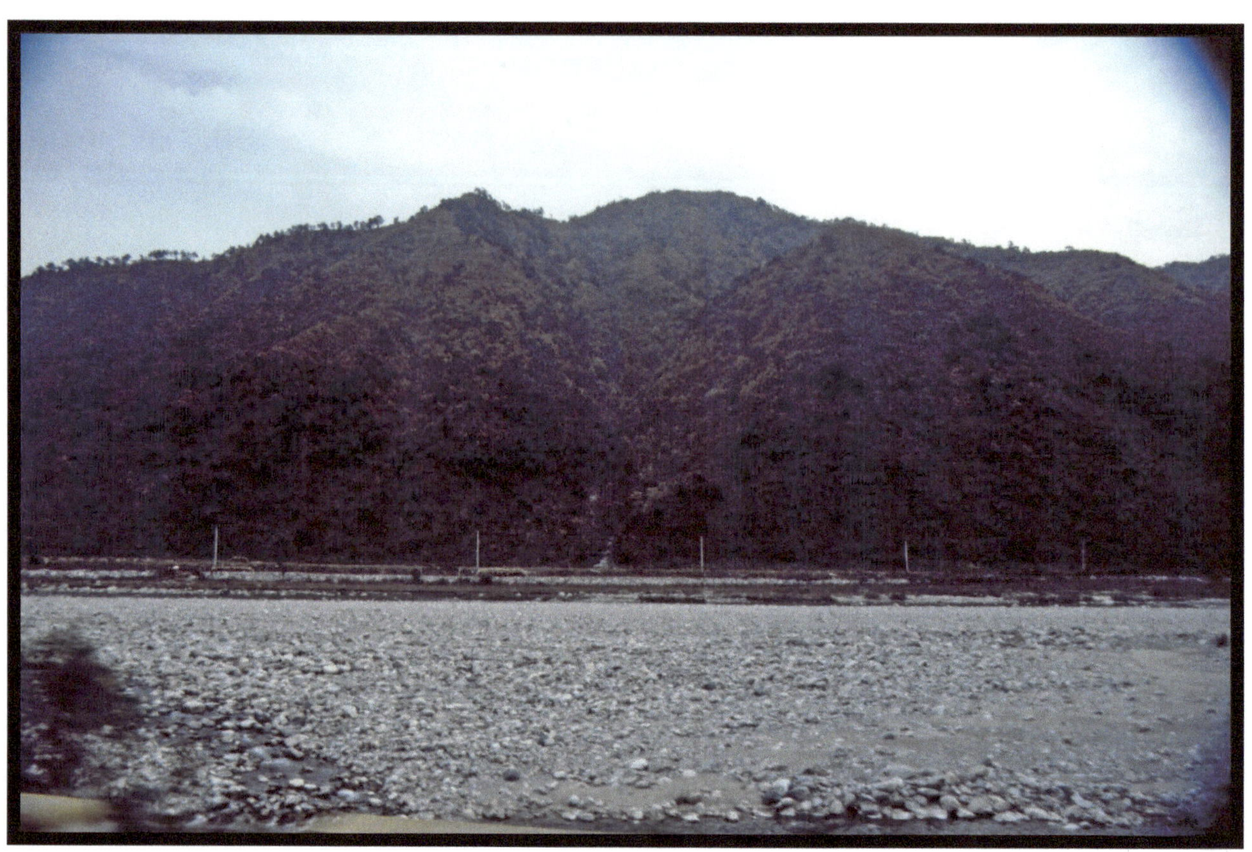

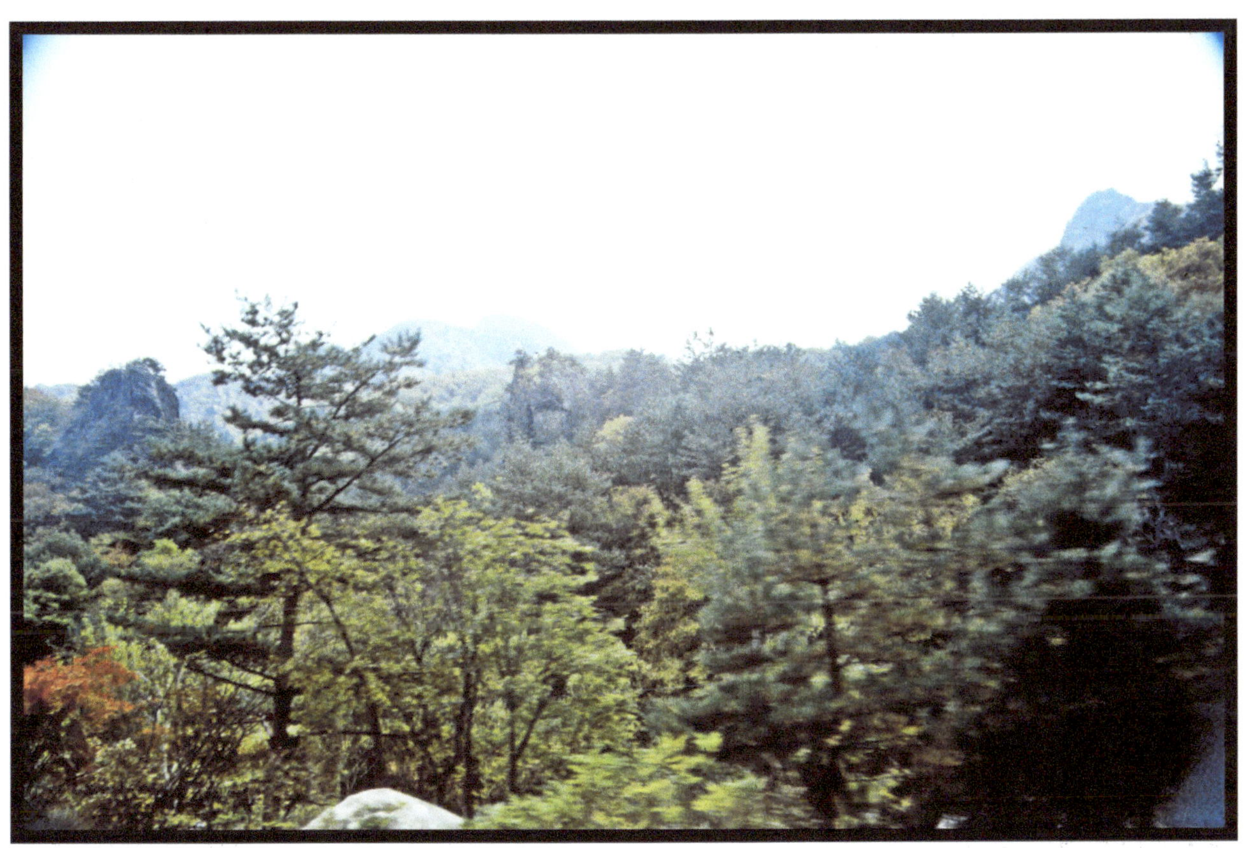

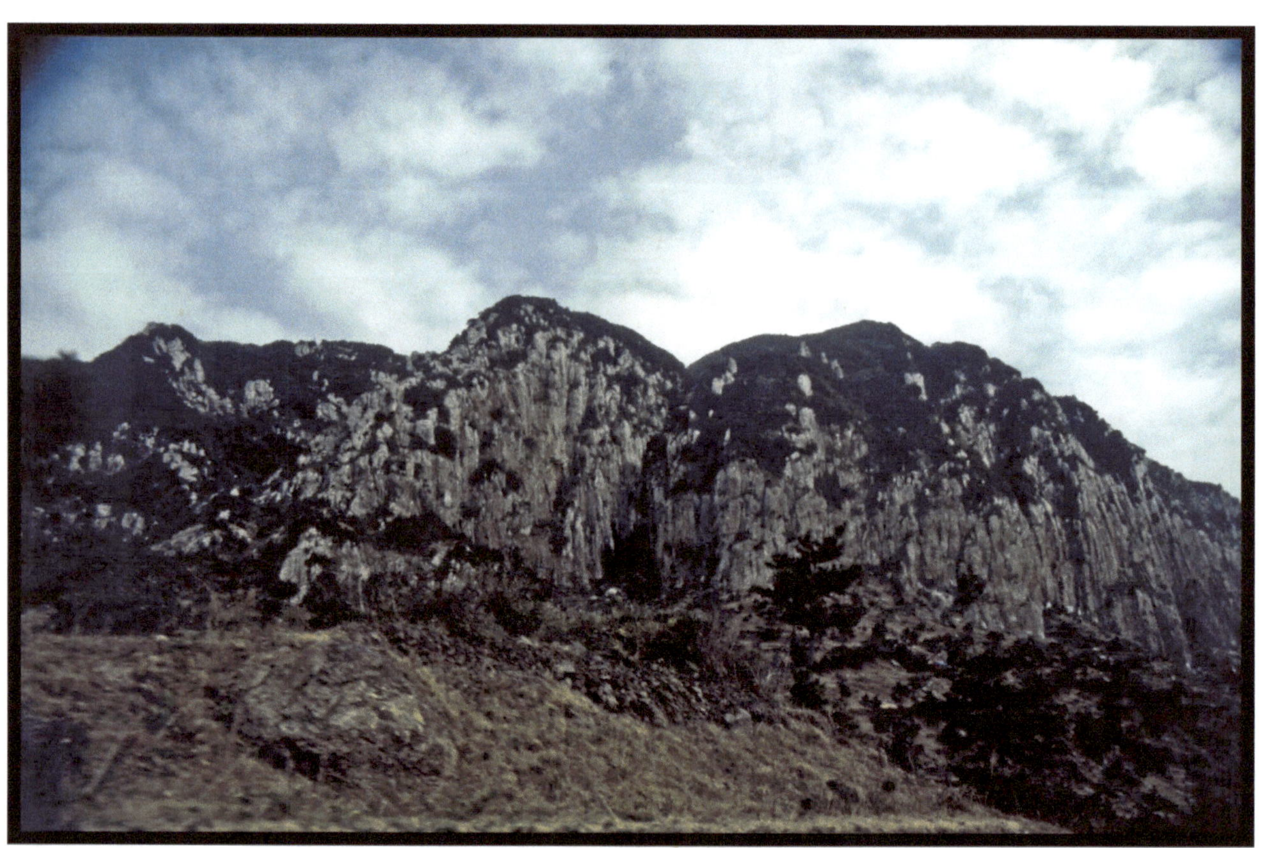

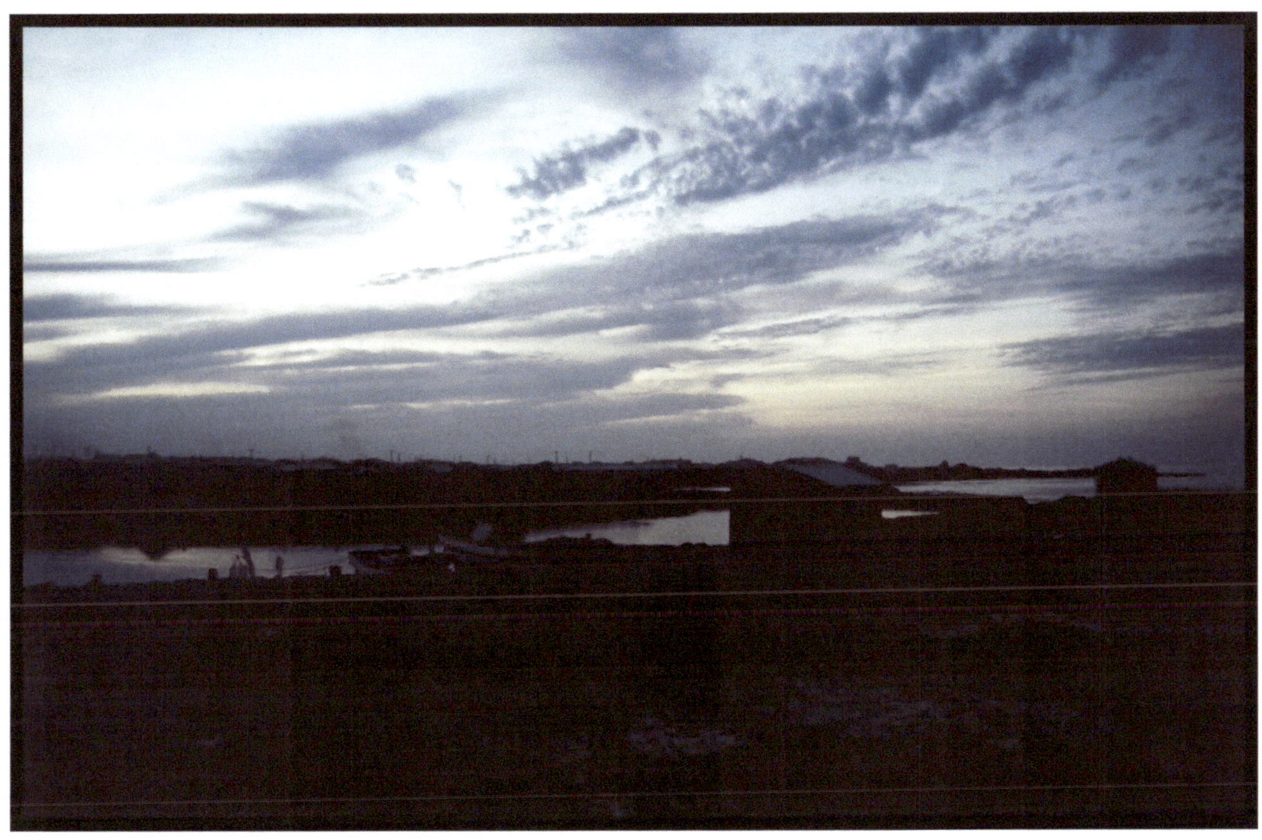

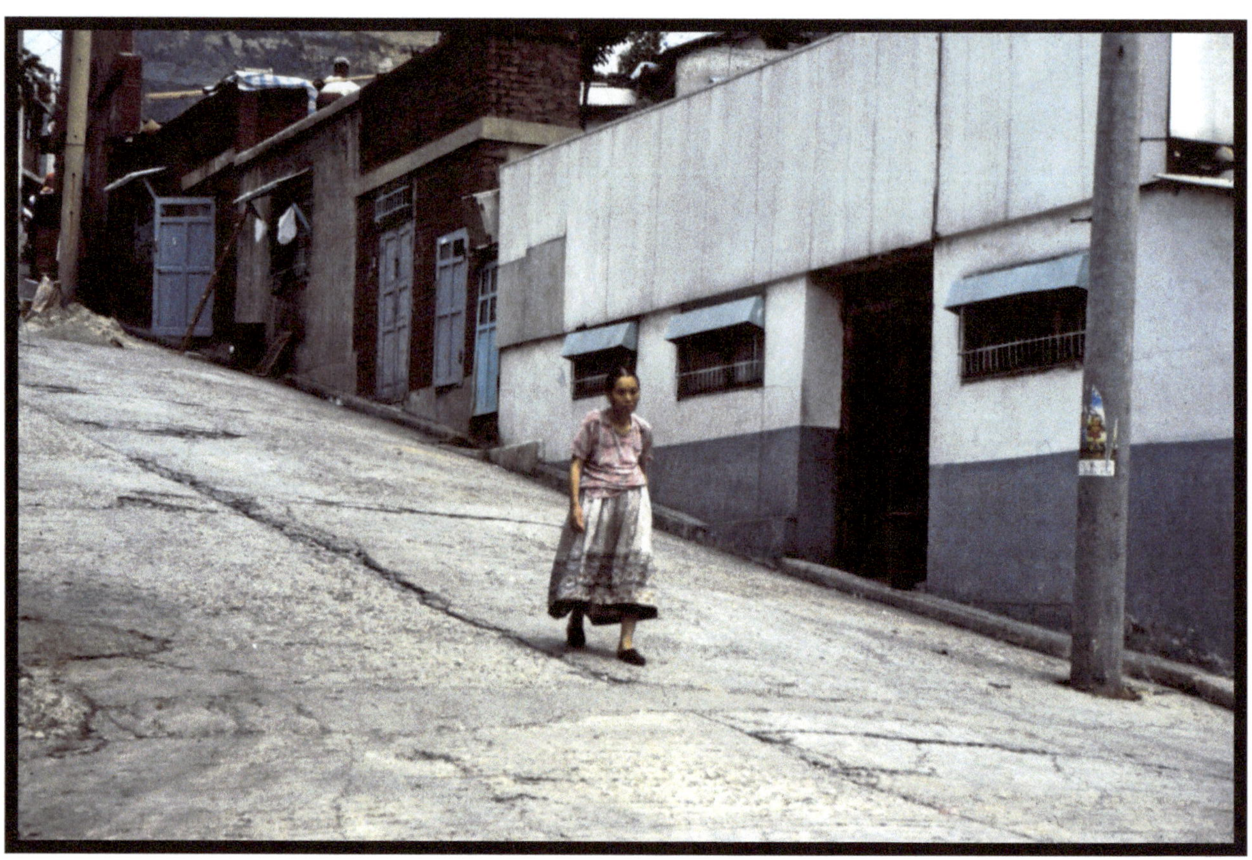

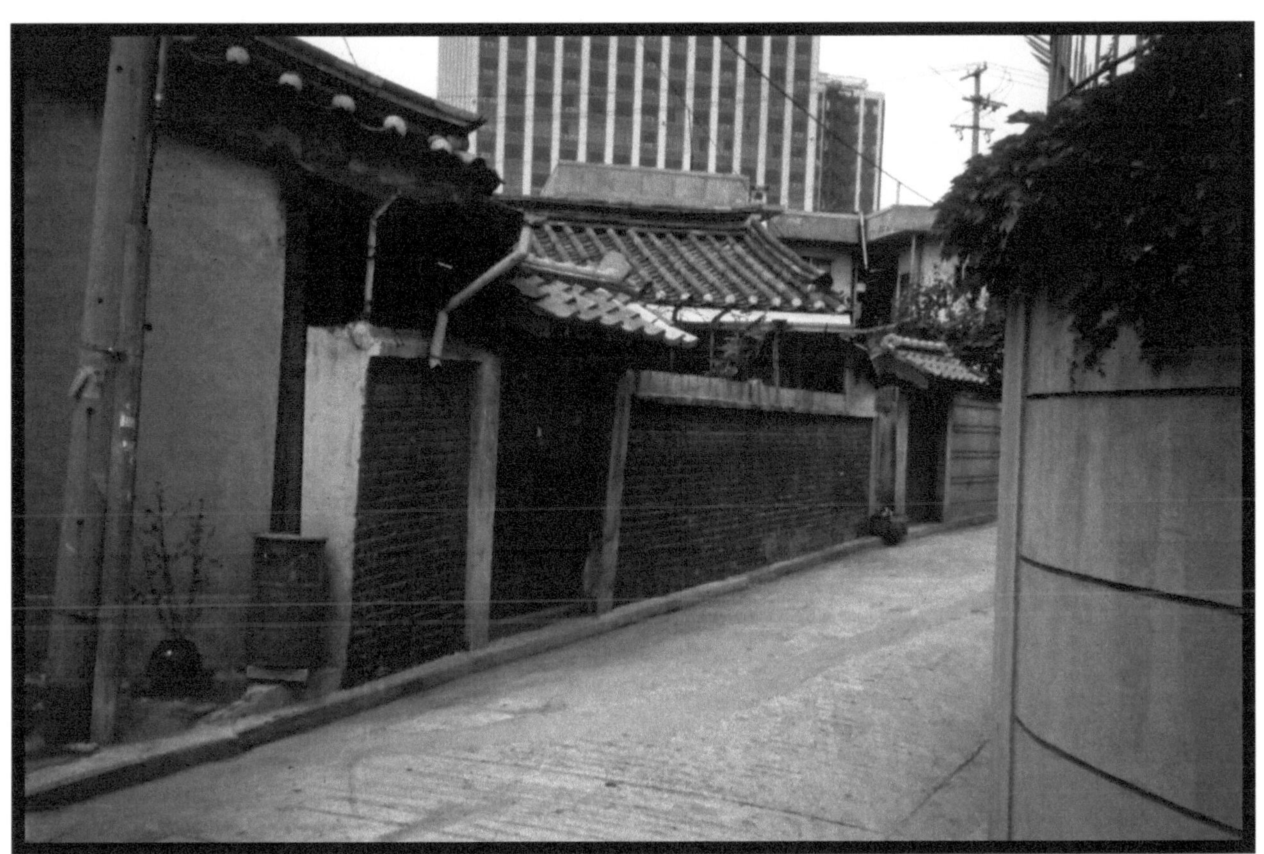

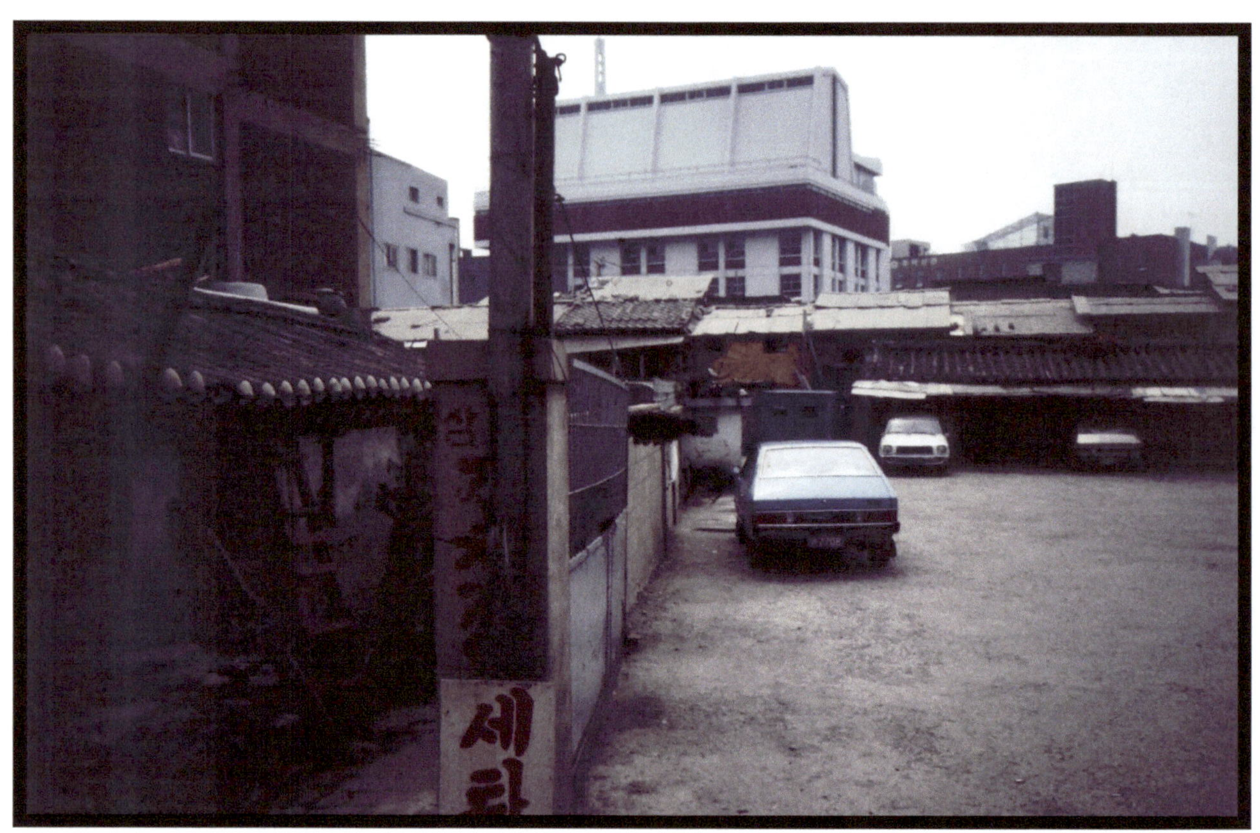
세

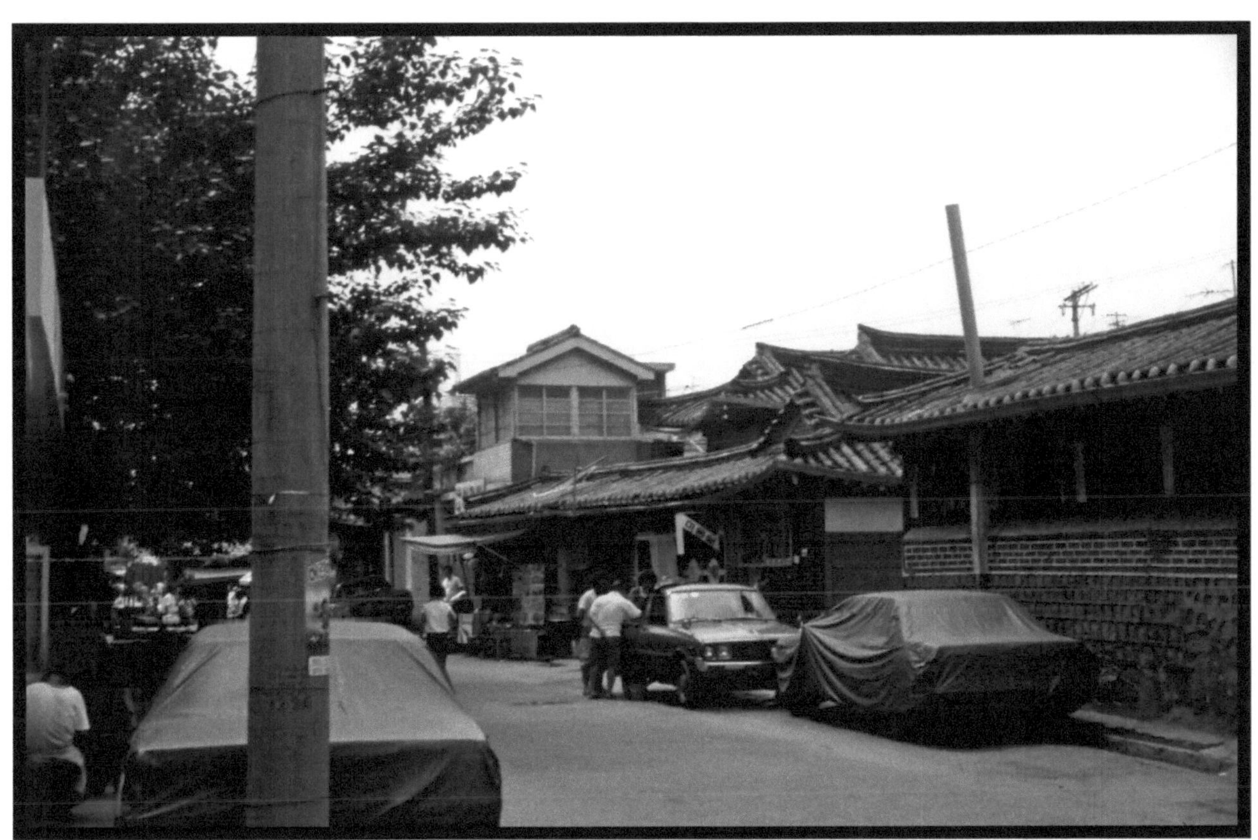

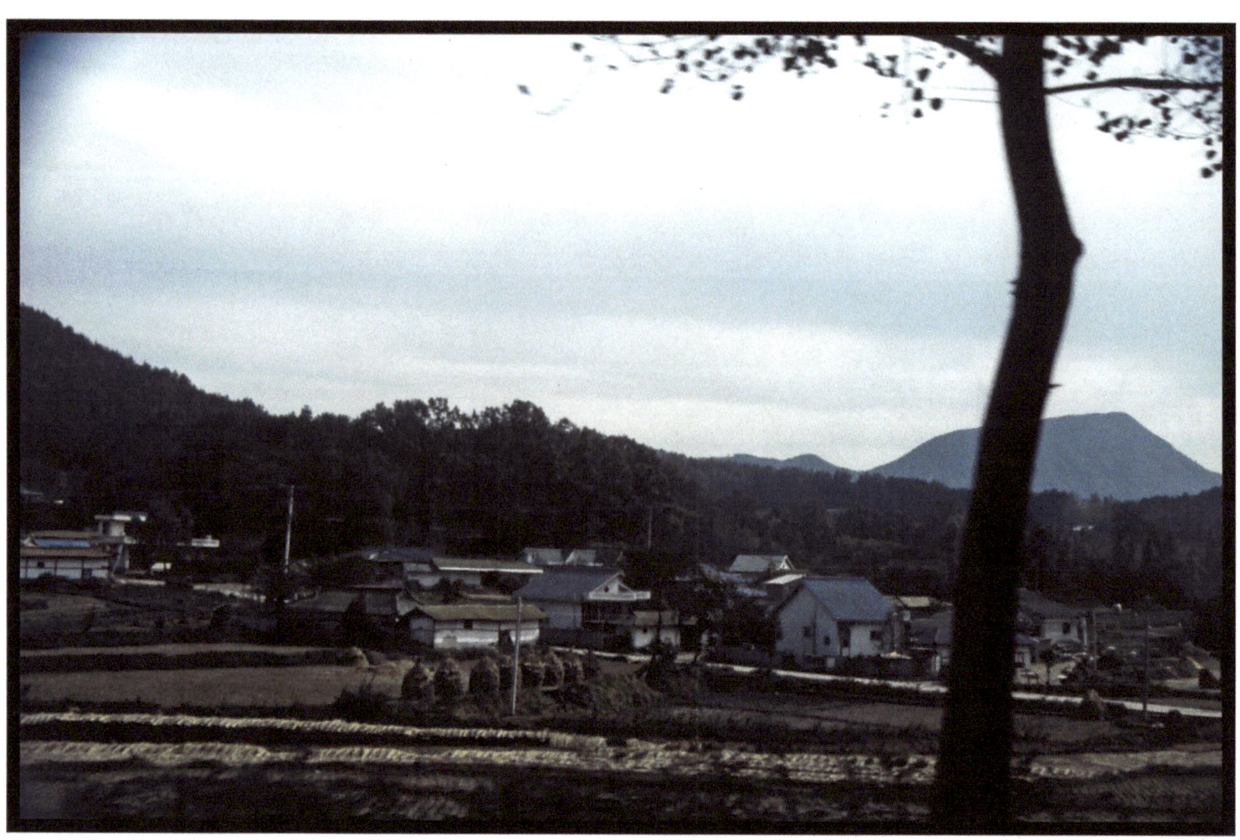

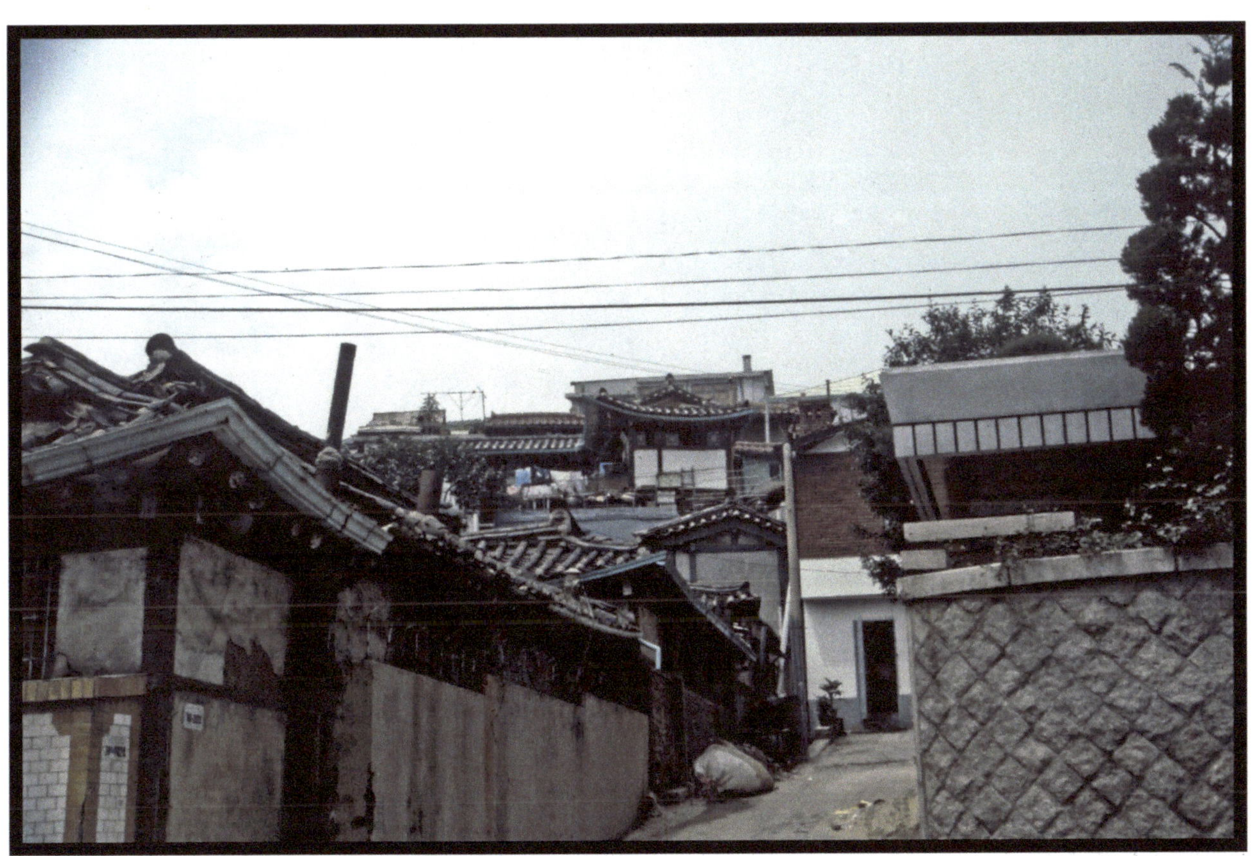

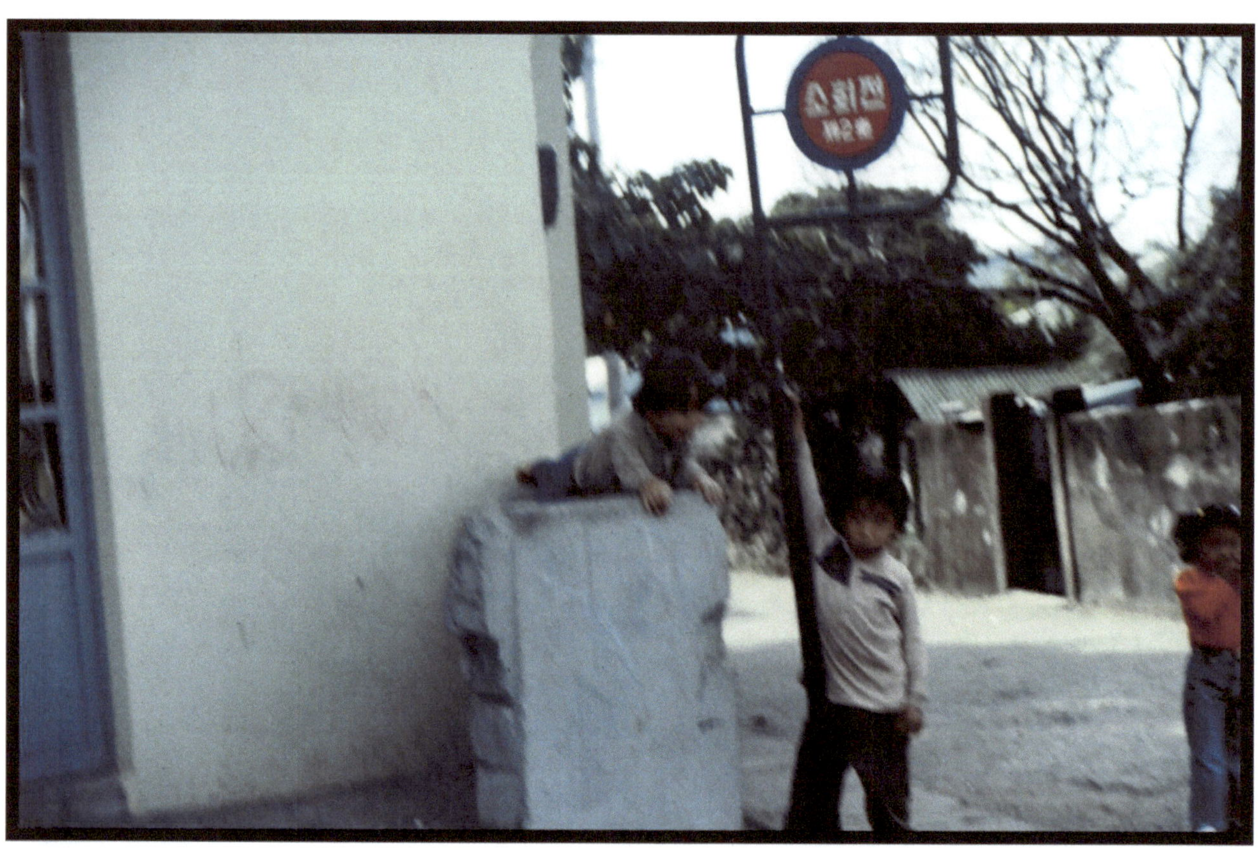

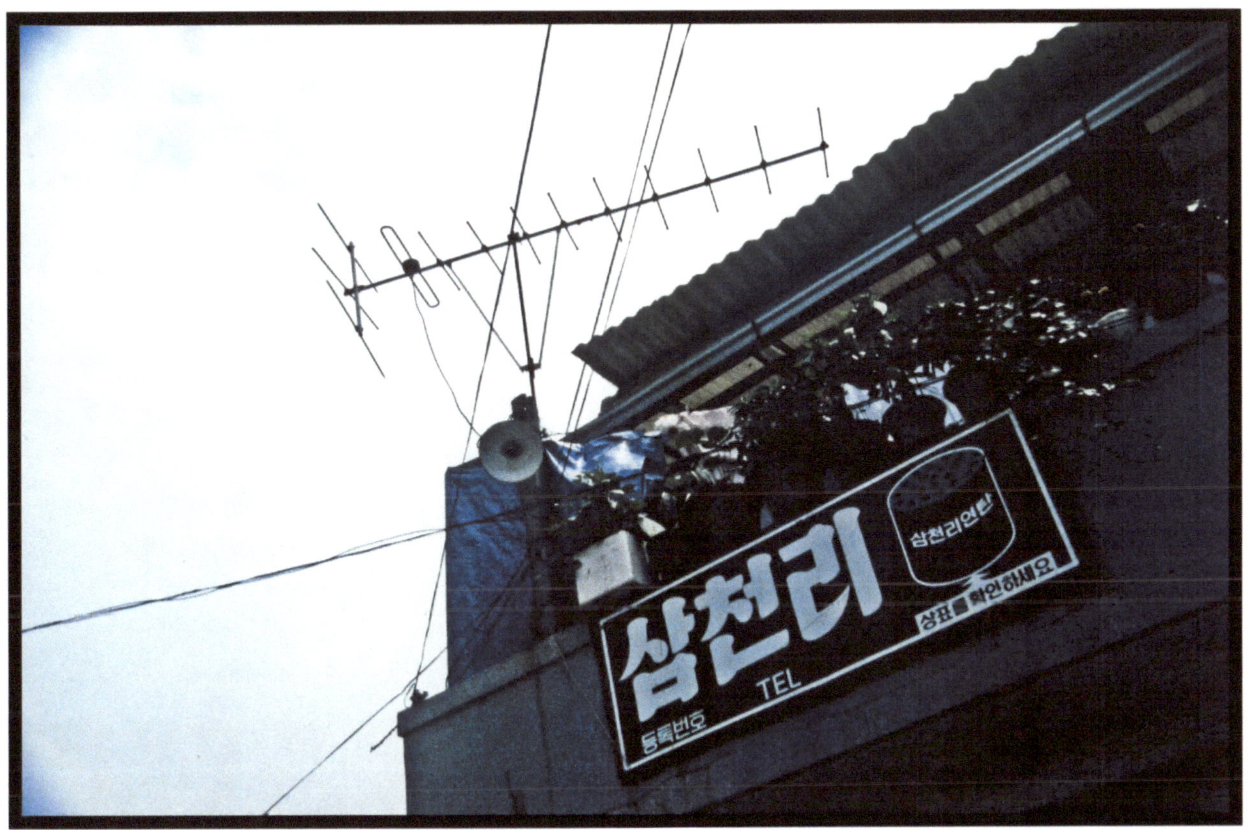
삼천리
삼천리연탄
상표를 확인하세요
TEL
등록번호

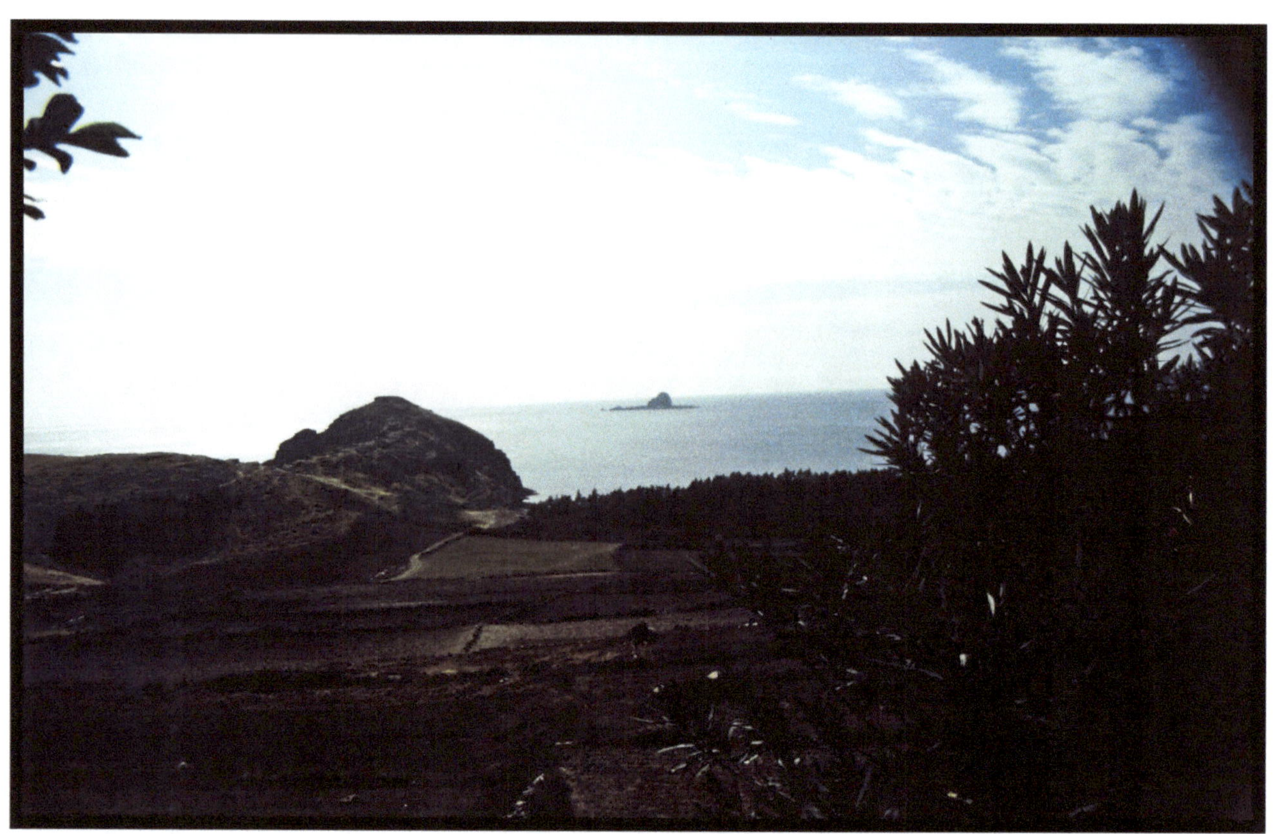

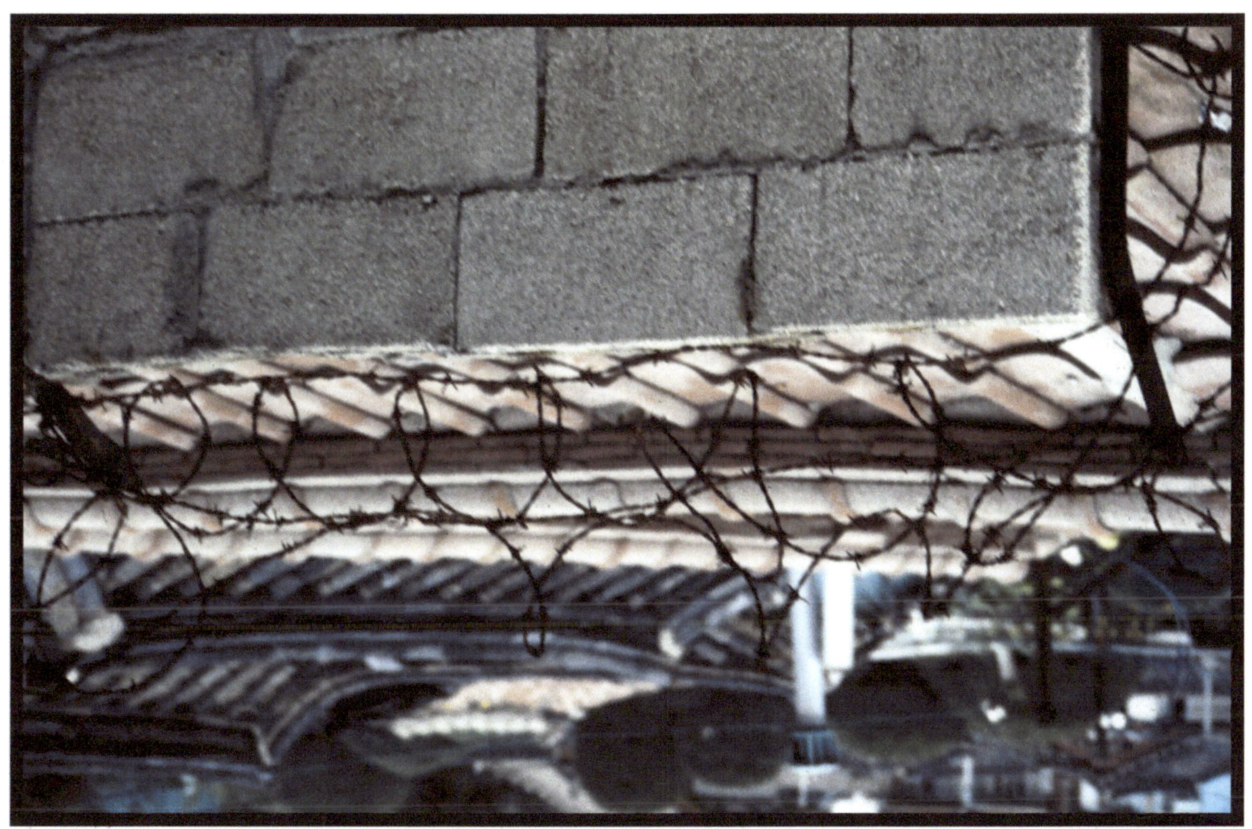

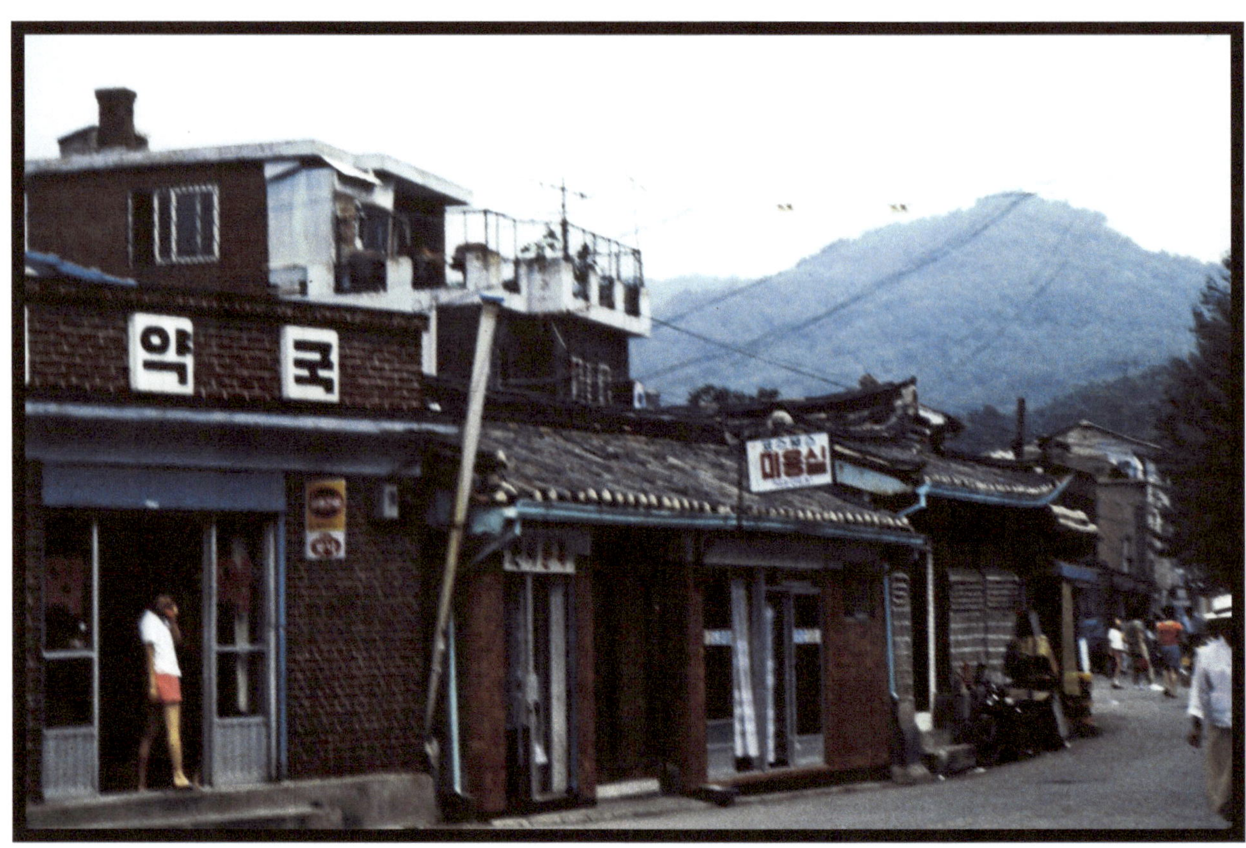
약 국
미용실

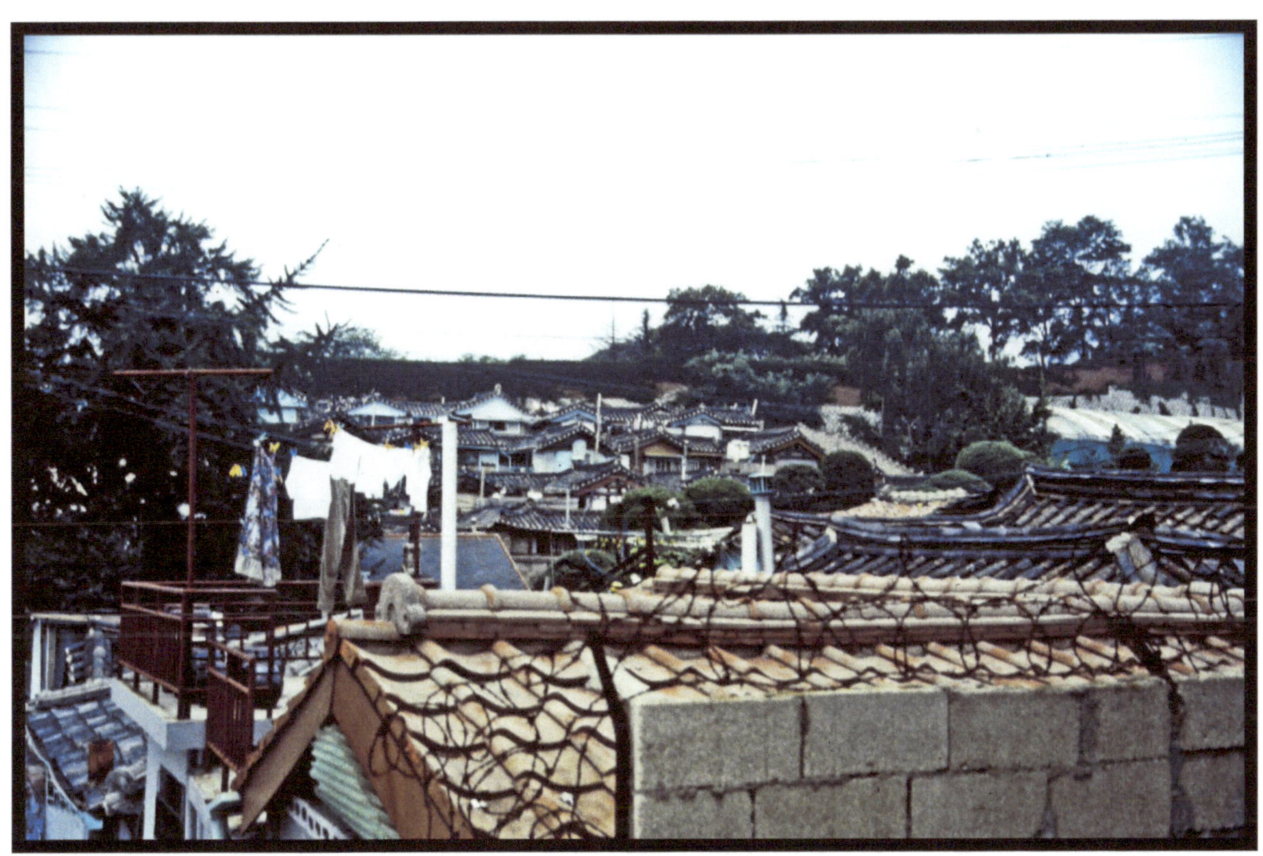

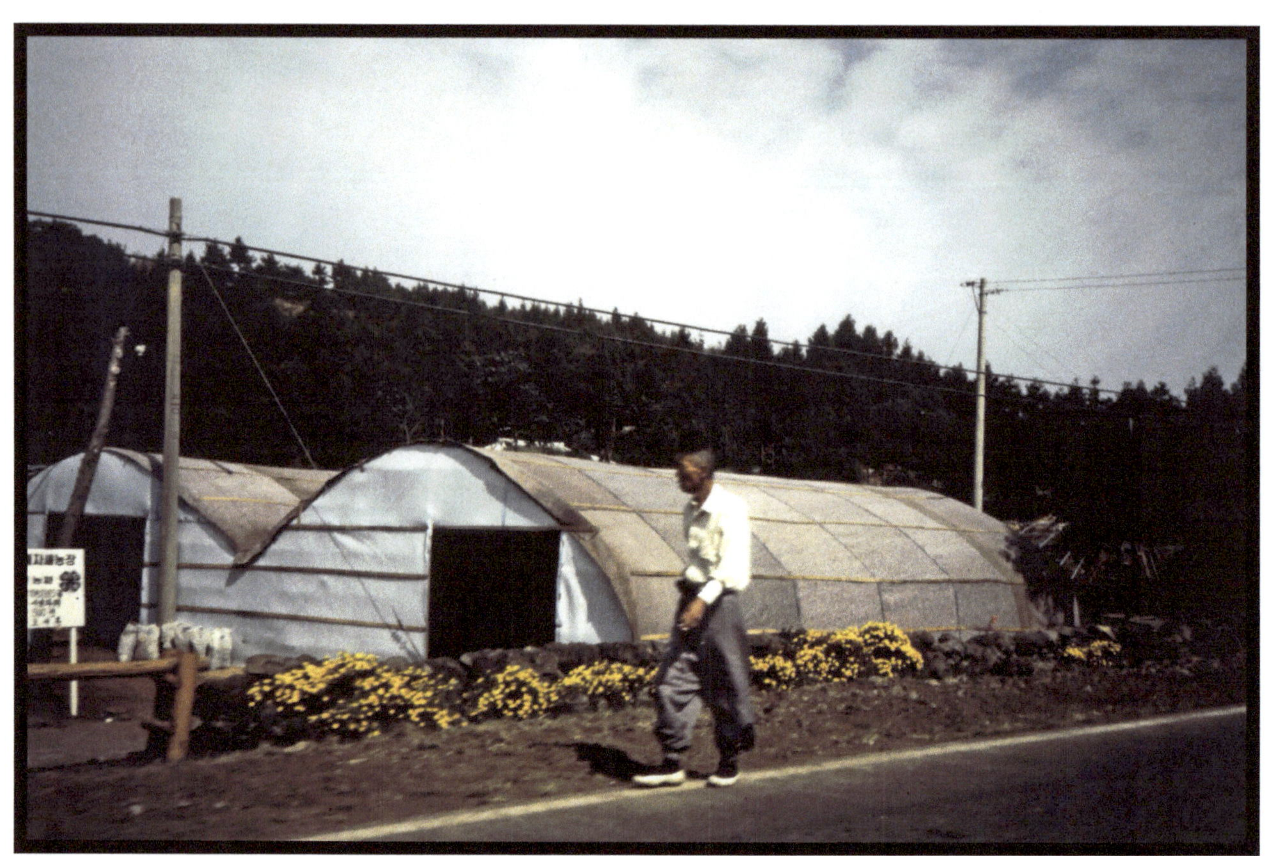

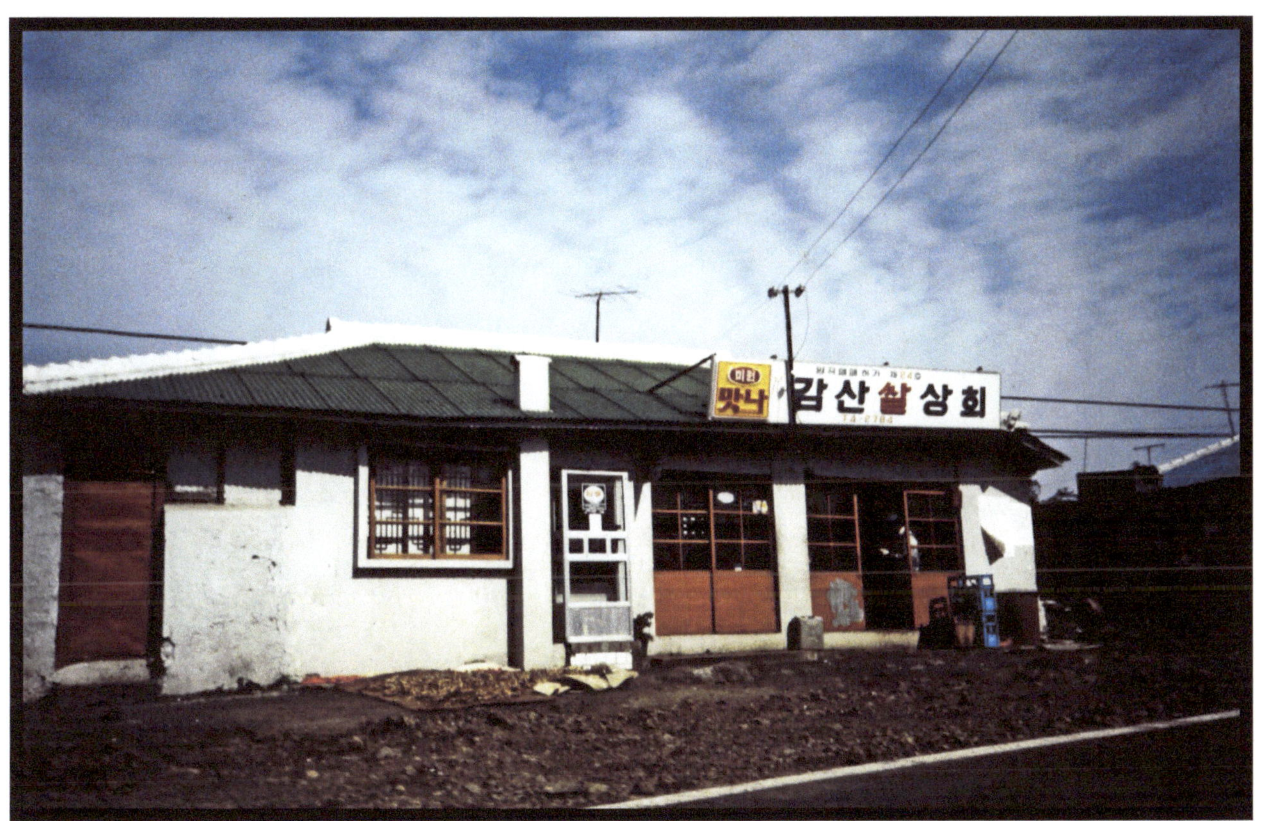
미원
맛나
감산쌀상회

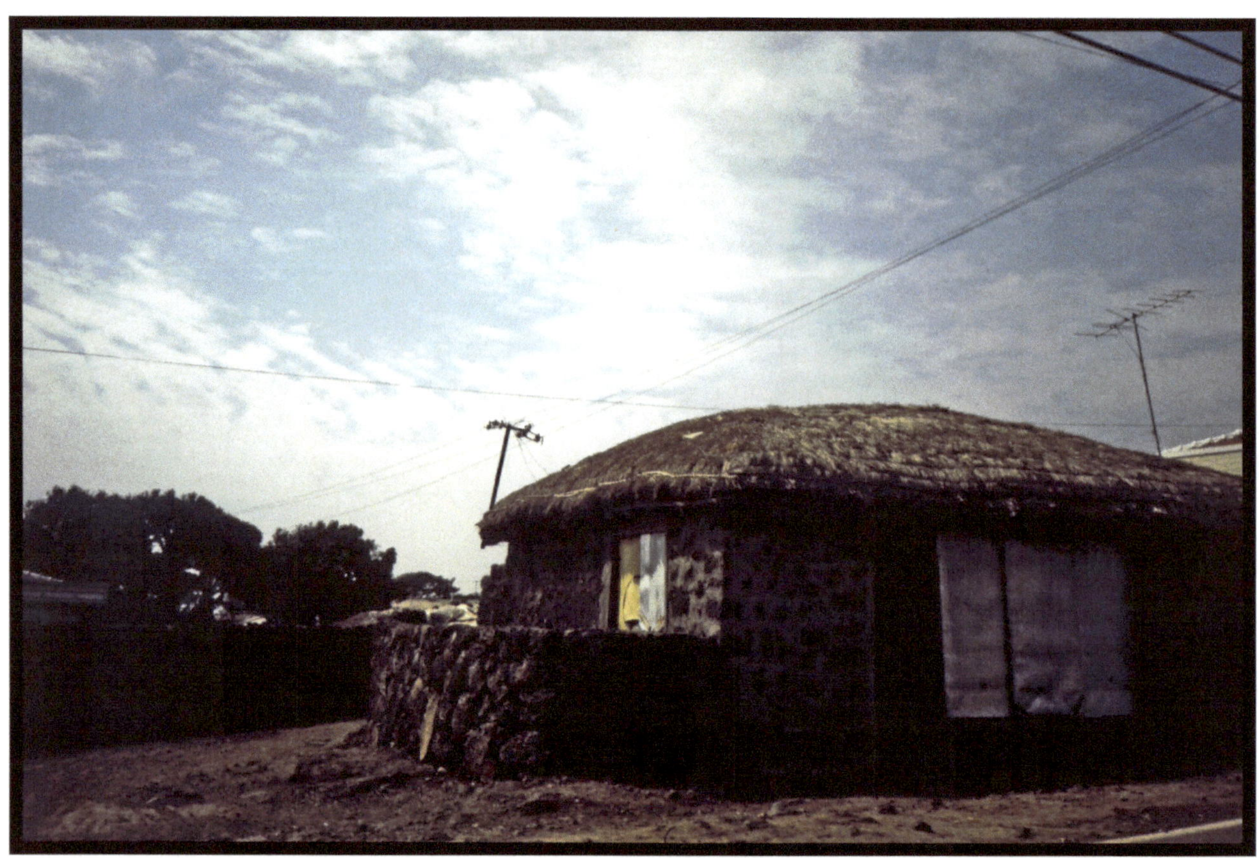

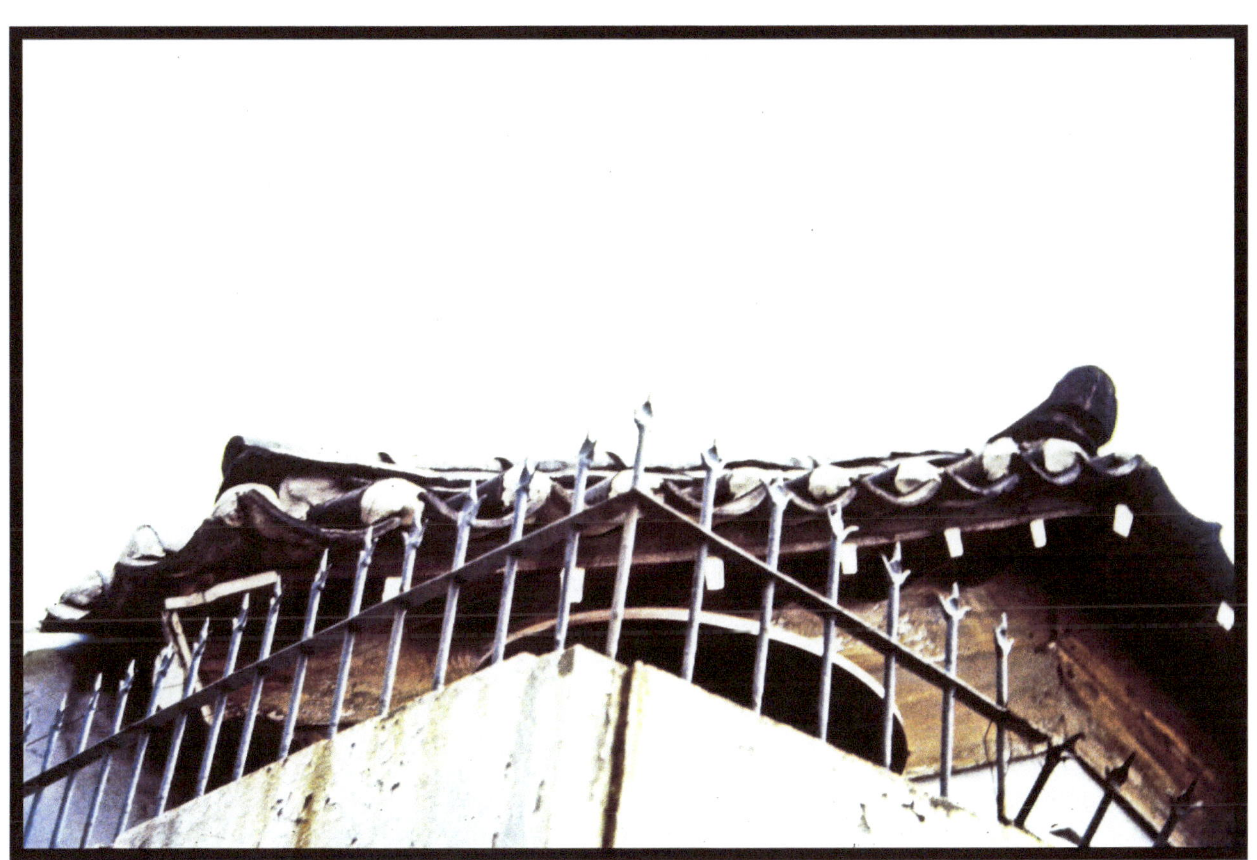

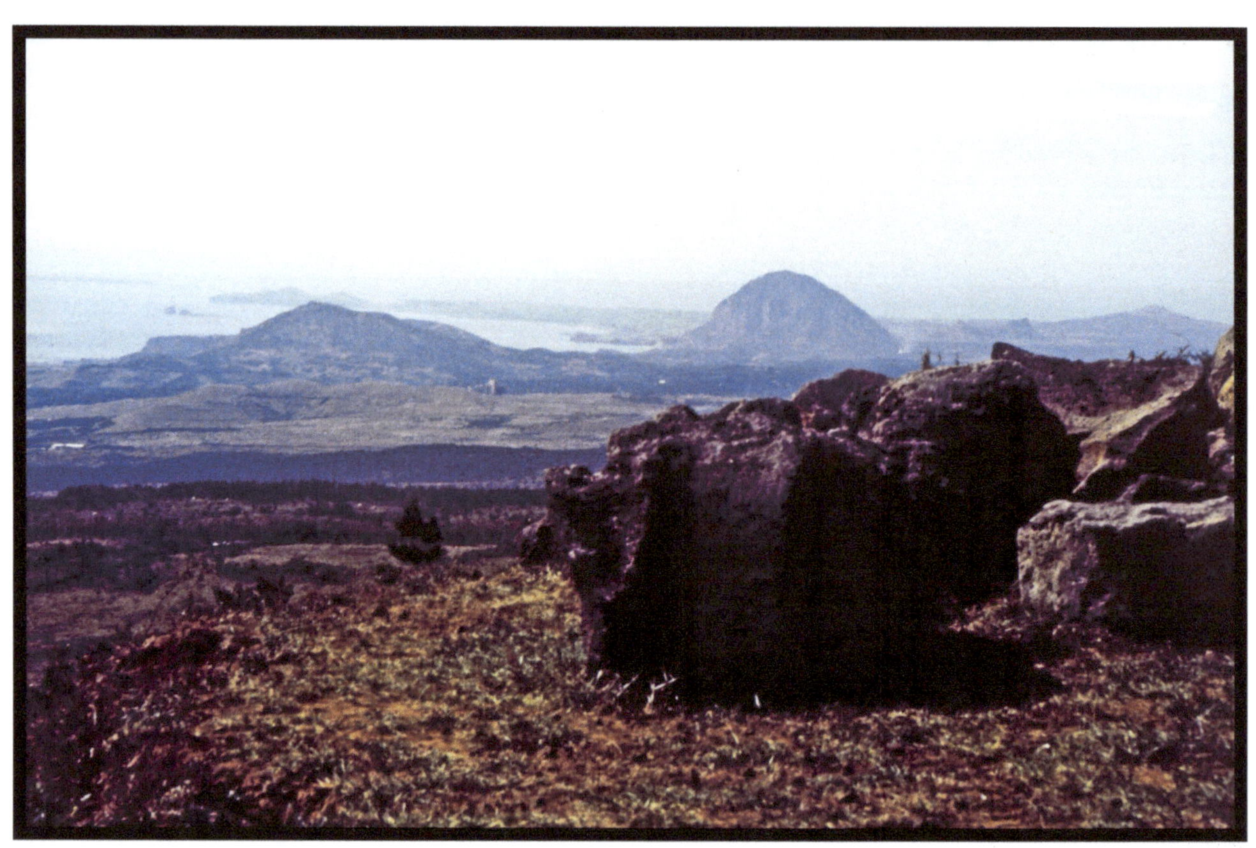

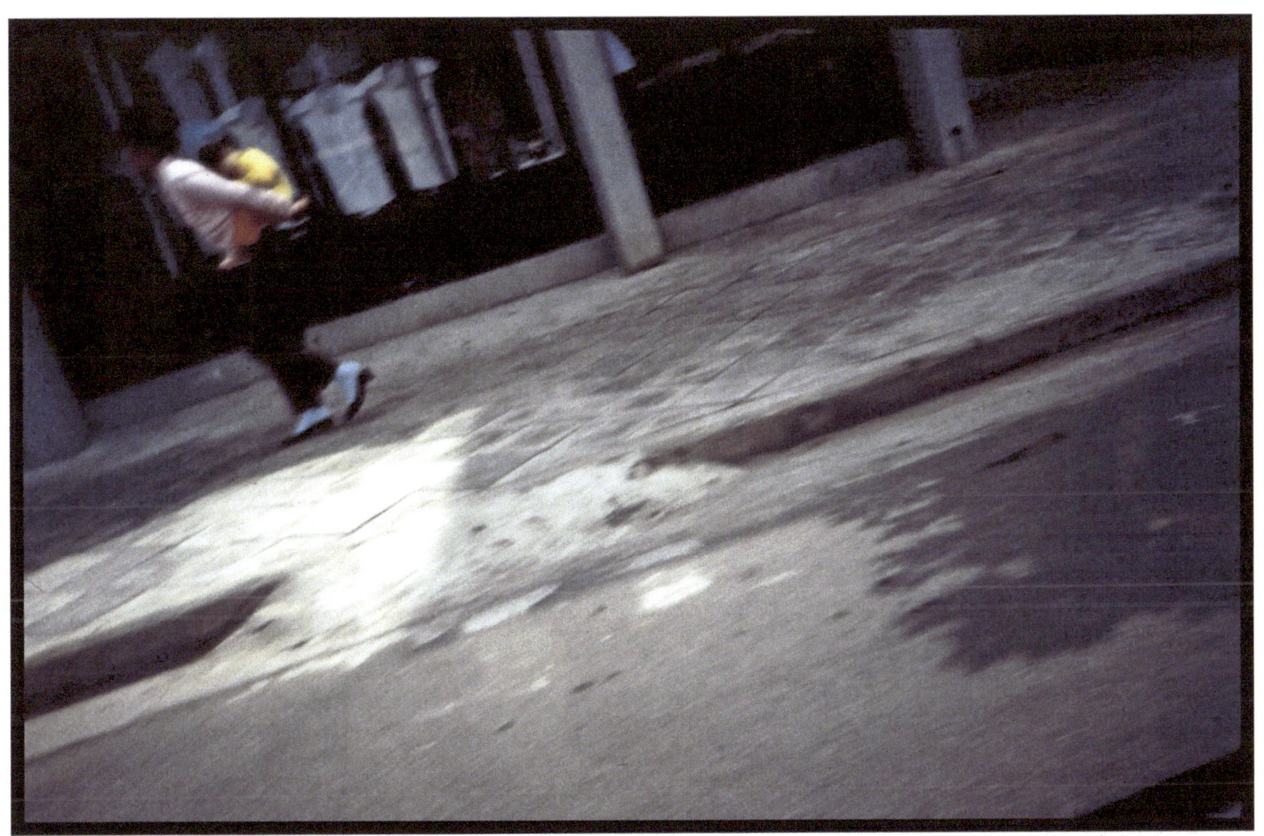

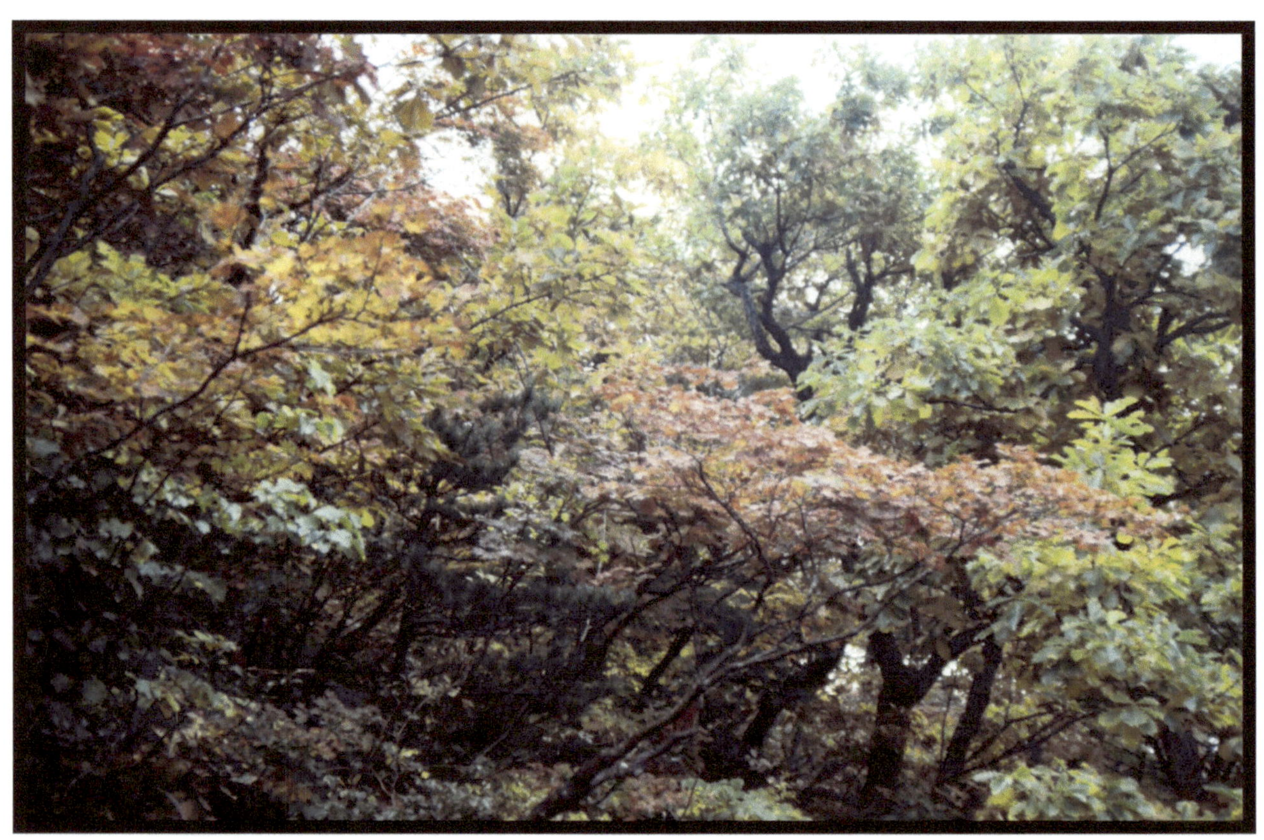

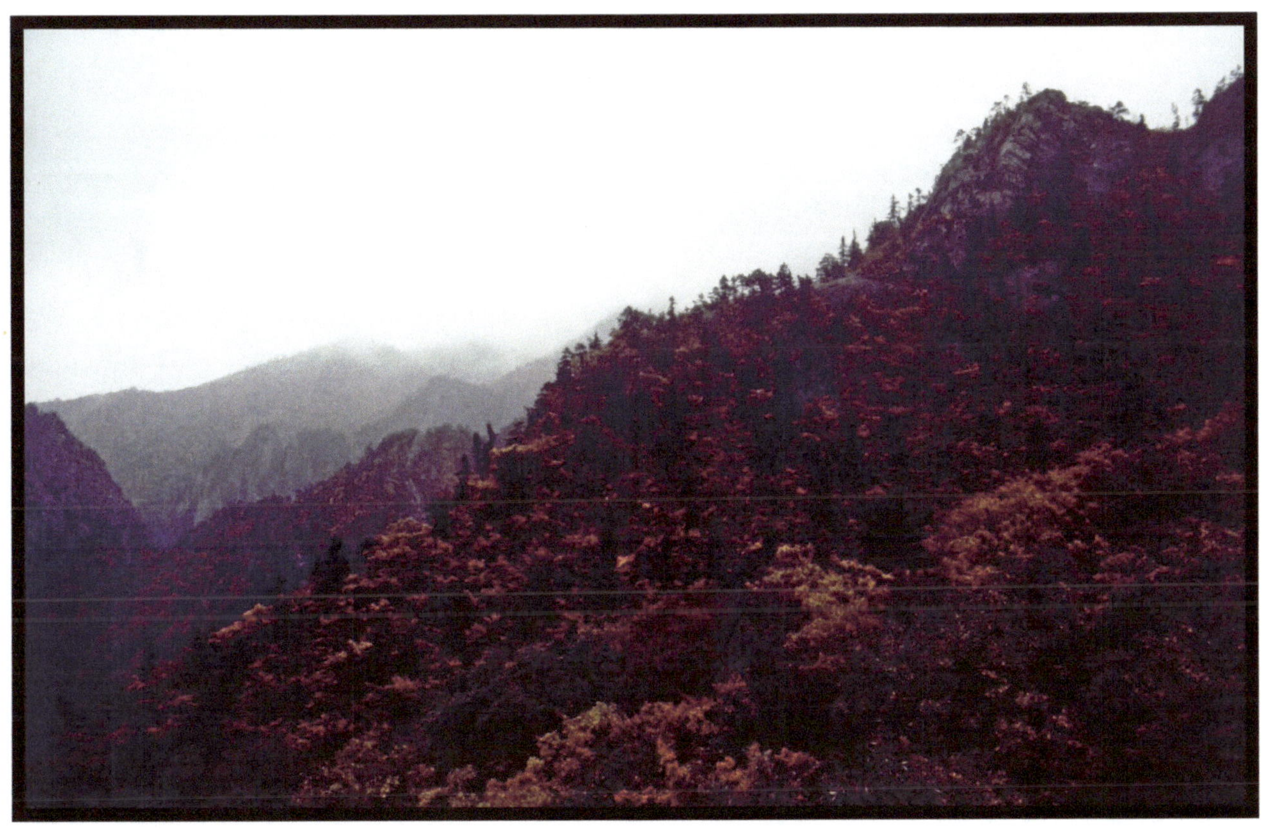

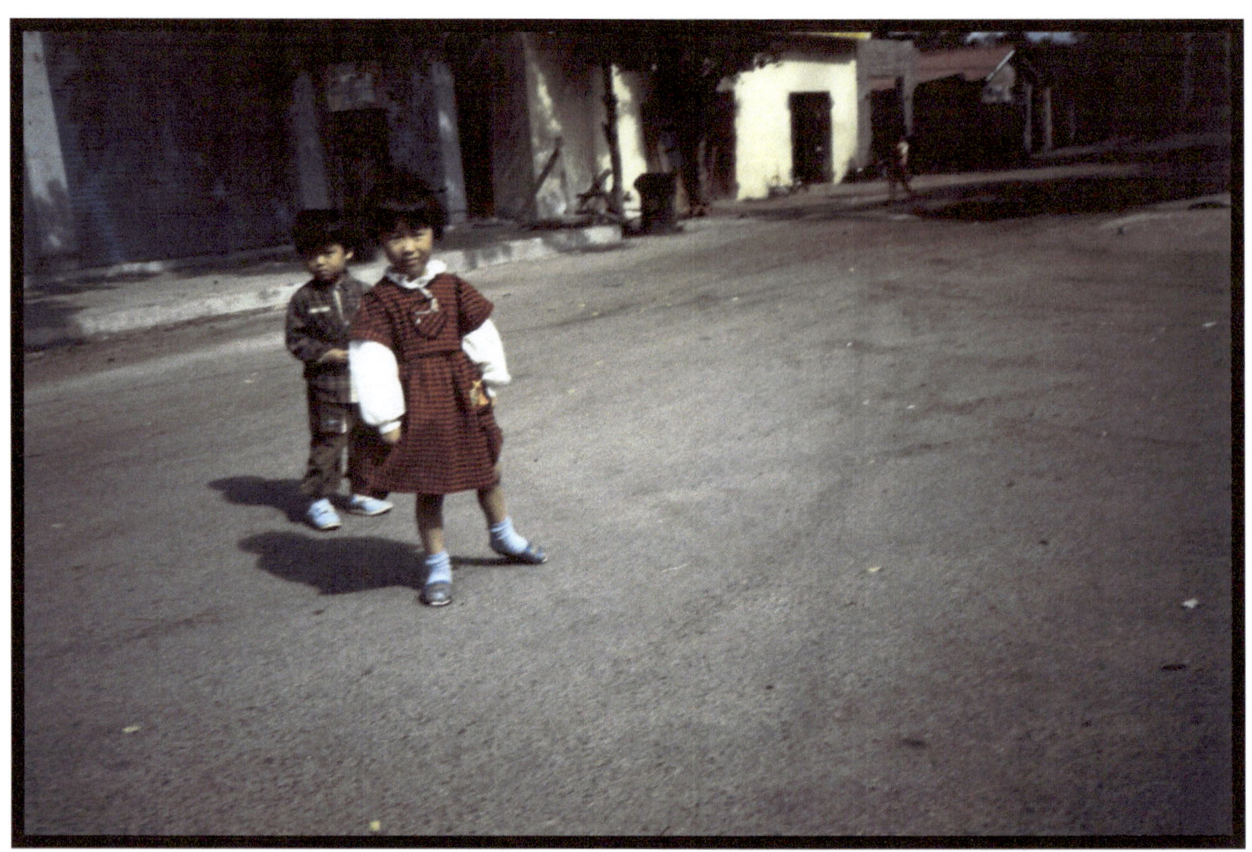

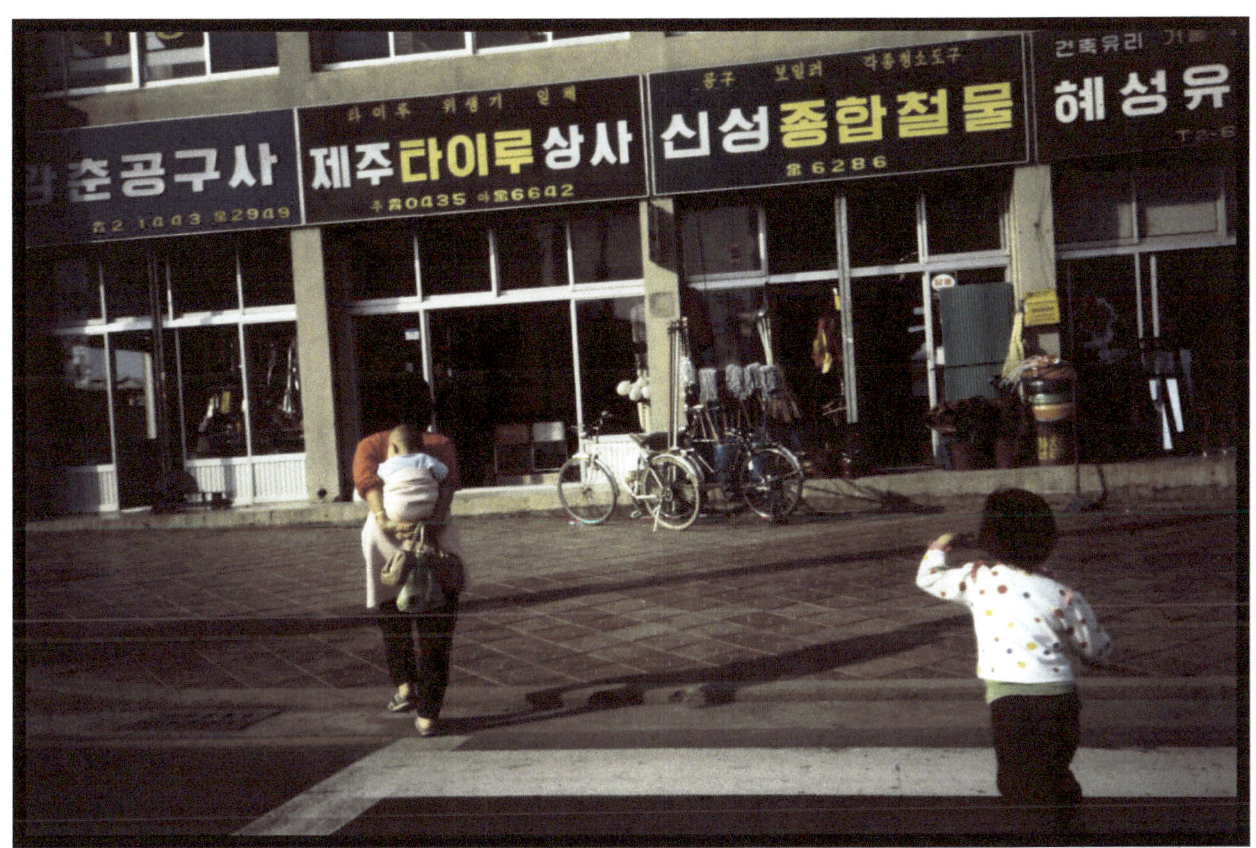
춘공구사
타이루 위생기 일체
제주타이루상사
신성종합철물
☎6286
건축유리
혜성유

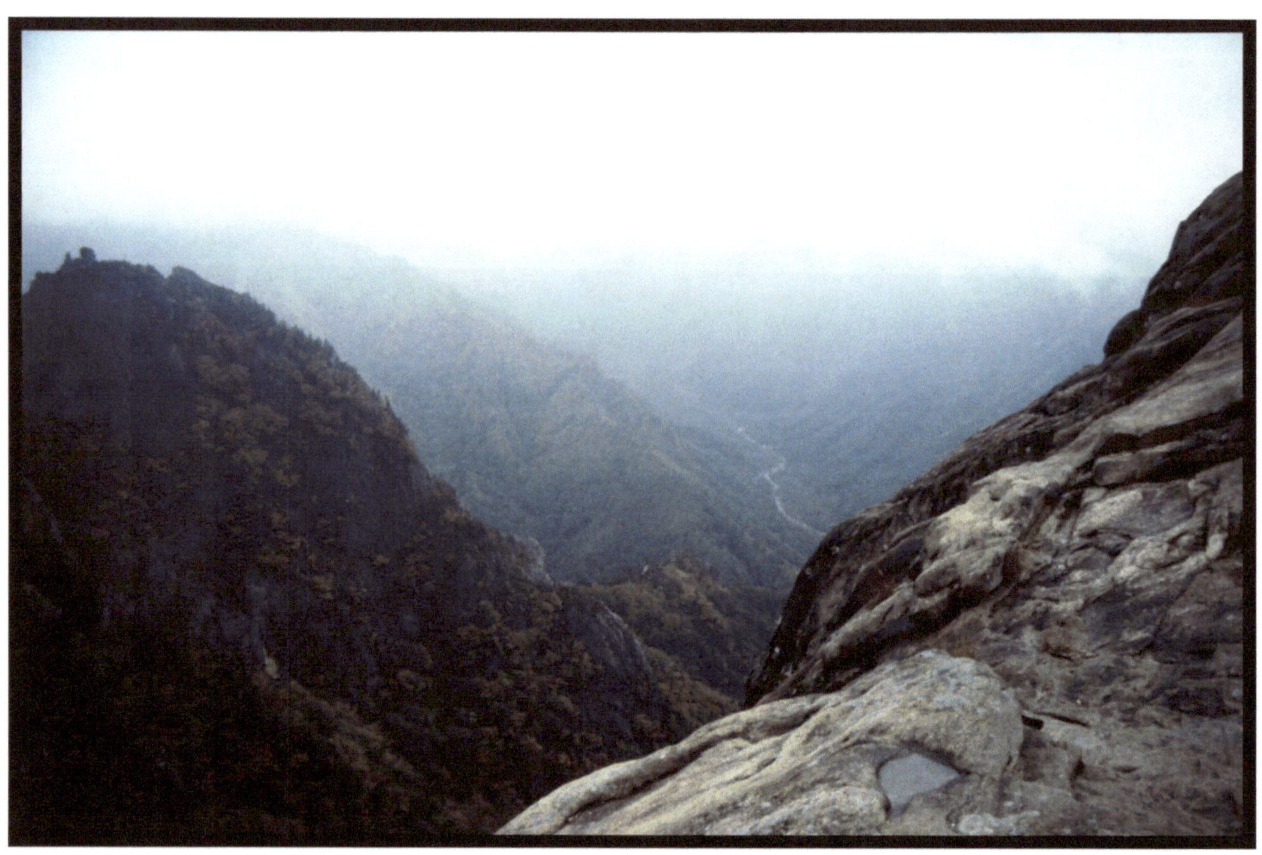

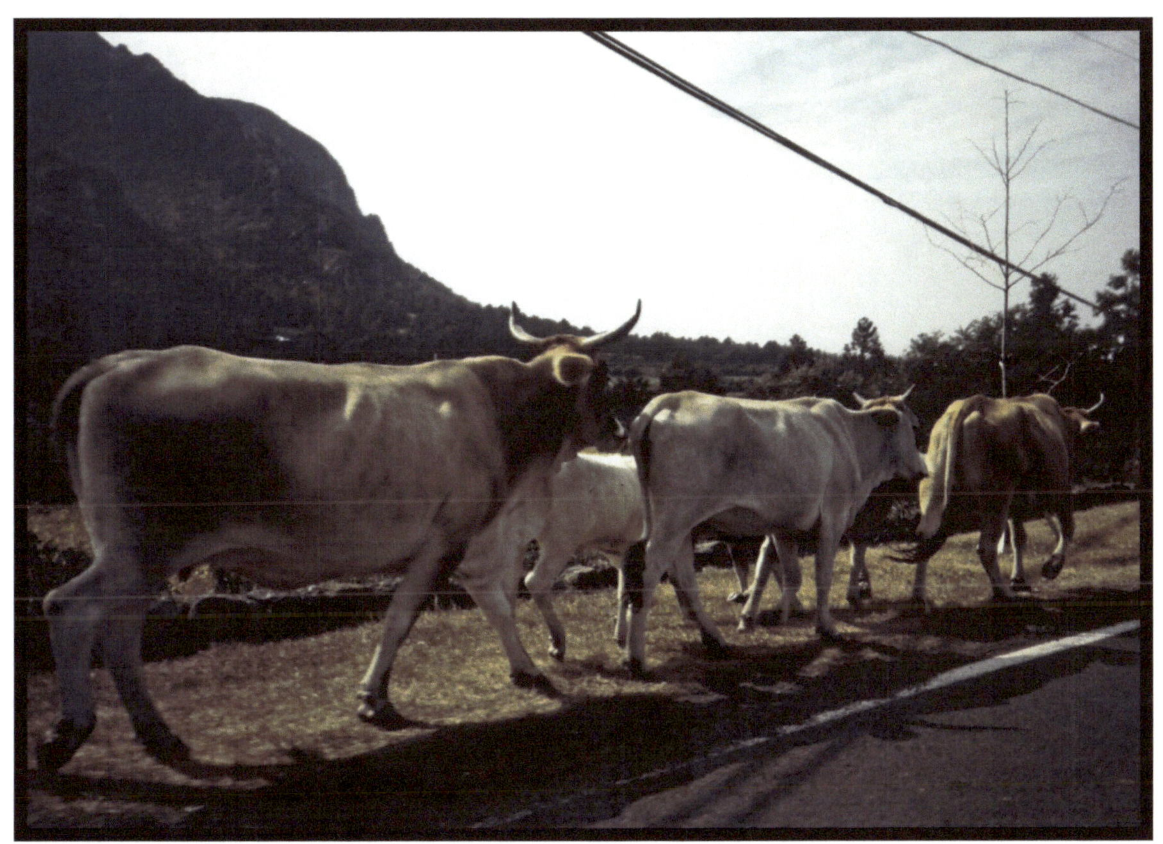

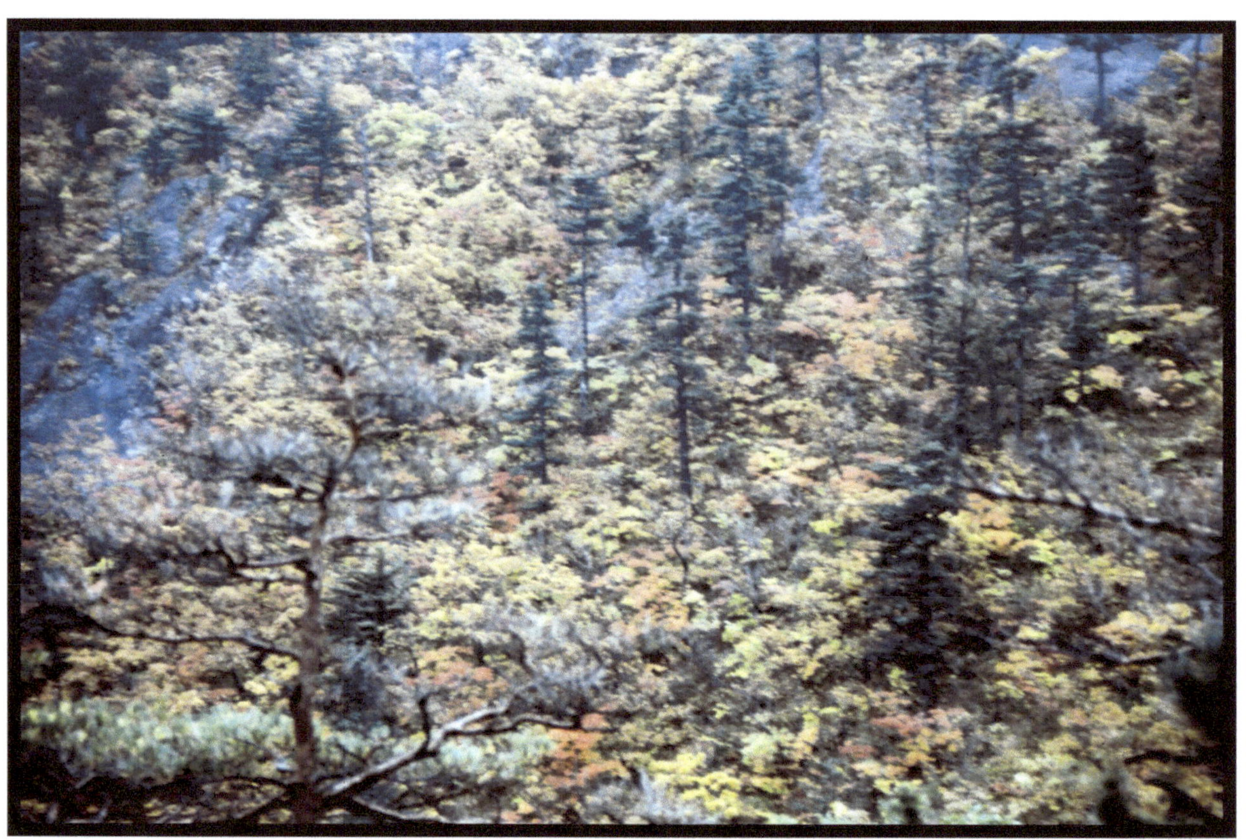

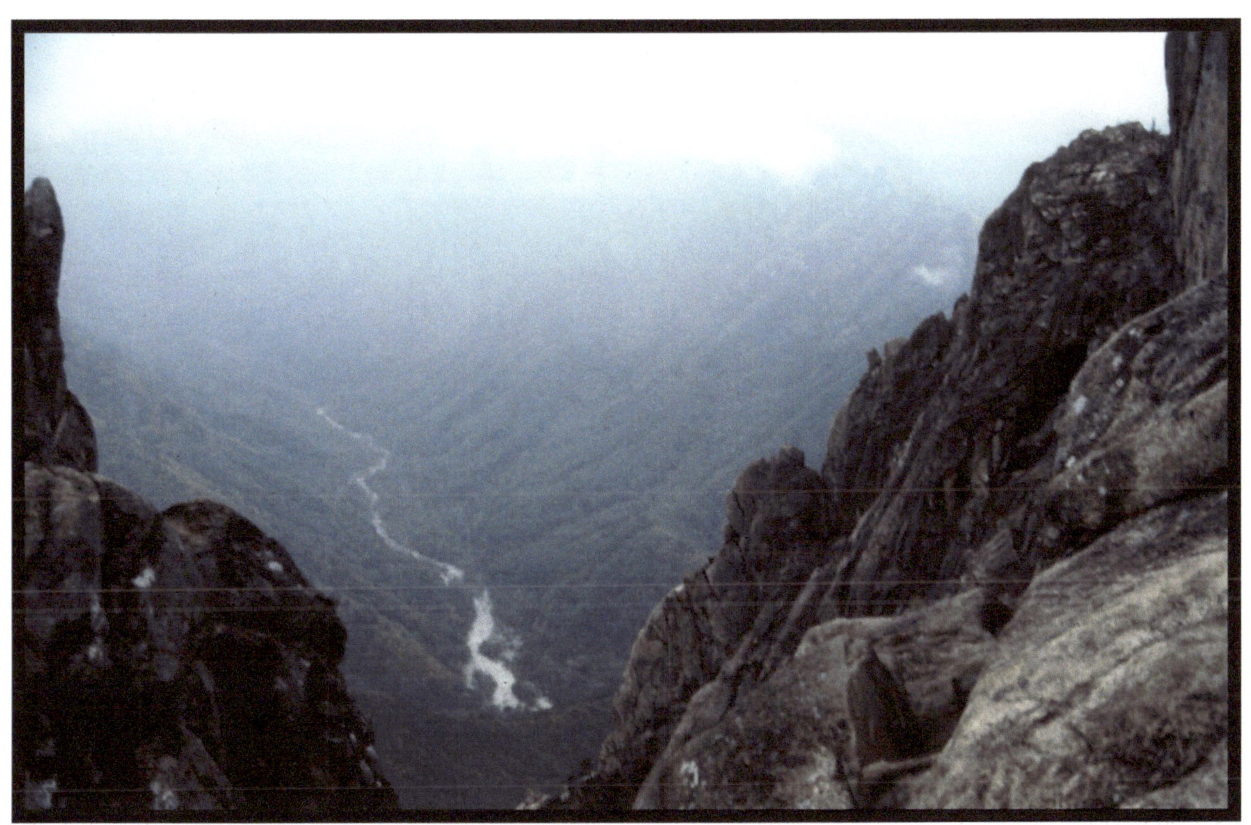

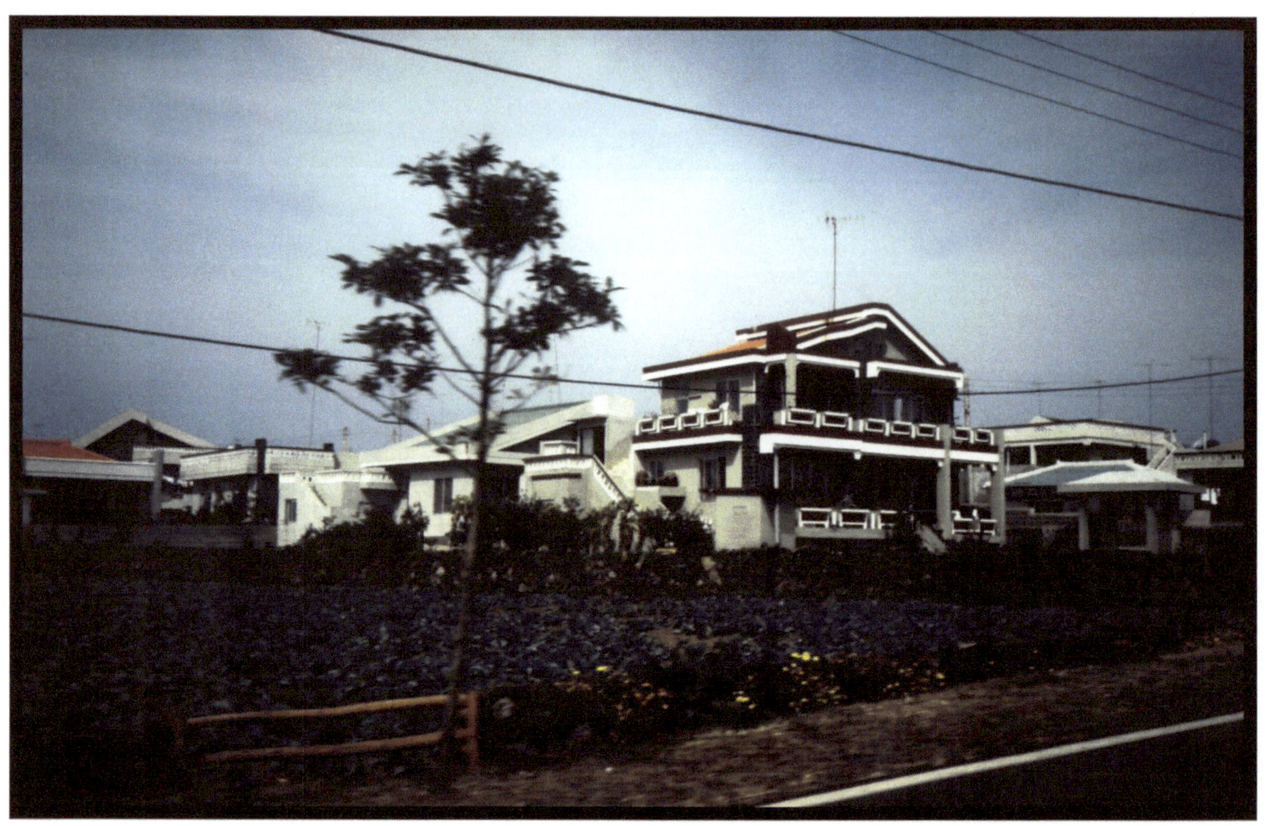

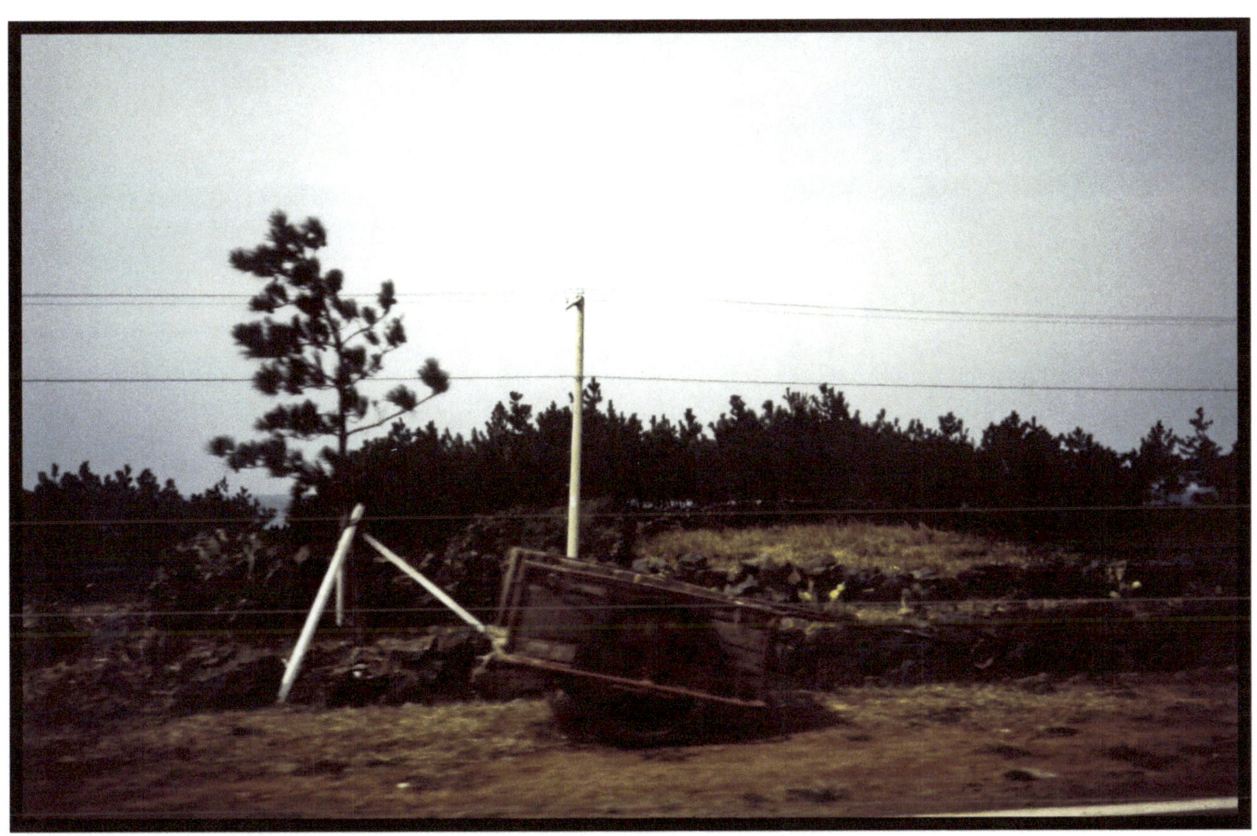

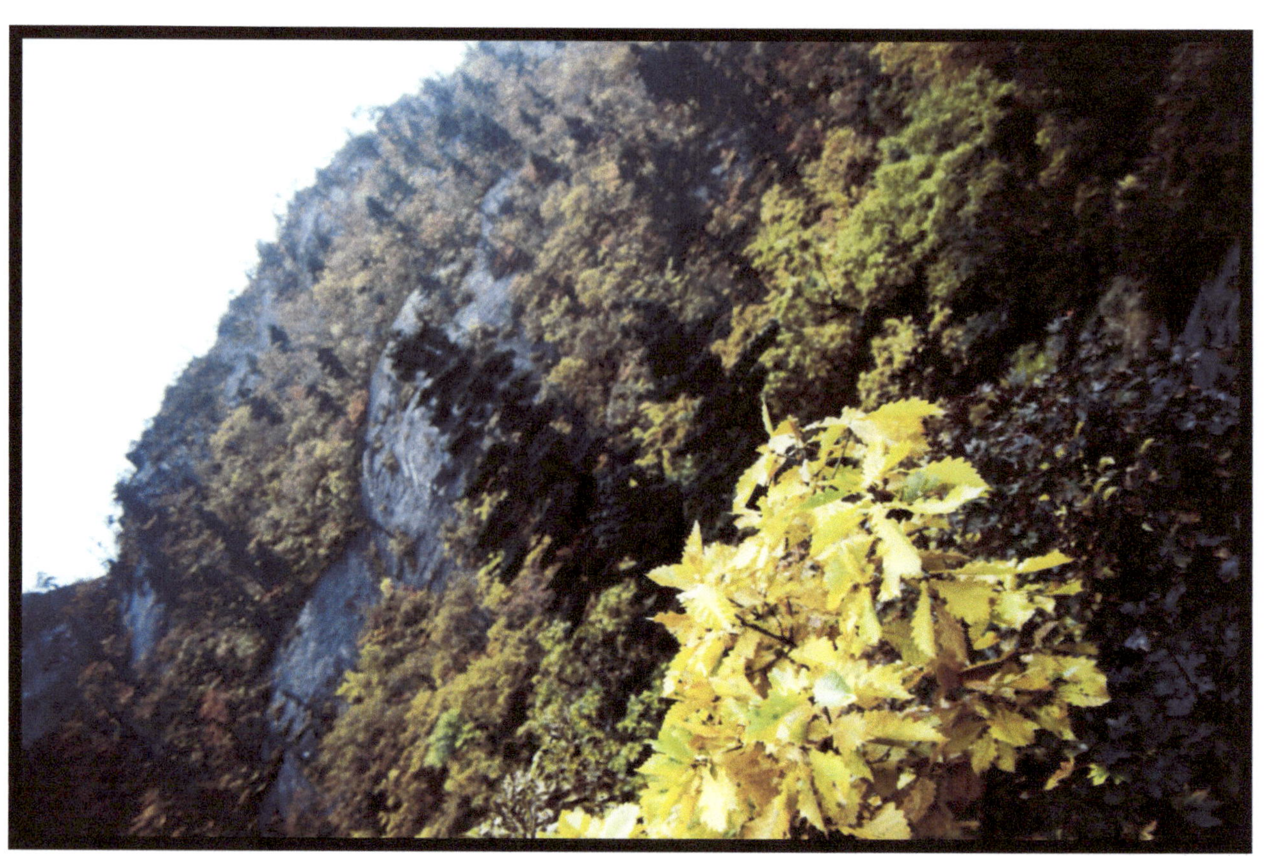

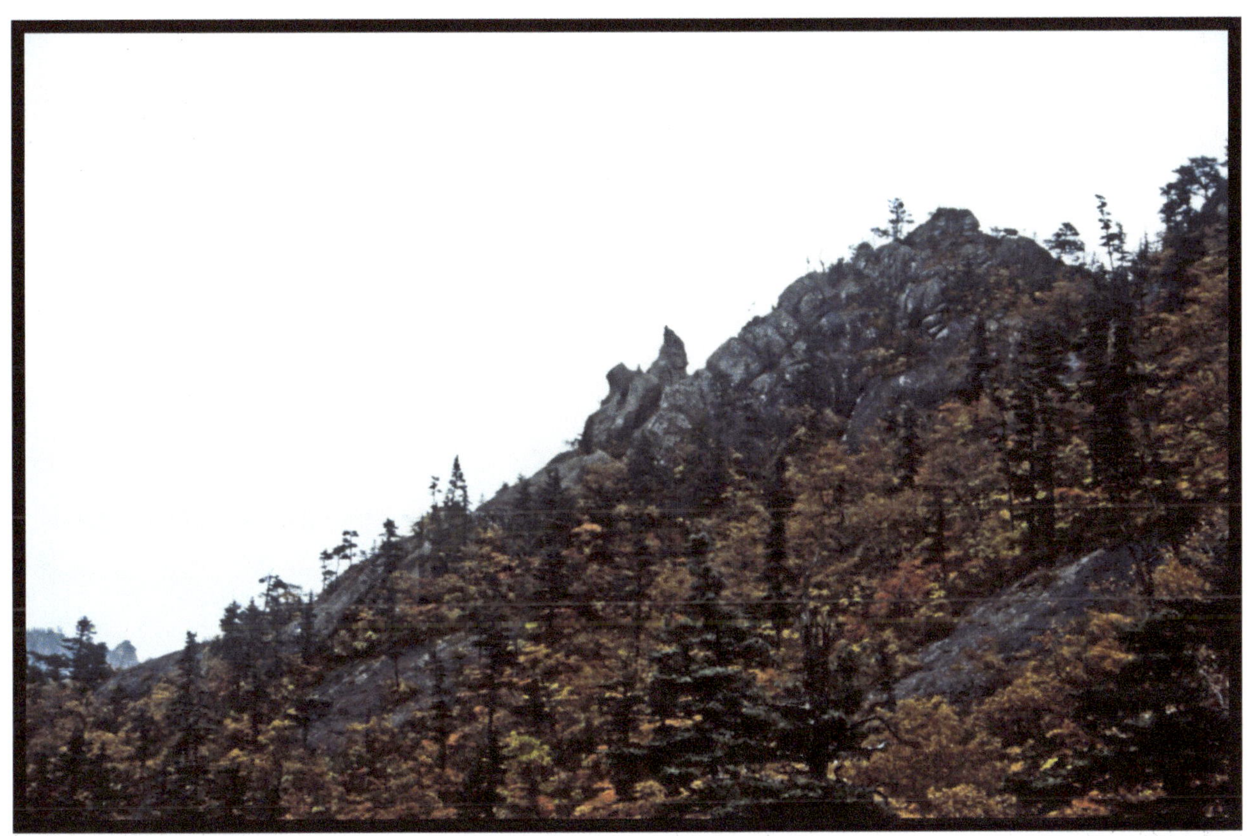

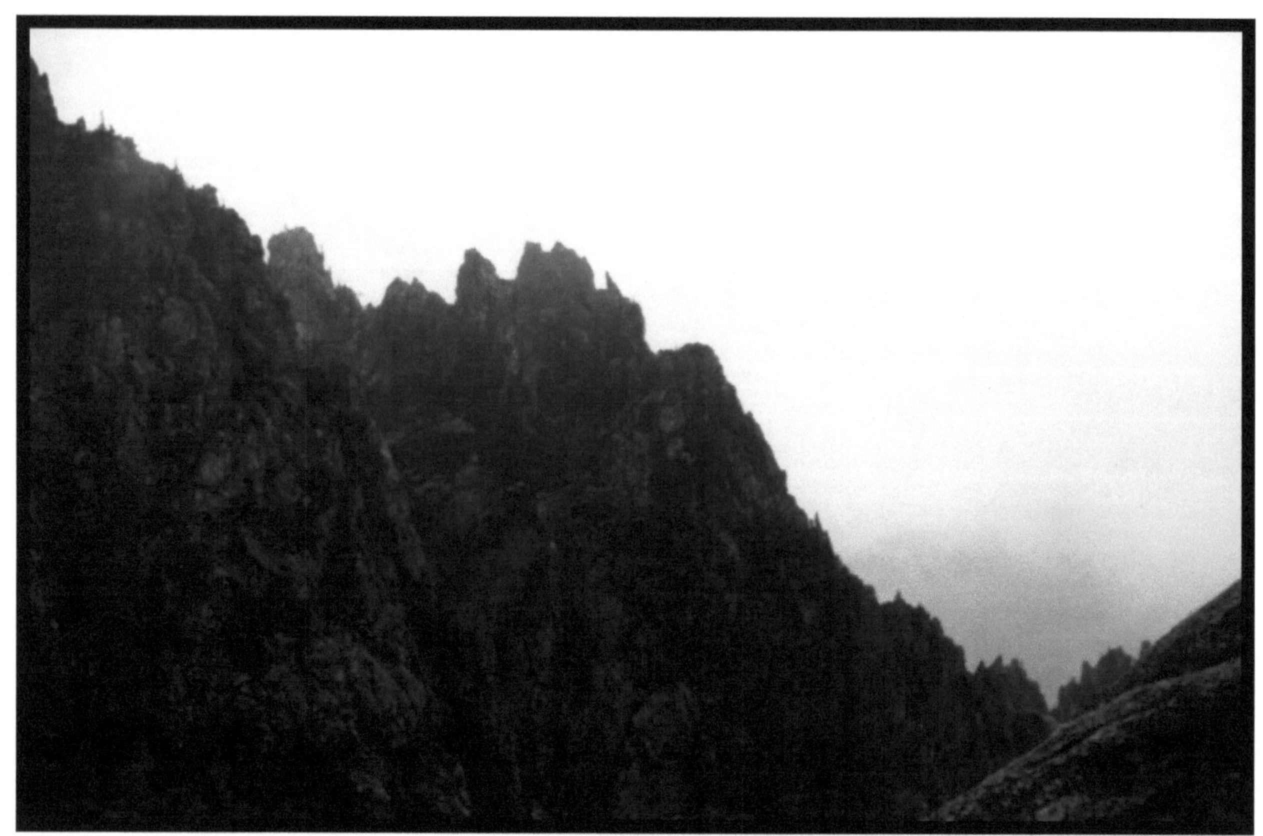

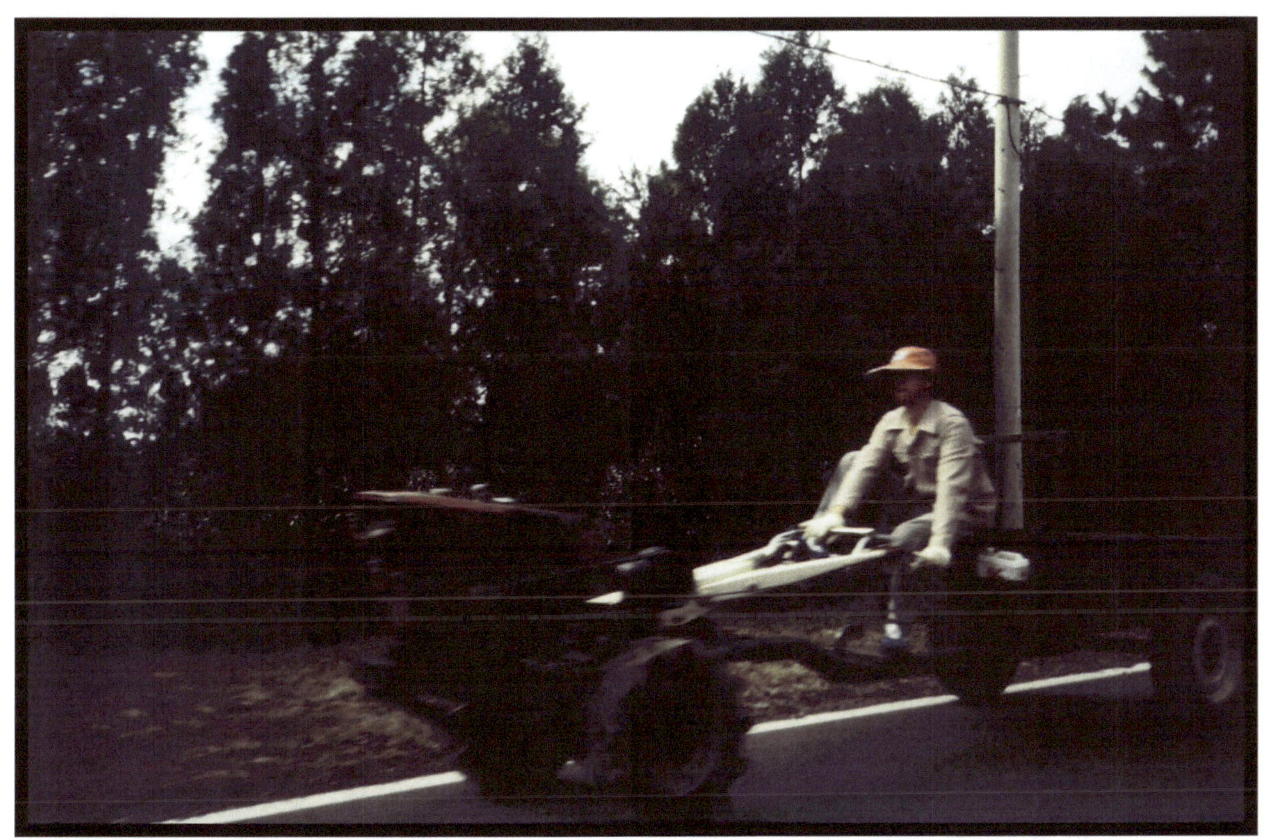

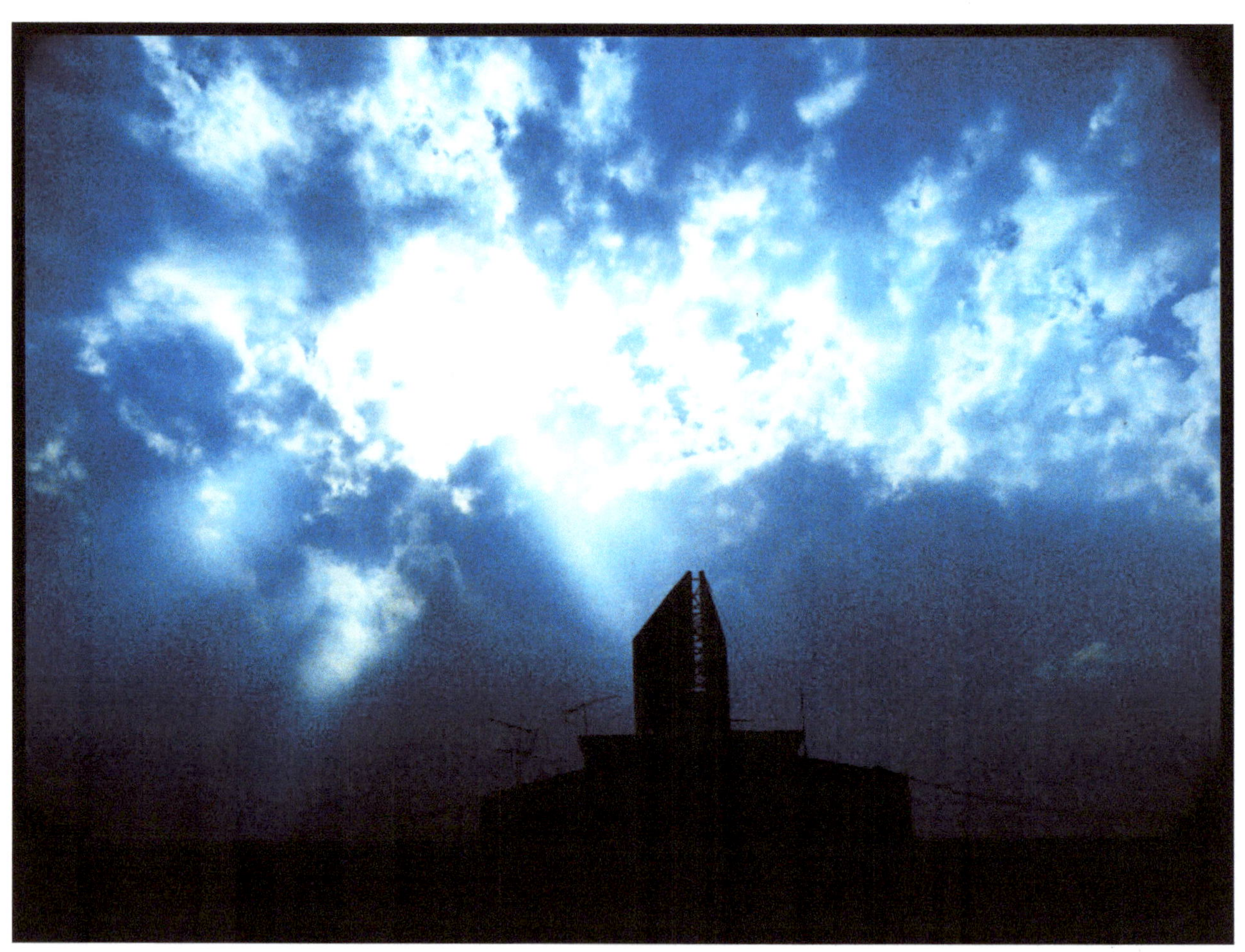

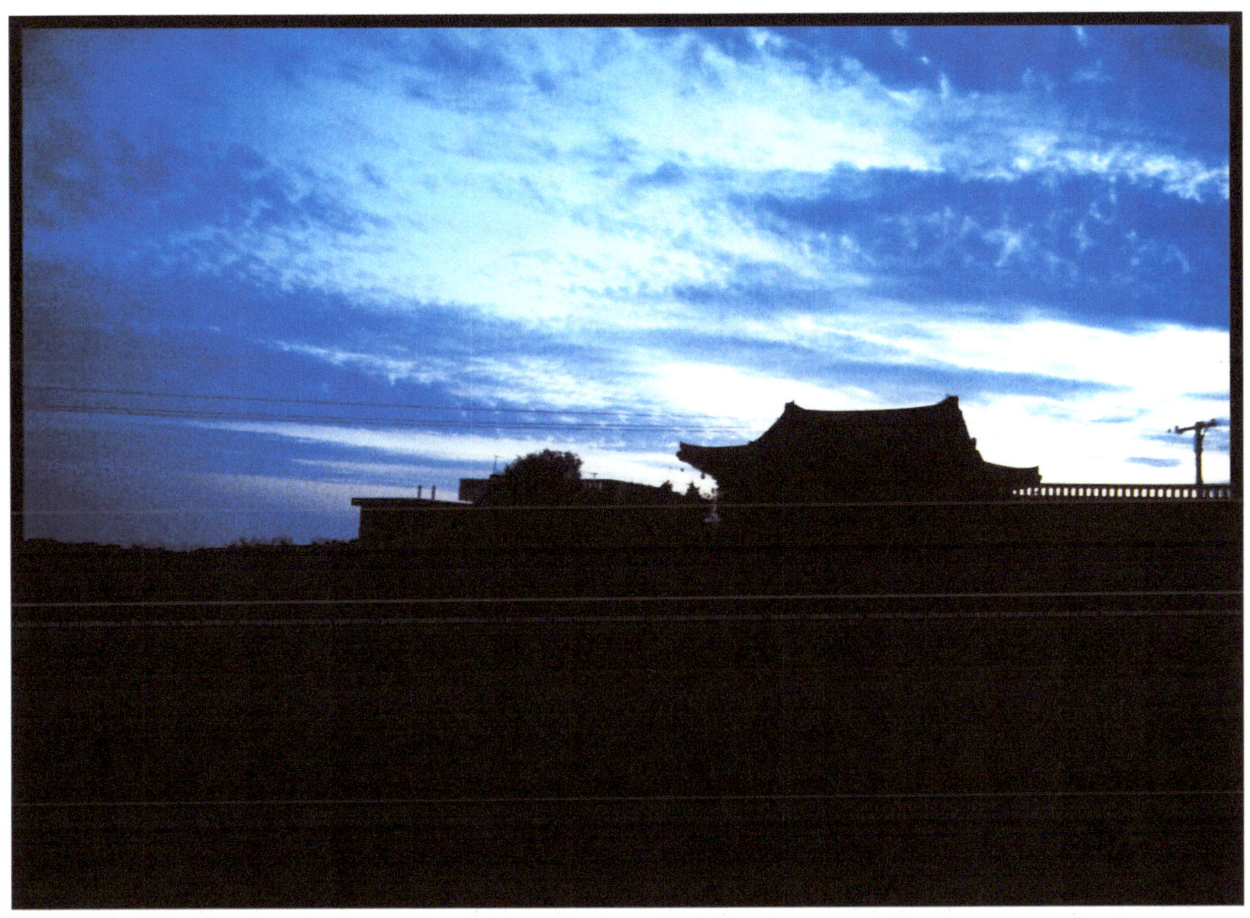

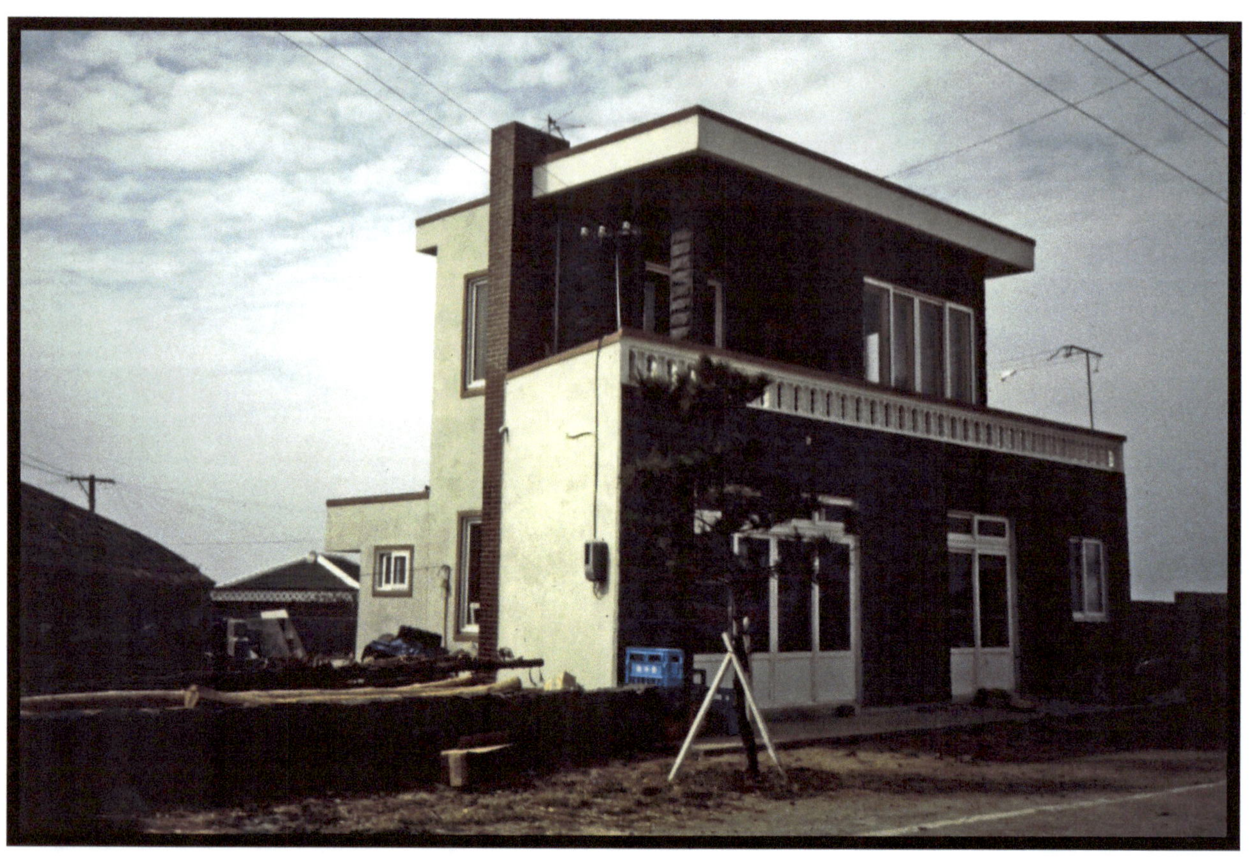

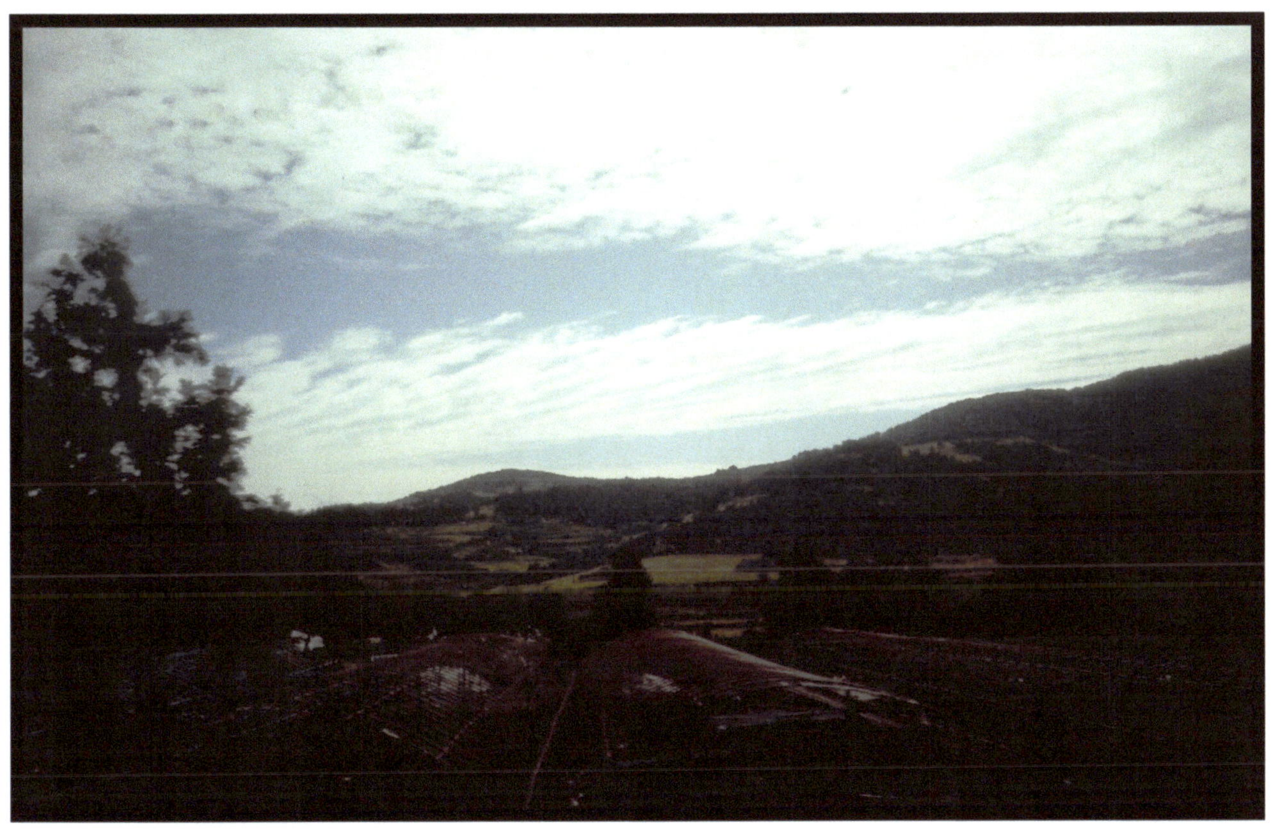

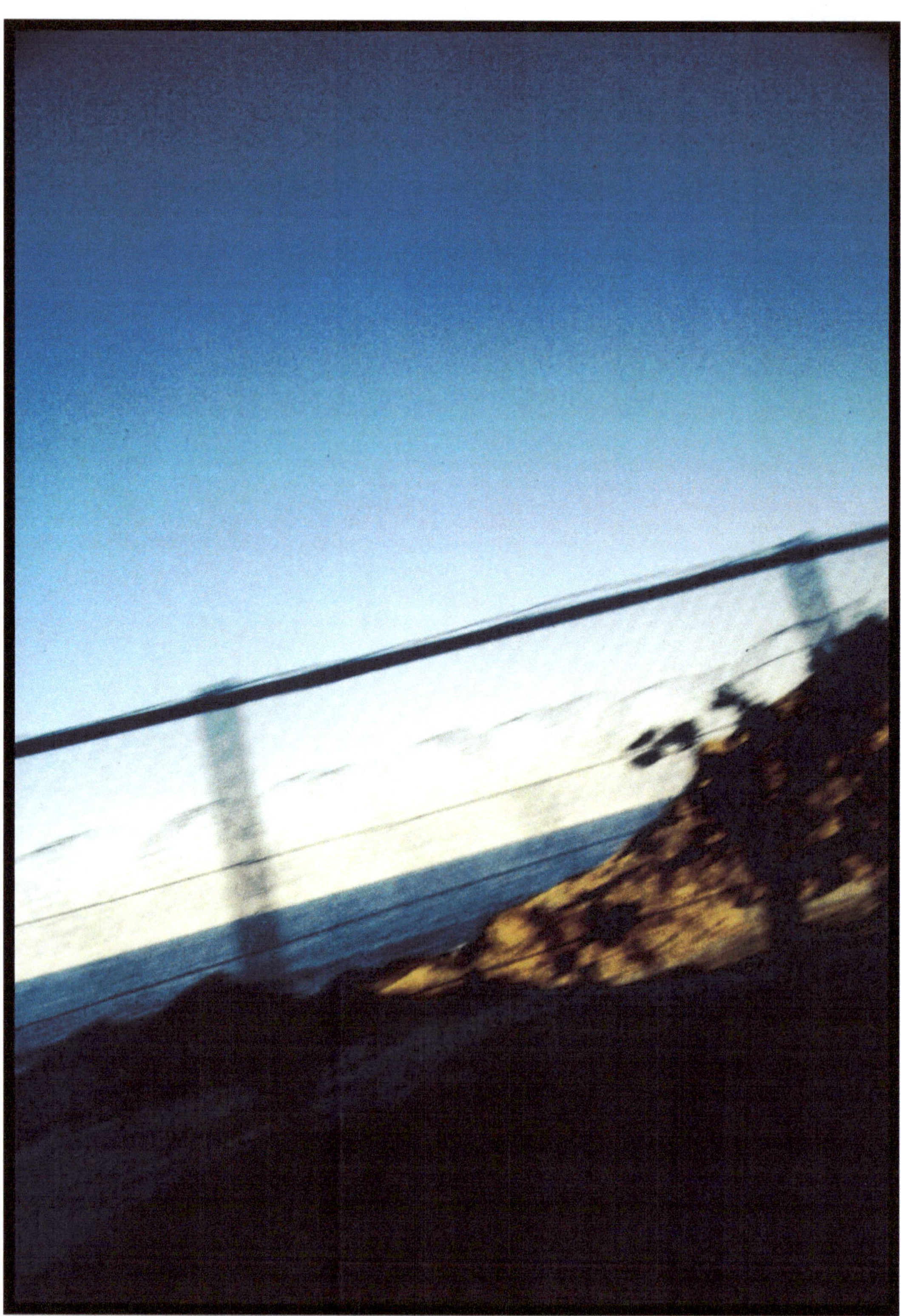

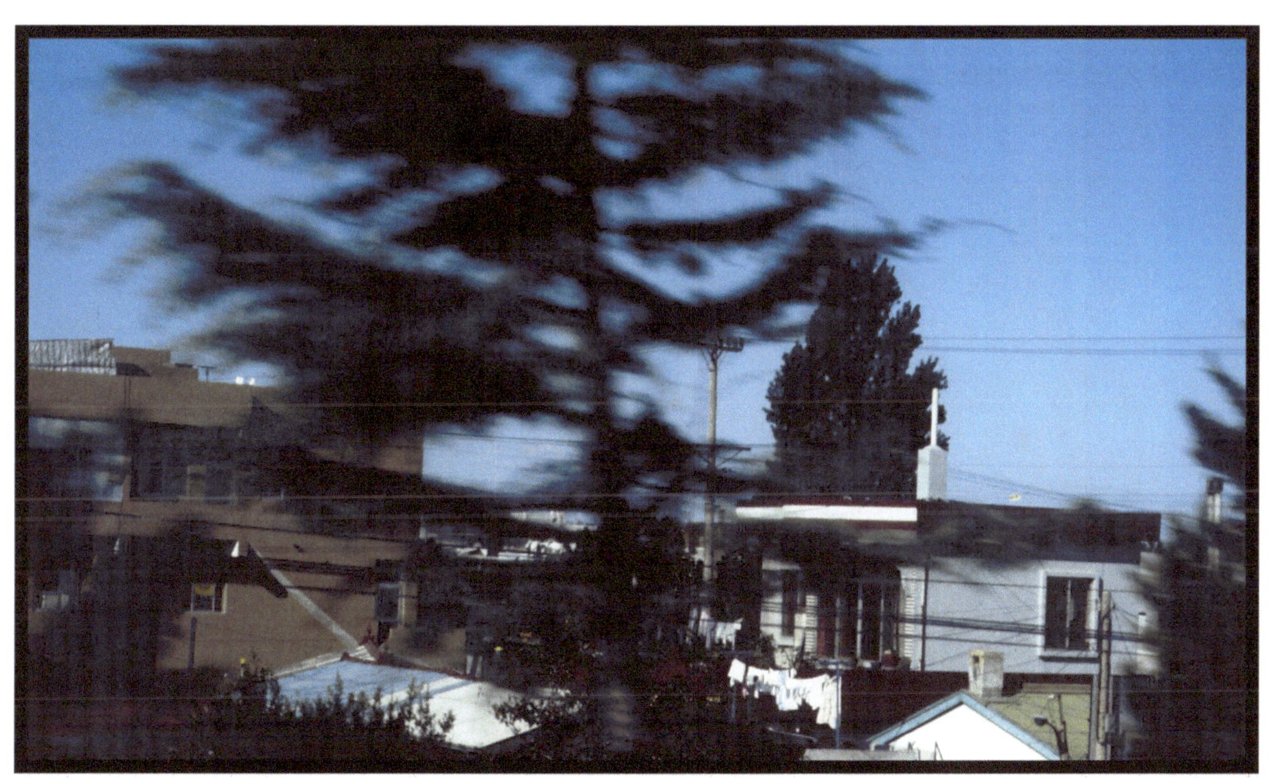

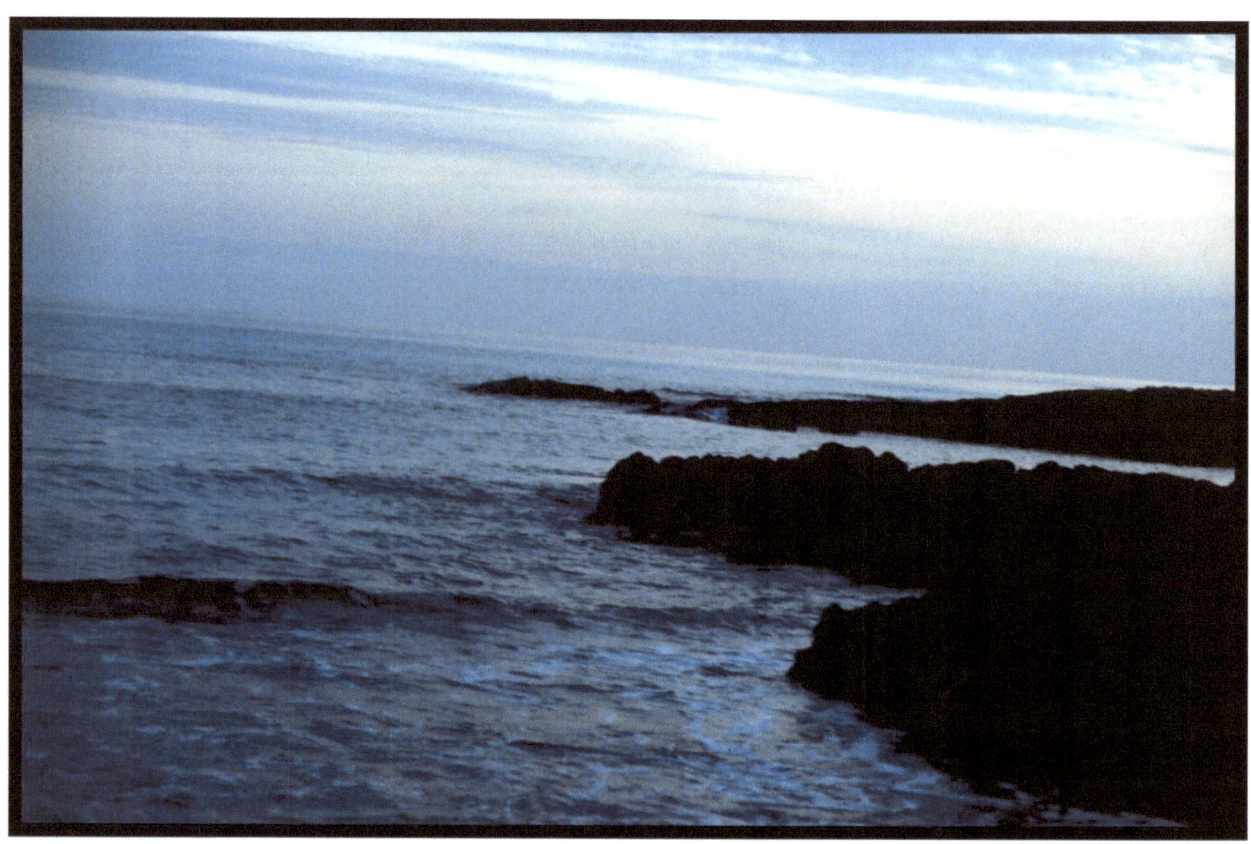

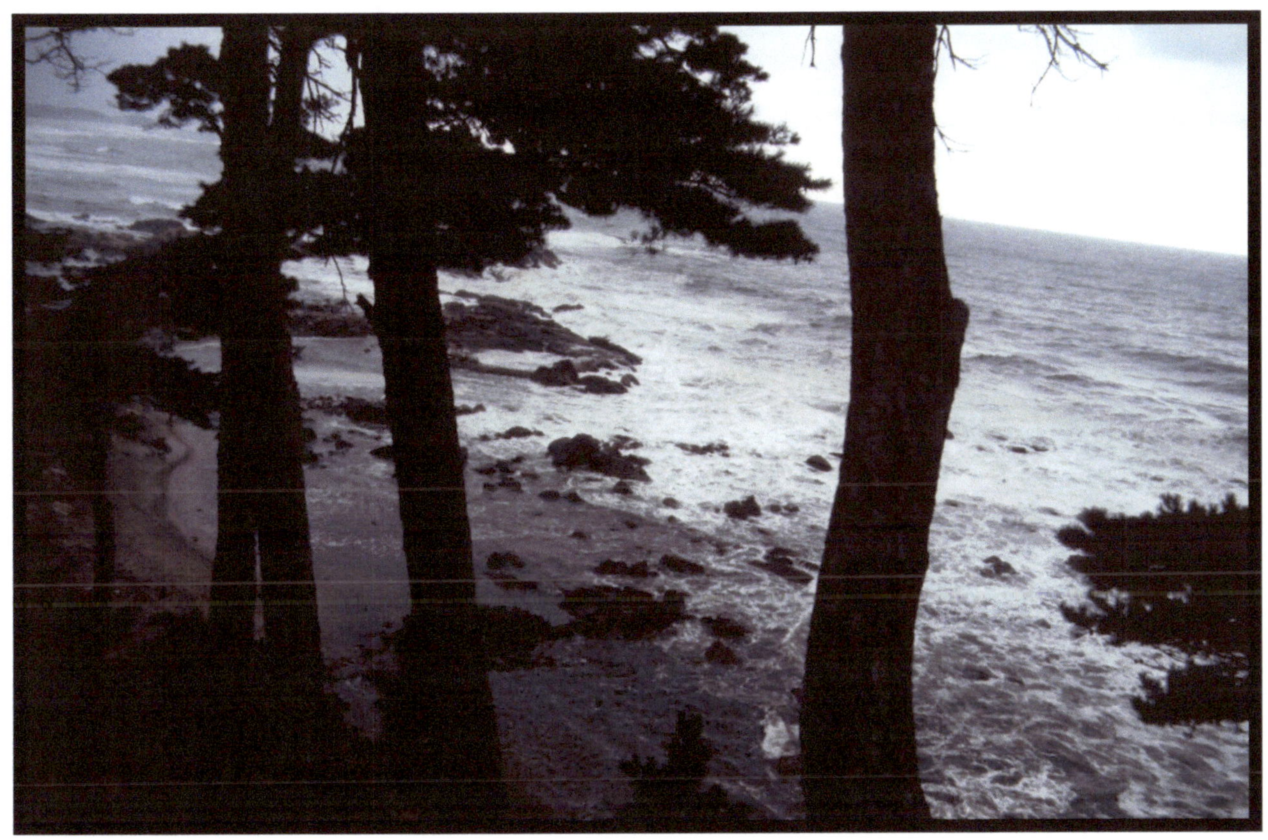

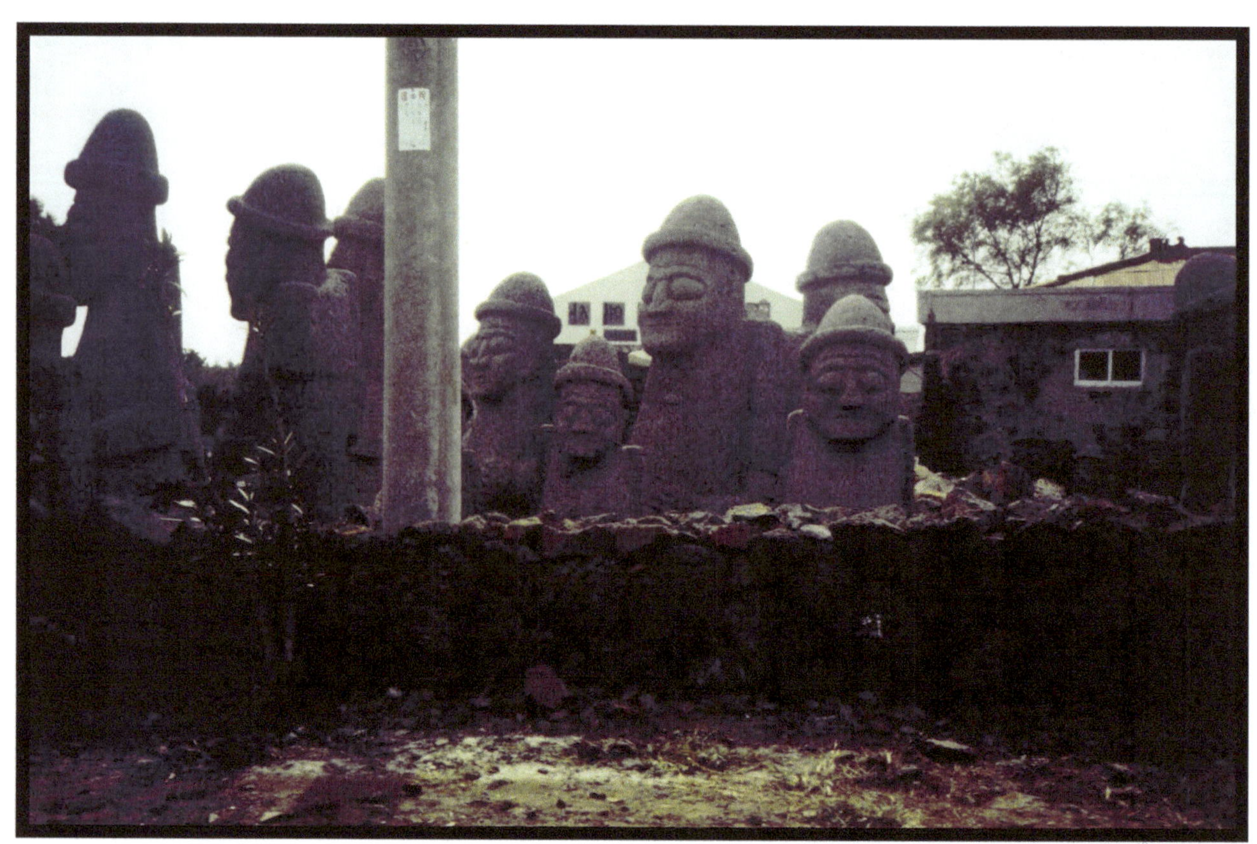

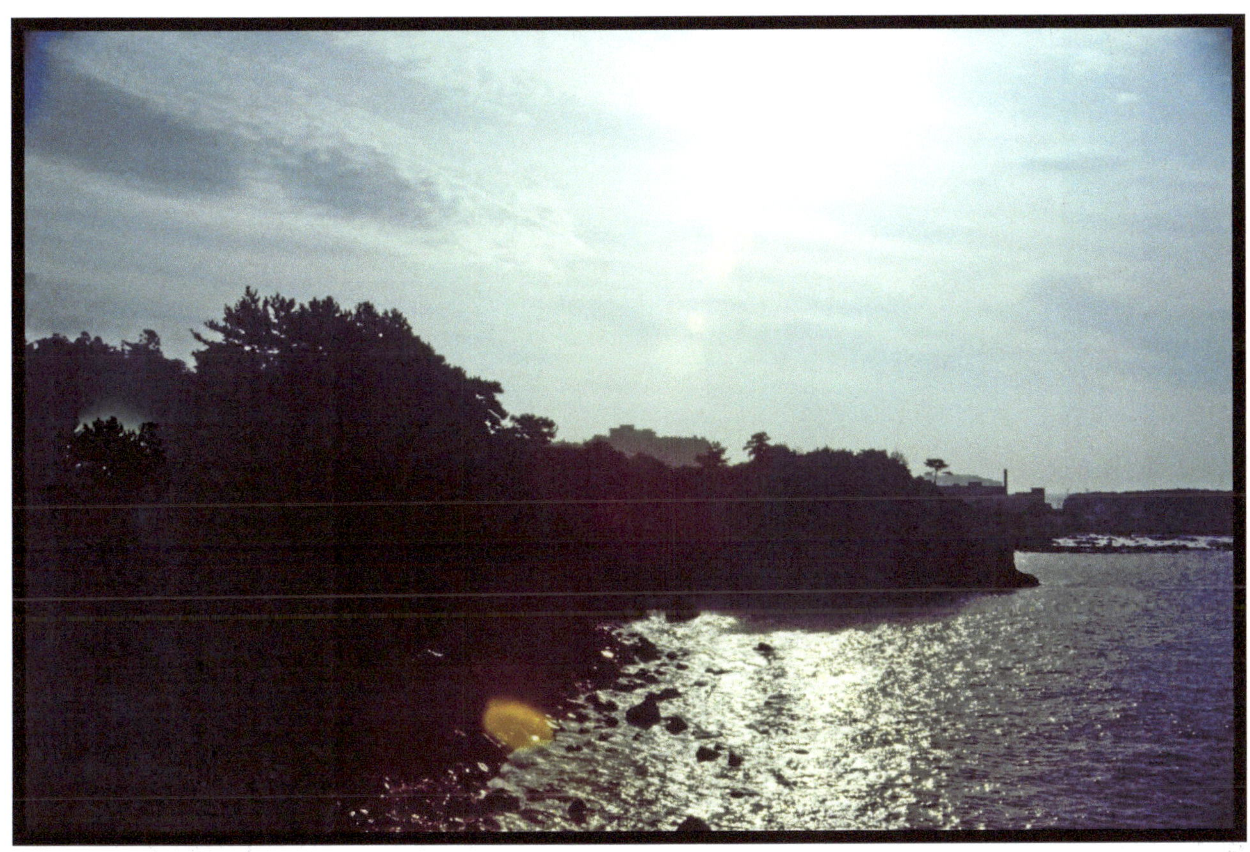

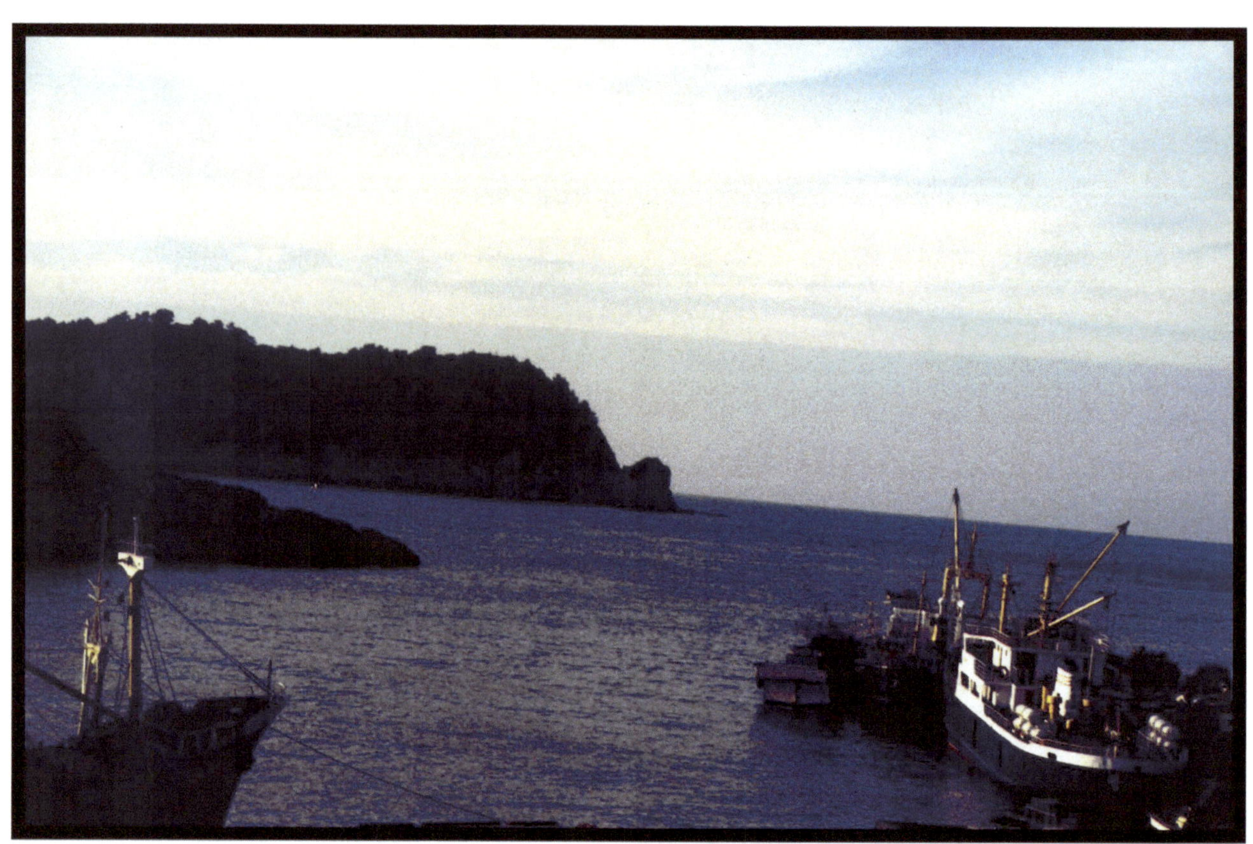

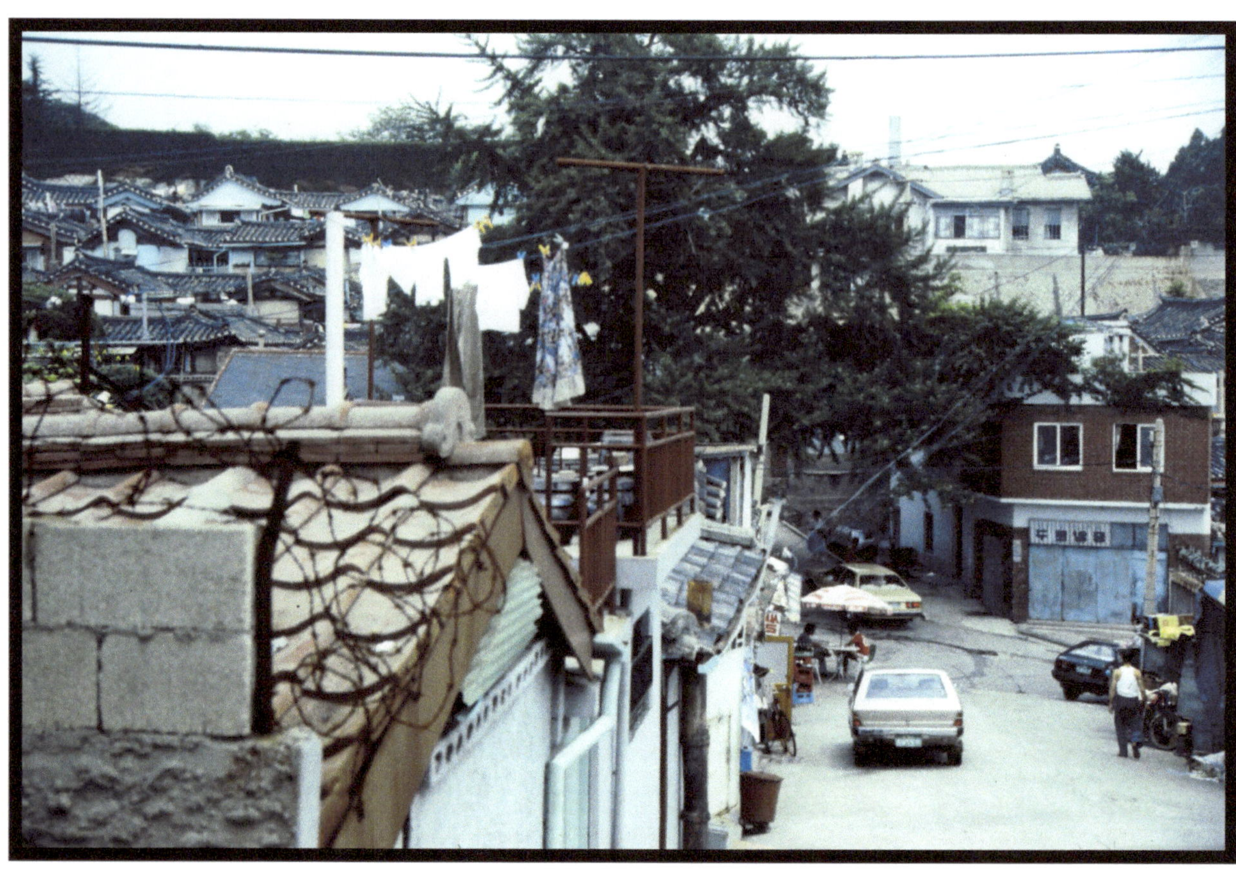

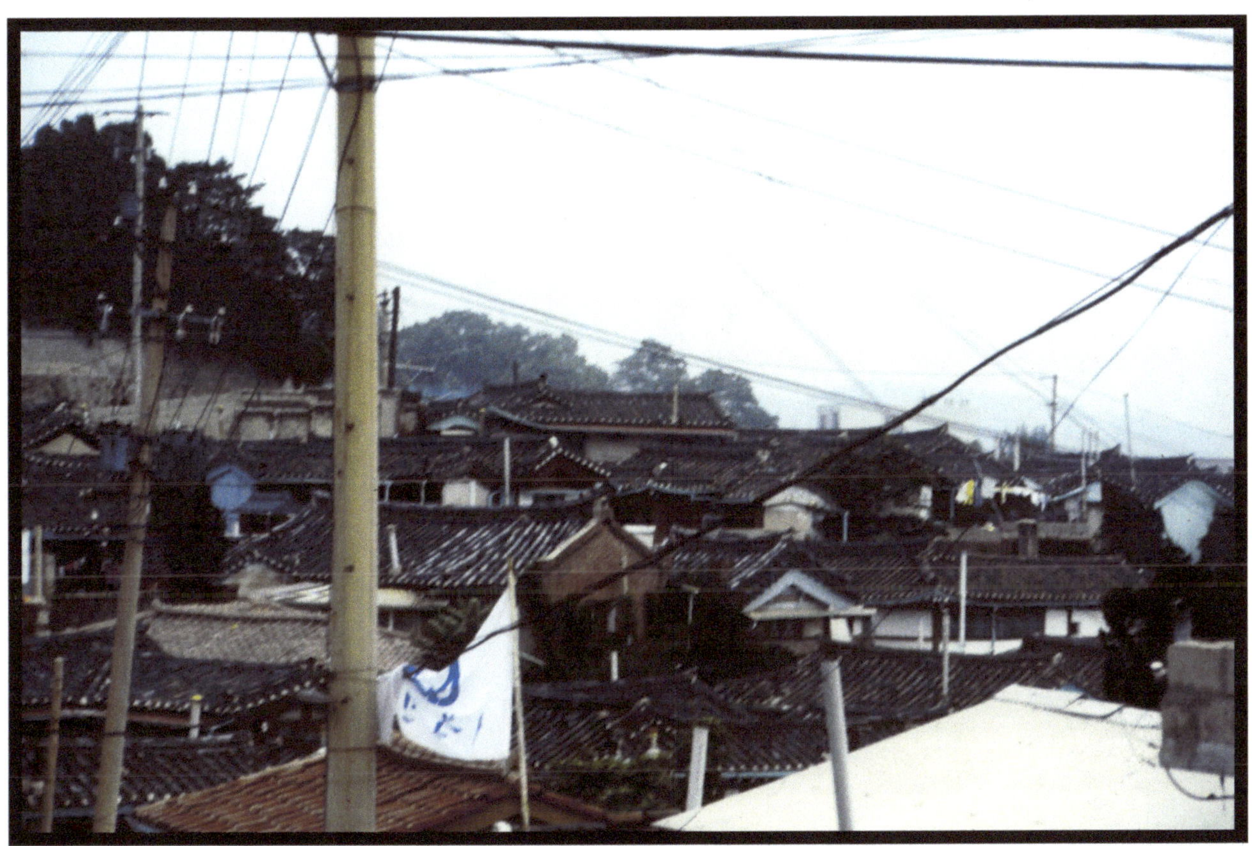

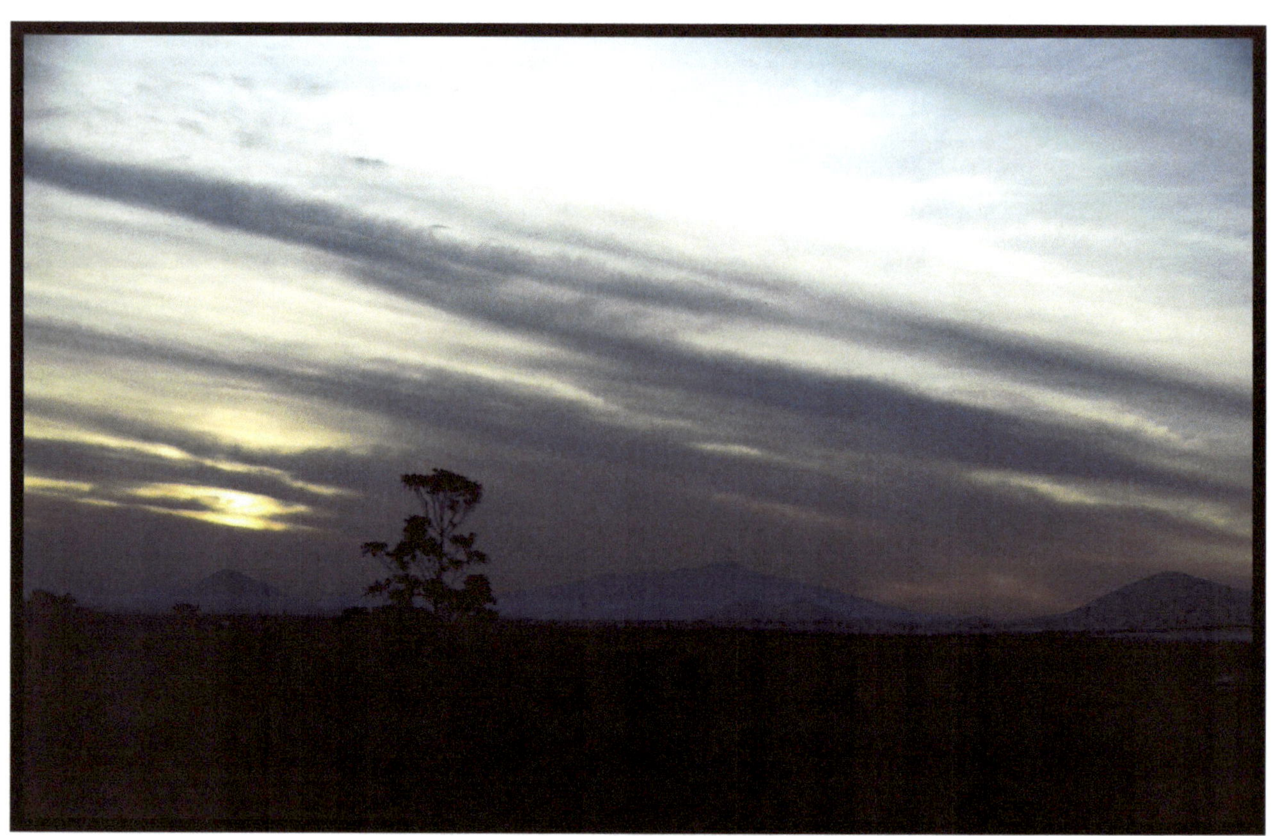

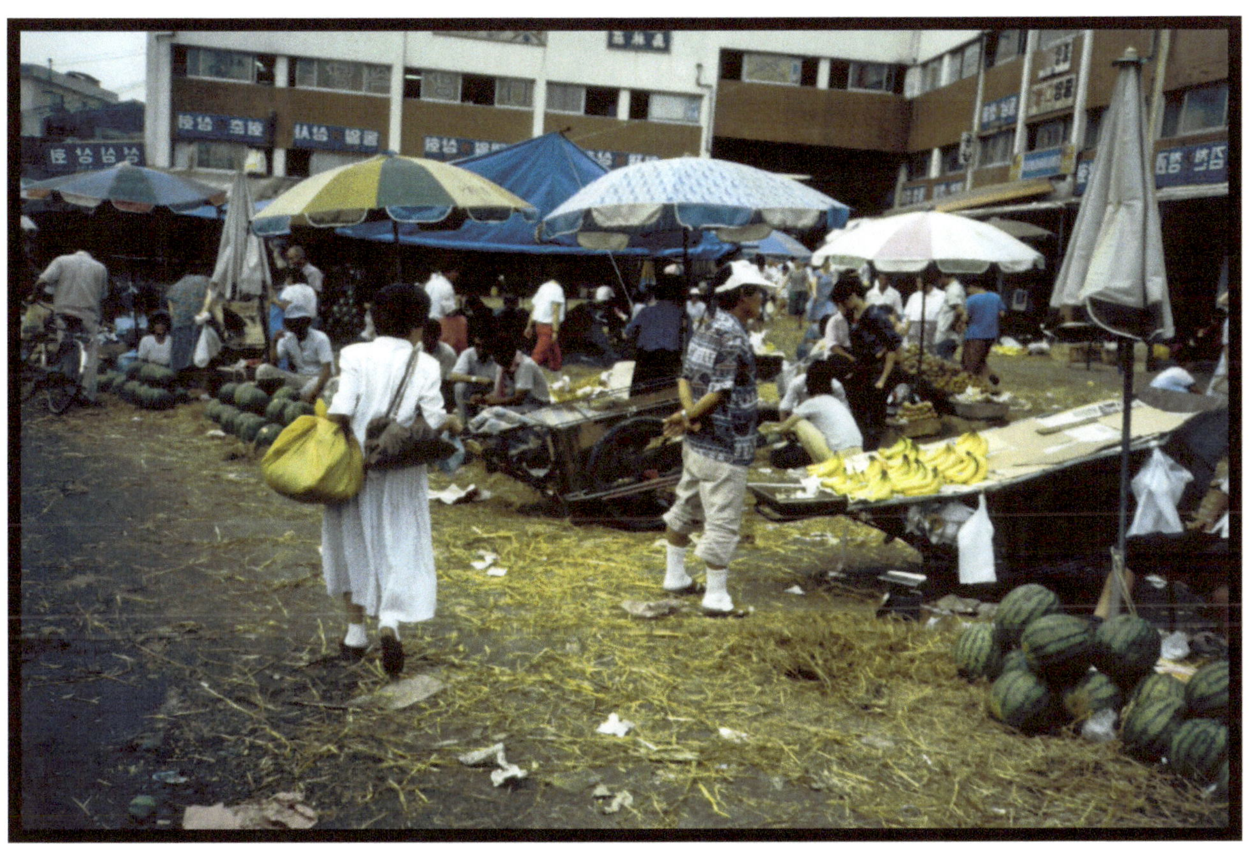

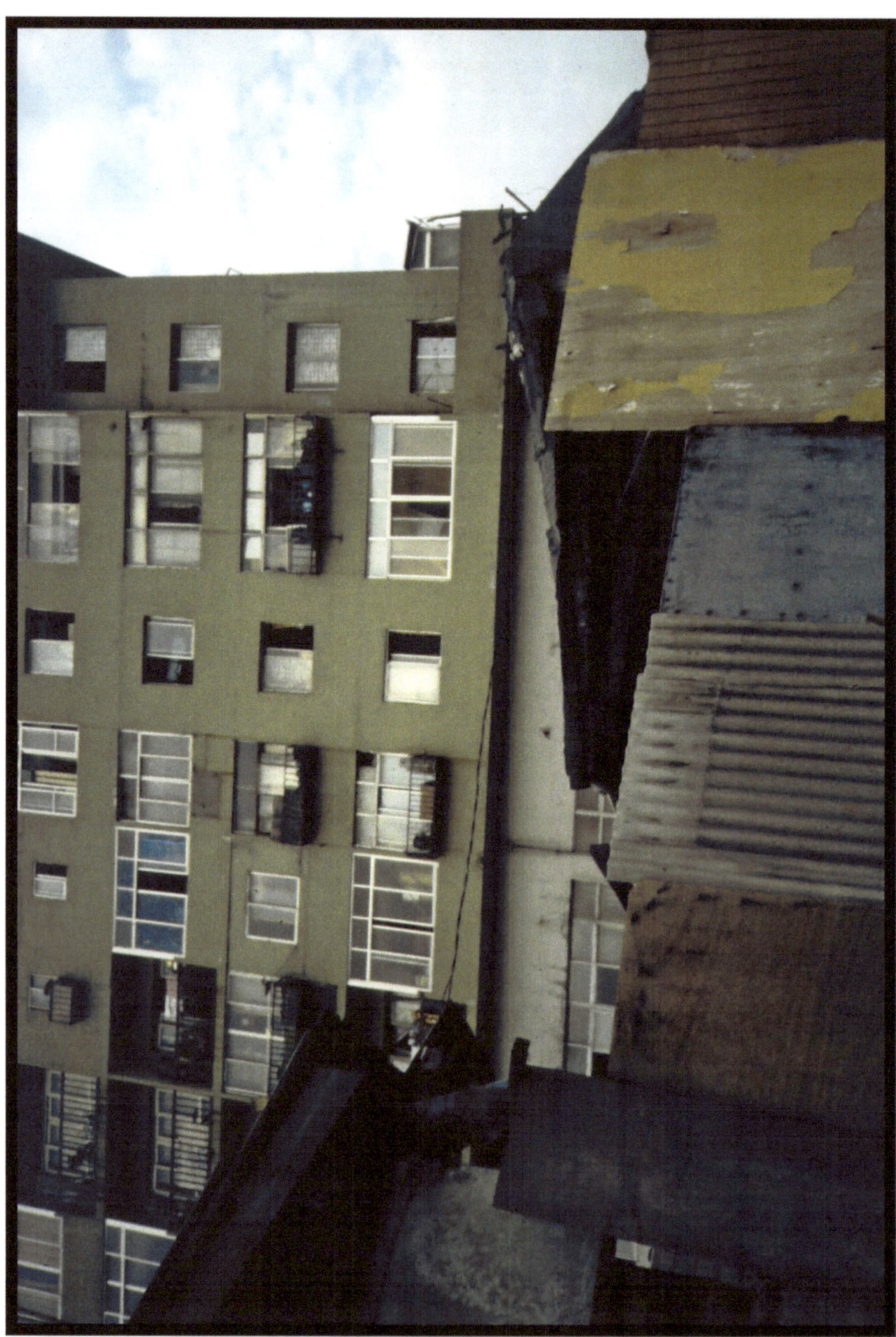

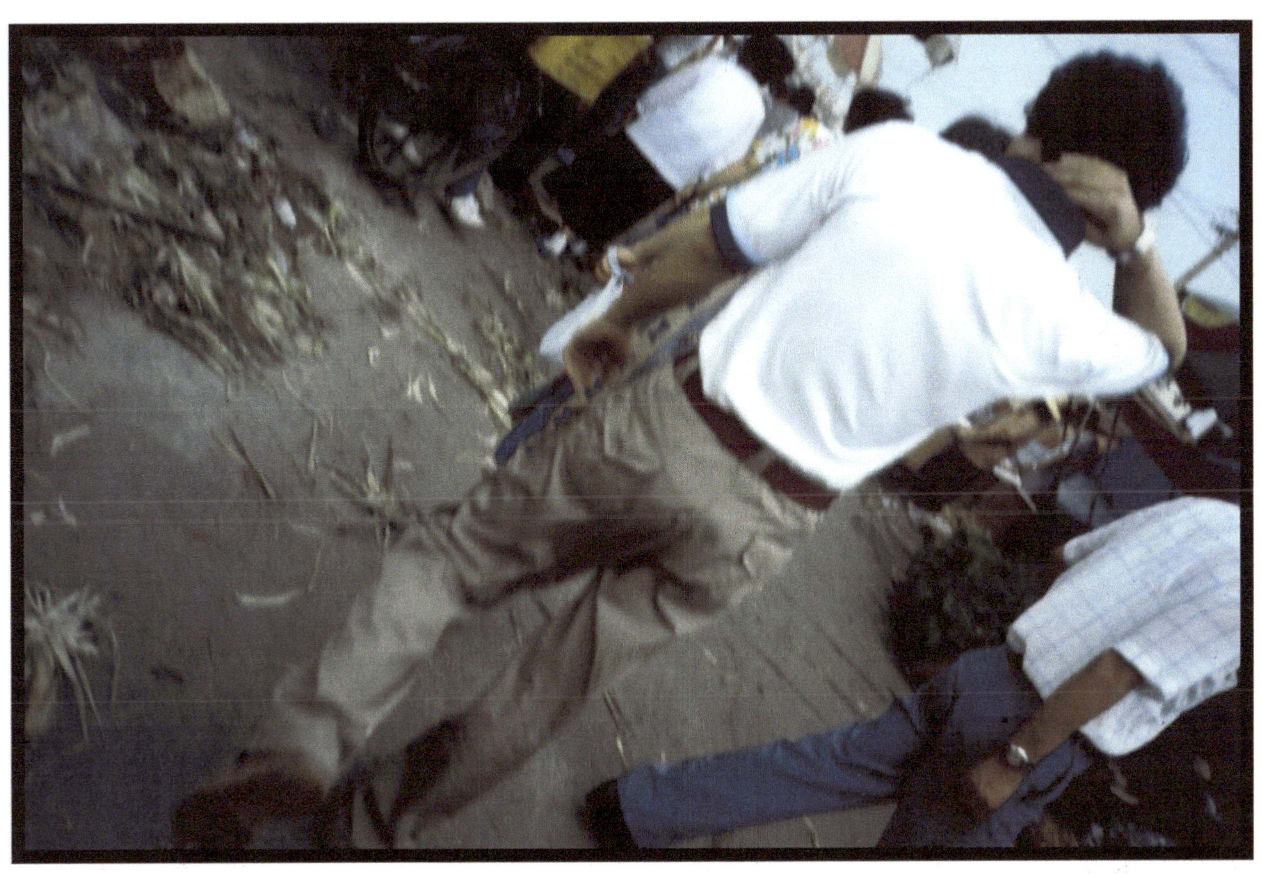

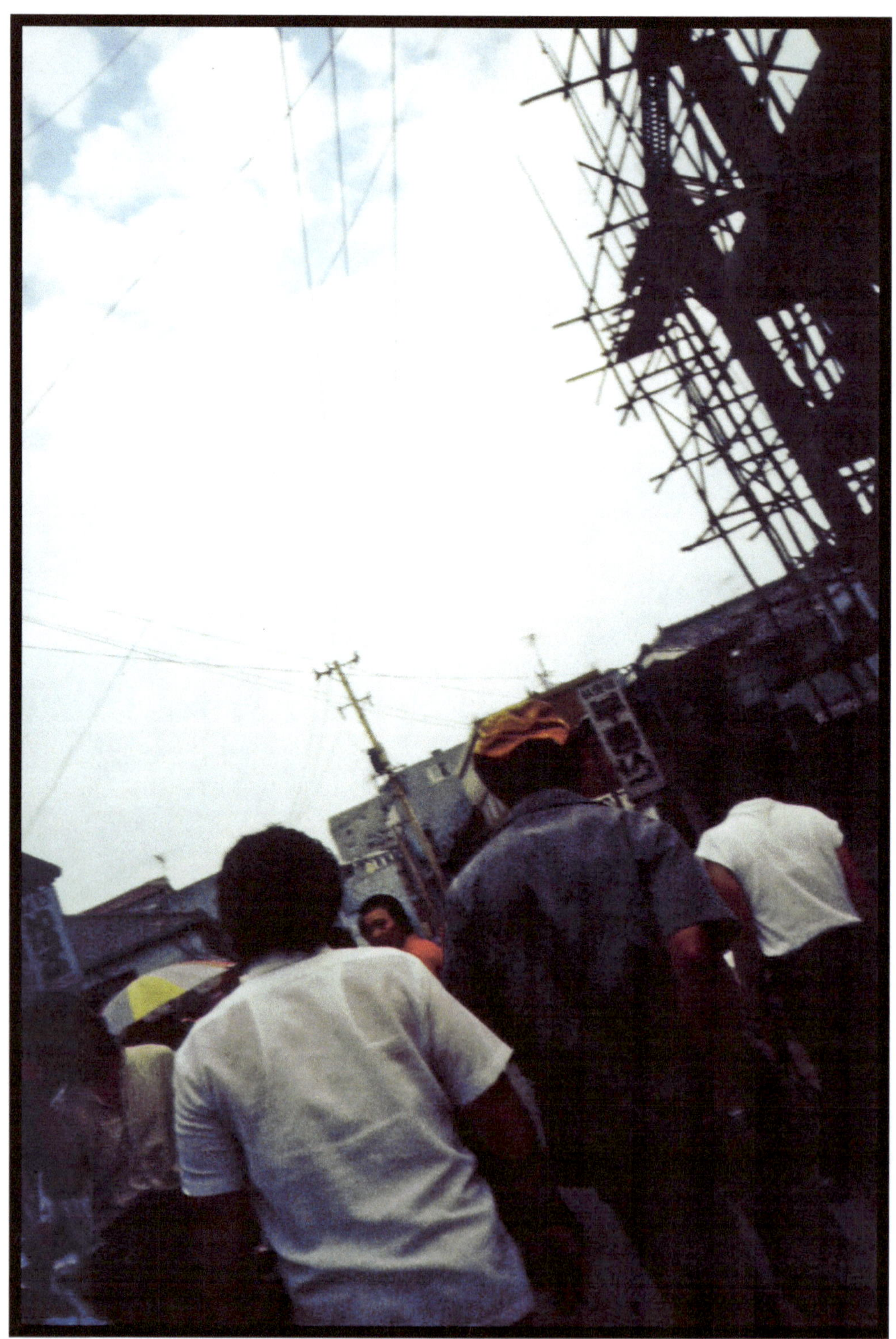

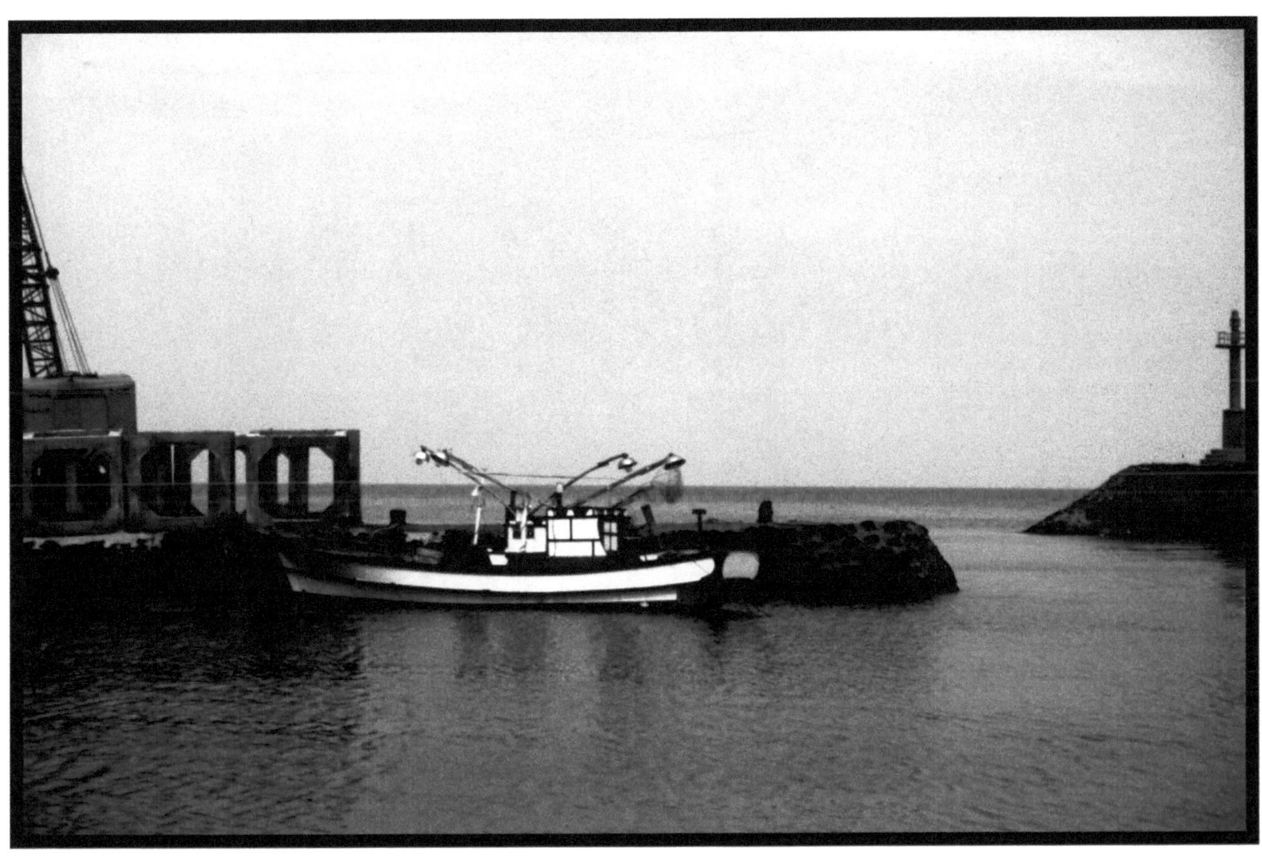

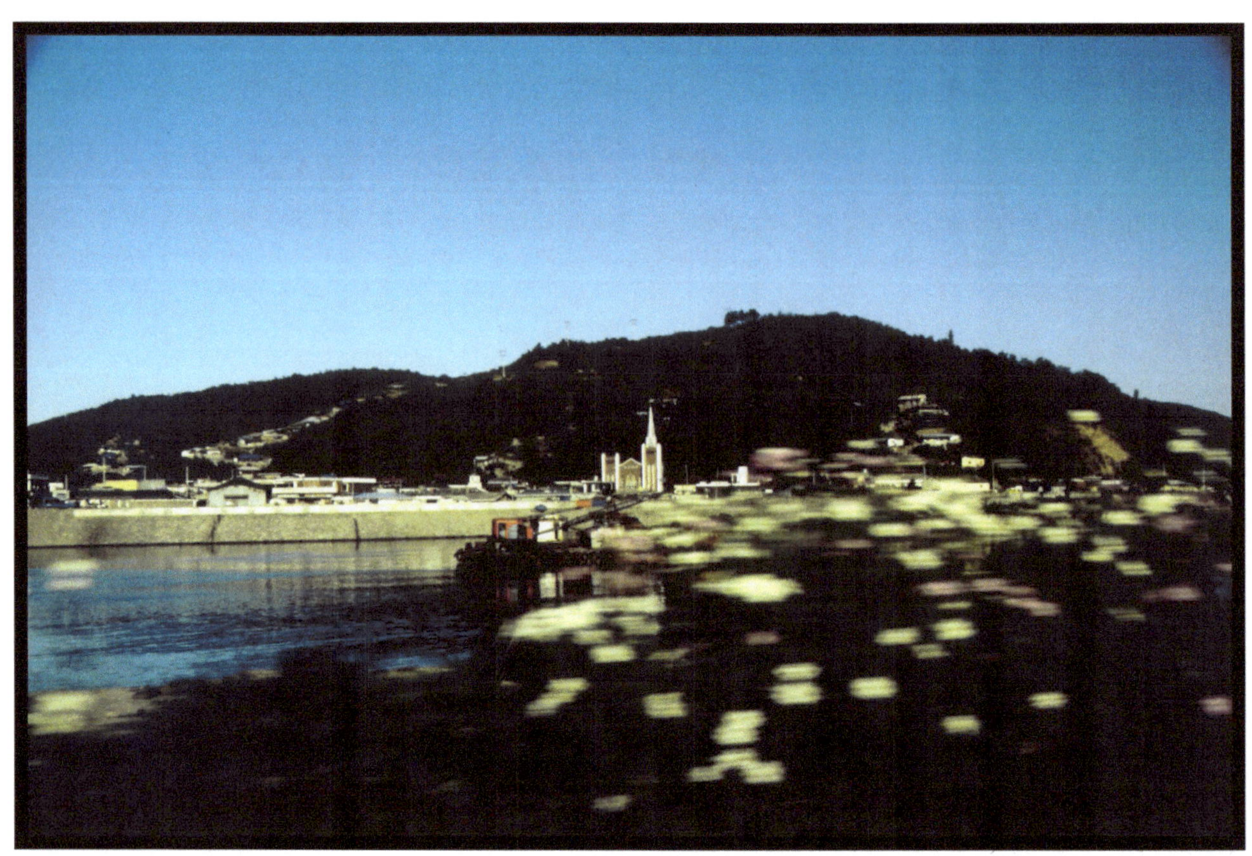

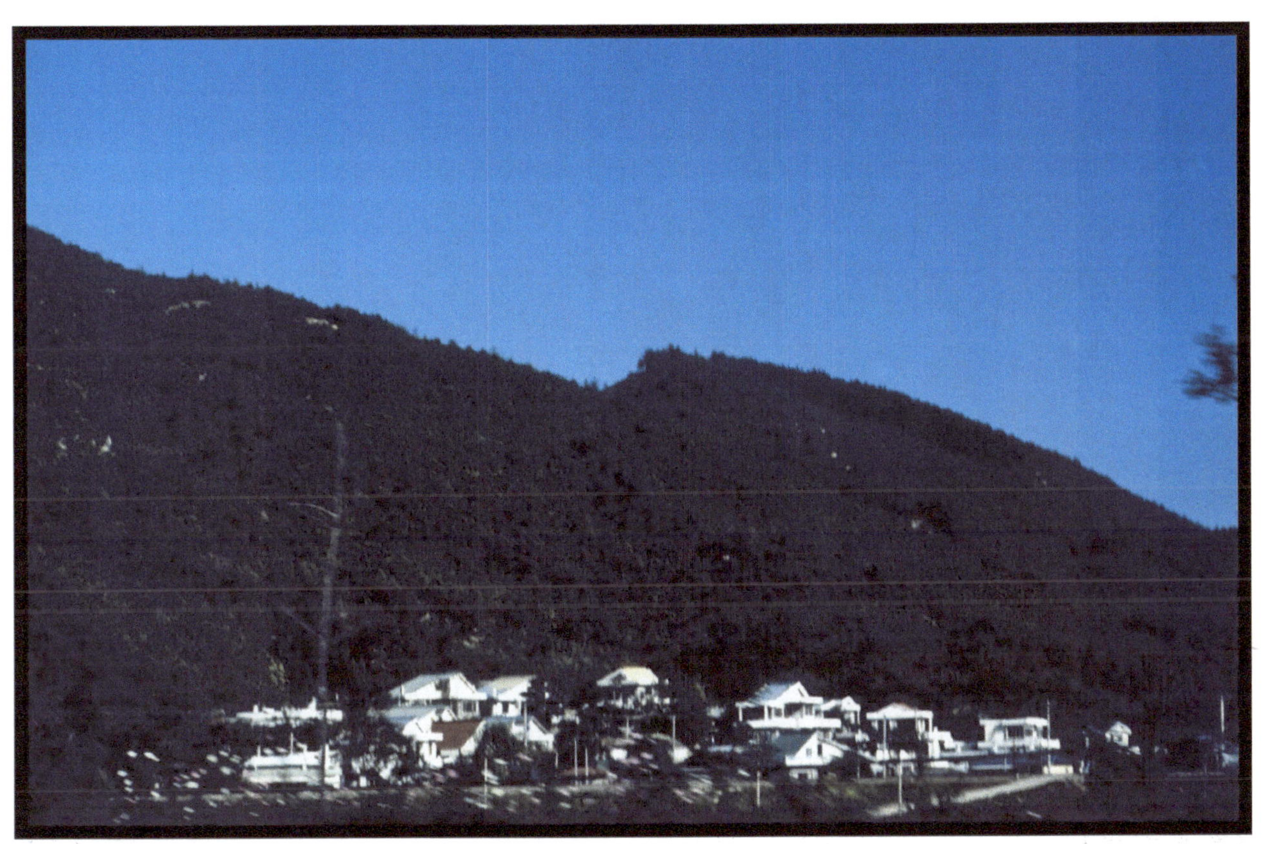

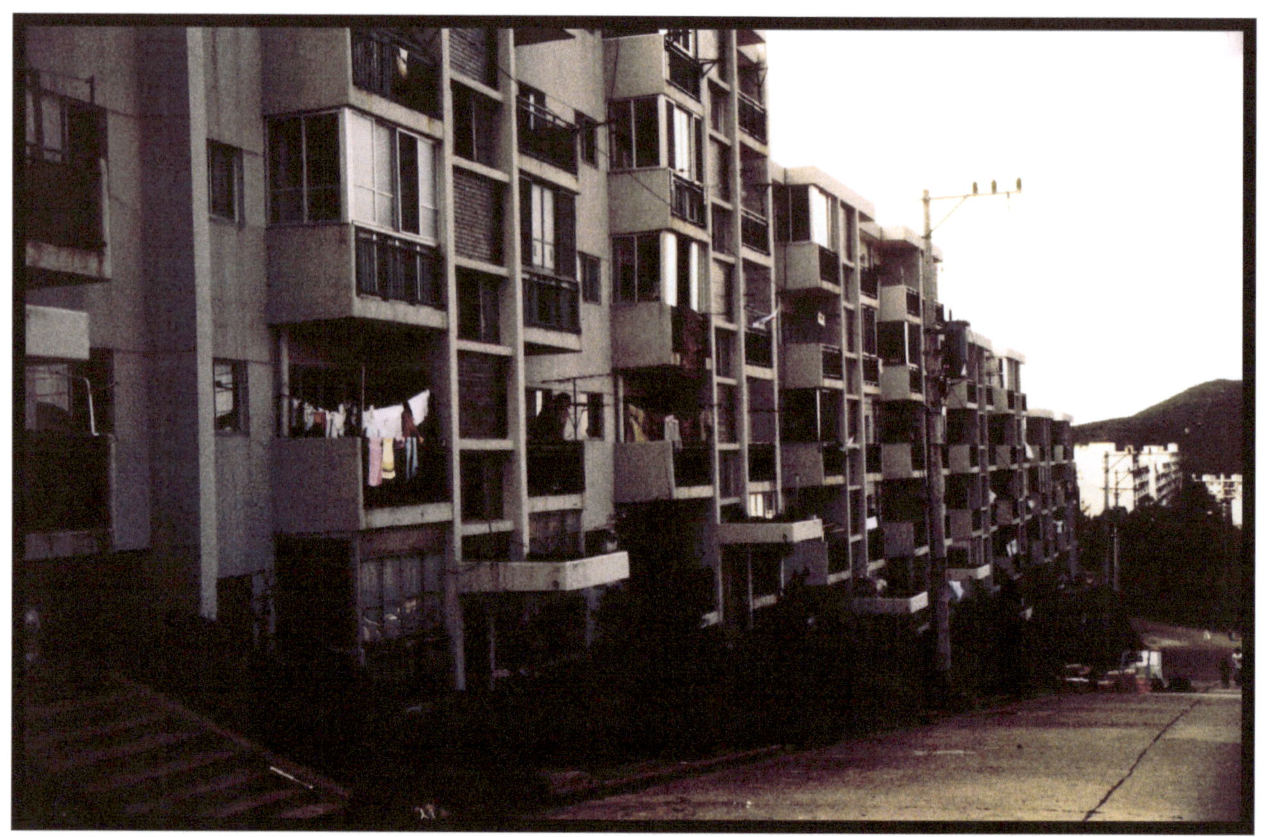

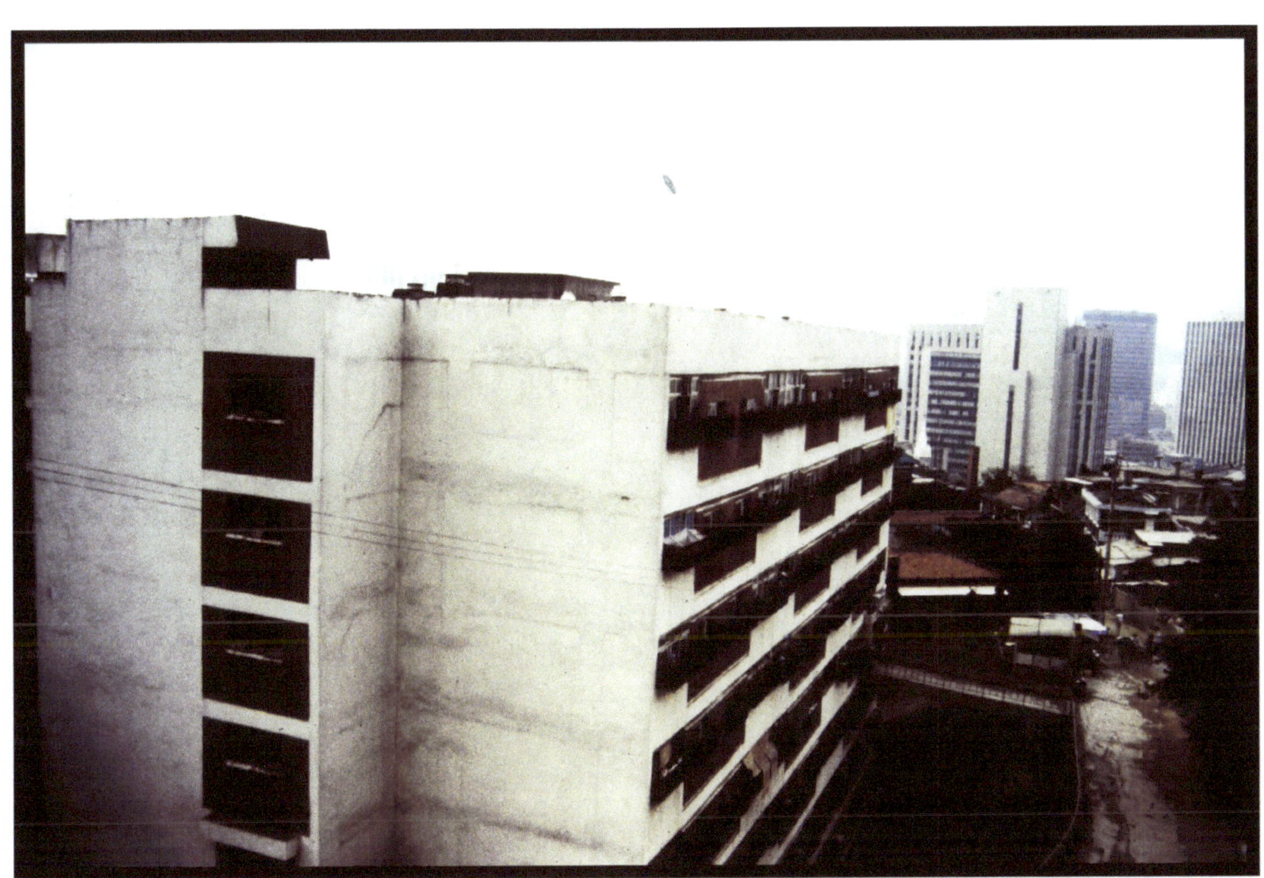

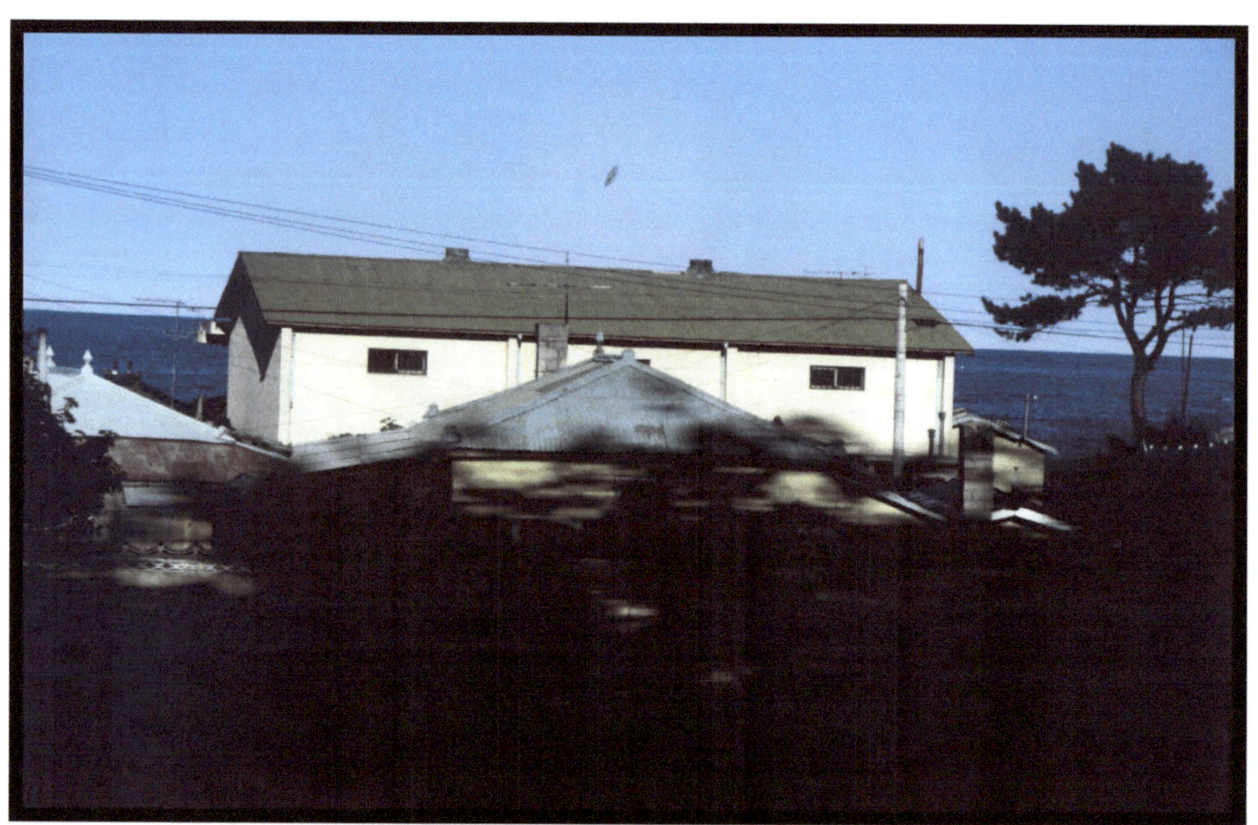

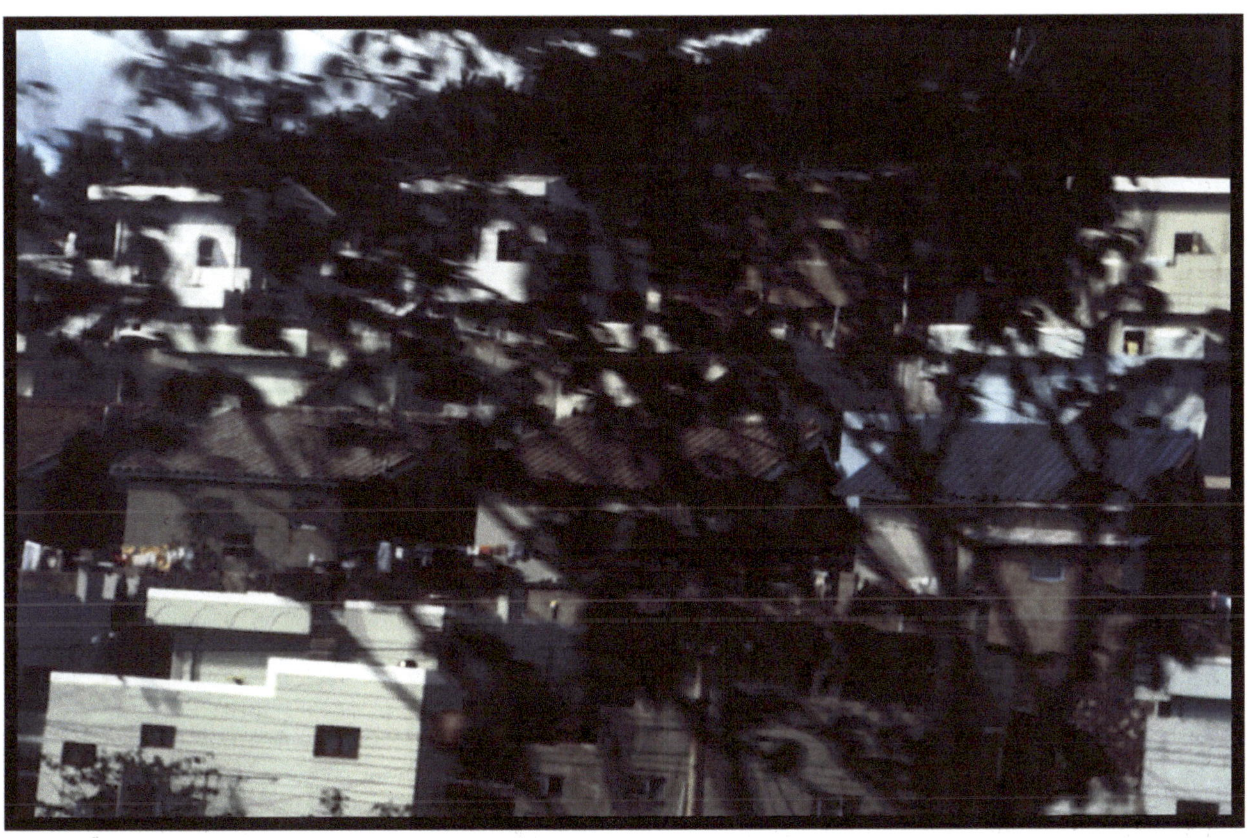

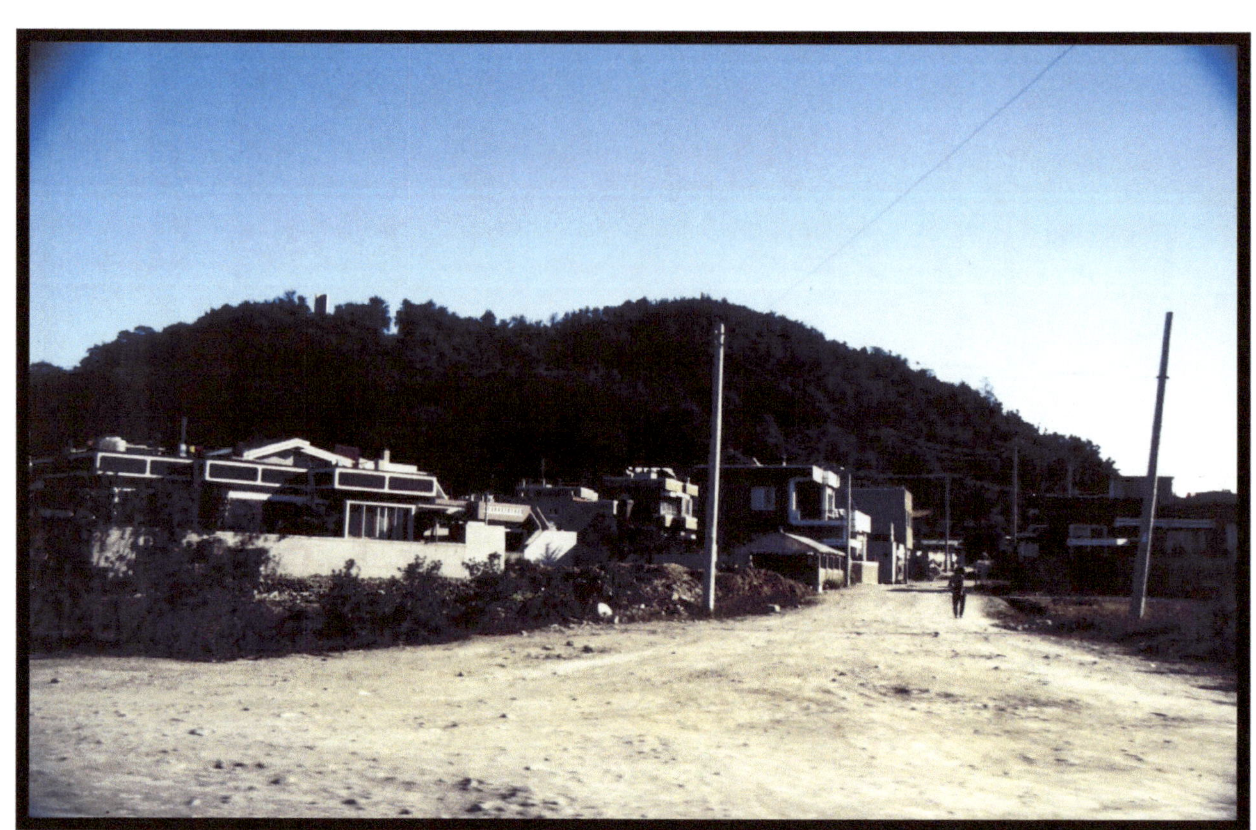

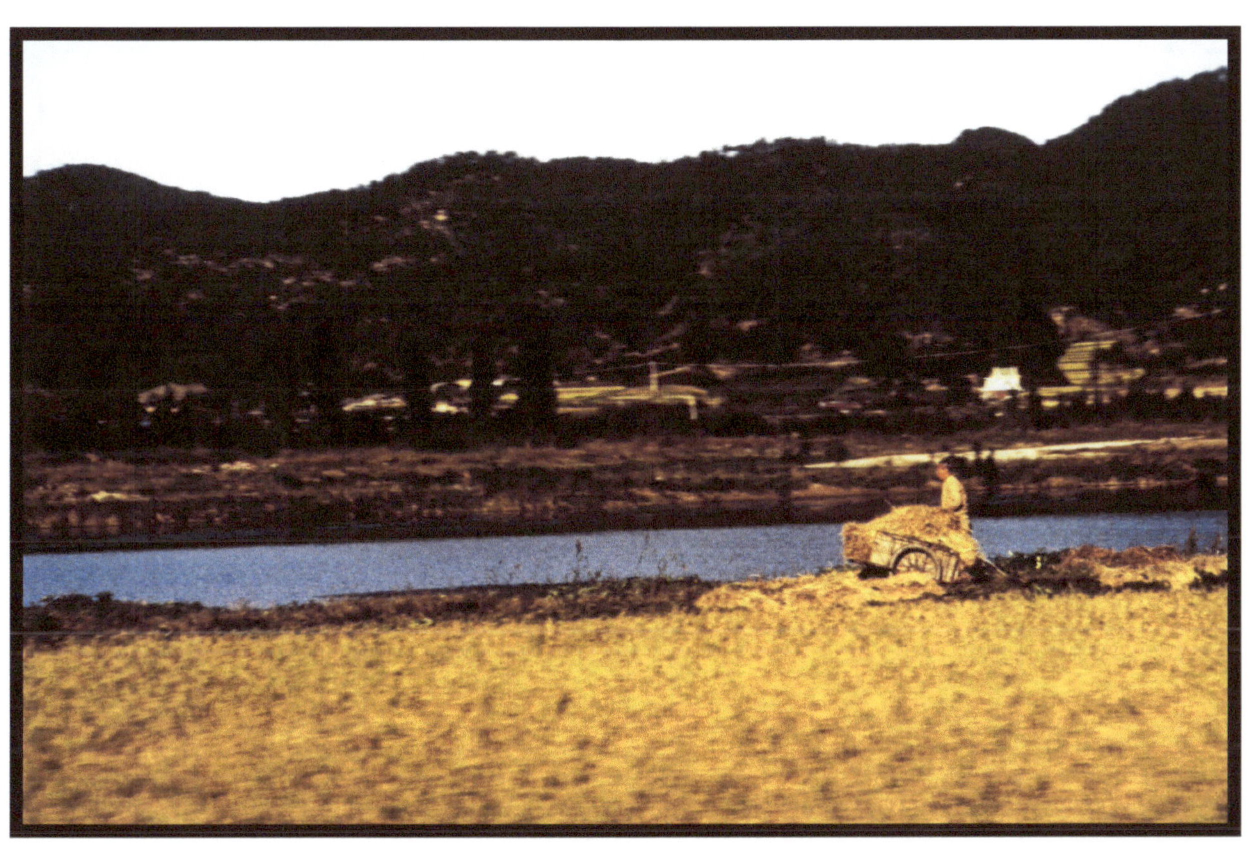

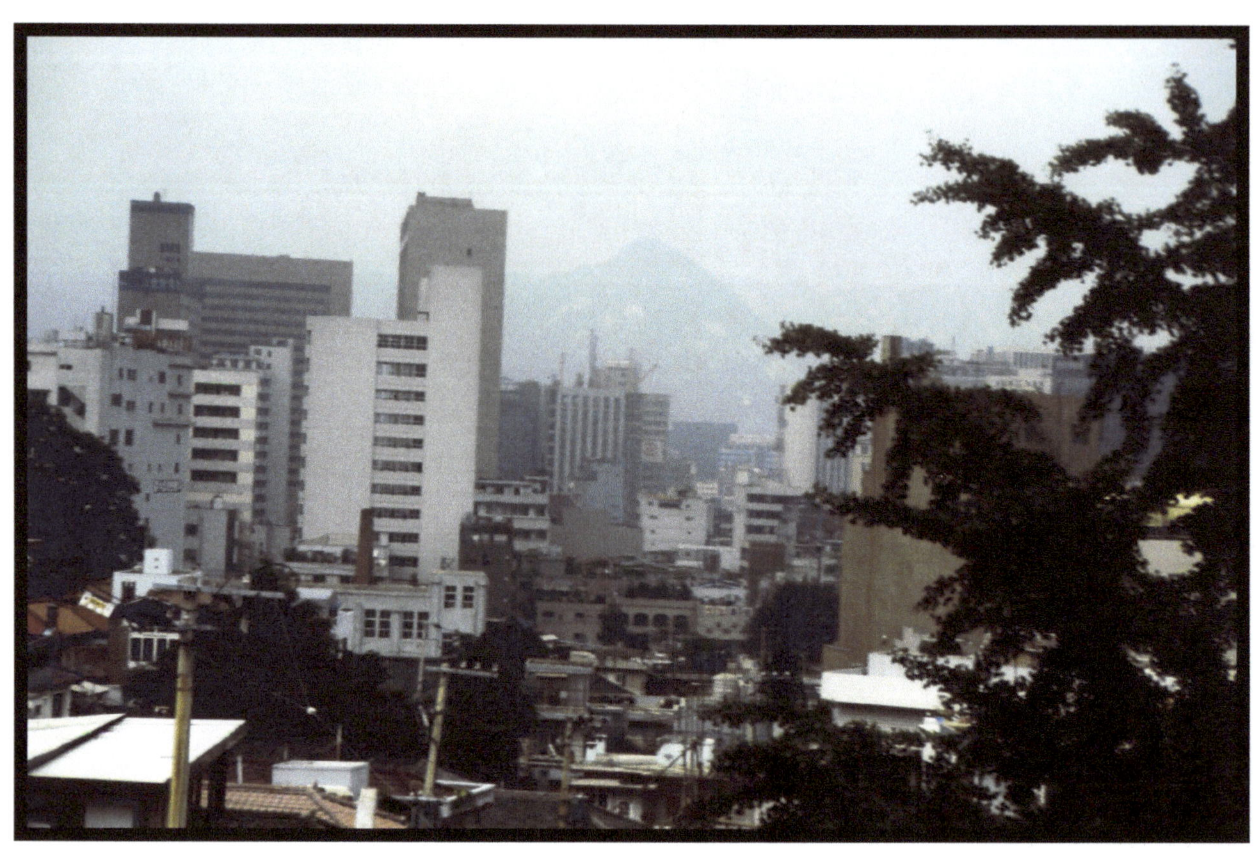

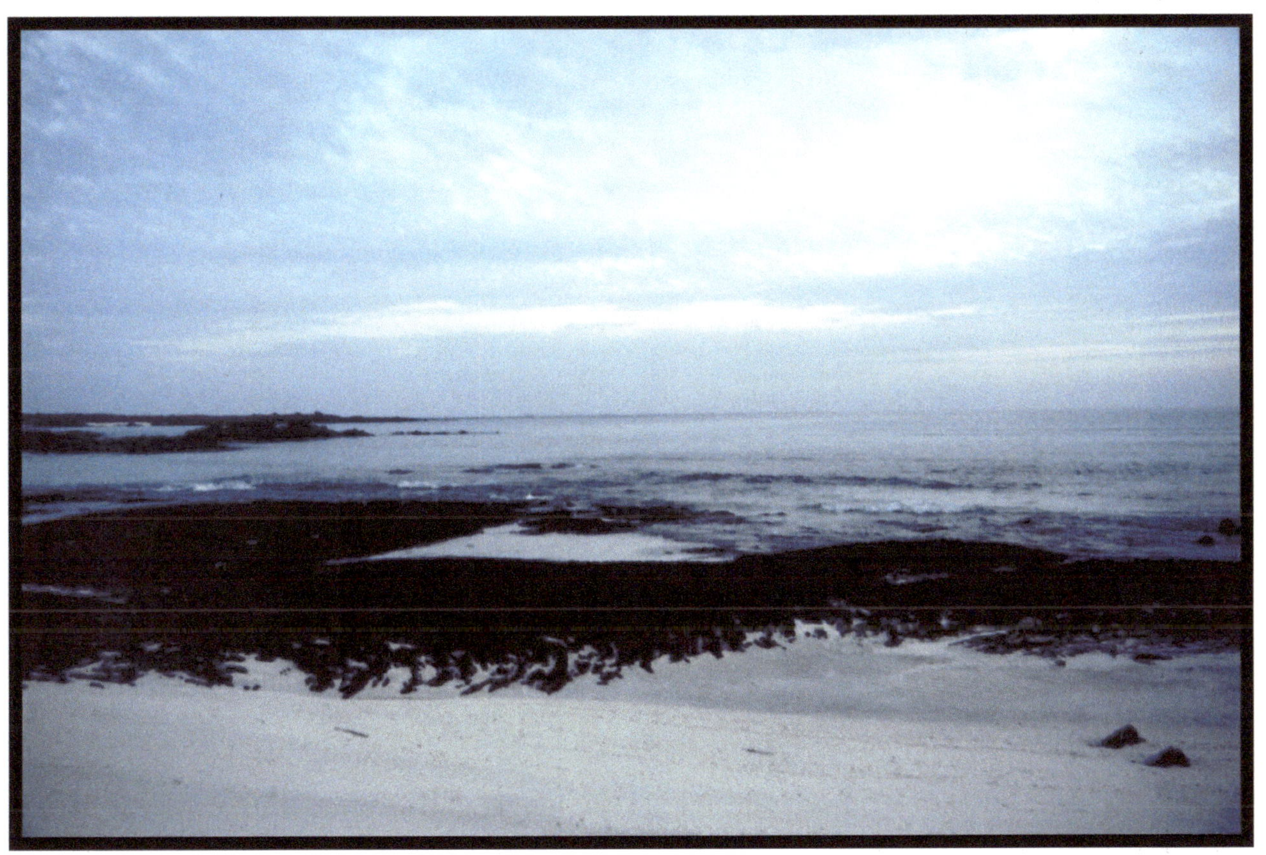

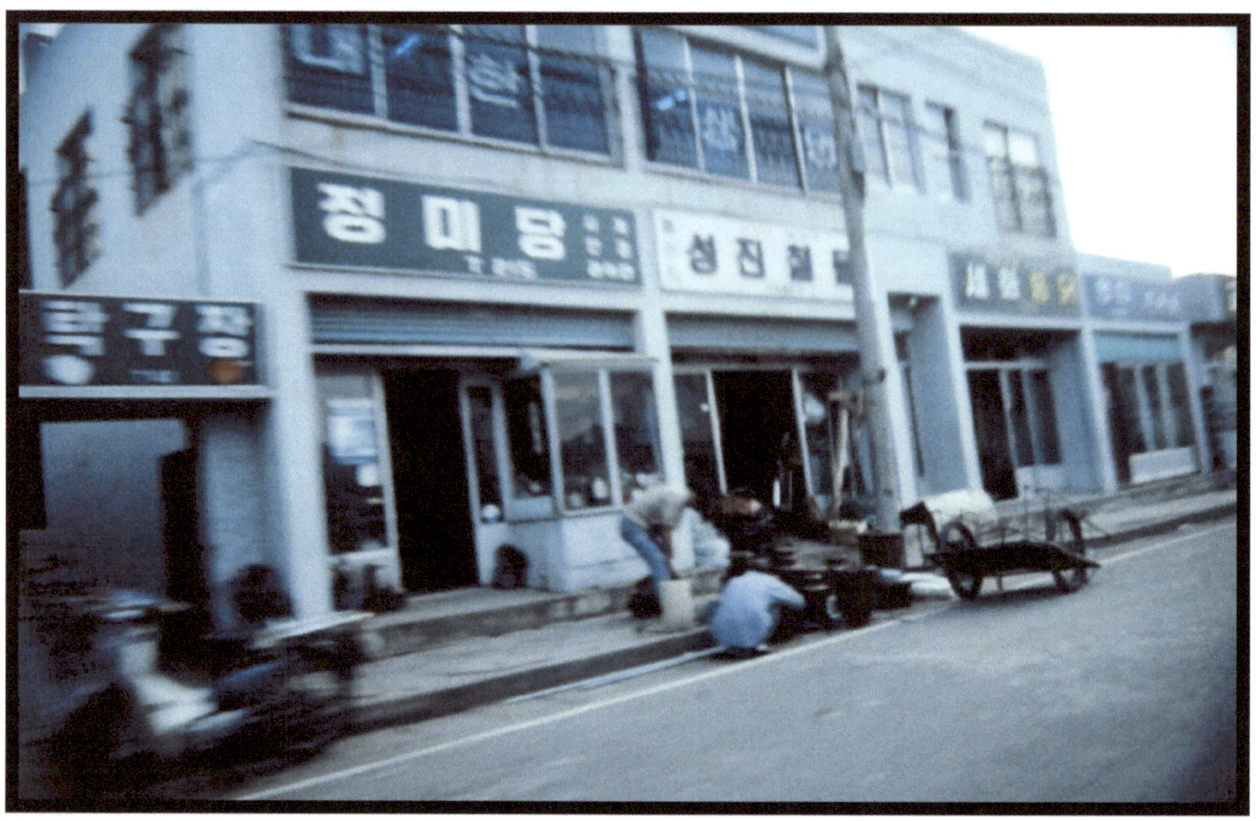
정미당

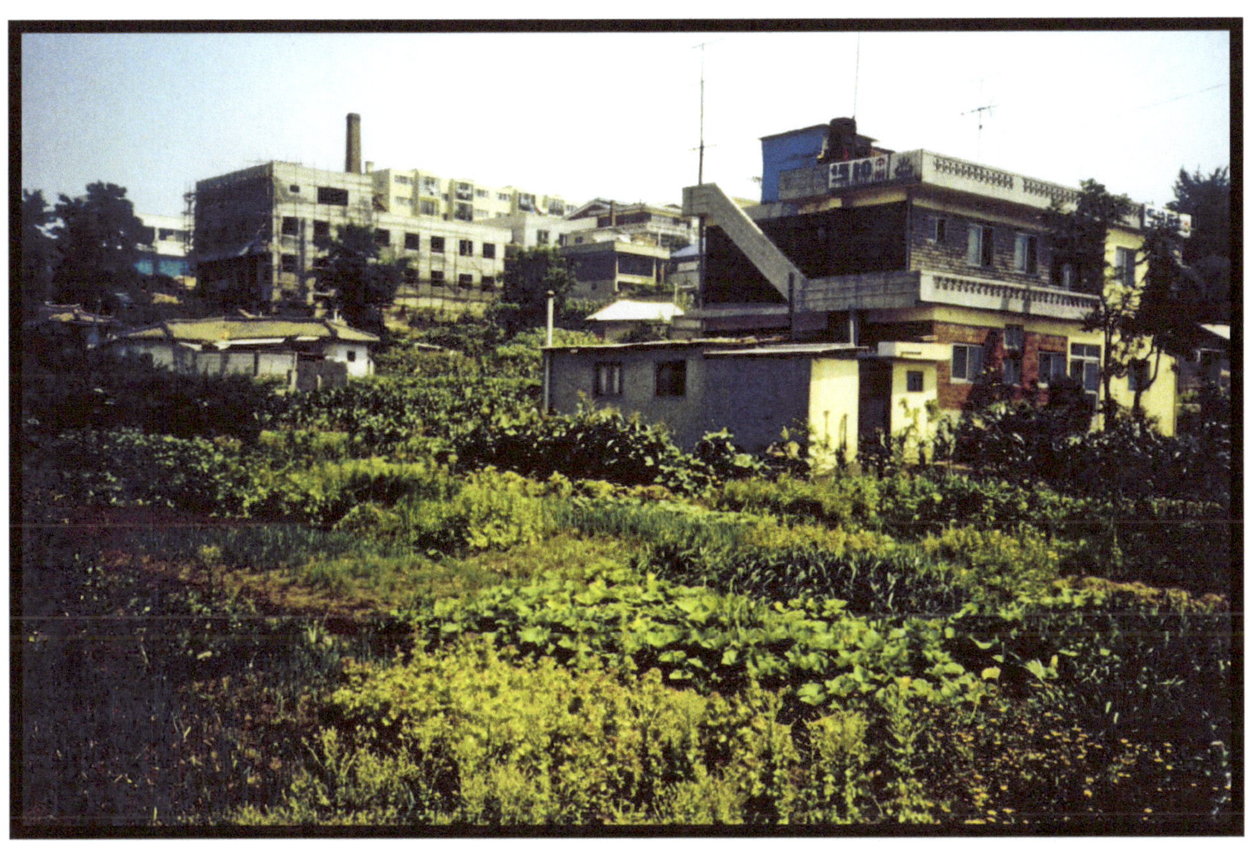

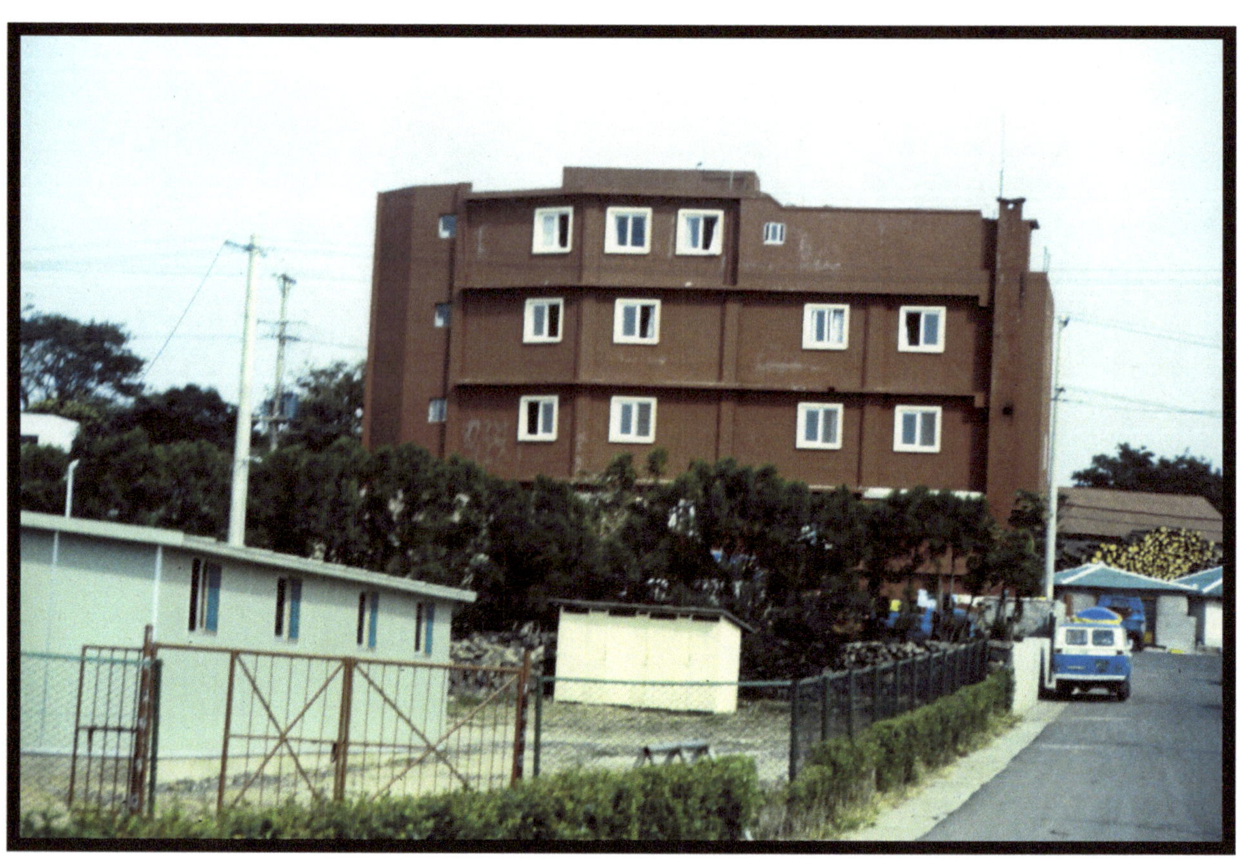

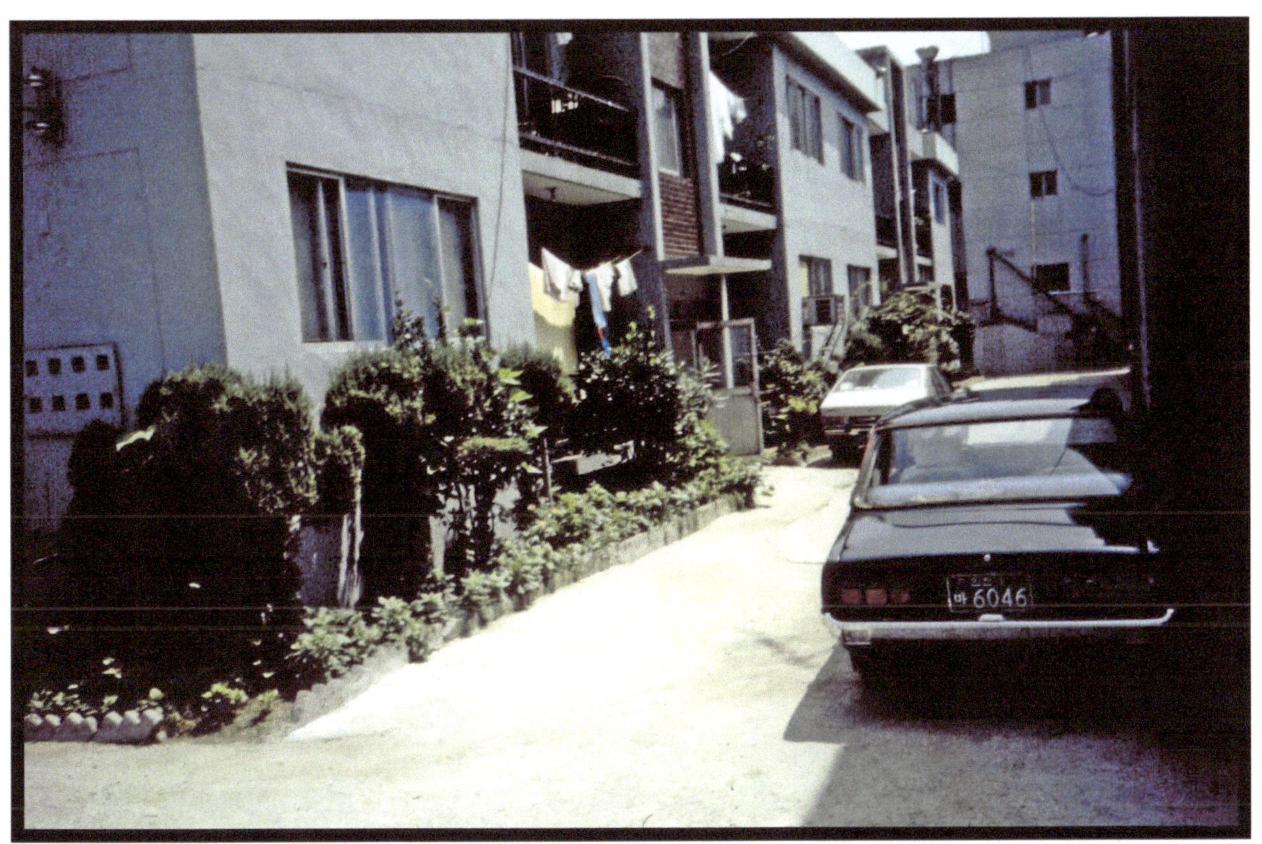
6046

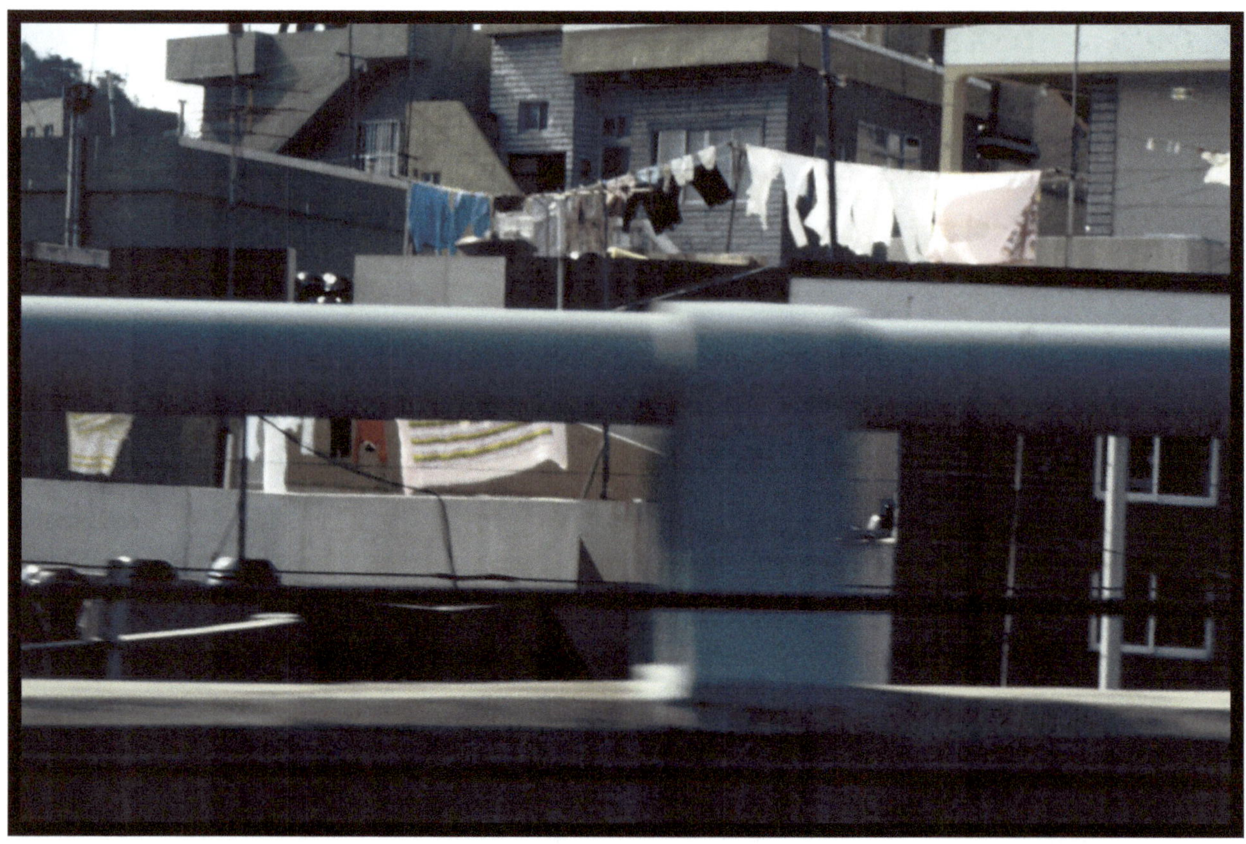

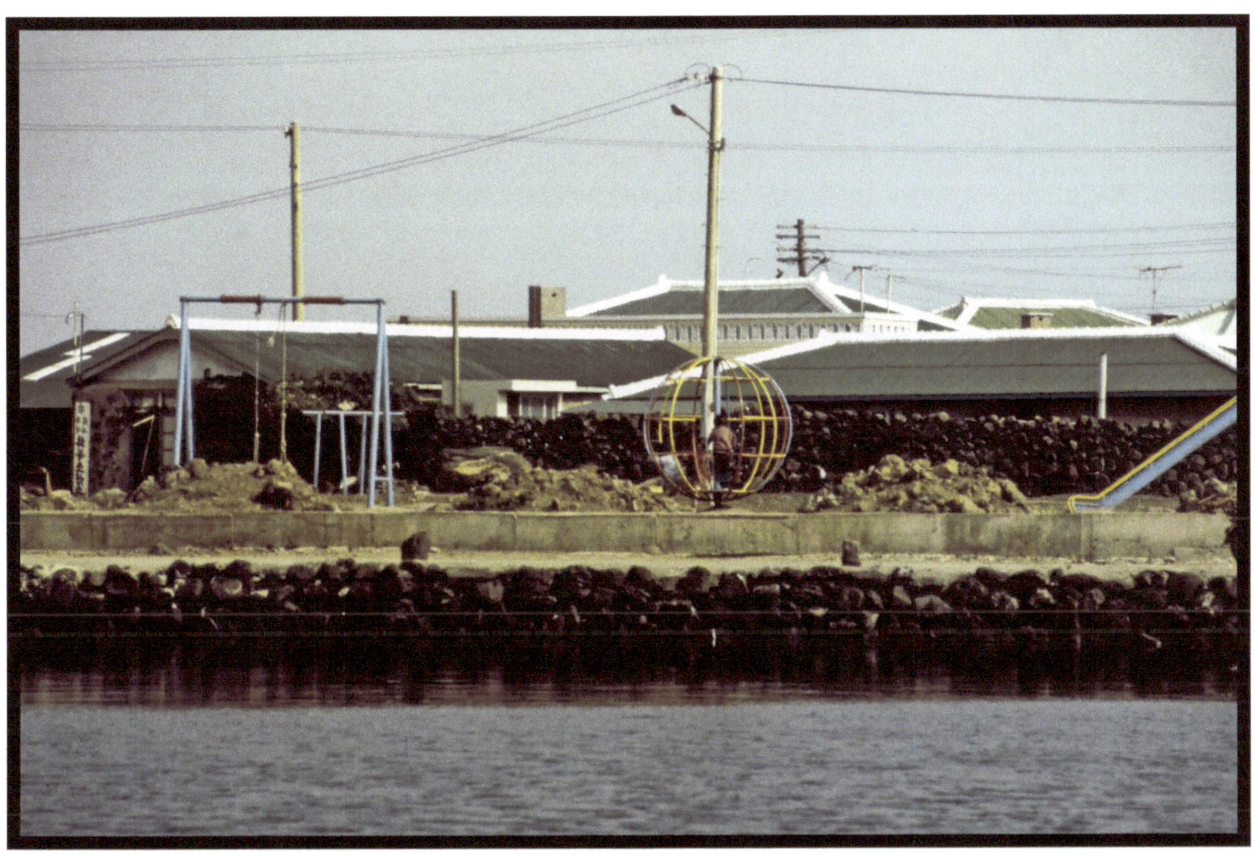

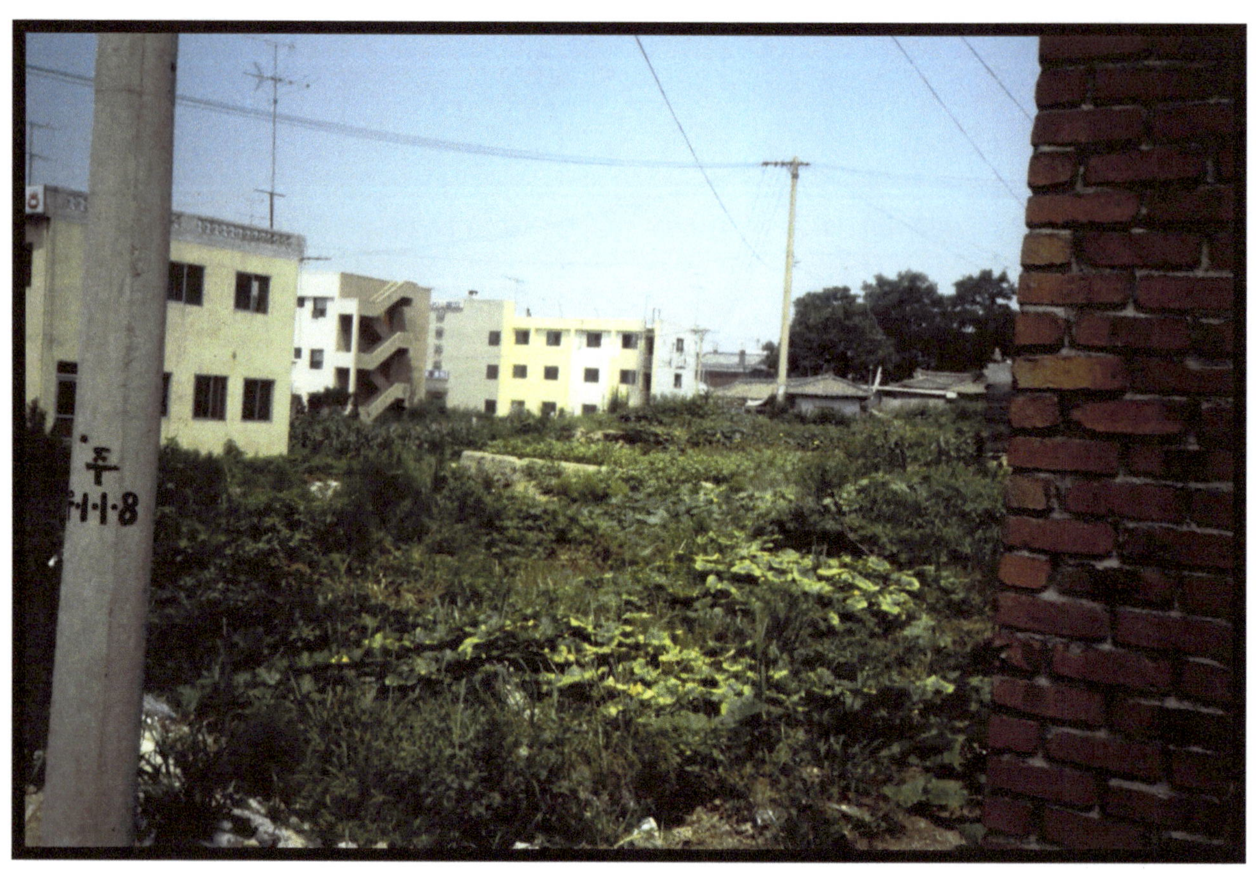
주
1·1·8

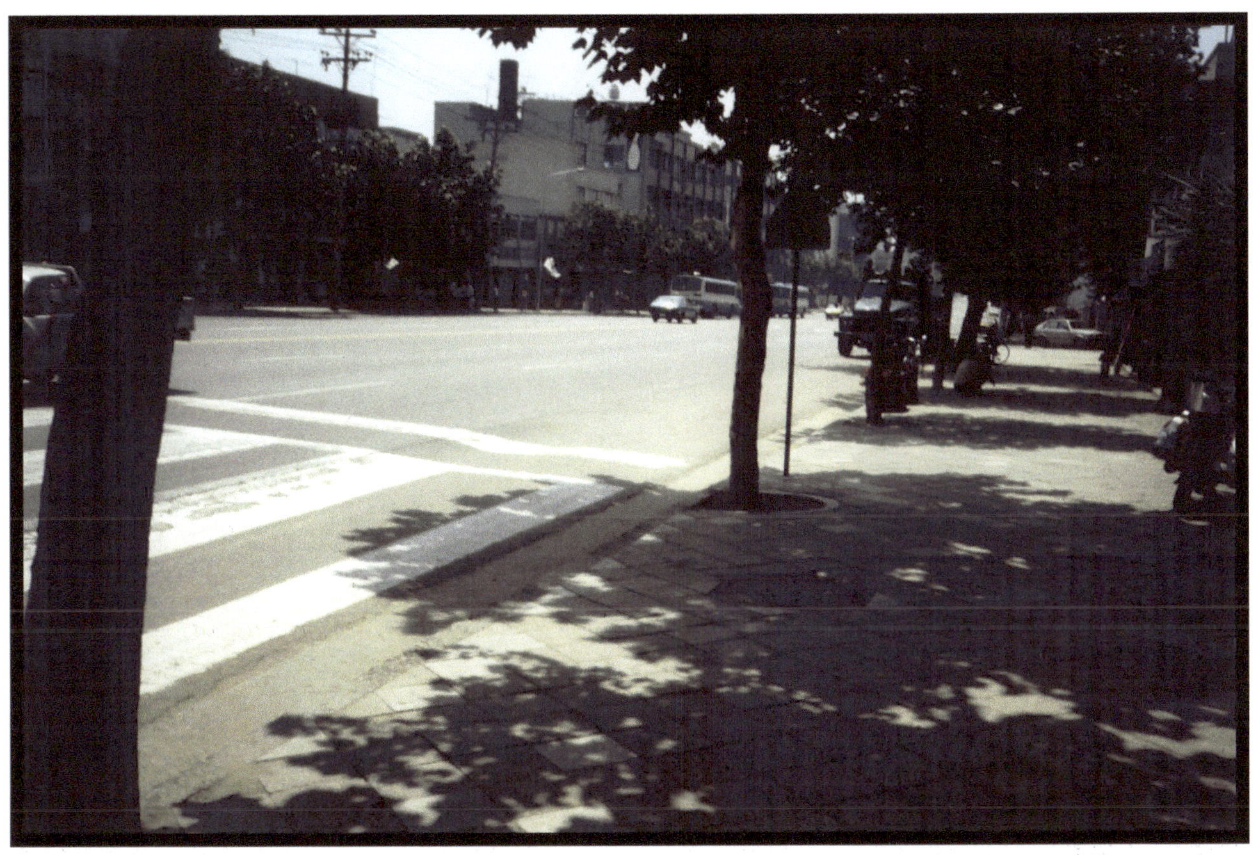

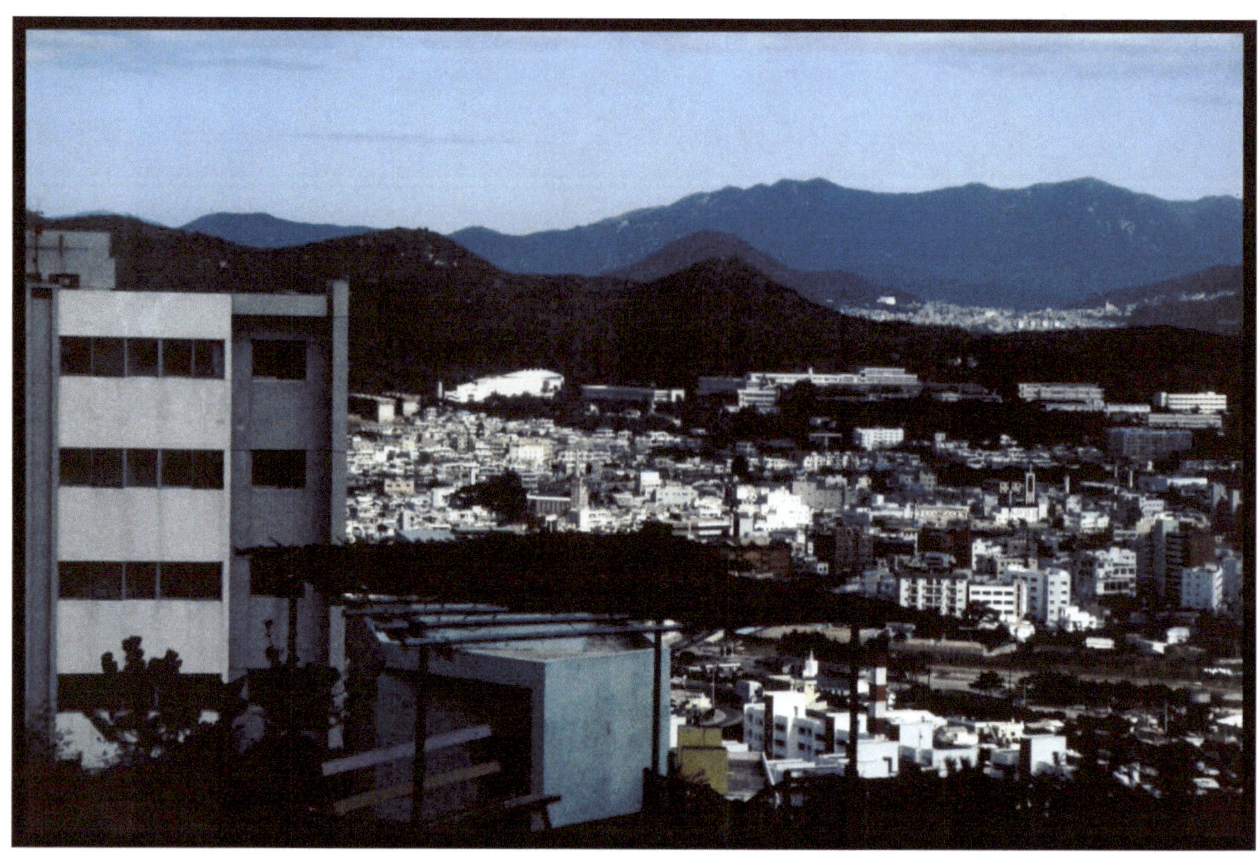

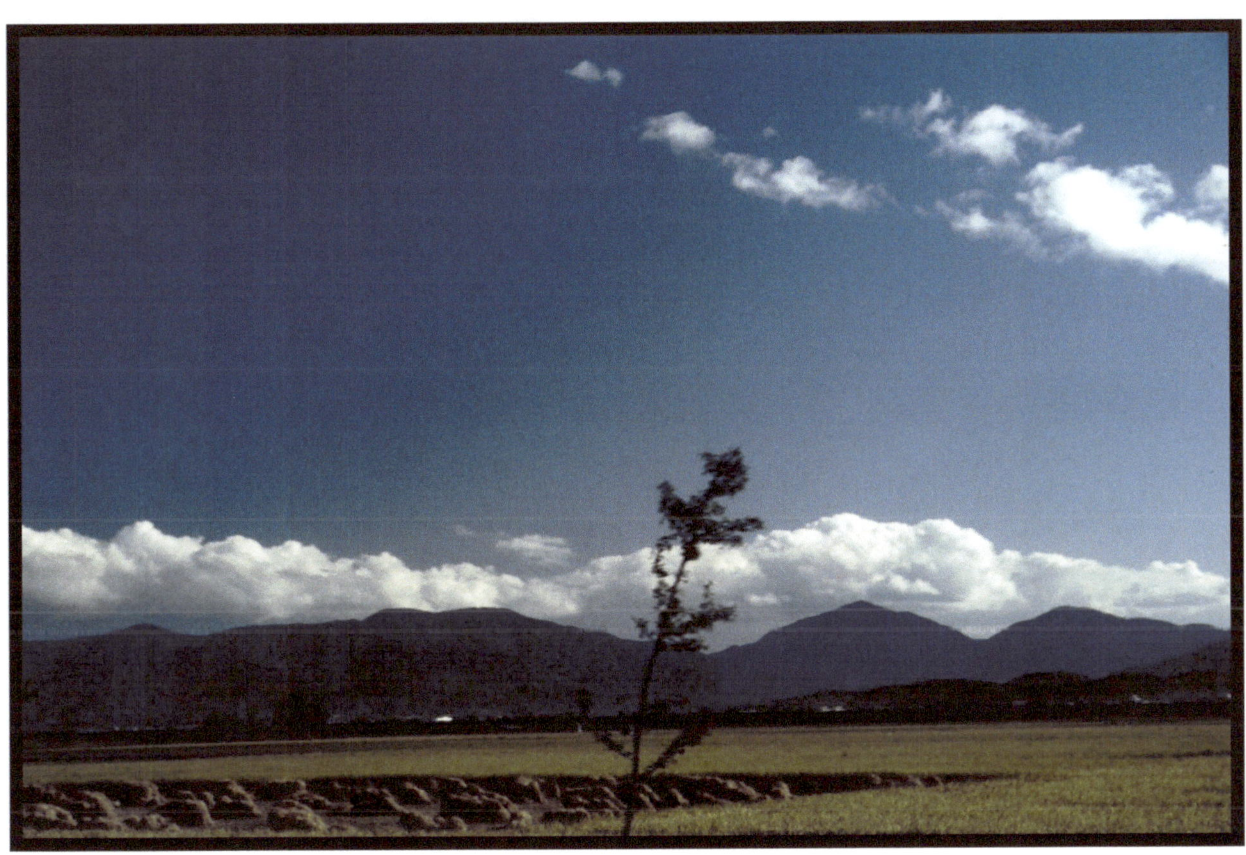

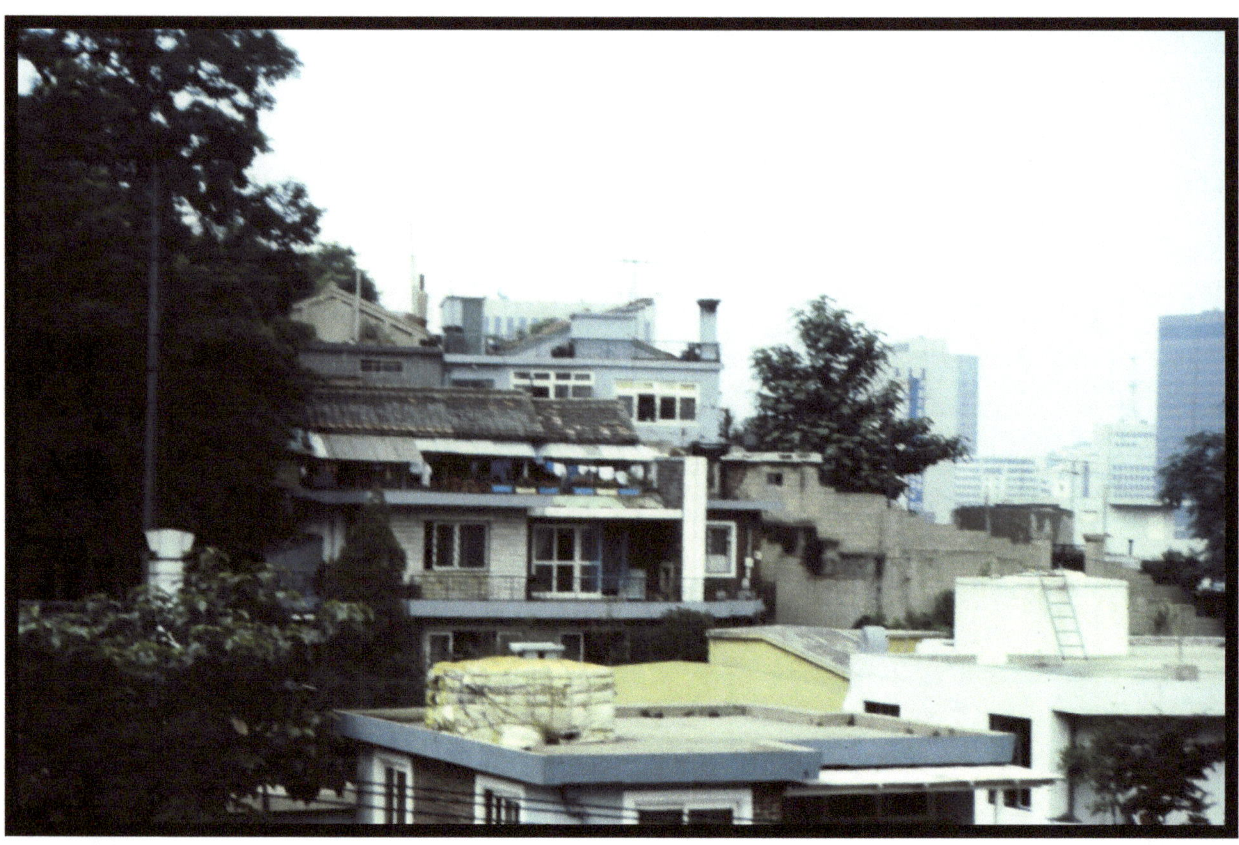

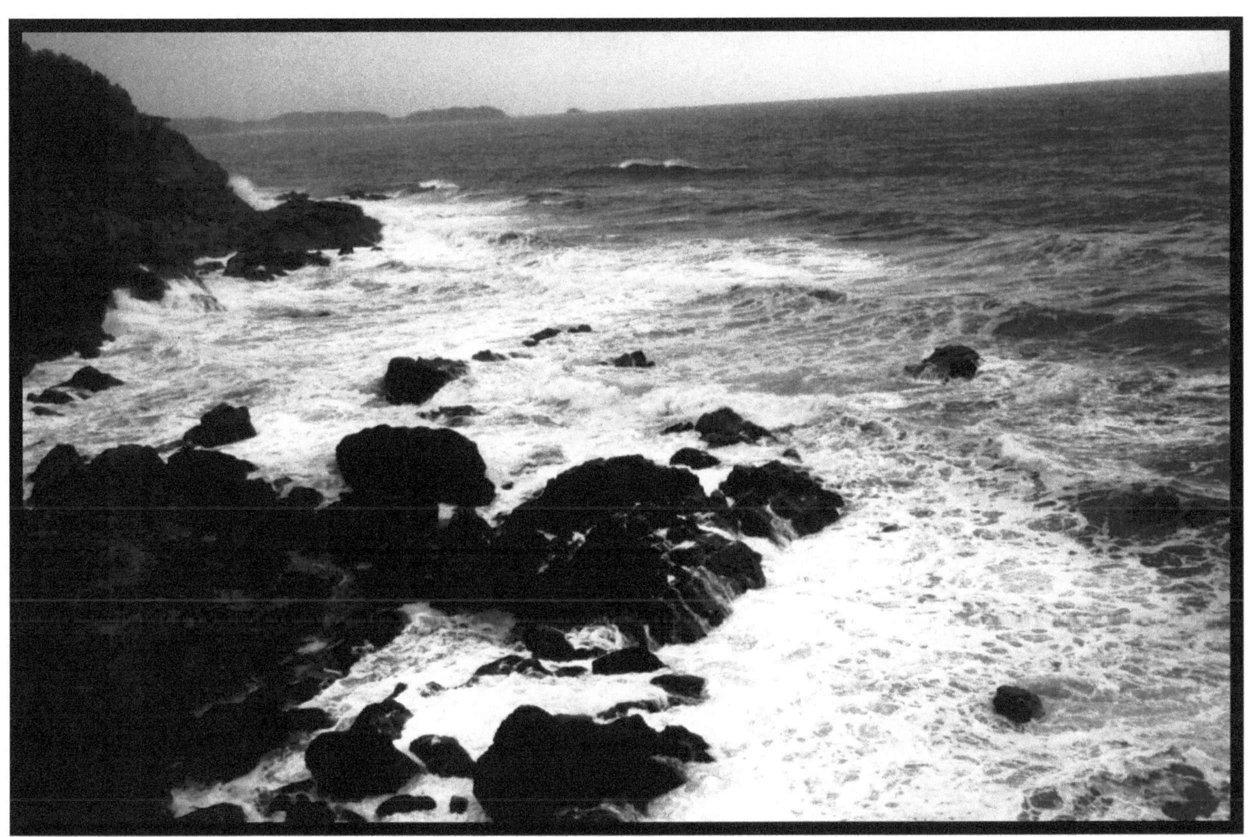

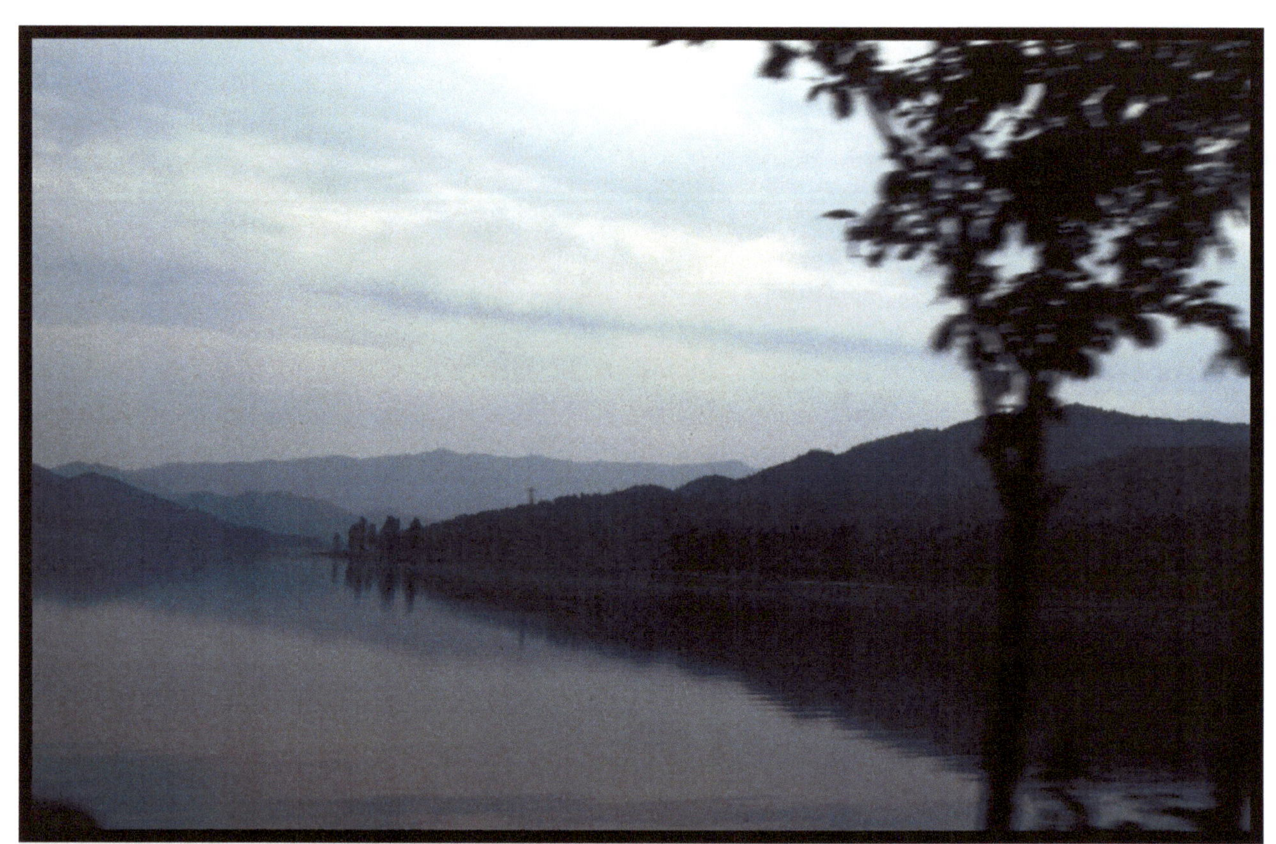

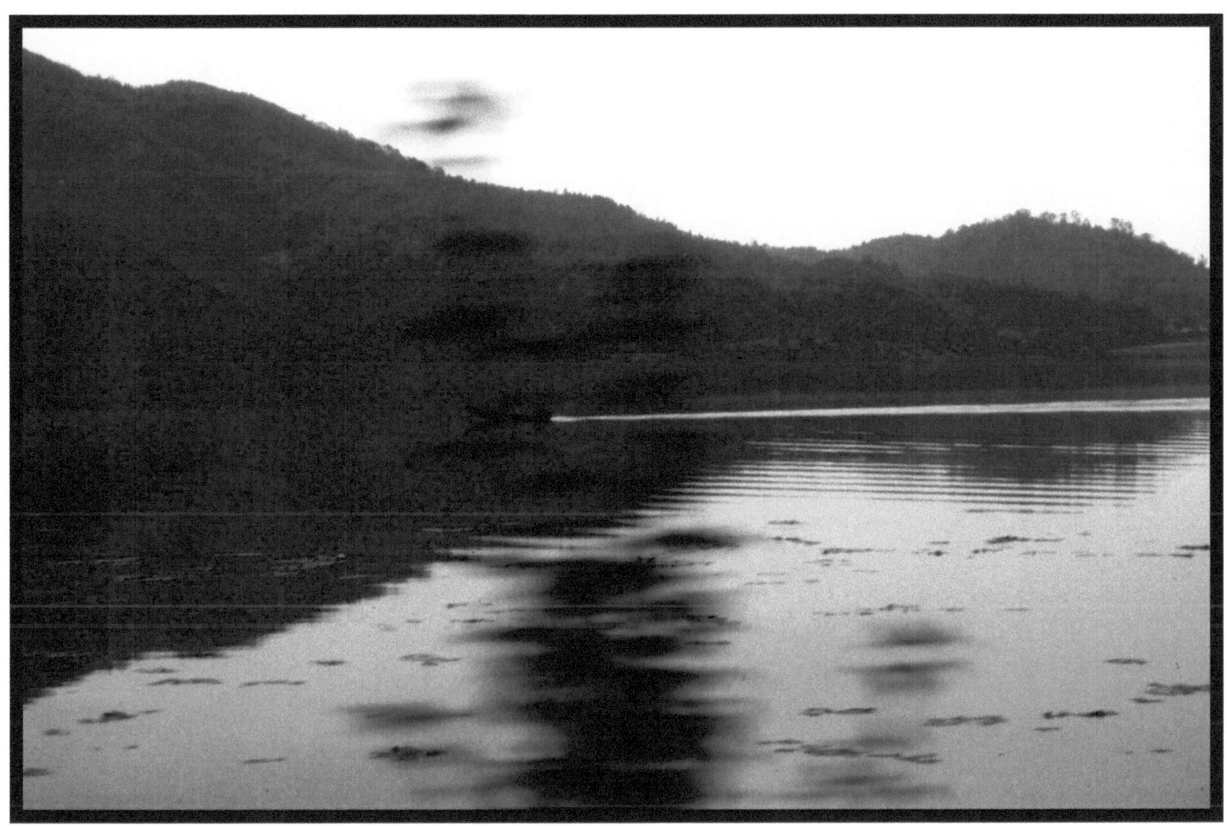

www.ingramcontent.com/pod-product-compliance
Lightning Source LLC
LaVergne TN
LVHW070118110826
845147LV00002B/148